"There are lots of books on organizational agility. But few are as comprehensive or thought-provoking as Jon Smart's tour de force, *Soon Safer Happier*. Jon has worked on the frontlines of the agile movement for almost thirty years, and he does a superb job of integrating his direct experience with the theories of organizational change. If you want to improve how your organization works, read this book!"

—**Julian Birkinshaw**, Professor and Deputy Dean,
London Business School

"*Sooner Safer Happier* is a must-read for leaders who have recognized the need to connect the cultural and the technological aspects of digital transformation. Jon Smart has established a critical set of patterns and antipatterns that are indispensable for an outcome-based shift from projects and waterfalls to products and innovation."

—**Mik Kersten**, CEO, Tasktop

"A true business-wide perspective on Digital Transformation and the need for whole business agility."

—**Adam Banks**, Non Executive Director and
Former CTIO of AP Møller Maersk

"If you are involved in the journey toward a safer, faster, happier organization that produces value at every step, this should be required reading. The 'patterns and antipatterns' approach means that you can easily spot where things may go wrong, and will have at hand some proven patterns to fix it. This is as close to a field guide as I have seen, and speaks of real and practical experience."

—**Dawie Olivier**, GM for Enterprise Transformation, Westpac

"This book is a treasure trove for anyone involved or interested in the theory and practice of business agility. Jon Smart and co-authors give a compelling 'Why?' for the need to change and clear, practical antipatterns and corresponding patterns of success. A game-changer for our organization and I'm confident for others' too."

—**Richard James**, Ways of Working Enablement Leader,
Nationwide Building Society

"As someone who works in a large financial services organization, many of the points raised in this book resonated with my personal experience. The antipattern versus pattern structure brings the principles to life and overlays real-world corporate culture with some of the 'hacks' to influence and drive change. This is a book that can be picked up by anyone across the business and is one that I will certainly be recommending to all our business and technology partners alike."

—**Chris Orson**, Head of Digital and Data, HSBC Securities Services

"While so many are trying to do Agile, experienced thought-leader Jon Smart illuminates how they miss the point and in great detail offers tangible ways for teams and companies to course correct. . . . Jon's book provides a logical, in-depth guide flagging the pitfalls of the plethora of antipatterns he has witnessed while generously sharing workarounds and better ways of working. [*Sooner Safer Happier*] has so many valuable enterprise agility lessons that it could be used for an MBA course. I wish this had been available when I started on my agility journey over a decade ago—it would have saved me learning many of these lessons the hard way."

—**Leah Jochim**, Experienced Enterprise Leader on Agile Ways of Working

"We've all seen these anti-patterns before—from organizations tackling agility with a 'one size fits all' approach to individuals putting their faith in tools and processes instead of people. Jon Smart brilliantly weaves theory and real-world experiences to provide antidotes that are focused on delivering better value sooner, safer, and happier. . . . Truly, a great and essential book for every agilist, leader, or change agent!"

—**Ahmed Sidkey**, PhD, President of the International Consortium for Agile (ICAgile) and Head of Business Agility at Riot Games

"Better Value Sooner Safer Happier. These five words, taken to heart, could very well change everything. . . . The book itself is a masterpiece of both insight and practical advice. From the opening of the introduction, I couldn't stop reading. Throughout the writing, complex concepts are made clear and accessible, which, in turn, sets the tone for the practical content. By intertwining patterns and antipatterns, anyone can open this book to a random chapter and apply the tactics within to improve their business."

—**Evan Leybourn**, Co-Founder and CEO, Business Agility Institute

SOONER
SAFER
HAPPIER

IT Revolution
Independent Publisher Since 2013
Portland, Oregon

SOONER

ANTIPATTERNS AND PATTERNS

SAFER

FOR BUSINESS AGILITY

HAPPIER

Jonathan Smart

*with Zsolt Berend, Myles Ogilvie
and Simon Rohrer*

25 NW 23rd Pl, Suite 6314
Portland, OR 97210

First Edition
Printed in the United States of America
25 24 23 22 21 20   1 2 3 4 5 6 7 8 9 10

Jacket Design by Devon Smith
Book Design by Devon Smith and Tamsin Ogilvie

Library of Congress Catalog-in-Publication Data

Names: Smart, Jon, author. | Berend, Zsolt, author. | Ogilvie, Myles,
author. | Rohrer, Simon, author.
Title: Sooner safer happier : anitpatterns and patterns for business agility
/ by Jonathan Smart with Zsolt Berend, Myles Ogilvie and Simon Rohrer.
Description: First edition. | Portland, OR : IT Revolution, [2020] |
Includes bibliographical references and index.
Identifiers: LCCN 2020023325 (print) | LCCN 2020023326 (ebook) | ISBN
9781942788911 (hardcover) | ISBN 9781942788928 (epub) | ISBN
9781942788935 (kindle edition) | ISBN 9781942788942 (pdf)
Subjects: LCSH: Success in business. | Agile project management.
Classification: LCC HF5386 .S6395 2020 (print) | LCC HF5386 (ebook) | DDC
658.4—dc23
LC record available at https://lccn.loc.gov/2020023325
LC ebook record available at https://lccn.loc.gov/2020023326

ISBN: 978-1942788911
eBook ISBN: 978-1942788928
Kindle ISBN: 978-1942788935
PDF: 978-1942788942
Audio: 978-1942788959

For information about special discounts for bulk purchases or for information on booking authors for an event, please visit our website at www.ITRevolution.com.

SOONER SAFER HAPPIER

To Kate, Annabelle, and Oscar,
thank you for your love and support
and for helping me to write this
sooner, safer, and happier.
—JS

To Tamsin, Rufus, and Phoebe,
my talented and wonderful family.
—MO

To Bronwyn, to the little bug,
and to the extended Rohrer family in London.
—SR

To Zsuzsa, Zsofi, and Dani.
—ZB

CONTENTS

LIST OF TABLES AND FIGURES

A SENSE OF URGENCY

The world changed on June 26, 2018. It happened quietly. Few people even noticed. But that was the day that, after more than a century, General Electric, the last original member of the Dow Jones Industrial Average, was removed from the index.[1]

GE was one of just a dozen firms that Charles Dow included in his list in 1896. The company appeared alongside giants such as American Tobacco, American Sugar Refining Company, and Tennessee Coal and Iron, companies that dominated what Carlota Perez, an expert on the effect of technology on socioeconomic development, calls the Age of Electricity and Engineering.[2]

As the previous age gave way to the Age of Oil and Mass Production, sugar refining lost its monopoly. Health concerns put out tobacco. General Electric, however, just kept going. It rode the change, feeding electricity into America's growing economy and transforming from an industrial conglomerate into a financial colossus. In 2004, GE was the largest firm in the world by market capitalization with a value of $382 billion.[3]

In 2016, it was one of the world's ten largest companies,[4] a symbol of how big and stable a company can become with expertise that suits the age. Just two years later, it was not. With a market value of $61 billion, only 15% of its peak value, and with its share price contributing less than half a percent to the Dow Jones's value, GE found itself relegated from industry's top league. Something had changed.

The reasons for GE's decline are numerous (bad bets in oil, junk mortgages, and the size of GE Capital's short-term borrowing leading up to the 2008 credit crisis[5] had much to do with it); however, it's not the only large, venerable company to find it was no longer leading the pack.

The rate of creative destruction is now faster than ever. In 1964, a firm listed on the S&P 500 Index could expect to remain on the index for thirty-three years. By 2016, that tenure had fallen to twenty-four years. By 2027, companies can expect to spend no more than twelve years on the index before they're replaced. At the current churn rate, between 2018 and 2028, about half the index will have changed.[6] With companies growing and shrinking faster than ever before, there is a need to be on the right side of change in order to survive and thrive.

A look at the current set of companies listed on the Dow Jones provides one clue to the source of the dramatic turnover on the S&P 500. Alongside stalwarts such as ExxonMobil and Procter & Gamble are Verizon, Cisco, IBM, and Intel, as well as Microsoft and Apple, two of the world's largest firms by market capitalization. Currently, seven of the world's ten largest firms by market capitalization are information technology companies, including (in addition to Microsoft and Apple) Google's parent company Alphabet, Facebook, Amazon, and China's Tencent and Alibaba.[7] An economy that used to be dominated by oil and repetitive mass production has given way to one dominated by a continuous stream of information technology innovation and unique product development.

It's not just *what* the technology companies are making. What characterizes today's most highly valued organizations is *how* they make what they make. Their behavioral norms and system of work are different from anything that's come before. They are applying better approaches to work by evolving their ways of working to deliver value in a way that suits the *nature* of their work. We are in the Age of Digital.

In this new age, every company is an information technology company, whether they know it yet or not. Today, nearly all change and nearly all product development in organizations (such as a new mortgage, a new vaccine, or a new model of car) includes information technology. For example, by 2030 it is forecasted that software will account for half of the total cost of a new car.[8] The organizations that are thriving are the ones that are leveraging information technology and treating software not as a cost center but rather as central to generating new business value.

Crucially, unlike in the age of repetitive mass production—where, for example, 1,500 cars are produced by one factory every day, one car a minute, twenty-four hours a day[9]—in the Digital Age, you don't write the same software thousands of times. Software is written *once*, rewritten a few times to improve it, and then *runs* thousands of times. Every software binary coming off the virtual assembly line is unique. People don't know what they want and you don't know how you're going to write the software until you've written it. Only once it's in the hands of people do they know what they *don't* want and do you realize how you *should* have written the code. Rather than the domain of work being repetitive, knowable, and deterministic with known-unknowns (you know how to fix it if something goes wrong), unique product development is unknowable and emergent with unknown-unknowns instead. For something that has not been done before, you don't know what you don't know until you do something and get feedback.

Over time, as compute power has increased, as we went from punch cards and valve-based computing with slow feedback loops (such as an overnight run) to microprocessors and the ability to have near-immediate feedback loops, an increasing number of software engineers realized that the then-conventional "heavyweight," sequential, stage-gate processes for software development were not optimal for the complex and emergent domain of digital knowledge work.

Practitioners felt and saw the pain. With inspiration from articles such as "The New New Product Development Game,"[10] software engineers in the late 1980s and early 1990s saw the benefits of better ways of working that were taking place in manufacturing firms like Toyota, Honda, and Xerox, with small empowered multidisciplinary teams and frequent small iterations, rather than the previous way of working with sequential, big-batch, stage-gate work passing by job role. This was in the context of product development and was heavily influenced by the legendary W. Edwards Deming, the godfather of Agile and Lean. With experimentation and experience, "lightweight" processes for software development became increasingly popular, being more suited to the emergent nature of digital work. In 2001, the values and principles of these lightweight processes were codified in the *Agile Manifesto*.

People doing product development found that these Agile principles helped them deliver value early and often with empowered teams. This led to better outcomes. These agile ways of working—suited to unique, emergent, product development—altered everything because they correctly optimize the *approach* to the work to the *type* of work. This way of working leads to the delivery of **Better Value Sooner Safer Happier**.

Increasingly old, traditional companies—the horses rather than the unicorns—are feeling the need to exhibit agility across the whole organization in order to keep up with the "born agile" disrupters who are not held back by legacy ways of working. Organized human endeavor in the Digital Age has increasingly shifted from *repetitive* production to *unique* product development. In addition, fueled by the same technological revolution, the pace of change has become faster.

To succeed, organizations are recognizing the importance of being proficient in *ways of working* suited to and leveraging the increasingly emergent nature of work and the continuous pace of change. Organizations are recognizing a need to exhibit business agility. These ways of working are not specific to IT, nor to any sector. They are essential to survive and thrive in the Age of Digital.

Living through the Tipping Point in the Age of Digital

In order to understand the macro picture, it is helpful to look at the work of Professor Carlota Perez. In 2002, Perez wrote *Technological Revolutions and Financial Capital: The Dynamics of Bubbles and Golden Ages*, an analysis of the relationship between financial bubbles and technological change. In it, Perez demonstrates how, since the first industrial revolution, approximately every forty to sixty years there is a new technology-led revolution that gives rise to a paradigm shift and a new economy with societal impact. There is a recurrence of financial bubbles bursting in the middle of each technology-led revolution, caused by overinvestment in the hype, leading to a recession and then a new golden age.[11] Each recession is a tipping point from a previous normal to a new normal. Since the beginning of the dot com crash in 2000, we've been living through the tipping point in the Age of Digital.

In each age, the ways of working evolve, suited to its context. Each advances on organized human endeavor, increasing productivity. We went from factory systems to subcontracting to Taylorism and Fordism and subsequently Lean in the Age of Oil & Mass Production. Now, we are emerging into *business agility* in the Age of Digital.

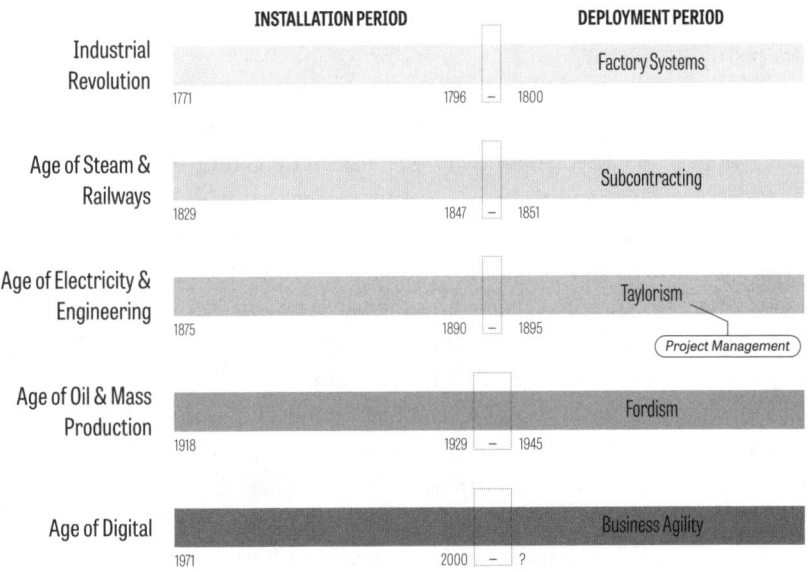

Figure A.1: Technological Revolutions

Adapted from Perez, *Technological Revolutions and Financial Capital.*

Project management and Gantt charts come from *two* technological revolutions ago, optimized for the primary context at the time, which was repetitive, knowable, deterministic, and generally physical activity. The evolution in ways of working, with time studies, reinforced the notion of managers versus workers, with a command-and-control, order-giver, order-taker, behavioral norm. Productivity improved, however, at a human cost, with workers treated as cogs in a machine.

Unfortunately, today, some organizations are still *misapplying* this way of working from more than a century ago to unique, unknowable, emergent, behavioral knowledge work: a type of activity that benefits from a wholly different approach, if there is a desire to deliver **Better Value Sooner Safer Happier**.

What This Book Is About

This book is here to help you on your unique journey to better ways of working in the Age of Digital in order to lead to better outcomes. It is a collection of antipatterns and patterns grouped into eight chapters, each chapter being a key learning.

These are lessons learned the hard way, and they are presented here to help you avoid potential potholes. Where work is emergent there is no such thing as best practice. There is no one size fits all. Your context is unique. These antipatterns and patterns are approaches that have been experienced by the authors and observed across hundreds of organizations to—more often than not—act as a headwind (antipattern) or a tailwind (pattern) to improving outcomes. This book, and the patterns and antipatterns within it, is shared learning. As your context is unique, your mileage may vary. No other organization has the same impediments, history, and culture as your organization. There is a need to apply an emergent mindset to this emergent domain of work. Take these learnings and optimize for fast learning. Amplify experiments that work and dampen experiments that don't.

The focus of this book is on *outcomes*, not on Agile for Agile's sake, or Lean for Lean's sake. These outcomes are expressed as **Better Value Sooner Safer Happier** (or **BVSSH** for short).

Better is quality. Quality is built in rather than inspected in later. With smaller slices of value and multidisciplinary teams, changes are within a team's cognitive load (that is, complexity that fits in your head) and there is a limited "impact radius." There are fewer incidents and outages. There is less rework, less failure demand. More time is spent proactively rather than reactively.

Value is unique; it's why you are doing what you are doing. It is of value to someone. It could be financial; it could be maintaining public safety; it could be charitable.

Sooner is time to market, time to learning, to pivoting, to de-risking, to avoiding a "sunk cost fallacy," to locking in progress and value early and often.

Safer is Governance, Risk, and Compliance (GRC), information security, data privacy, regulatory compliance and resilience in chaos, be that a cyber-attack or a global pandemic. It is customers *trusting* your organization. It is agile rather than fragile. It is speed *and* control, not one or the other. It is cultural, keeping the conversation on risk alive. The better the brakes, the faster you can go.

Happier covers customers, colleagues, citizens, and climate, as it is not about "more for less" at any human or climatic cost. It is high levels of customer advocacy and colleague engagement with a positive impact to society and the one planet we live on. It is a more humane way of working.

Each of these elements balances the other. You can't force Sooner, as there will be a downward trend in Better and Happier. Improving on **BVSSH** is not prescriptive. Measures are vector metrics (trends) rather than absolutes so that improvement over time can be compared. No one is exempt from improving. Within guardrails, teams are empowered and supported to build a muscle memory of continuous improvement in line with **BVSSH**. Sometimes it's more agile and lean; sometimes it's smaller waterfalls due to history, a command and control culture of fear, and lack of psychological safety. It depends on your unique culture, history, and context.

A key theme in this book that is worth highlighting is *"Go Slower to Go Faster."* This is explored in particular in Chapters 2 and 7. There will be quick wins, and it is a fallacy to try to do too much too soon. *People have a limited velocity to unlearn and relearn.* You cannot force the pace of change in the same way that King Canute could not hold back the tide. Forcing the pace of change will likely lead to real, lasting change either not happening at all (with new labels on the same old behavior) or taking longer and with more risk. Lasting behavioral change takes as long as it takes, based on actions taken to nurture it, ignore it, force it, or sabotage it. It can be given a tailwind or a headwind. The intent is that this book gives you a tailwind.

What this book does *not* attempt to do is to touch on each body of knowledge. This is such a rich, deep, fascinating topic that it could fill a library. And if you are holding a physical copy, you are probably grateful that it doesn't weigh more! While in particular agile, lean, and DevOps are spoken of, there is no explicit attempt to cover in depth topics such as systems thinking, design thinking, user experience (UX) design, Eli Goldratt's Theory of Constraints, W. Edwards Deming's System of Profound Knowledge, and so on. It is a beautiful, never-ending learning journey, which you too can contribute to, should you wish to.

The intent is that this book will give you a tailwind for improved ways of working. This book is not just about agile. Or just about lean. It is about ways of working for better outcomes in the Age of Digital.

Who Are We?

I started out as a developer on the trading floor in investment banking in the early 1990s. I was part of a multidisciplinary, single-digit-sized team, physically sitting together, with a tribal team identity. We were the swaps trading desk.

We were all "the business" irrespective of specialism. We were naturally agile, with many-times-a-day deployments of technology-enabled value. We followed an adaptive "lightweight" process, which today would be recognized as agile and lean. It was a case of "you build it, you run it," which incentivized writing software that was supportable and resilient. It was fun and engaging.

Over time I've repeatedly taken multi-disciplinary teams on the journey from traditional to better ways of working to optimize for outcomes within the financial services industry. I have approximately thirty years of experience as an agile and lean practitioner, as a "business technologist" delivering software to generate business value, with lessons learned the hard way: by trying, sometimes succeeding, sometimes failing, learning, pivoting, and trying again.

Most recently I was leading Ways of Working at Barclays, a universal bank that dates as far back as 1690 and employs about 80,000 people globally across multiple business units. It's a large, highly regulated business. My role was to increase agility and help everyone in the bank deliver better services to Barclays' customers, release value sooner, and ensure that change was safe and compliant, with happier customers and colleagues. The benefits we saw are mentioned in the next chapter. I am currently helping organizations across industry sectors improve their ways of working, applying principles in context to optimize for **Better Value Sooner Safer Happier**.

It's teamwork, and I'm delighted that three people who have been on the same shared journey have contributed to this book. Together with Zsolt Berend, Myles Ogilvie, and Simon Rohrer—colleagues and friends—we will share in this book the most important lessons that we've been able to draw from our experiences developing and adopting better ways of working.

In the decades that Zsolt, Myles, Simon, and I have been agile and lean practitioners, we've seen the benefits that better ways of working can bring. We've repeatedly seen initiatives with a deterministic mindset, work passing by job role silos, and Think Big, Start Big, Learn Slow ways of working where hundreds of people fail at very high cost. We've also seen thousands of small, empowered teams and teams of teams improve their ways of working within guardrails, with strategic alignment, with intrinsic motivation, growing together, increasing engagement and satisfaction, regularly delivering value, and improving on **BVSSH** outcomes. We've seen how better, more humane ways of working are adopted through an organization, and we've also experienced the impediments that are a headwind for improving outcomes, and how they can be alleviated.

We've implemented many mandatory, regulatory initiatives with a fixed scope and fixed date, with a need to cease business activities if not implemented in time, all implemented with agile and lean principles, all early and all successful. In these situations, a waterfall approach would have been too risky, with late learning and back-loaded risk. Due to agility and fast time to learning, having got early learning on the least understood and the riskiest bit of these activities, we were able to go back to the UK regulator and suggest that for the benefit of global competitiveness, they might want to update the legislation, which they did. Even regulation isn't always immutable if you're learning fast enough.

Who This Book Is For

This book is aimed at leaders at all levels, in all roles, in large, complex organizations, who are on or are about to go on the journey of reinvention in the Age of Digital. You might be having some issues or you're not seeing the expected outcomes you desire or you want to set out with a guide for your journey.

This book is aimed at a broad spectrum of experience, including those who do and don't have decades of experience in agile and lean ways of working or organizational change at scale. For those who do, as per the Dunning-Kruger effect (see Chapter 3), you will realize how much you still have to learn and that you're never done learning. It is a huge pivot, how people work together, a mindset shift with a focus on outcomes over output, with finance, HR, compliance, internal audit, and real estate implications. This is a once-in-a-lifetime pivot in how human endeavor is organized. Therefore, building on all the bodies of knowledge to date, it is still a nascent topic and there is still much to learn. My intent is that this book will be updated in the future as we all continue to learn.

This book is for people organization-wide, not just IT. Nothing is out of scope if it is an impediment to delivering **Better Value Sooner Safer Happier**. Marketing, sales, legal, compliance, internal audit, HR, finance, procurement, real estate, executive committee members, non-executive directors, strategy, business units, product managers, digital, data, back office operations, the PMO, and so on should all find benefit in the antipatterns and patterns in this book.

If you are feeling that you are living through an antipattern, the intent is that this book can support you in making your case to bosses, peers, and stakeholders to help amplify ways of working that should lead to better outcomes.

How This Book Is Organized

Antipatterns and Patterns

Organizations are complex adaptive systems. There is no one way of working that suits every context. Change is emergent. Changing how you do change is emergent. Organizations are emergent, with a memory. It's emergence tripled. The only feasible way to progress is by running experiments, being sensitive to context with a fast feedback loop, and a safe-to-learn environment. There is no such thing as "best practice"; there is no one-size-fits-all set of practices that optimizes for all contexts.

What I have observed from learning the hard way and shared learning from the agile, lean, and DevOps communities is that there are common antipatterns and patterns.

An *antipattern* is a common response to a situation that, more often than not, is ineffective and risks being highly counterproductive. Antipatterns are approaches that have been seen many times to not optimize for outcomes, sometimes setting an organization back many years and creating organizational scar tissue and a strong headwind. Very occasionally an antipattern for the majority of organizations might be a pattern for one organization: for example, perhaps a scenario where cashflow is running short, and it's a high-risk, do-or-die strategy for an organization.

A *pattern* is a response to a situation that, more often than not, is effective and improves desired outcomes, of course with ups and downs, backs and forths, and swings and roundabouts, as it's all about people. A pattern can help create a tailwind. It has repeatedly improved outcomes and become "sticky." It can help create a tailwind for change. As with the antipatterns, your mileage may vary. In some rare contexts, a pattern might be an antipattern. However, I would advise caution and not use this as a rationale to knowingly adopt an antipattern with a command-and-control, deterministic mindset. I would suggest starting with the patterns and experiment with fast feedback.

This book is laid out as a series of antipatterns and their corresponding patterns. If you are reading a particular antipattern and are feeling the pain, you can look at the corresponding pattern for a suggestion on an approach that will likely generate better outcomes.

Each chapter looks at a related set of antipatterns and patterns. My aim is that you will be able to use this book as a guide on your own unique, never ending journey. You'll be able to learn from others, avoid potholes, and accelerate while remembering that this is not a cookbook or a manual. It can't do the work for you. You should interpret the antipatterns and patterns in your own unique context. A bit like learning to ski, it's advisable to have coaching from a ski instructor, someone who can anticipate the bumps or turns ahead and help people learn to ski for themselves.

I believe these antipatterns and patterns are applicable in the context of large, bureaucratic enterprises—the economy's horses rather than its unicorns. That said, as some unicorns grow rapidly, hiring people from larger, more traditional firms, I've seen a meeting in the middle. The horses exhibit more agility and the unicorns become more bureaucratic. Even unicorns are not exempt from continuously improving. You will need to probe, sense, and respond.

Principles

With each chapter comes a number of principles. They distill the essence of the chapter to its *guiding principles*, to guide behavior and the millions of decisions that are made every day. For example, "Invite over Inflict" and "One Size Does Not Fit All." They apply across contexts.

Specific *practices* emerge by applying the *principles* to a unique context and by using coaching and experimentation, leveraging many bodies of knowledge. As Dan Terhorst-North has said: "Practices = Principles + Context."[12] The successful pattern is to identify the top ten or so principles that you feel are most important to encourage across your organization, communicate them relentlessly, and recognize behaviors in line with them. They are positive behavioral guardrails.

The intentionally long list provided in this book is intended to help you get started. The principles themselves are self-referential. You are invited to use them, and there is no one size fits all. Your context and impediments will determine which are more important to encourage.

How to Read This Book

Just as there is no one size fits all, there is no one way to read this book. It could be read left to right in a linear manner. Equally, it is intended to be "dippable." The idea is that you can hone in on an area of interest, reading the relevant antipatterns and patterns.

The book is organized into three parts.

- **Chapter 0** covers how we got here and takes a closer look at agile, lean, and DevOps.
- **Chapters 1 to 8** are the lessons learned, comprised of antipatterns and patterns.
- **Chapter 9** is advice on how to get going.

We'll now take a closer look at Chapters 1 to 8.

In Chapter 1, I start by looking at how agile and lean are not the goal and how, instead, it is important to start with why and focus on outcomes.

In Chapter 2, I talk about achieving big through small. It's not about scaling agile on top of the current bureaucracy; it's about descaling in order to scale agility and applying an agile approach to agility.

In Chapter 3, I talk about how one size does not fit all and how it is better to invite change rather than inflict it. One of the core tenets of this book is that a practice that works in one context won't necessarily optimize for outcomes in another context. Also, forcing ways of working on people is less likely to be successful than inviting participation with incentivization. Here, we look at a pragmatic approach with the VOICE acronym.

In Chapter 4, I discuss the importance of leadership, including role modeling desired behaviors, creating a psychologically safe culture where safe-to-learn experimentation is rewarded, and being less commander, more servant leader, ensuring that there is high alignment and high autonomy.

In Chapter 5, I discuss building the right thing and explain how to move from discrete output to continuous outcomes. This is the pivot from project to product, from output to outcomes.

In Chapter 6, Myles Ogilvie talks about building the thing right: how continuous compliance keeps teams on track while also keeping them free to innovate and respond. These are the minimal viable guardrails that enable safe autonomy and empowerment.

In Chapter 7, Simon Rohrer explores how continuous attention to technical excellence is essential to exhibit agility and deliver better outcomes.

In Chapter 8, Zsolt Berend explains how to become a learning organization. This is intentionally the final chapter of antipatterns and patterns, as for any organization this is an aspirational state to achieve: to become a continuously unlearning and relearning organization, in order to be the best at being better.

Throughout this book, you'll find case studies, examples, and scenarios drawn from across different industries. This is a book that, should you choose, will put you on the right side of change, create a tailwind, and help you deliver **Better Value Sooner Safer Happier**.

0 HOW WE GOT HERE

In 1992 the representatives of China's National People's Congress voted to build a hydroelectric dam at the site of the Three Gorges on the Yangtze River. Engineers drew up their plans. Work got underway. A small cofferdam was built to create a channel that would divert the flow of China's most powerful river. A new ship lock on the left bank allowed navigation to continue. Five years after the vote to start the project, the flow of the Yangtze River was blocked. A second cofferdam was used to build the dam itself together with a power station. A permanent ship lock replaced the first lock. Ten years after the vote, the second cofferdam was removed and the Yangtze River flowed again, filling the reservoir.[1]

During the construction, the Chinese government relocated more than 1.3 million people and over a thousand towns and villages were flooded. By the time the dam opened, construction had cost around $24 billion and, at its peak, employed over 26,000 workers. The dam reached as high as 185 meters and stretched more than two kilometers across the river. With twenty-six turbines, it could generate twenty times the power of the Hoover Dam. It now has thirty-two turbines and is the world's most powerful dam.[2]

It was always clear that an economy growing as quickly as China's would need new energy sources, and ideally those energy sources would need to be cleaner than coal. By implementing one stage of construction after another, China was able to successfully complete the production of one of the most complicated engineering projects ever undertaken.

While the Chinese government was building a giant dam across its most powerful river, the British government was also undertaking an ambitious project of its own: it was trying to computerize post offices so that they could improve benefit payments. The seventeen million people who then collected benefits would be given special "swipe cards." The system would reduce fraud, lower costs, and be more convenient for both government and claimants.

The card was announced in 1996. The IT project was run by the Department of Social Security (DSS) and by post office counters. Pathway, a subsidiary of International Computers Limited (ICL), won the contract to develop and install the technology. By the time the project was canceled three years later in 1999, post office counters had lost £571 million, ICL wrote off £180 million, and the DSS had laid out about £127 million. Because the system was supposed to have saved £100 million in fraudulent claims, which didn't happen, the total cost to the taxpayer of the failed project was put at about £1 billion.[3]

The cancellation of the post office benefit card project was followed by the publication of a report later that year that listed twenty-five government IT projects that had "resulted in delay, confusion, and inconvenience to the citizen and, in many cases, poor value for money for the taxpayer." The report goes on to say that "for more than two decades, implementing IT systems successfully has proved difficult" and that "problems continue to occur in areas where recommendations have been made in the past."[4]

Those challenges aren't unique to the UK's IT initiatives. In 2013, the US government launched HealthCare.gov, a health insurance shopping site that would enable Americans to take advantage of the new Affordable Care Act. Despite the budget for the site ballooning from $93.7 million to $1.7 billion during development, it was only four days before launch that officials realized the site still had too little capacity. It crashed as soon as it opened. By the end of the day, only six of the 250,000 people who had tried to access the site were able to select an insurance plan and submit an application.[5]

In the cases above, it was a Think Big, Start Big, Learn Slow approach. The future was determined at the moment when the least was known, and there was insufficient learning until right at or after the theoretical end, which is really just the beginning. There was insufficient realization of early and often slices of value and learning. A deterministic mindset was being repeatedly applied to an emergent domain of work. And the same poor outcomes resulted.

That doesn't necessarily mean that the Chinese government is better at building things than the UK or US governments. Building a dam is knowable. There are more than 57,000 large dams worldwide.[6] China is the most dammed country in the world, with more than 23,000 large dams. Dam-building requires expertise. And having built concrete structures to hold back water 22,999 times before, those building it know what to expect, including what problems or challenges might occur. They might not be able to avoid every problem and every delay, but they know where and why delays are likely to occur. There are known-unknowns; people know what they don't know, due to having performed this activity previously many times.

Digitizing benefit payments for seventeen million people and all post offices in the UK had not been done 57,000 times before. It had *never* been done before. Building HealthCare.gov had *never* been done before. Not only that, HealthCare.gov was expected to go live on day one in the thirty-six states in the US that had declined to build their own exchanges. From zero to 250,000 users overnight in one THINK BIG, BUILD BIG, BIG BANG release.

With this work, which has never been done before, people don't know what they don't know. There are unknown-unknowns. Both of these initiatives tried to force a deterministic-way-of-working peg into an emergent-domain-of-work hole, but that does not make it magically work. As Albert Einstein is credited with saying, "the definition of insanity is doing the same thing over and over again but expecting different results."

Instead, it is necessary to optimize for early and often learning in a real environment with real customers or consumers. This lowers the risk of delivery, generates value earlier, enables pivoting to maximize value, and locks in progress as you go. The best part is that, unlike pouring concrete, which sets, with knowledge-based products and services, such as software, this way of working is easy to do. Actually, it's the *easiest* to do.

In order to understand traditional ways of working in most large organizations today in the context of change, it's helpful to understand how we got here.

Previous Ways of Working Were Optimized for Repetitive Labor

One of the leaders of the Efficiency Movement, Frederick Winslow Taylor, did much to improve industrial processes. Working first as a machinist and then as a consultant in the 1890s, Taylor applied a scientific approach to work by using a stopwatch to analyze repetitive work, such as shoveling iron ore or inspecting ball bearings. The result, Taylorism, was a top-down, us-and-them, command-and-control management system. Workers were told when to start and stop working, managers set quotas instead of workers setting the pace of work, and tasks were increasingly specialized. Managers would watch the workers, measure their performance, and order changes. Managers planned and workers worked. Employees did what they were told. As Taylor put it:

> The work of every workman is fully planned out by the management at least one day in advance, and each man receives in most cases complete written instructions, describing in detail the task which he is to accomplish, as well as the means to be used in doing the work. This task specifies not only what is to be done but how it is to be done and the exact time allowed for doing it.[7]

While Taylor's methods increased productivity, they did little to increase happiness or satisfaction in the workplace. Indeed, it is clear that Taylor looked down on workers: "A man who is fit to handle pig iron . . . shall be so stupid . . . that he more nearly resembles in his mental makeup the ox than any other type."[8]

Henry Gantt, the creator of Gantt charts, worked with Taylor in the early 1900s. According to Wallace Clark in *The Gantt Chart: A Working Tool of Management* (written in 1923), what we call a Gantt chart used to be called the Man Record Chart. The horizontal lines represented a worker's actual output versus what the manager (not the worker) viewed to be a reasonable quota. If you moved enough crude iron today, you could go home. If not, you had to keep working. "Long line men" were promoted and "short line men [were] very apt to do everything possible to distract the attention of others from their inferiority."[9]

The premise of the Man Record Chart was to watch over workers and follow up on perceived idleness—a continuation of the command-and-control culture of Taylorism, with managers telling workers exactly what to do. While the result was greater efficiency, it also drove a strong "us and them, managers versus workers" culture and unrest from unions.

The time study approach that Taylor championed was then built upon and improved by others, leading to the specialized production lines of Ford's Model T and eventually the pull-based, just-in-time supply methods pioneered by Toyota that now power modern automotive factories.

While Taylorism turned workers into subservient machines, advances in technology led to machines that could do the work better. The automatic loom replaced handweavers. The internal combustion engine revolutionized travel and delivery times. Telegrams and telephones increased the speed at which information could flow. The forklift and automation replaced the muscles of Taylor's steelworkers. Eventually, with the invention of the microprocessor and the arrival of the Age of Digital, labor's comparative advantage switched from following orders and moving lumps of iron to the ability to create unique products and services that deliver outcomes for customers. The means of production changed from brawn to brain.

From Repetitive Manufacturing to Unique Product Development

In Taylor's time, work was repetitive and performed by hand. Today, more and more of human endeavor is done with the head and is never the same twice, with automation taking on repetitive tasks. Today's most dynamic industrial workplaces are no longer steel mills and fields of discarded iron. They're more likely to resemble hipster cafés with espresso machines and shared tables. In many cities, the warehouses that used to store physical goods are now trendy, bare-brick hotbeds of information technology innovation. Work has moved away from hand-making the same thing repeatedly—effort that's deterministic and has known-unknowns—to unique, knowledge-based work that is emergent and full of unknown-unknowns.

In the same way that going from the Stone Age to the Bronze Age meant not just better tools but also an entirely new society with new ways of living, organizing, and working, so the shift into today's Digital Age has produced equally large social and economic effects.

In 2011, Marc Andreessen, coauthor of the first widely used web browser (Mosaic) and cofounder of the venture capital firm Andreessen Horowitz, told *The Wall Street Journal*:

> Software is eating the world. Six decades into the computer revolution, four decades since the invention of the microprocessor, and two decades into the rise of the modern Internet, all of the technology required to transform industries through software finally works and can be widely delivered at global scale.[10]

Organizations that have applied ways of working that suit the domain of work have not just survived, they've thrived to a degree rarely seen before. Alphabet, Amazon, Apple, and Microsoft have all been valued at over $1 trillion. Apple was the first publicly traded company to hit this landmark in August 2018, with the other three firms surpassing this valuation within eighteen months. Alphabet (Google) and Amazon went from zero to a $1 trillion valuation in just over twenty years. It is interesting to look back in time and see how for each landmark valuation there is a new normal and organizations with new ways of working that are suited to the technology revolution and type of work. The first $100 billion company was IBM in 1987, in the Age of Digital. General Motors was the first $10 billion company in 1955, in the Age of Oil & Mass Production. US Steel was the first $1 billion company in 1901, in the Age of Electricity & Engineering (and was removed from the S&P 500 Index in 2014).[11]

That doesn't mean that businesses must adopt new ways of working in this new Digital Age. Firms can choose to not adapt. A quote often attributed to W. Edwards Deming states: "It is not necessary to change. Survival is not mandatory."

For example, in the retail apocalypse that started in 2010, approximately 10,000 stores closed in the US and 16,000 in the UK in 2019 alone prior to the COVID-19 pandemic.[12] That's five hundred stores closing every single week. The main factor cited was the shift to ecommerce. Thomas Cook, HMV, Debenhams, Bonmarche, Mothercare, Clintons, Karen Millen, Jack Wills, Bathstore, Sears, Borders, Topshop US, and Barneys are just some examples of retailers who have shut up shop or have needed to be rescued in the past few. The pandemic is accelerating the trend with as many 25,000 stores predicted to close in the US alone in 2020.[13] Meanwhile, digital natives are set to open 850 stores by 2023 in "clicks to bricks" expansion plans.[14] There are plenty of vacant stores for them to choose from.

What Are You Optimizing For?

This is an important question to ask. Within your organization, what are you optimizing for? Are you optimizing for the fast flow of safe value with high levels of customer advocacy and colleague engagement? Or for role-based silos, where work is passed over the wall to the next role-based silo with little notion of end-to-end ownership? Are you optimizing for value and time to value, or for pushing a "promise for a future solution" through endless gates and committees for years? Are you optimizing for fast learning and pivoting in order to maximize outcomes in the shortest possible time and with the least effort and least risk? Or for following a predetermined project plan with learning and risks back-loaded to the end with a large impact radius, big-bang implementation? Are you optimizing for everyone using their brains to run safe-to-learn experiments to continuously improve or for following orders?

As we've seen, organizations that have optimized their ways of working to suit the type of work have thrived. This results in higher customer expectations, raising the bar. There is a new normal, further fueled by the COVID-19 pandemic, accelerating the Age of Digital.

Given the importance of taking an optimal approach for the type of work, it is important to understand what agile, lean, DevOps, and waterfall are and their history. As this book is for leaders at all levels and in all roles in large, complex organizations, it assumes no, or little, prior knowledge of ways of working.

Certainly this is what I find in practice. People, historically, have spent very little time thinking about or improving *how* they do what they do.

What Is Agile?

Agile (along with Lean) has origins in manufacturing in Japan, heavily influenced by the teachings of W. Edwards Deming from the 1950s onwards. As we saw in "A Sense of Urgency," the 1986 *Harvard Business Review* article "The New New Product Development Game" articulates the benefits of better ways of working that were taking place in manufacturing firms like Toyota, Honda, and Xerox. The article is still remarkably up to date. These organizations, *in the context of new product development*, had small, empowered, multidisciplinary teams working in small iterations and with a clear North Star outcome. They were empowered as to *how* to achieve the mission, within guardrails, and with a high degree of experimentation. As of the date of the article, Xerox was developing new products with half the number of people and in half the time compared to the previous sequential, stage-gate process.[15]

The article uses the sport of rugby as an analogy, with the team moving together up the pitch with the ball. This led Ken Schwaber and Jeff Sutherland in the early 1990s to call their iterative and incremental approach to software product development Scrum, as per the scrum in rugby.[16]

At the same time, others in software development, myself included, were experimenting with "lightweight processes" (versus heavyweight, sequential, stage-gate processes), finding that more value was delivered sooner with less delivery risk, higher levels of engagement, and no "sunk cost fallacy." With experimentation and experience, "lightweight" processes for software development became increasingly popular, being more suited to the emergent nature of digital work. As Barry O'Reilly, author of *Unlearn*, has subsequently put it, "Think Big, Start Small, Learn Fast."[17]

In 2001, seventeen leading software developers met in Snowbird, Utah, to discuss new, lightweight methods of developing software. They produced what became known as the *Agile Manifesto*.[18] This manifesto is a set of four values and twelve principles that optimize outcomes where the type of work is unique product development. Teams who follow these principles welcome changes to requirements late in product development; trust motivated individuals to get the job done; believe that the best architectures, requirements, and designs emerge from self-organizing teams; and adjust behavior at regular intervals in order to become more effective. While the manifesto was put together by software developers, the values and principles apply to any unique emergent type of work, not only software.

The principles laid out in the manifesto are the very opposite of the top-down management methods advanced by Taylorism. Instead of supervisors giving orders, multidisciplinary teams work together toward a clear outcome aligned to business strategy. They determine safe-to-learn experiments to test the outcome hypothesis (*probe*), measure results (*sense*), and react accordingly (*respond*). Teams are empowered within minimal viable guardrails (for example, compliance, standards, and regulation). Change and changing how you change, based on feedback loops, is essential to optimize outcomes. The principles leverage emergence to your advantage to reduce risk early and pivot to realize more value sooner.

The *Agile Manifesto* intentionally leaves it to people to figure out *how* to apply the principles because organizations are complex adaptive systems and each context is unique. It acknowledges that there is no one-size-fits-all set of practices.

One of the principles states: "Simplicity, the art of maximizing the amount of work not done, is essential." The focus is on *outcomes* over output. That is, maximizing outcomes with *minimal* output, the most value for the least effort. The definition of "productivity" is the number of units of output for each unit of input, which for unique emergent work is not optimal. Instead, the focus should be on "value-tivity," maximizing outcomes for the least output.

As we passed the tipping point in the Age of Digital, to quote Dan Mezick, an "Agile Industrial Complex" developed.[19] This is a top-down imposition of Agile practices and one-size-fits-all processes with no empowerment for teams. It is push, not pull. It is prescriptive and formulaic, not emergent or empowering, and rarely optimizes for desired outcomes in context. It is a forced infliction of emergent ways of working, done with a traditional, deterministic mindset. It is Agile snake oil, cookie-cutter Agile, Agile-in-a-box. Install it and you will be Agile. It is Agile for Agile's sake, Agile as the goal, measuring "how Agile are we." It does not necessarily lead to agility, to better outcomes.

The word "Agile" itself has collected a lot of baggage since its first inception, and I come across many people who have been burnt by an overzealous infliction of it in the past. The word generates resistance. To quote Peter Senge, author of *The Fifth Discipline*, "The harder you push against a system, the harder it pushes back."[20] To increase agility, to optimize for outcomes, given history and culture, *sometimes* the best approach is not Agile at all.

In this book, capital "A" Agile is used to refer to agility in this sense: as a noun, a product, a process, a set of practices, *doing Agile*. This alone does not necessarily translate into better outcomes. I prefer "agile" with a lower case "a," as a verb, rather than a noun, as in *being agile*, as in exhibiting *agility*. It refers to behavior, to culture, to principles, which inform millions of decisions every day. How that manifests will be unique, as your context is unique, and as we will see throughout this book.

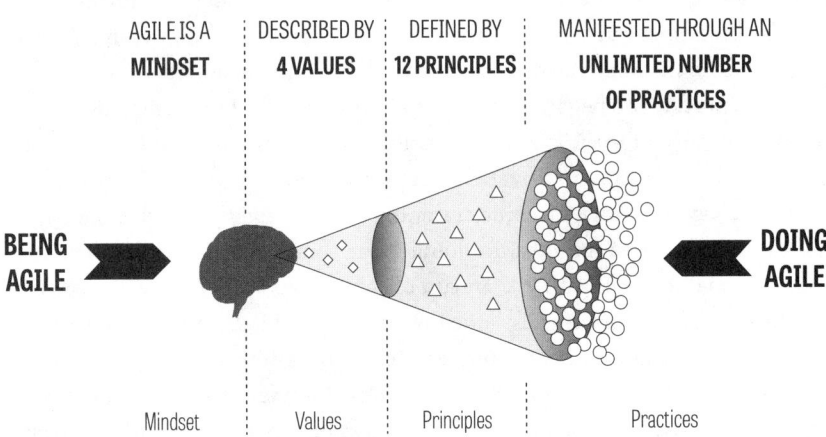

Figure 0.1: Being Agile versus Doing Agile

Adapted from Ahmed Sidky.

Sometimes, I will use the word "nimble" in place of agile in order to sense check. For example, we want to be nimble (i.e., we want to learn fast, continuously improve, and pivot), rather than we want to do Agile (we're doing standups, counting points, and doing mandated, top-down two-week sprints, but not necessarily improving and still working within a broader deterministic mindset). Equally, we don't necessarily want to "do Nimble" or run a Nimble Transformation. We *do* want to improve ways of working suited to our unique context in order to optimize for outcomes.

As organizations are complex adaptive systems, there is no one best way. The majority of agility is about behavioral norms, culture, rather than processes or tools. It's people, process, and tools, in that order.

From Mass Production to Lean Production

"Lean production" was a term coined by John Krafcick, the first American engineer hired at the Toyota-General Motors joint venture, NUMMI. His training at NUMMI included lengthy periods in Japan at Toyota factories, where he learned the fundamentals of Lean production at the source. The term first appeared in the book *The Machine That Changed the World.*[21] One description states that "Lean production is lean, because it uses less of everything compared with mass production. Half the human effort in the factory, half the manufacturing space, half the investment in tools, half the engineering hours, in half the time."[22] The core idea is to maximize customer value while minimizing waste.

Lean production began in the Toyota Production System where, due to economic necessity in the 1950s, with smaller volumes than in the US or Europe and with limited capital, Toyota's chief production engineer, Taiichi Ohno, devised a way to change machine stamping dies for body panels from a day to an astonishing three minutes. In doing so he found that it cost less per part to make small batches rather than run off enormous lots. This was because it eliminated the cost of carrying large inventories, and it meant that any stamping mistakes showed up almost immediately with minimal waste.

Building on concepts from Sakichi Toyoda (founder of Toyota) and his son, Kiichiro, Ohno also instigated a *kaizen* process of constant improvement with all workers, rather than improvement being a job role that someone else did, as was the case in the US car industry and Taylorism. Finally, Ohno developed new ways to coordinate the flow of parts within the supply chains, moving to a just-in-time, pull-based system, further eliminating costly inventory and waste and optimizing for flow. It took Ohno more than twenty years to fully implement these concepts. The result: in 2008 Toyota was the number one car manufacturer globally, stripping GM of the sales crown for the first time in seventy-eight years. Currently, Toyota has the highest market value of any automotive manufacturer, worth four times more than GM and seven times more than Ford.

In *Lean Thinking*, Daniel Jones and James Womack outline five lean principles:[23]

1. **Value**: specify value from the point of view of the customer.
2. **Value Stream**: identify the value stream and all the steps in it, from concept to cash.

3. **Flow**: limit work in progress; stabilize flow; focus on lead time, throughput, and flow efficiency; alleviate impediments to flow.
4. **Pull**: move from a push-based system of work to a pull-based system of work; go at the capacity of the system of work and don't over-produce.
5. **Perfection**: the relentless pursuit of perfection.

Lean and agile, with a common root in post–World War II Japan, have a lot in common, such as a focus on building quality in, value, flow, respect for people, a pull-based system of work, and a *kaizen* process of continuous improvement and visualizing work. However, a key area where they differ is the focus on "standardized work" in lean. Mass production looks for "good enough," and lean production looks for perfection. This is desirable for repetitive production; however, for the unique, unknowable, emergent domain of product development, "perfect is the enemy of good," to quote Voltaire. Lean production (suited to knowable, repetitive work) seeks to minimize variability, striving for perfection, in some cases targeting Six Sigma levels of perfection. Agility (suited to unknowable unique work) actively seeks and benefits from variability with multiple minimally viable, safe-to-learn experiments in order to optimize for outcomes.

What Is DevOps?

DevOps is a portmanteau that combines Development and Operations. DevOps focuses on breaking down the barriers between the teams responsible for developing a product and the teams responsible for deploying and operating the product. The term was coined by Patrick Debois when he created the DevOpsDays conference in Ghent, Belgium, in 2009. Agile in software development had alleviated the impediments to flow between customers, business analysts, developers, and testers; however, in many traditional organizations there was still a metaphorical brick wall between those building software and those running it, with a lack of shared understanding, accountability, or end-to-end flow.

Developers would build a product and then throw it over the wall at an increasing cadence, often with no notice or advice on supportability, for someone in a different role to deploy to production and support. IT Operations would tend to repetitively and manually fix issues in production without the Development team's awareness such that many issues were rarely permanently addressed. The cost of IT Ops ("lights on") would continue to rise, squeezing discretionary spending. Typically IT build and IT run would not sit together, limiting collaboration and the ability to overhear (or even directly handle) repetitive support queries. Not surprisingly, getting closer to "you build it, you run it," sitting people together in multidisciplinary teams, automating testing and deployment, and having a focus on failure demand, supportability, resilience, and observability all lead to better outcomes. Having to support your own product is a strong motivator to maintain high quality and supportability. The primary tribal identity is aligned to the customer, the value stream, and the product(s), not the job role. The team succeeds and learns together.

In *The Unicorn Project*, Gene Kim defines five ideals of DevOps:[24]

1. **Locality and Simplicity**: alleviate dependencies between teams and components.
2. **Focus, Flow, and Joy**: the smooth flow of work that enables focus and joy.
3. **Improvement of Daily Work**: continuously improve and pay down technical debt.
4. **Psychological Safety**: a top predictor of team performance; enables improvement.
5. **Customer Focus**: optimize for customer value, not for a role-based silo.

In my experience, DevOps can have a narrow IT Dev plus IT Ops meaning and a broader enterprise DevOps meaning. The broader meaning of DevOps is delivering **Better Value Sooner Safer Happier**. It is the application of better ways of working, end to end, to deliver business and customer value, leveraging many bodies of knowledge, including agile and lean. The biggest impediment to flow, to better outcomes, might be in behavioral norms, leadership, finance, HR, PMO, real estate, governance committees, and so on. If in your context DevOps is being used in the narrow meaning, be wary of local optimization. Once the weakest link in the chain is no longer the weakest link, little value will come from continuing to strengthen it. Identify the next weakest link, which could be project-based funding for example and alleviate that, before repeating forever!

Agile, Lean, DevOps, and other bodies of knowledge are all a means to an end, not the end itself. They are shared learning in human endeavor, which can be used in context to improve outcomes, to deliver **Better Value Sooner Safer Happier**.

What Is Waterfall?

Most large, old, traditional organizations either used to take, or still take, a waterfall approach in the context of unique change. The word "waterfall" is used as there is a sequential, stage-gate process, where work is completed at one stage before flowing to the next stage and so on. It is one-way, with big batches of work passing by job role. There is big, up-front planning and design, predicting time, cost, scope, and quality at the point when there has been the least actual learning. There is change control on the plan that inhibits agility. "Scope creep" occurs (because people are discovering the unknowable as they go) and is inhibited. Time to value is typically measured in years. The focus is on achieving a predetermined plan rather than on early and often learning to maximize value and the outcome—or to stop working on it early and move on at the lowest cost of failure.

There is sunk cost fallacy ("We've invested $100 million already. We can't write it off. Let's keep on going."). Learning is late, with a high-stakes, big-bang implementation and a large impact radius. Late learning delays the realization of value and reduces the likelihood of maximizing value. It also significantly increases delivery risk, back-loading it to when there is the least time to respond. People end up cutting corners to hit a predetermined "deadline" or feel demoralized at slipping the plan (which in reality is the gap between what is knowable and what is unknowable). The later the learning, the higher the probability of being wrong and the higher cost of being wrong. By the time something is delivered, the world has moved on. "IT doesn't move as fast as the business" is a frequent comment associated with waterfall change delivery.

Engagement is low as employees don't get to see the fruits of their labor adding value until much later, if they are lucky. People are stuck in role-based silos, with no feeling of or actual end-to-end accountability. People are promoted and incentivized within their role-based silos, leading to finger pointing. "It's not my problem. I did my bit. The hole is on their side of the boat." The problem with big-bang, waterfall failures has been described as "the application development crisis."[25]

Applying a waterfall approach in the context of unique change is a thinking error. It is miscategorizing emergent work (unknowable) as deterministic (knowable). It is taking an approach that came about in the context of manual labor shoveling iron ore or building dam number 57,001 (tasks that have been done sufficient times before to be knowable) and applying it to unique product development (which has never been done before and is unknowable).

In the same category as waterfall is water-scrum-fall. While it is a slight improvement on a fully sequential, stage-gate process, it is not agile. It usually manifests as a waterfall project with big, up-front planning and big, up-front design, the word "sprint" ten times in the middle of the gantt chart, the work for each "sprint" having been pre-planned, and then late learning with big-bang testing and implementation. It does not exhibit agility and does not optimize for outcomes. It is still applying a deterministic mindset to an emergent domain of work.

Winston Royce, one of the first to document the waterfall sequential process, wrote in 1970 that "the implementation described is risky and invites failure."[26]

When considering the optimal approach to the type of work, it's not about agile or waterfall. It's about agile (unknowable, unique) and lean (knowable, repetitive). Waterfall is "Think Big, Start Big, Learn Slow," for which, in my opinion, there is no excuse. Why would you not optimize for early and often learning, continuous improvement, and the ability to pivot for unique change in order to de-risk and realize more value sooner and improve outcomes? Even construction has adopted agile and lean principles and practices.[27]

As we've seen, to deliver **Better Value Sooner Safer Happier**, it is important to apply the optimal approach to the work based on the type of work. In the next section, we take a look at the Cynefin framework, which is a helpful way to frame this question.

Approaching Work Based on the Domain of Work

As we've seen, product development, unique change, is *emergent*, not *deterministic*. The work is filled with unknown-unknowns and acting in the space changes the space. Conversely, a worker making wheels all day long on an assembly line knows when the wheel is built and when it's not. Likewise an organization processing ten million payment transactions a day. In that context, you want standardized work, not variability.

It's much harder when each thing you build is unique. Only once the product is built can you realize a better way of building it, or even realize that building something entirely different would better meet the needs of the consumer. In an emergent domain, you want variability to learn and then amplify the experiments that optimize for the desired outcomes.

This means there is no one-size-fits-all way of working. It's not about Agile-everything or Lean-everything or DevOps-everything. It's about optimizing the way of working based on the type of work and your unique context.

The Cynefin Framework

In 1999, while working as a management consultant for IBM Global Services, Dave Snowden produced the "Cynefin" (pronounced kuh-nev-in) framework to categorize the different domains in which work today takes place. Named after the Welsh word for "habitat," the framework provides a model of five domains for problem-solving and decision-making (see Figure 0.2). It is a very useful way to determine when to take an agile approach, a lean approach, or neither.

Figure 0.2: Cynefin
Adapted from Dave Snowden.

Clear: Child's Play

The "clear" domain of the Cynefin framework is straightforward and has predictable results. This is child's play. There is no need for a project plan, a sprint, or a backlog. A child knows that if she turns left, then right, then left again, she will arrive at school. The route is the same every day and so is the result. This domain has known-knowns and a best practice. In the UK you drive on the left. In the US you drive on the right. The relationship between cause and effect is clear. In this domain it is possible to *sense* the situation and the environment (e.g., I'm in the UK), *categorize* it based on what you know (in this country people drive on the left), and *respond* by following the rules or applying best practices (set off, driving on the left).

Complicated: Sweet Spot for Lean

The Complicated domain requires more judgment. It is knowable because this activity has been done many times before in this context. However, it's not child's play; it requires expertise. There are known-unknowns. The relationship between cause and effect needs analysis or knowledge. In this domain, you *sense*, *analyze*, and then *respond*, applying the appropriate good operating practice. There is *good* practice here, but there is no *best* practice. As it is non-trivial, there is still room for improvement, to eliminate waste, to improve quality, and to optimize flow.

For example, an IT firm installing servers in a datacenter; an automotive manufacturer building cars; an investment bank trading and processing equity trades; the HR department onboarding new employees. These activities are knowable because they've all been done many times before; however, the work requires expertise, especially when things go wrong. Even then, the failure patterns have been experienced before. This is ordered, repetitive, knowable activity. This is the sweet spot for lean.

Complex: Sweet Spot for Agile

Unique product development takes place in the Complex Domain. This is where there are unknown-unknowns and acting in the space changes the space. Cause and effect can only be deduced in retrospect. Whereas the previous two domains are *ordered*, this domain is *unordered*. There is no such thing as best practice or even good practice because activity in this domain is emergent. The best approach here is to *probe* by running a safe-to-learn experiment to test a hypothesis, to *sense* the results, and then to *respond* by amplifying or dampening the experiment.

In the Age of Digital, all software development is unique. You don't write the same code twice. People don't know what they want until they see it. You don't know how you're going to write it until you've written it, and then it needs to be refactored as you realize how it could have been written to be more usable, maintainable, or resilient. Even installing a third-party application, such as an ERP system, is novel: that code has never been installed in that context with those data feeds, those people, and those processes before. Minimizing time to learning is key; fast feedback loops de-risk delivery and enable optimizing for outcomes. This is the sweet spot for agility.

Chaos: Act First

Sometimes decisions have to be made in a domain that is "chaotic." Knowledge here is less important than rapid action that returns order. We *act* to establish order, to stem the bleeding; *sense* where stability lies; and *respond* to turn the Chaotic into Complex. Like the Complex domain, this domain is also *unordered*.

The global COVID-19 pandemic is a good example of this domain. With mandated lockdowns in force globally and people required to stay at home, organizations scrambled remarkably quickly to act. That could have been to open up more network connections to enable huge numbers of people to work from home, or in industries such as aviation, automotive, and hospitality to shut down operations, or supermarkets and suppliers working to keep the supply chains operating. There was no time for months of planning and multiple committee-based approvals. Organizations often comment that they are at their best in these situations, with people coming together, irrespective of job role or business unit, working as one multidisciplinary team to quickly address the issue. Most then go back to their previous ways of working. Techniques stumbled upon in Chaos can end up becoming a new good or best practice in the Complicated or Clear domains for business as usual.

Confused

The last of the domains in the Cynefin framework is Confused, when it's not clear which of the domains currently apply. This can be authentic (you're really not sure, in which case break the situation down into smaller parts) or inauthentic (which means that you are complacently ignoring any distinction and carry on managing Complex situations as if they were Complicated or Clear.)

Work Moves Around Domains

Work is rarely stationary in one domain. For example, the creation of a new product, such as a new model of car, will start in the Complex domain. In an agile manner, there will be customer focus groups, pencil sketches, computer-aided design (or "digital twin" simulation), and eventually a small-scale prototype and wind tunnel testing for quickest time and cheapest cost of learning, avoiding a sunk cost fallacy. At some point there will be a full-size prototype and eventually testing in the extremes of the Sahara and Alaska, all the time making updates to maximize the desired outcomes. Later 100,000 instances of that model are built each year, which is into the Complicated domain. Then there is a shallow dip into Chaos with a recall of certain models due to a fault, some Complex domain experimentation to fix it, and then back into Complicated domain with lean production.

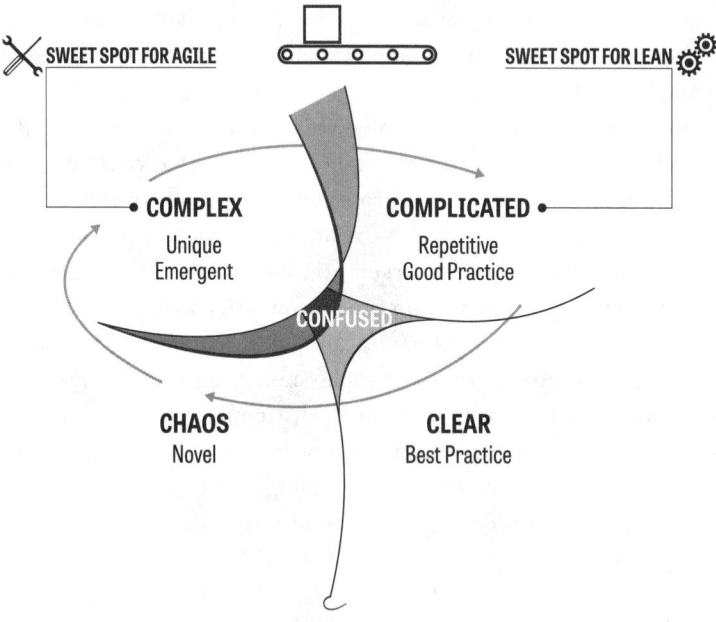

Figure 0.3: Work Moves around Domains

Software benefits from both an agile and lean approach. The software binary is agile-created and the path to production is lean, as the build, test, deploy process should run repetitively and with a high degree of automation many times a day. Periodically there will be step-change agile experimentation in the path to production and then back into lean again. Software is an agile-created box on a lean conveyor belt.

Surviving and Thriving in the Age of Digital

For those who choose to leverage the latest technological revolution and adopt ways of working that suit the nature of more of today's work, the benefits are clear. *The State of DevOps Report 2019* shows that elite performers compared to low performers deliver business value through technology 208 times more frequently, are 2,604 times faster to recover from incidents, and have a seven times lower change failure rate.[28] There is quicker learning, feedback, value, and ability to pivot to maximize desired outcomes. There is greater resilience and stability, which leads to increased satisfaction by both customers and colleagues. These factors, along with psychological safety, are positively correlated to overall organizational performance.

In my own experience, several years into being a servant leader on better ways of working across Barclays, in the context of unique product development, we saw the lead time, the time from starting work to getting it into the hands of the customer, the time to learning, to pivot, to reduce risk, reduce by two-thirds on average. The time to value and feedback was three times faster than it used to be. We saw a corresponding average 300% increase in throughput of items of value across thousands of teams for product development. The number of incidents fell by a factor of twenty, and the independently surveyed colleague engagement scores were the highest they had ever been. The teams that made the most progress reduced time to value by a factor of twenty, with throughput rising by a similar amount. Learning was twenty times faster, as was de-risking, the ability to pivot, to respond to feedback, to learn, to change direction, and to stop. Like the high performers in *The State of DevOps Report 2019*, teams were delivering **Better Value Sooner Safer Happier**.

This was after our fair share of learning the hard way and observing many Kübler-Ross curves, with peaks of excitement, troughs of disillusionment, and then, usually, climbing up to a higher point of mastery. (See Chapter 3 for more on this.) As we looked at in "A Sense of Urgency" and will explore throughout this book, lasting behavior change cannot be forced. It is not a short-term activity; it is continuous.

With the new means of production, the pace of change is getting ever faster. Change is no longer staccato, as it was in the past. Product development in particular, with a pivot from project to product, is no longer a case of big-bang builds, leaving it to go into obsolescence, letting the weeds grow, until another big-bang slash, burn, rewrite is required. Organizations are moving to "continuous everything."

Both software systems and human systems lose information over time. Left alone they become less efficient and less maintainable. Software becomes obsolete and people, with a charitable intent, introduce bureaucracy, often with unintended consequences. The weeds grow back. Instead, we need to be tending to the garden continuously, keeping it "evergreen," nurturing culture, upgrading the plane while flying, and avoiding behavioral, process, and technical debt, which accumulates with compound interest. Change and continuous improvement should be a sustainable habit, a constant process of experimentation, feedback, learning, and pivoting to optimize for outcomes. After all, customers are not just buying a point-in-time product, they are buying ongoing innovation and an experience. And people want to work somewhere where the way of working is sustainable, engaging, and humane.

Some organizations are still using ways of working from two technological revolutions ago, misapplying them to the type of work. Others have adopted ways of working suited to the increasingly emergent nature of work in the Age of Digital. We've gone from Taylorism in the Age of Electricity & Engineering to Fordism and then Lean Production in the Age of Oil & Mass Production and now to Business Agility in the Age of Digital. Repeatedly, efficiently, sustainably, and continuously delivering **Better Value Sooner Safer Happier**. There is a new normal.

I'll talk about **BVSSH** in more detail in the next chapter; it's at the heart of this book and it should be the focus of any business that wants to survive and thrive in the Age of Digital.

FOCUS ON OUTCOMES:
BETTER VALUE SOONER
SAFER HAPPIER

Do you want to do or are you currently doing an Agile, Lean, or DevOps Transformation? If so, my best advice is:

Don't.

Instead, focus on the *outcomes* you want to achieve. Then you will achieve agility.

Focus on:

Better Value Sooner Safer Happier

This is the number one lesson I've learned after almost thirty years as an agile and lean practitioner delivering business value through software in the Age of Digital, from leading Ways of Working at a large, old, global, regulated organization to working with many large firms across different industry sectors. Together as a team-of-teams, as servant leaders, we experimented, learned, and pivoted.

Agile, Lean, and DevOps are not the goal. An organization can score highly on a "How Agile Are We?" test (or worse, "How Much Are We Rigidly Complying to a Specific Agile Framework?" test, or "How Many Scrum Teams Do We Have?" test) without producing better business outcomes. I've seen it happen time and time again. The wrong thing can be produced more quickly. Teams can become feature factories, a self-fulfilling prophecy of backlog replenishment with a focus on "More output!" rather than a focus on better outcomes. In addition, Agile can be viewed as an IT-only thing, no more than a local optimization, an agile bubble in a sea of traditional approaches. Or teams can exhibit cargo cult behaviors, with new labels and rituals but with the same old behaviors as before.

Agile, Lean, DevOps, design thinking, systems thinking, Theory of Constraints, and so on are all proverbial tools in a toolbox that organizations can employ to achieve desired outcomes. They are bodies of knowledge, years of wisdom acquired in the field of organized human endeavor, articulated as principles and practices. As we've seen, they are suited to specific contexts—contexts that are the new normal in the Age of Digital—as venerable old firms (the "horses" of a previous age rather than new digital "unicorns") move on from ways of working that are more than a hundred years old, originating from two technological revolutions ago in the late 1800s.

Every organization is unique and is a *complex adaptive system*. Culture change is emergent. So the interventions chosen need to be applied *uniquely in context*. There is no cookie-cutter, one-size-fits-all approach. There is no silver bullet, no snake oil, no panacea. To know whether the bodies of knowledge, the principles and practices you're using, are having the desired impact, you need to know what your desired outcomes are and keep your eye on that ball. What job are you using the bodies of knowledge for? What result do you want to produce?

At every organization I've worked for or with, those desired outcomes can be articulated as **Better Value Sooner Safer Happier (BVSSH)**.

What Is Better Value Sooner Safer Happier?

So what is **Better Value Sooner Safer Happier**? What do the terms represent and how are they measured? An important point to note is that they are *not only* IT outcomes and measures. They apply across organizations, anywhere work is being done to deliver value. They're about a collective "*our* business," not an us-and-them "*the* business," irrespective of job role. In the Age of Digital every company is a software company directly or indirectly, and there are few cases where value delivery does not in some way involve Information Technology.

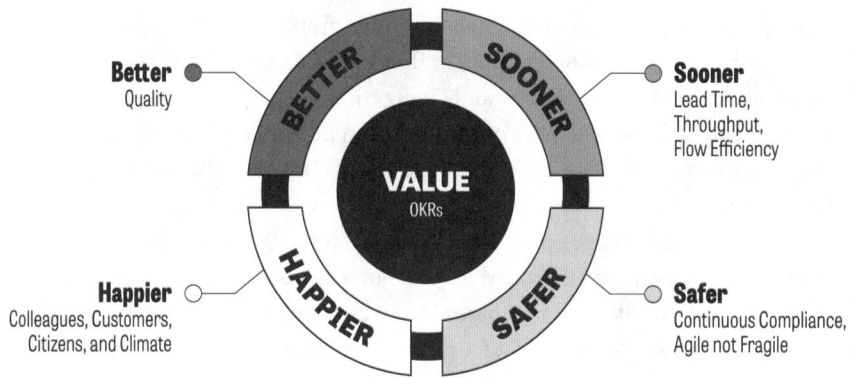

Fig 1.1: Better Value Sooner Safer Happier

Better is quality. For example, for a software product "better" could mean fewer production incidents, a faster mean time to recovery, and improved static code analysis measures. For internal audit, "better" could be less rework of internal reports. For an operational area of an organization, such as processing payments, transactions, or loan applications, "better" could be a lower error rate. The lower the "failure demand," the lower the cost of keeping the lights on and the greater the percentage of the budget that can be spent on new value-adding activities. Quality should be built in, rather than inspected in later.

Value is in the eye of the beholder. It is unique and it is articulated via quarterly business outcome (also known as Objective & Key Results or OKRs). It's why you're in business. "Value" could be market share, revenue, units sold, P&L, margin, diversity, carbon emissions, app downloads, minutes streamed, subscribers, and so on. Value should cover the perspective of the consumer and producer.

Business outcomes are hypotheses, as we're in the emergent domain. They are nested, with a lineage up to longer-term, organization wide strategic outcome hypotheses (yearly and multi-year). There is fast feedback with daily releases of value into the hands of customers to test the hypotheses. The value measures are the KRs in OKR with leading and lagging measures. Daily, weekly, monthly nested cadences enable pivoting based on fast learning. Typically there is a monthly cadence on the quarterly business outcomes to inspect and adapt. With daily releases of value, it is possible to have daily feedback on multi-year strategic hypotheses. See Chapter 5 for more on this.

Sooner is flow, which is at the heart of agile and lean. It's about optimizing for fast and efficient flow of safe value with respect for people. There are three key measures that can be aggregated up to the organization level or disaggregated down to the team level:

- **Flow efficiency** is the percentage of time that work is actively being worked on during its elapsed end-to-end lead time, as opposed to waiting to be worked on. It is one of the most important measures, yet it is rare to find an organization that knows its flow efficiency for knowledge work. For most large service-based organizations, in my experience, flow efficiency is typically 10% or lower. This means that work is waiting at least 90% of the time. This is where significant gains can be made. Focus on where the work *isn't*, not where the work is. Focus on the work, not the worker. The wait time is usually caused by impediments to flow, such as role-based or time-zone handoffs or multiple committee review steps, leading to work being queued. A high wait time is also caused by organizations attempting to do too much work in parallel. The more cars on the road, the slower they go. Identify and alleviate the impediments to flow and limit concurrent work in progress.

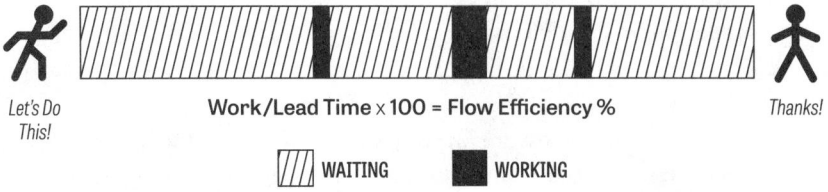

Figure 1.2 Flow (In)Efficiency

- **Lead time** is time to market, the time from starting work on an item of value to getting it into the hands of a customer. Reducing lead time enables faster feedback, quicker learning, reduced risk, earlier monetization, and the ability to pivot sooner to maximize outcomes. Lead time is a distribution—typically a Weibull distribution, a type of continuous probability distribution—that resembles a normal distribution skewed to the left and with a long tail. The recommended measure is the 85th percentile lead time and its change over time.

- **Throughput** is a count of items of value delivered into the hands of a customer in a given time period. As lead time comes down, throughput should go up. If it doesn't, then flow has an upstream impediment. Ideally, throughput should not increase directly in line with reduction in lead time. Instead, some of the time gained from reducing lead time should be used for innovation, time with customers, and continuing to improve the system of work, further alleviating impediments to flow. We want to maximize outcomes with minimal output.

Note that the word "faster" does not appear here. "Faster" can have negative connotations. A "feature factory" can work fast, churning out features that no one wants, working harder rather than smarter.

Safer means continuous compliance, agile not fragile, a topic we cover in Chapter 6. It is about not making the news headlines due to leaking customer data. Safer is Information Security, cyber, data privacy, General Data Protection Regulation, know-your-client, anti-money laundering, fraud, and so on. It is Governance, Risk, and Compliance (GRC). Safer is speed *and* control, not choosing one at the expense of the other. Safer is cultural, with a continuous conversation on risk.

Happier is happier colleagues, customers, citizens, and climate. Improving ways of working is not at any human, societal, or climatic cost. It is about a more humane, engaging way of working, with multidisciplinary, empowered teams centered around the customer. Happier is working smarter not harder; it is improving the system of work and removing impediments. Happier is obsessing about customer satisfaction (which will lead to revenue, rather than a primary focus on short-term financial measures). Happier is also about social and climatic responsibility.

Together, **Better Value Sooner Safer Happier** balance each other. If Sooner is achieved by working people harder or cutting corners, the result will be a reduction in Better and Happier.

BVSSH contains two sets of outcomes. **Better Sooner Safer Happier** are the *how* outcomes. They measure the improvement in the system of work. **Value** is the *what*, the business outcome hypotheses that the system of work produces and that I discuss in Chapter 5. The two sets of outcomes form a virtuous circle. Improvements in the *how* leads to improvement in the *what* due to faster feedback, the ability to pivot, higher quality, and more engaged colleagues and customers.

Note that just as I don't mention "faster," I also never use the word "cheaper." A lesson learned by organizations adopting lean principles and practices in Japan is that "cheaper" is an antipattern. It will create a headwind. People don't want to work themselves or a colleague out of a job. It is not a motivating call to action. Cheaper has negative connotations on quality and happiness.

Also, a focus on reducing visible costs often increases hidden costs via a reduction in flow efficiency. There is a hidden cost to cost-cutting. For example, introducing more handoffs, communication paths, time-zone challenges, differing incentivization, and so on all reduce flow efficiency. It increases the time that work is waiting. This reduces throughput and makes lead time longer. The system of work becomes less efficient. Learning and pivoting is slower. The company spends less, but it's also doing less and has made the system of work less effective. It's a double whammy on the ability to generate value. The organization has throttled back, both with a step change down in value production and a reduction in the gradient of adding value over time, due to reduced flow efficiency. This reduces income, which puts further challenges on cost.

Improving ways of working for product development is about "value-tivity." We want to optimize for value and time to learning. Outcomes over output. We want to maximize outcomes in the shortest time and with the least output. We want to maximize the value curve, cut the tail, and pivot to the next value curve. Typically, a focus on "cheaper" has the opposite effect, making time to value and time to learning longer.

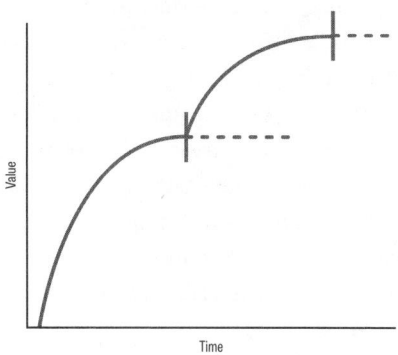

Figure 1.3: Maximize the Value Curve; Cut the Tail

Instead of cheapness, focus on **Better Value Sooner Safer Happier** outcomes and improve the system of work. As lead time reduces and throughput increases, striving for the highest value in the shortest time, with greater agility, the "income" in cost-income ratio should improve, all other things being equal and compared to maintaining the status quo.

If an organization doesn't have the runway to improve first, or macro drivers (such as a global pandemic), to change the business fundamentals and force a need to spend less and do less, my advice is to pay very close attention to the system of work. Don't increase the hidden costs with a reduction in flow efficiency and a longer time to value and learning. Don't prioritize cutting costs at the expense of flow. The result will be increased hidden costs. Do have a focus on throughput accounting as well as traditional cost accounting.

Now that you have a deeper understanding of **Better Value Sooner Safer Happier**, and you are ready to focus on outcomes rather than Agile, we will look at two of the most important, most fundamental, antipatterns. They generate a significant headwind. They are detrimental, as they do not apply an agile mindset to agility. These antipatterns (as with all antipatterns) are approaches that more often than not reduce the likelihood of achieving desired outcomes. They make a hard job harder.

ANTIPATTERN 1.1

Doing an Agile Transformation

I've met with many organizations and leadership teams that want to undertake an "Agile Transformation." The process usually begins in the same way. We sit with senior leaders and ask them *why* they want to change. The response is often silence. A couple of people will stare at the ceiling. Someone will stretch their legs. Then, eventually, one brave person will raise a hand, and say:

"It takes us too long to get new ideas to market. We're slow and inefficient."

"Good," I'll say, and write that on the board. "Anyone else?"

More replies usually come in then, and they are written down in turn:

"Everyone else is doing it."

"We're struggling to stem attrition and attract talent."

"Our customer satisfaction is trending in the wrong way."

"We don't want to be left behind."

"Beats me. I think we're doing fine as we are," says the person with their arms crossed and brow furrowed.

Each of those answers is reasonable and understandable (even the last one). We continue asking why the company might want to change how it does what it does. Eventually someone lands on the existential point: "We're being disrupted. If we don't change how we do things here, we won't survive."

Often, the organization is about to embark—or has already embarked—on an "Agile Transformation." Or they've had a bitter experience in the past with a "Lean Transformation" or Six Sigma or tried to become more "DevOps" with a focus on tooling. Typically, desired outcomes have not been articulated other than "How many Agile, Lean, DevOps teams do we have?" There are bubbles of agile in a sea of Gantt charts with predetermined solutions, dates, and spending predicted at the point of knowing the least, an annual, bottom-up financial planning process that takes six months of the year to plan and re-plan and focuses on output over outcomes. There are "drop dead dates" and "deadlines" (in *most* cases it's not life or death); RAG (red, amber, green) statuses and change control processes; a change lifecycle with twenty mandatory artifacts, most with their own stage-gate governance committee; a traditional waterfall Project Management Office; sixty-page Steering Committee decks; project plans with the word "sprint" ten times in the middle; a lack of psychological safety; a performance appraisal model that incentivizes mediocrity (underpromise to overdeliver) and uses a Think Big, Start Big, Learn Slow approach. The good news, with a charitable intent, is that the organization wants to improve.

1: Tools in the Toolbox

It's not about "Agile," or "Lean," or "DevOps" for "Agile's" or "Lean's" or "DevOps's" sake. Figuratively speaking, they are tools in a toolbox. Of course, they are much more than tools; they are behavioral principles, practices, and tools. The point is that you have a collection of bodies of knowledge to deploy optimally in context. A tool transformation, such as an "Agile Transformation," is not optimizing for outcomes, it's optimizing for the tool.

For example, let's say you want to hang more pictures on your wall, so you do a "drill transformation." To stretch the analogy further, the make of drill denotes a particular agile framework. For example, a "Bosch drill transformation" or a "Black & Decker drill transformation." At the end of your drill transformation, you may have a multidisciplinary team creating a wall full of quarter-inch holes faster, meeting hole-drilling commitments, but it doesn't mean that the pictures are going up. Agile and lean principles, practices, methods, and frameworks are bodies of knowledge to achieve a goal, but they are not the goal. Equally, success is not defined as teams using actual tools, such as JIRA and Jenkins. A tool-led transformation does not equate to agility.

2: Cargo Cult Behavior

During World War II, America had airbases on a number of Melanesian islands in the South Pacific. Planes would land regularly, dropping off cargo such as medicine, foodstuffs, tents, and weapons that the islanders had never seen before. Once the war ended, the planes stopped coming. The islanders responded by creating what anthropologists called a "cargo cult."[1] They built wooden control towers, wore headphones made from coconuts, performed parades and ground drills with wooden rifles, and built life-sized replicas of airplanes out of straw. They had seen that when the Americans performed similar behavior, planes arrived with boxes full of goods. Despite their attempts at re-enacting this activity, the flying machines did not return to drop their cargo.

This cargo cult behavior can occur in organizations undergoing Agile Transformations. It can happen when organizations "do Agile," pursue Agile for Agile's sake, or focus on "How Agile are we?" rather than on desired outcomes. Staff might not wear coconut headphones, however, there are new role titles, iterations, standups, retrospectives, and stickies, which by themselves do not necessarily translate into better business outcomes. People are practicing the ceremonies, but the planes don't land and the cargo never arrives.

It happens at both large and small organizations. Until 2010, Nokia had the number one market share for smartphones.[2] Nokia development teams had adopted agile ways of working and, with a positive intent as an improvement on previous ways of working, would apply a "Nokia Test,"[3] which measured the company's agility in relation to the Scrum agile framework.[4] In the space of just two years, during 2011 and 2012, Nokia's Symbian operating system fell from the largest market share to extinction.[5] The last Nokia phone with the Symbian OS was unveiled in February 2012. In the UK, not a single major operator stocked it. Nokia sold its mobile phone business to Microsoft in September 2013.

In his book, *Transforming Nokia*, Risto Siilasmaa, Nokia's chairman since 2012, described how he felt when he learned that it took *two days* to compile the Symbian operating system and *two weeks* to do a complete build:

It was as though someone had hit me in the head with a sledgehammer. . . . There were fundamental flaws in how we developed the platform that most of our profitability and near-term growth depended on. . . . As I later learned, the overall build time was two weeks! This was a recipe for catastrophe and a catastrophe was exactly what we had staring straight into our eyes.[6]

The teams could "do Agile" as much as they liked. They had Product Owners, standups, sprints, and so on, all of which are improvements on a traditional waterfall approach with a very long concept-to-cash time and a long time to learning. However, it didn't save Symbian or Nokia mobile. According to Siilasmaa, the bigger problem was a lack of psychological safety.[7] Bad news was being buried instead of exposed, discussed, and dealt with. No one had bubbled up the fact that the overall build time was two weeks. Doing Agile will not address that problem.

In my experience, the behavioral norms in an organization are the biggest lever in transforming ways of working. As I'll explain in Chapter 4, they're also the hardest to move. Had there been a primary focus at Nokia on the *outcomes* instead of on the tools, the results might have been different. A focus on Sooner might have shone a light on the long lead time to learning for Symbian features. A focus on Happier might have exposed a lack of psychological safety. Focusing on all of **BVSSH** might have kept Symbian competing with Android and iOS.

I've experienced this cargo cult behavior firsthand. It was one of my biggest lessons learned. At Barclays in 2015, I was leading an "Agile Transformation." We ran a "How Agile Are You?" self-assessment survey with four levels. The test had a positive intent, and it gave a rough indicator of who was working with agile principles and practices and who was still working with old, waterfall ways of working.

In hindsight, I wouldn't do it again. The test led to cargo cult behaviors with new labels on the same old practices. We also had teams who had adopted agile principles and methods but, for a wide range of reasons that I'll describe in later chapters, didn't produce the expected beneficial outcomes. They were focused on agile practices but not on the outcomes.

Worse still, we had targets on the four agility levels—and you get what you measure. Teams found ways to game the system, and in some cases that produced even more cargo cult behavior. Every business unit achieved their "How

Agile Are You?" targets, with some miraculous, almost unbelievable, jumps just before the end-of-year performance appraisals. The survey might have had a positive intent; however, with the benefit of hindsight, it turned out to be misguided. We learned and we pivoted.

ANTIPATTERN 1.2

Using Old Ways of Thinking to Apply New Ways of Working

Focusing on "Agile," "Lean," or "DevOps" as the end rather than the means to an end is using old ways of thinking to apply new ways of working.

A capital "A," capital "T" Agile Transformation, from the perspective of employees, infers involuntary, mandatory change being done to them, whether they like it or not. The capital "A" denotes *how* they are going to change. The capital "T" tells them they *have* to change. Both of these words carry baggage. They suggest extrinsic (push) rather than intrinsic (pull) motivation.

Capital "A" Agile in this antipattern tells employees that they *have to be* a Product Owner, Scrum Master, or Team Member. They *have to* adopt stand-ups, retrospectives, stories, epics, and stickies. They *must* learn new jargon and become comfortable talking about velocity, story points, story mapping, planning poker, burn up, burn down, spikes, MVP, OKR, VSM, XP, CI/CD, squads, tribes, chapters, guilds, Dojo, Kata, *kaizen*, Obeya Room, and cumulative flow diagrams. It's revolution, not evolution, and you don't have a choice. Not quite as extreme as the Spanish Inquisition, it's an Agile Imposition.

Capital "T" Transformation in this antipattern represents an imposed change. It represents a program of work with a start date and an end date when the firm will have magically and permanently transformed, like a caterpillar turning into a butterfly. It is a top-down mandate, treated as a project like any other, with a deterministic mindset; big up-front planning with "deadlines" (that death analogy again); and an eighteen-month countdown. In some cases, it's a dressed-up cost-cutting exercise as a big-bang change, with a reorganization into squads and tribes, new roles, and staff layoffs. In some cases, people need to reapply for their own jobs with months of uncertainty. Are your top talent, who are able to get a job next door, likely to hang around with that degree of instability? In at least one organization that I know of, they didn't.

Typically the response in large, old organizations is a cynical: "Here we go again, yet another Transformation program. I'll sit tight, put my head in the sand, and wait for it to blow over." I've observed some long-tenured colleagues who have developed an incredible skill and mastery in maintaining the status quo. The force is strong. For some people who are at the tail end of the job-for-life generation, and who are now in sight of their final salary pension, there is no incentive to rock the boat. Quite the opposite.

Transformation as a mandated program uses old ways of thinking to apply new ways of working. It is applying a way of working that originated in the Age of Electricity and Engineering in the late 1800s, evolved from repetitive manual labor in factories to unique emergent change in the Age of Digital. It is not applying an agile mindset to agility. To quote Martin Fowler, one of the *Agile Manifesto* signatories, "*Imposing* agile methods introduces a conflict with the values and principles that underlie agile methods."[8]

That conflict generates a number of emotional reactions, as I discuss next.

1: Fear and Resistance

Not surprisingly, mandated change and mandated *how* trigger fear and resistance. There are worries about a loss of control, uncertainty, changing habits, fear of failure, fear of incompetence, more work ("I have to do this work AND you're asking me to change how I do the work?"), change fatigue, and "better the devil you know."[9]

Managers used to traditional ways of working—to a command-and-control culture in which they give orders and see those orders carried out—fear that the change will result in a loss of control. Leaders and stakeholders accustomed to a theater of control that plans each step of a project up front (at the point of knowing the least) and assumes that the future is predictable fear embracing the reality that the domain is emergent and requires experimentation. It's easier to try to command and control the future. Leaders of role-based silos feel threatened, fearing for the empire that they've built and what that means for them. Everyone fears changing habits that they're used to and are comfortable with. Even the most confident employees can suffer from imposter syndrome. There is fear that changing a system of work that has brought them to their current position will reveal an inability, a weakness, or a vulnerability.

Other fears include concerns that the change will increase workload. With an existing need to deliver value come hell or high water, people are now being asked to change *how* that business value is delivered with jargon like "velocity," "sprint," and "points." Inertia plays a role too. For many people, "the devil you know" looks better than an agile and lean devil they don't know.

From an evolutionary perspective, depending on the messaging of the why and depending on how the change is approached, especially for those with a fixed mindset, change drives a fear of survival. That leads to resistance and less rational thought as the primitive brain takes over: *Can I change? What if I can't adapt? Will I still be able to pay the bills?*

As Robert Maurer explains in *One Small Step Can Change Your Life: The Kaizen Way*, the problem with the amygdala and its fight-or-flight response is that it triggers alarm bells whenever we want to make a departure from our usual, safe routines:[10]

> The brain is designed so that any new challenge or opportunity triggers some degree of fear. Whether the challenge is a new job or just meeting a new person, the amygdala alerts parts of the body to prepare for action—and our access to the cortex, the thinking part of the brain, is restricted, and sometimes shut down.[11]

2: Loss Aversion

This evolutionary fear of change is also seen in loss aversion: people's tendency to prefer avoiding losses to acquiring gains of similar value. Studies have suggested that losses are twice as powerful, psychologically, as gains.[12] The fear may be an evolutionary holdover. For our ancestors on the edge of survival, the loss of a day's food could be enough to cause starvation. The gain of additional food would be nice, but they've already survived. The extra food now needs to be stored and protected, and it's not going to add years to their life. In this scenario, the implications of loss far outweigh the benefits of gains. This evolutionary tendency to avoid losses, even to obtain gains, further cements people's desire to maintain the status quo.

3: Agentic State

Forcing change on people and dictating *how* they have to change creates extrinsic rather than intrinsic motivation. In some people this leads to an "agentic state," in which they feel compelled to obey orders, sometimes even when they think those instructions won't lead to the best or even morally right outcomes.

They pass off the responsibility for the consequences to the person giving the orders.

In 1961, Yale University psychologist Stanley Milgram began conducting a series of experiments to see whether volunteers would be willing to obey an instruction from an experimenter in a white coat to deliver high levels of electric shocks to a stranger who had answered a question wrong. In one experiment, Milgram reported that as many as 65% of the volunteers agreed to deliver what they thought was a 450-volt shock even though they feared it could be fatal.[13]

Since then, researcher Gina Perry has been through Milgram's notes and interviewed participants, publishing her findings in 2013. According to Perry, looking at the many variations of the experiment, about half the people who undertook the experiment believed that the shocks they were giving were real, and in some cases two-thirds of those refused to administer them. However, people still exhibited a state of agency, of obedience. While some people were complicit in doing something they believed was harmful, others still went through the motions, doing what they were told. They were playing their role in taking and carrying out orders from a person in perceived authority.[14]

Be wary of generating an agentic state in people. If new ways of working are imposed with an old way of behaving, as a command-and-control order, as a dictate, allowing for some national cultural differences in obedience, the majority of people will obey the order even if they don't believe it will necessarily result in a good outcome. I've come across cases where people are following orders while also wanting a change to fail. They are sabotaging it specifically by following it to the letter in order to prove their point.

A similar psychological state is "learned helplessness," where people are frozen while waiting for the next order, due to a lack of psychological safety and a command-and-control culture. If old ways of behaving and thinking are used for new ways of working, people will not think for themselves; they will not improve; they will follow orders and wait for the next one. I've seen this a number of times, with teams following mandated robotic maneuvers of agile. It did not optimize for outcomes, and it is not living the values of agile and lean.

4: Removing the Top Three Motivators: Autonomy, Mastery, Purpose

In his book *Drive: The Surprising Truth About What Motivates Us*, Daniel Pink explains that what motivates workers today, and especially workers in the knowledge industry, isn't the promise of financial rewards.[15] Frederick Winslow Taylor's model famously used a few more dollars' salary as an incentive for manual laborers, but a couple more dollars won't motivate today's workers to move more lines of code. What will have people delivering better outcomes are *autonomy*, *mastery*, and *purpose*. We all want to feel that we control our own lives, that we're good at what we do, and that what we do matters. These are all intrinsic motivators.

When employees hear that they're undergoing an "Agile Transformation," at least two of those top three motivators are taken away. There is a lack of *autonomy* (you have to do this thing, you have no choice) and there is a lack of *mastery* (you're a beginner again, possibly after a long career).

So increasing agility can feel like a big price to pay. What are people getting for that price? Why are they being asked to pay it? If the *why* is articulated as the achievement of cost reduction or an increase in profitability—if the reason for the transformation is only to make more money for the company, perhaps also to work themselves or their colleagues out of a job—then *purpose* is also removed, taking away all three categories of human motivation: *autonomy*, *mastery*, and *purpose*.

Often, people are being forced to adopt agile or lean practices instead of being invited and incentivized to create better outcomes. As Peter Senge put it in *The Fifth Discipline*: "The harder you push, the harder the system pushes back."[16]

From Antipatterns to Patterns

Focus on Outcomes, Start with Why, Empower the How

We've seen that Agile, Lean, and DevOps are, figuratively speaking, tools in the toolbox. They are a means to an end, not the end. Doing Agile does not make you agile. A frog march of Agile leads to cargo cult behavior: the robotic maneuvers of agile are being followed, but the planes are not dropping cargo.

We've also seen that imposing Agile is not agile. It leads to fear and resistance. It is not empowering; instead, it can lead to people being in an "agentic state," complying with orders without question, thought, or ownership of the outcome. It also removes the top three motivators of work: autonomy, mastery, and purpose.

Agile and lean are bodies of knowledge, which have been accumulating for many decades, with principles, practices, ways of thinking, and behaving that, when done well and applied in context, lead to better business outcomes. Those outcomes—and how they're balanced so that it's not at any human, societal, or climatic cost—are where the focus needs to be.

At one organization, for example, I found that adopting agile for product development was not the best way to improve outcomes. The organization had undergone multiple failed Agile Transformation attempts previously and there was history with emotional scar tissue. Instead, honoring the current roles and responsibilities and pursuing evolutionary improvement, initially with smaller, traditional waterfalls and a focus on outcomes with autonomy on the how, was the best approach to delivering **Better Value Sooner Safer Happier**. There was no revolution and thus little to fear or resist. Eventually the organization pivoted from project to product and exhibited agility with multidisciplinary teams and shorter time to market. Agile principles and practices had been adopted; however, it was done without using the A-word. Instead, it was done by people using their own brains to work out how best, in context, to improve on **BVSSH** outcomes, with support and feedback loops on **BVSSH** measures. In the process, a new and lasting muscle memory was formed, the ability of an organization to improve by itself, not waiting for an order, which is a new "learned self-helpfulness" capability. This is what you really want.

In addition to being clear on the desired outcomes and empowering *how* those outcomes are improved, there is also a need to clearly articulate the unique *why*. The organization needs to understand the reasons for being asked to improve ways of working, and those reasons need to appeal to people's intrinsic motivators. Talking about cost-cutting and layoffs will likely kill the change dead in the water. If the organization does not face an existential threat, why would someone put a lot of effort into working themselves or their colleagues out of a job? Why should they make sacrifices in order to pay institutional investors a greater dividend or meet some other short-term financial commitment made by the board? The *why* matters.

Agility needs to emerge in an agile way. Empowerment, experimentation, respect for people, self-determination, learning, everybody bringing their brains to work and continuously improving how they do what they do, are core tenets of an agile and lean mindset. The work itself is emergent and so is improving the system of work for that work.

Remember, a pattern is an approach that more often than not is successful. As every context is unique and there is no one size fits all, your mileage may vary.

PATTERN 1.1:

Focus on Outcomes

Focus on the outcomes, on **Better Value Sooner Safer Happier**, as the goal, not on Agile, Lean, or DevOps as the goal.

In his 1962 book *Diffusion of Innovations*, sociologist Everett Rogers described how innovation tended to spread first to a small number of Innovators, then reached Early Adopters, was taken up by equal numbers of Early Majority and Late Majority, before finally being used by Laggards.[17] (See Figure 1.4.)

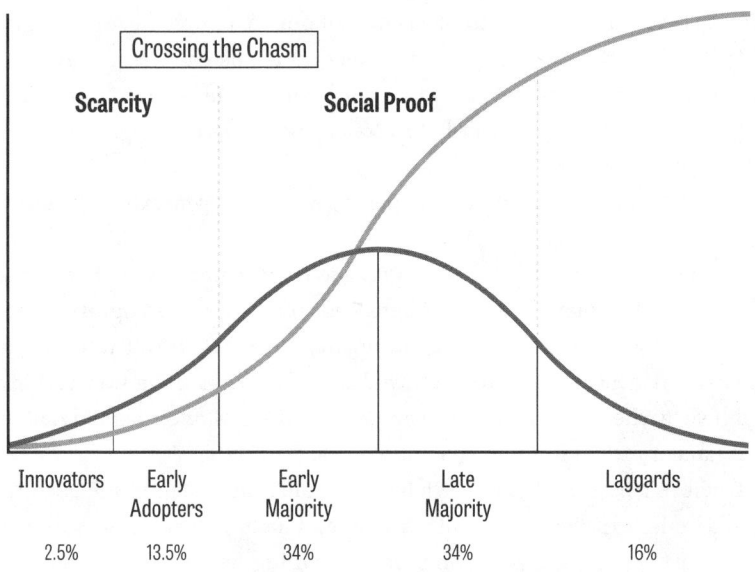

Figure 1.4: Diffusion of Innovations

As we passed the midpoint at Barclays and were getting into the Late Majority and Laggards, we recognized the need to pivot. The A-word (Agile) was an anchor, not an accelerator. It was like a magnet. The Innovators, Early Adopters, and Early Majority had one polarity. They were attracted to the new ways of working and had embraced the support the firm was providing. It helped them do what they had long been trying to do in the past. The Late Majority and the Laggards had the opposite polarity.

PATTERN **1.1**

We pivoted to focus on outcomes. We changed our headline focus and all the visible, cultural signposts. We replaced the posters and floor-standing banners, changed the name of the team, the internal communications, and so on. We were already measuring **BVSSH** outcomes; however, we hadn't made them the headline. With the benefit of hindsight, I would have started with a headline focus on the outcomes, on **Better Value Sooner Safer Happier**.

We had previously avoided imposing a particular agile framework or approach, preferring to empower teams to decide the *how* for themselves according to their context, while we supplied support and the minimal viable guardrails that are discussed in Chapters 5 and 6. Pivoting to focus on the outcomes further increased empowerment and reduced resistance. We weren't imposing a way of working, and especially not one that might have had baggage.

My narrative when speaking to leadership teams changed from: "Hi, I'm Jon, and I'm here to make you adopt agile; you choose how." to "Hi, I'm Jon, and I'm here to help you deliver Better Value Sooner Safer Happier if you want to and if you want help."

As you can imagine, those two opening sentences generate very different responses.

No one in their right mind is not going to want to improve on **Better Value Sooner Safer Happier** outcomes. There was an incentive to improve, without mandate and without targets. The optionality at the end is full autonomy and hence intrinsic motivation. Resistance dropped away as there was nothing to resist. I've learned that the words "convince" and "resistance" should not enter the vocabulary when improving on outcomes.

It doesn't matter if you are delivering value on a mainframe with fifty-year-old code, experimenting with a new mobile app, producing an internal audit report, processing payments, or onboarding new customers, no one is exempt from choosing to improve, to be the best at being better. It's not about agile for systems of innovation and waterfall for systems of record. I find this to be an irresponsible approach. Think Big, Start Big, Learn Slow is never okay. A key part of an agile and lean mindset is continuous improvement. Irrespective of starting point and context, everyone can and should continually improve on delivering **Better Value Sooner Safer Happier**.

We made **BVSSH** outcome data transparent across business units. We showed an improvement trend (or not) over time and went from push to pull. We dropped targets and agility levels and made improving outcomes a strategic priority, looking at trends over time rather than absolute values. There

PATTERN 1.1

was incentivization to improve the system of work; it was no longer about agile or lean for their own sake. Having removed targets, there was empowerment in how much to improve or even to not improve at all. Making the **BVSSH** data transparent was key. It's hard data and it's hard to argue with it. And human nature means that no one wants to be the one improving the least.

The level of pull from the late majority and the laggards shot up almost overnight. After issuing the outcome data trends twice, I got a call requesting support where previous efforts had stalled. In my view, this was entirely because the focus was on the outcomes, on improving **Better Value Sooner Safer Happier**, rather than on adopting agile.

Based on this learning, from similar learnings at a range of organizations, and from case studies at conferences and sharing in the community, I've yet to find an organization where **Better Value Sooner Safer Happier** does not encapsulate the desired outcomes from better ways of working in the Age of Digital.

PATTERN 1.2:

Start with Why; Empower the How

In Antipattern 1.2, we saw how a capital "A," capital "T" Agile Transformation feels to an employee like involuntary, mandatory change being inflicted upon them, whether they like it or not. The capital "A" denotes *how* they are going to change and the capital "T" denotes that they have to change. Often organizations treat a Transformation (with a capital T) as a project with a start date and an end date, applying an old way of thinking to new ways of working. Imposing Agile is not agile, nor is treating it as a deterministic project. In addition, humans have an evolutionary bias to be averse to loss. Collectively, all of this can generate fear, resistance, and an agentic state. Forced change removes the top three motivators for people at work: *autonomy*, *mastery*, and *purpose*.[18]

In addition to being clear on the desired outcomes and empowering how those outcomes are improved, there is a need to clearly articulate the unique why for your organization in a way which appeals to intrinsic motivators. Cutting costs, increasing earnings per share, increasing return on equity, and prioritizing shareholders' short-term financial interests may not be a sufficient *purpose* for most employees. So what is?

PATTERN **1.2**

1: Start with Why

In his book *Start with Why: How Great Leaders Inspire Everyone to Take Action*, Simon Sinek compares a company that sells what it does with a company that sells *why* it does.[19]

For example, most PC manufacturers sell computers where you select the microprocessor, the amount of memory, the size of the hard drive, and the price. The PC is a commodity and margins are low. Most PC manufacturers sell the *what*.

Apple's products, however, look like nothing else on the market. They have a design ethos, a style, and a cult following. Apple has had a strong *why* from the beginning. The company was born at a time of revolutionary, anti-establishment sentiment in Northern California. "The Apple gave an individual the power to do the same things as any company," Apple's co-founder Steve Wozniak explained to Sinek in *Start with Why*. "For the first time ever, one person could take on a corporation simply because they had the ability to use the technology."[20] Within three years Apple was a $100 million company.

In 2009, Apple's *why* was: "Everything we do, we believe in challenging the status quo, we believe in thinking differently." Today the why is: "Apple's employees are dedicated to making the best products on Earth and to leaving the world better than we found it."[21] The company has been one of the top three most highly valued, publicly traded companies every quarter since Q2 2010, and in most of those quarters it was the most highly valued company. It was the first company with a trillion-dollar market valuation and in 2019 topped *Forbes's* list of the most valuable brand for the ninth year in a row.[22]

"People don't buy what you do," Sinek says, "they buy why you do it."[23] People buy Apple's *why*.

The "buy" here could mean purchasing a product or a service, or it could equally mean buying into change. Edgar Schein, former professor at MIT's Sloan School of Management, said: "Learning only happens when survival anxiety is greater than learning anxiety. Learning anxiety comes from being afraid to try something new for fear that we will look stupid in the attempt. It can threaten our self-esteem and even our identity."[24] That anxiety is a threshold that has to be overcome in order to be willing to unlearn, relearn, and take action. If learning anxiety is higher than survival anxiety, there will be inaction. Ideally, that learning anxiety should be lowered by creating a psychologically safe environment in which to learn, with support and coaching, rather than by increasing survival anxiety, which is what most organizations intentionally or unintentionally do.

In addition, to overcome learning anxiety, the *why*, the call to action, needs to be articulated in a form that appeals to all primary motivators. However, research has shown that the *why* for most change doesn't.[25] What the leader cares about (and typically bases at least 80% of his or her messaging on) does not tap into roughly 80% of the workforce's primary motivators for overcoming learning anxiety.

The *why* has to be about more than higher profitability, shareholder returns, or stock price. It can't only be about the company's short-term financial returns. When employees are asked what motivates them most in their work, their answers are split equally between five forms of impact:

- **Society**: They want their work to have a positive effect on society (for example, creating or protecting employment, helping those less fortunate, or improving sustainability for the benefit of our planet).
- **Customer**: They want to positively impact customer satisfaction and create brand advocates.
- **Company**: They want to have an effect on the company and its shareholders, which enables the other four forms of positive impact.
- **Team**: They want to have a positive impact on their colleagues, such as by creating a more engaging and rewarding environment or by helping team members to improve. That's an effect that people can see around them each day on people they value.
- **Individual**: They want a *why* that has a positive impact on themselves, on their levels of autonomy, purpose, and mastery, on their growth and personal development.

The pattern here is to craft a *why* for change, that people will buy and that is unique to your organization.

And then repeat that *why*. Communicate this why three more times than you think you need to and you're a third of the way done. A tip here is that when training for any way of working, whether that training is run internally or externally, have the organization's unique why at the start of every session. You cannot over-communicate the *why*. Follow it up with social proof, recognition, and reward for those who have overcome learning anxiety. Show that it's

PATTERN **1.2**

safe for people to choose to come into the water and that others have already jumped in and are benefiting. They have an incentive to join them.

2: Improving Ways of Working Is Emergent; Empower the How

There is a need to apply new ways of thinking and behaving to new ways of working.

Change—and changing how you change—in human systems is not deterministic or reductionist. You can't take change apart, see how it works, swap a few bits, and put it all back together again. Change is emergent. The best approach to changing ways of working is not as a capital "T" Transformation, as a "project," or as a "program" with a start date and an end date. In this domain, there is no such thing as best practice, and there is no one-size-fits-all solution that optimizes outcomes for the many unique contexts in which the change takes place. It is not a case of applying a reorganization, new job titles, ceremonies, the so-called Spotify Model, and declaring that the horse has transformed into a unicorn. You'll only have glued a fake horn to the horse's head. It still won't poop rainbows.

Organizations are complex adaptive systems. The behavior of a complex adaptive system is emergent. It is not predicted by the behavior of its parts, which, for large companies, are networks of complex adaptive systems themselves. Organizations are adaptive because behavior mutates in response to change events. They look to increase what they perceive to be their survivability. Acting in the space changes the space. Any experiments that take place in a complex adaptive system are not really experiments because you can't undo them, like adding milk to coffee.

Nor is a complex adaptive system linear. It's susceptible to the butterfly effect, where a butterfly flaps its wings and there's a tornado a thousand miles away. The trick is to find the small changes that have a large *positive* effect. Complex adaptive systems have a history. They evolve and their past has a bearing on their present behavior. History and folklore are important. People don't forget. Especially if they really didn't want milk in their coffee.

As change is emergent and changing how change is done is also emergent, once you are clear on your **BVSSH** outcomes and your organization's unique *why*, the optimal approach is to apply agility to agility. As we saw in the previous chapter, this is the Complex domain of the Cynefin Framework. You have to

Think Big, Start Small, Learn Fast in your unique context. Probe, sense, and respond. Run safe-to-learn experiments with support and coaching and from within guardrails. Don't bet the farm on a big bang. At the beginning the force is strong and the corporate antibodies are powerful.

The key to success here is to invite participation. It will be the Innovators on the left of the Diffusion of Innovation Curve (Figure 1.4), that 2.5% sliver, who will volunteer to go first. They have the appetite. They are motivated by the buzz of being first and have probably been working this way formally or informally for some time. A great way to identify Innovators is to run a voluntary Community of Practice. Organize one per region, meeting in person where possible, and see who turns up every time. I previously created and chaired an internal, global, Agile Community of Practice that grew to 2,500 people. It had a three-year head start on the adoption of better ways of working firm wide, and it meant that we already knew who the Innovators and Early Adopters were across multiple business areas globally. These were people with a passionate belief derived from having been agile and lean practitioners for in some cases up to twenty years. There was social proof, in context, of how agility resulted in better business outcomes, and these people wanted to help lead the change.

Having invited the Innovators, keep the change gradient low as experiments are proven in your unique context and within risk appetite. Nail it before you scale it. Humans have a limited velocity to unlearn and relearn. You cannot force the pace of change. Seek more Innovators and Early Adopters who want to opt in from across the organization. Ensure that there are people from "our business," IT, compliance, finance, and so on, not a local optimization in one function or job role. Avoid the need to play catch-up with the Finance Department in eighteen months.

With volunteers identified, provide support. It is advisable to have a central Ways of Working Center of Enablement (WoW CoE) and coaching. (Note that it's called a "Center of Enablement," not a "Center of Excellence.") The WoW CoE is a central, small, servant leadership function for ways of working. The servant part is that it is there to support colleagues, to help mobilize the organization to remove impediments to **Better Value Sooner Safer Happier**. The leadership part is that it is there to lead the way, to shine a light, to recognize, reward, communicate, share learning, build community, and be knowledgeable on ways of working that improve on **BVSSH** outcomes. Coaching should be made available on a pull, not push basis, because like learning to ski, it's much easier if you have someone who can coach you: ski in front,

PATTERN **1.2**

side by side, behind, then move on to the next learner. Otherwise you fall over a lot, hurt yourself, and want to go back to the hotel for a mulled wine.

Over time, as the innovators and early adopters make progress, others see the results, the recognition, the incentives, and the social proof. They join in. The **BVSSH** outcome data shows the effect that the experiments implemented so far are having. Outcome measures inch up further. More people are willing to join in. Those who were willing are now enthusiastic. Eventually, the Laggards, those who wanted a comfortable life doing what they've always done, realize that they're being left behind. When much of the company is working with new ways of working, when teams are delivering **Better Value Sooner Safer Happier**, and the Laggards have not improved when there is no reason for not improving, they stand out. That's the last thing a Laggard wants to do. In my experience, they either choose to opt out of the firm, which is fine, or they choose to join in with improving outcomes, which is preferable.

Inviting improving ways of working in order to deliver **Better Value Sooner Safer Happier** is ongoing, outcome-oriented, lower-case "t" transformation. Human systems entropy. The work never stops. You are never done improving. A former knowledge worker from Toyota in Japan once told me that all "office workers" were expected to spend 40% of their time on continuous improvement activities. I found this astounding. Two days out of every five on continuous improvement. You are never done at being the best at being better.

Case Study: Ways of Working Enablement at Nationwide Building Society

Nationwide Building Society, a large financial services organization, which is over 135 years old with more than 15 million members, is on a journey to transform ways of working. Richard James, the Ways of Working Enablement Leader, explains:

The organization recognized a need to adapt to a rapidly evolving market and keep pace with newer entrants while simplifying and reducing the cost and complexity of change—all while improving the stability and resilience of service we provide. Historically, relatively traditional in structure and approach, Nationwide was comprised of a functional set of Business communities (divisions) with a large, centralized Change team and separate IT Development and IT Operations communities leveraging a high degree of outsourcing for engineering resources. Almost all change was project-managed and delivered centrally using a waterfall approach, with Business stakeholders engaged through business analysis for requirements documentation and subsequently developed through one or more IT Development centers with a large manual release process ahead of the transition to IT Operations. This approach was said to lack flexibility, with high costs and a slow speed to market. It needed to change.

In response to the challenge, the different communities looked at improving pace and cost through targeted change initiatives. The Technology community proposed a greater focus on agile methods, automation, in-sourcing engineering talent, and DevOps practices. The Change community put the focus on simplifying methodology and reducing handoffs between Business, Change, and IT Development. The Digital community focused on speed to market, member-centricity, and flexibility by introducing cross-functional product teams focused on customer journey re-engineering and bringing together Business, Change, and IT Development colleagues into long-lived teams. Each of these separate programmatic initiatives had deterministic plans to demonstrate marked improvements over twelve to twenty-four months.

While these separate programs were similar in intent, they overlapped in delivery, confusing colleagues and suppliers as each progressed on their respective timelines. Each initiative had a partial focus on "test and learn" but with deterministic plans of execution that sought to systematically implement improvements at an increasing pace and scale once initial learnings had been incorporated. The delivery approach for each program assumed consistent returns for all impacted areas, with all changes completed within two years of inception. While progress was made in all three programs, the net result was not as hoped. Change fatigue set in for colleagues. The board's patience eroded.

The arrival of a new COO in 2019 saw a rethink. In the first twelve months, Change, IT Development, and IT Operations were brought together alongside Controls as part of a repurposed Resilience and Agility community, with a focus on collaborating on a set of ambitions to increase pace and simplify change. A new CIO role acted as the catalyst for accelerating the move toward DevOps, alongside the introduction of a Ways of Working Center of Enablement (WoW CoE) to support teams in improving end-to-end flow while embedding a culture of continuous learning and experimentation.

PATTERN **1.2**

The approach to ways of working pivoted from a deterministic change program to a facilitative enabling team, working at all levels, on a hypothesis-led evolution over time, focused on enabling teams to achieve Better Value Sooner Safer and Happier. Recognizing that all teams and colleagues are at different stages of their own journey, the WoW CoE doesn't seek a "one size fits all" design for agility—forming long-lived Enablement Team partnerships with teams to test, learn, and adapt while sharing emerging patterns of success across the wider organization.

With a belief in "Think Big, Start Small, Learn Fast," experimentation is the approach taken, with teams seeking to resolve impediments to flow, based on hypotheses with leading and lagging indicators aligned to outcomes, aligned to BVSSH. The benefits of descaling the evolution to fit within teams' daily working lives has been profound—tackling larger issues in context and incrementally has led to a more sustainable change where learning and experimentation are celebrated.

Summary

Want To Do a *Thing* Transformation? Don't. Focus On Outcomes.

In this chapter we've seen that the goal is not agile or lean for their own sakes. That kind of transformation can lead to cargo cult behavior and unimproved outcomes. Imposing Agile is not agile. Instead, focus on the outcomes. Focus on delivering **Better Value Sooner Safer Happier**, making use of the most appropriate proverbial tools in the toolbox in your many unique contexts, with coaching and support.

We also looked at a capital "T" Transformation and applying old ways of thinking and behaving to new ways of working. There is a mandate from the top, a traditional project or program with a deterministic mindset, a one-size-fits-all approach, and lacking a compelling why or colleague engagement. This drives fear, resistance, and can result in the removal of all of the top three motivators for people at work: autonomy, mastery, and purpose.

Instead, start with a *why* for your organization that appeals to intrinsic motivators. Focus on **BVSSH** outcomes. Invite participation and empower the how. Start with safe-to-learn experiments within guardrails and with support such as a Ways of Working Center of Enablement and coaching.

Then, keep going! Impediments are not in the path; impediments *are* the path. Take your foot off the gas and the weeds will grow back fast, so you have to keep moving. It's essential to dedicate ongoing bandwidth to support the organization in continually improving ways of working to deliver **Better Value Sooner Safer Happier**. The ultimate goal is to become a learning organization where both change and improvement is continuous. Be the best at being better.

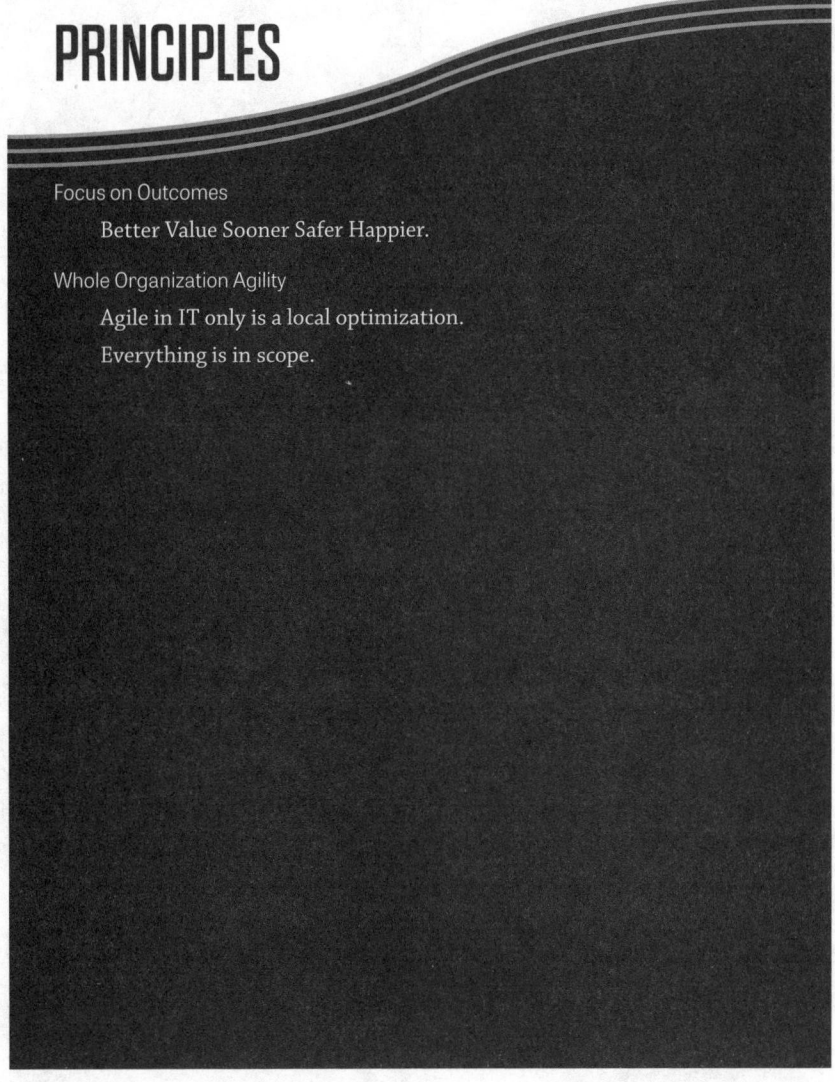

PRINCIPLES

Focus on Outcomes

Better Value Sooner Safer Happier.

Whole Organization Agility

Agile in IT only is a local optimization.

Everything is in scope.

2 ACHIEVE BIG THROUGH SMALL

In 1962, Elisabeth Kübler-Ross was teaching at the School of Medicine at the University of Colorado when she was asked to fill in for another professor. She was nervous. Born in Zurich and only thirty-four, she still spoke with a thick German accent. The professor she was replacing was a popular lecturer who could fill and dominate a lecture hall. Kübler-Ross could barely make herself heard.

To help her communicate her lesson, Kübler-Ross called on the help of a sixteen-year-old medical patient. The girl was dying of leukemia, and Kübler-Ross invited the students to ask her about her condition.

The lecture hall fell silent. There was a lot of shuffling in seats, but slowly the students started to question the teenager about her blood tests and her chemotherapy. They focused on her medical procedures and on her symptoms. They saw only the disease. Eventually, the patient had had enough. She angrily started to ask her own questions:

"What's it like not to be able to dream about the high school prom?" she demanded.

"What's it like to know you'll never go on a date?"

"What's it like to know you'll never grow up?"

"Why is everyone always lying to me?"

By the time the lecture ended, many of the students were in tears and Kübler-Ross had given the students a demonstration of what would go on to become the second of her five stages of grief. People facing death or the loss of a loved one, she argued in her 1969 book *On Death and Dying*, pass through denial, anger, bargaining, and depression before reaching an acceptance of the situation.[1] The order may change and not everyone experiences each stage, but those feelings will be familiar to anyone who suffers a loss.

Now, changing the way you work isn't the same as facing bereavement or the loss of your own life. However, the human reaction to change is the same. Kübler-Ross herself expanded her model to include any loss, including the loss of a job or the end of a relationship.[2]

In feedback from regular colleague surveys, I have observed this pattern many times. It is pronounced when change is inflicted. There is a peak of emotion that takes the form of interest (or head-in-the-sand denial), then a dip as people realize that changing habits is hard. There is learning anxiety as we saw in Chapter 1, followed in most cases by a climbing up and out of the hole with a steady improvement in delivering **Better Value Sooner Safer Happier** outcomes as the new situation is accepted and mastery of the new normal grows.

Change is always difficult. Changing ways of working is hard. Colleagues with long careers can suddenly find themselves experiencing a lack of mastery, learning anxiety, a feeling that they're beginning again as though they were arriving at a company for the first time straight out of university, college, or school. At least some of their intrinsic motivators, that sense they're in control of their destiny and are good at what they do, are coming under pressure.

In the previous chapter, I looked at a capital "A," capital "T" Agile Transformation. I explored what motivates people and discussed the importance of focusing not on Agile or Lean for their own sake but on the **Better Value Sooner Safer Happier** outcomes to be improved through better ways of working. In this chapter, I'm going to examine how that change is implemented and why I've found that it happens best when work is first descaled before agility is scaled, so that a series of early, often, and safe-to-learn changes produce a lasting S-curve of change, with quick time to value, quick time to learning, lower risk, and the ability to pivot to maximize outcomes.

ANTIPATTERN 2.1

The Bigger the Capital "T" Transformation, the Bigger the Change Curve

So, what happens when an employee hears that their company is undergoing a large transformation? How do they experience Kübler-Ross's model in a context of workplace change?

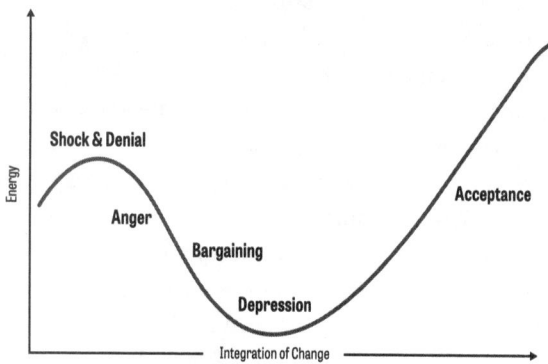

Figure 2.1: The Kübler-Ross Curve

Adapted from Kübler-Ross, *On Death and Dying*.

1. Shock and Denial

The first stage is the shortest. An employee faced with the prospect of a forced change that might put job, status, and competence on the line will need time to absorb the news. They're being told that what got them to this point might not move them further forward. There is denial. They tell themselves that this is just another Transformation Program; it happens every two to three years and they've managed to avoid previous ones. The proposed change still seems far away and nothing has happened yet. For some, there is a high degree of cynicism. They put their head in the sand and continue, at least for a while longer, to pretend that everything is the same. Following the initial shock of change, for some there may be a rise in morale with a fanfare of announcements, town halls, excitement, and a buzz. The hard work, the unlearning and relearning, the harder impediments to overcome, the reality of the situation has not yet kicked in.

2. Anger

As employees see that the Transformation is not going away, that the situation is real, some may become angry. They might blame the company. They might blame the change agents. They might blame some leaders. They might blame trendy tech ideas and the people who think they have all the solutions. They might blame their colleagues. Surely this is just a fad, isn't it? We've always worked this way, so why do we need to change now? As their frustration grows, they can become irritable and even difficult to work with. They're certain that all the people who support the change must be wrong. Their morale drops. Their anger is an indication that change is being acknowledged, rather than denied.

3. Bargaining

People facing death or terminal illness have little to bargain with, but patients are known to pray for more time and offer to perform good deeds if they get it. Some employees facing inflicted changes will try to bargain with those around them. "Your ideas are fine," they say. "But we're special." They'll try to hold on to as much of their way of working as they can in return for accepting some elements of change. This stage is further mental acceptance that at least some change is coming, and they're starting to figure out how to minimize it, rather than deny it or fight it off.

4. Depression

The next stage is depression. This is when team members know that the change is inevitable, that it's going to affect them, and they believe that there's nothing they can do to prevent it. They stop caring and feel that there's no point in being enthusiastic or making plans for the future. It can also come about as the reality of unlearning and learning is felt, with a change of habits. People feel vulnerable being a learner again and needing to rebuild mastery. There are broader organizational impediments. It's hard and it's not in their comfort zone. This is the lowest moment during a process of change. Without support and coaching, or if the dip is too big and too long, some teams give up here.

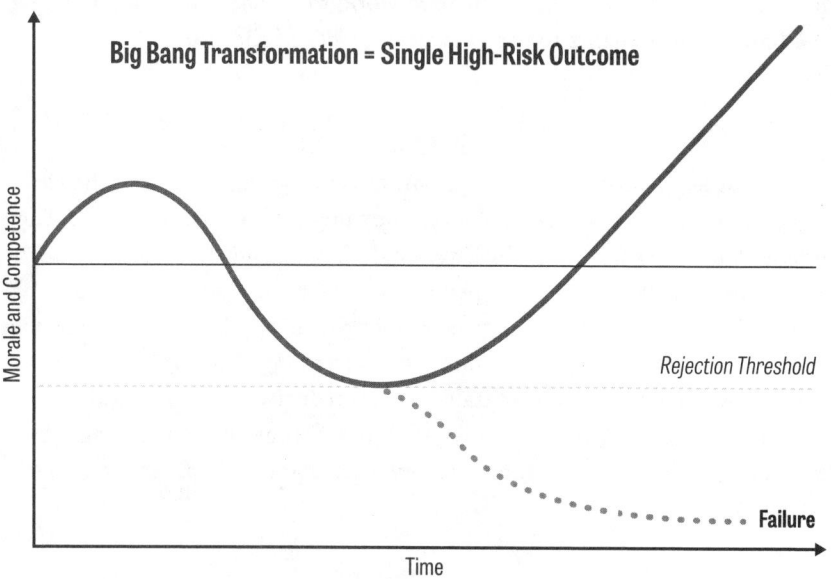

Figure 2.2: Rejection Threshold

5: Acceptance

Finally, through experimenting with better ways of working; with empowerment, support, and coaching; through starting to see the green shoots of better outcomes; through shared learning with other teams, community support, and social proof, people start to climb out of the trough. Empowering people to use their own brains to discover how to improve on outcomes, supported with coaching, reduces the time in the dip. If there is learned helplessness, an infliction of rigid ways of working, a lack of psychological safety, and no support, it will be harder.

It's important to remember that people don't always pass through each of these stages in order, and they can begin in different places. We saw in the previous chapter that people are at different places on the Diffusion of Innovation curve. An Innovator will experience a much shallower and shorter Kübler-Ross Curve. A Laggard will have a deeper and longer curve (with some people wanting to sabotage change, which is why it's a good idea to start with the Innovators). Nor do people always move forward. It's not unusual to fall back to a previous stage, and each stage can last for a different period of time. Equally, it will be a case of cycling through all the stages repeatedly as more people come on the journey and as new people join an organization. Each time the before and after points are higher than they were previously.

The Bigger the Change, the Deeper and Longer the Dip

The bigger the change, the deeper and longer the dive into chaos. In my experience, if done as a big bang across the whole firm, the time for collective learning anxiety, the time for unlearning, the time for behaviors and processes to become fit for purpose, the time for morale to fall through depression and return to the place where it started before the change process began—and before it rises through the stage of acceptance—is several years depending on the size and culture of the organization. This assumes that the organization does climb out of the hole.

The tenure of a CEO, COO, or CIO can be less than that; the end tends to coincide with the lowest point of depression, with the dip in the curve. A CXO can find themselves moving on before the company climbs out of the hole, and the new person comes in just as people are working out how to pull out of the dip. Lucky them. Or, the new leader says that this agile thing isn't working and takes the company back to traditional ways of working. Back to Think Big, Start Big, Learn Slow, with a deterministic mindset and a system of work suited for repetitive, unskilled, manual labor in factories in the late 1800s.

The depth of the depression and the speed with which the company crashes into it depend on the size of the bang with which it starts the Transformation. Or, to put it another way, the bigger the capital "T" Transformation, the bigger the change curve.

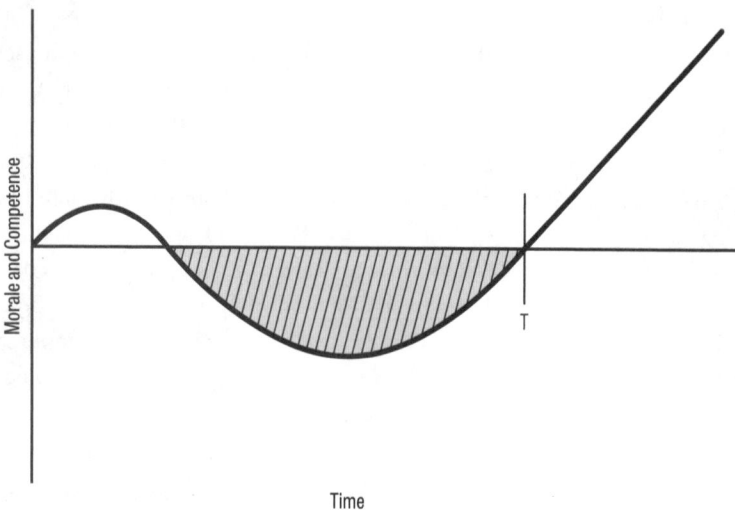

Figure 2.3: The Bigger the "T" in Transformation, the Deeper and Longer the Dip

If you're embarking on one large, broad, big-bang transformation, you can expect an almighty, deep dip in the curve. The depression comes on faster, falls deeper, lasts longer, and affects far more people. Everyone is unlearning at the same time. Behaviors, processes, and tools are not set up to support new ways of working. Impediments are at their greatest. There is a high level of risk.

The deeper the dip, the harder it is to climb out of it and the longer it takes. Because some firms don't even start to consider change until they're already facing an existential threat, there may not be sufficient time to climb out of that trough. "We don't have time. We need to go big," could be a fallacy and a self-fulfilling prophecy. Going big may ensure that you don't have time.

In the vast majority of cases, a start big, all-in, bet-the-farm approach is an antipattern. It is not applying an agile mindset to agility. It fails to acknowledge that organizations are complex adaptive systems, that both change itself and changing how you perform that change are emergent, that humans have a limited velocity to unlearn and relearn, and that the pace of change cannot be forced. This approach is applying a deterministic mindset to an emergent domain. At best, it just puts new labels on the same old behavior.

If changing behaviors to deliver **Better Value Sooner Safer Happier** is to be successful, sustainable, safe, and sticky, you may find that applying an agile mindset to agility leads to better outcomes.

You Probably Don't Want Everyone Learning to Ski at the Same Time

Imagine that you're a ski instructor. You're given an entire organization or an entire business unit and told that you need to make everyone proficient at skiing as quickly as possible.

Now, you know that the first skiing lessons are always the hardest. They're cold, painful, and slow. There's a lot of falling over. It can hurt. Snowplowing uses up the most energy, so it's tiring too. You know that once the students have broken past snowplowing, once they've learned to link their turns and started to almost parallel ski, the enjoyment will increase. Their speed will go up. Energy usage for the same distance and time will come down. Their skiing will become fun and addictive. They'll quickly forget about those painful first attempts, and they'll be grateful to have this fun new skill.

So how do you get from those difficult first skiing lessons on the nursery slopes to the fun stuff on the powder snow?

There are a few options. One is to skip the snowplow entirely. Take everyone who wants to learn to ski—or who *has* to learn to ski—to the top of the ski lift. Line them all up at the top of the black run, point their skis straight ahead, and give each one a big push.

Anyone who makes it to the bottom of the slope will have learned to ski on their way down. There won't be too many of them, but they'll all be very talented.

Your goal, though, is to keep as many people in the group (and in one piece) as possible. So you could try to teach everyone at once: take everyone who's going to learn to ski and bring them all up to standard at the same time. You could mandate that everyone attends classroom training, to be taught about skiing (without actually skiing). At the end of it everyone gets a certification. In theory, that should get the hard part out of the way at once and then everyone will be able to move forward together at the same pace.

There are a few problems, however. Once people are attempting to ski, it turns out that the nursery slopes only have so much capacity. There's a limited amount of snow, instruction time, and oversight available. If you try to schedule everyone at the same time, you'll have a large number of people all snowplowing in the same space at the same hour, and in an environment not yet optimized for that many people. Without enough ski instructors to go around, and without enough space to learn and make mistakes in a safe environment, the students will ski over each other, bump into each other, and knock each other down. There are not enough helicopters for the airlifts to hospitals, and for those who are still mobile, there are insufficient lifts, restaurants, and pharmacies to cater to the huge demand. There will be queueing and chaos. Most people will get hurt, feel disillusioned, and give up. Instead of heading out onto the slopes keen to learn something new, they'll find a bar and seek solace at the bottom of a glass of schnapps.

That is what a big-bang transformation does. It front-loads the biggest challenges. It piles them all into the toughest stage and spreads them across the largest number of people at the same time. It's the hardest way for employees to change, and the hardest way for the company to change. The beginning is a time when the antibodies to change are at their strongest. There are vested interests at stake. The impediments to better ways of working and flow will be at their highest. Behaviors, processes, and tools will be supporting traditional ways of working. Understanding is low and the force is strong with cognitive biases that have no lessons learned through doing or empirical data from the organization to challenge them, there is no social proof in context.

In large, diverse, regulated, multinational organizations where the cultural norm is mostly command and control, you can expect a capital "T" Transformation to generate denial, frustration, and anger. A big change stands a higher chance of cultural tissue rejection, with more ammunition for those averse to change. The impact radius is about as big as it can get. The organization needs to have a big risk appetite. Things will get significantly worse before they get better. Someone will break a leg.

Cognitive Overload

Changing from a caterpillar to a butterfly requires many people to unlearn and relearn. People need time to undergo that process. Behavioral scientists have shown that cognitive overload is a major theme in the rejection of change. Cognitive reasoning is finite and easily depleted. According to research by psychologist Wendy Wood, approximately 40% of decisions that people make every day are not made consciously. They're habits, and most of them have to be unlearned in order to continuously improve ways of working.[3] "The thoughtful intentional mind is easily derailed, and people tend to fall back on habitual behaviors," Wood says. "Willpower is a limited resource, and when it runs out you fall back on habits."[4]

Where the change has not been internalized and embedded, where it has been forced across an organization in a broad manner, it stretches like an elastic band. As soon as the leader mandating the capital "T" Transformation moves on, the organization's habits and codified processes snap back. It takes at least three to five years for a large, traditional organization to develop new muscle memory and months to slip back. The continuous improvement never ends.

That's why big capital "T" Transformations are less likely to be successful, take longer, and generate more chaos than starting small and learning fast, which is more likely to lead to sooner, more sustainable, and stickier outcomes. Starting big is an approach that doesn't live its own values or apply its own principles. It is not applying an agile mindset to increasing organizational agility. It is a deterministic approach to an emergent domain. It is big batch, big bang, and big risk. It is approaching change in a manner counter to the change being asked of colleagues.

Case Study: ANZ Bank Goes Big ■

In 2017, ANZ Bank announced that it would reorganize its workforce and adopt a "scaled agile methodology." The aim was to respond faster to customer expectations, to improve speed to market, and to empower team members to do the best they could with the resources available.

The transformation would be rolled out through 2018 and, according to *iTnews*, a technology news site, would "dramatically increase the bank's current use of agile methodology from 20 percent, mostly in technology and digital teams."[5]

The bank went big. Within a year, 9,000 people—half of its Australian workforce—had been told that they needed to re-apply for their jobs, including senior leadership executives. Not all the people who underwent the video interviews made it back into the company. "The 'rock stars' who got the big bonuses every year, who rode roughshod over people and left a trail of bodies in their wake, didn't get the jobs," Christian Venter, one of the executives who led the Agile

Transformation, said. "Instead, it was a new kind of leader. And when we did that, the organization knew we were serious. That's where the cultural transformation starts."

But it wasn't just the "rock stars" who didn't come back. Altogether, the bank lost 11% of its Australian workforce in that twelve-month period. Those who remained were trained in New Ways of Leading, a kind of servant leadership that emphasized curiosity, shared clarity, empowerment, empathy, and selfless growth. The New Ways of Working that ANZ introduced was inspired by the so-called Spotify model and other organizations, such as ING Bank. Under this model, ANZ arranged workers into "tribes" of 150 people divided into squads of five to nine people, fully dedicated. The company found cross-tribe collaboration a challenge, observing that people are tribal.

In May 2019 the bank's chief executive, Shayne Elliott, told a media conference that it had essentially completed the rollout of New Ways of Working. "I don't have a target. I don't really care what the number is; if it works, we want more of it and we just go," he said.[6]

Although the bank had reduced headcount by 30% while doing the same amount of work, it had found that the New Ways of Working didn't work in branches, in contact centers, or in dealing rooms. The transformation would continue but not "in a way that we impose on you because it looks good on an org chart."

ANTIPATTERN 2.2

Scaling Agile Before Descaling the Work

Most of the businesses that I help guide toward better ways of working are big companies. They're enterprises that have been around for more than a century. They have many years of organizational scar tissue and ways of working that are almost ingrained into the walls. That's not to say anything against the businesses themselves. It's just what happens over time.

Writing in *The Economist* in 1955, C. Northcote Parkinson explained that work expands to fill the time available for its completion. An "elderly person of leisure" he says could spend an entire day writing and mailing a postcard to a niece at Bognor Regis (a seaside resort on the English coast). "He or she would spend an hour finding the postcard, another hour hunting for spectacles, half-an-hour looking for the address, an hour-and-a-quarter writing the message, then twenty minutes deciding whether or not to take an umbrella for the walk to the postbox. . . . A busy [person]," he adds, "would finish the same task in three minutes."[7]

Parkinson went even further. Not only does work expand to fill the time available, he argued, bureaucracies also expand at a rate of 5% to 7% each year "irrespective of any variation in the amount of work (if any) to be done."[8] By way of example, he cites the growth of the British Colonial Office, which expanded at an average rate of 5.89% each year between 1935 and 1954, even as the size of the British Empire shrank from 17 million square miles to 4 million square miles.[9] The Colonial Office was at its smallest when the British Empire was at its largest and at its largest when the British Empire was at its smallest.

Officials, he argued, make work for each other, and no official ever wants to multiply rivals; they only want to increase subordinates. They expect to manage ever-growing numbers of people.[10]

Parkinson was talking about the British civil service, and I'd like to add a contemporary corollary that I've observed in large organizations: "Policies, Standards, and Controls expand with the number of control staff employed."

When there is no group of people focused on improving the system of work, impediments to **Better Value Sooner Safer Happier** start to creep back in. It's a bit like playing whack-a-mole, with well-intentioned but poorly implemented controls or processes, which are not optimized for **Better Value Sooner Safer Happier**. Human systems entropy; the bureaucracy grows back unchecked. There is a need for continual gardening.

Large, old, traditional organizations, with their years of organizational scar tissue and their century-old ways of working, will be at the highest level of inefficiency and bureaucracy that their revenues can support. Now that we're past the tipping point in the Age of Digital, organizations are finding that they can no longer support that inefficiency and remain competitive.

It is suboptimal to take such an inefficient and bureaucratic organization and apply one set of practices, a prescriptive framework, or methodology on top, across the whole organization in one go. In this context, the scale, the bureaucracy, the number of communication paths are *themselves* all impediments to optimizing for **Better Value Sooner Safer Happier**. It's like trying to teach an elephant to dance.

An agile framework is not a magic cure for the surrounding processes, controls, handoffs, cultural norms, committees, mandatory artifacts, review boards, and six months of detailed planning with a once-a-year, project-based funding cycle, locking in predetermined output. It can also lead to a fallacy of "Well, we had a hundred people working on this before, now we need those same hundred people doing Agile." As we'll see in Pattern 2.2, the problem may be that it's not a hundred-person problem.

Instead, it is important to *descale* the work before scaling agility. That's not the same as scaling capital "A" Agile, which is "doing Agile" rather than exhibiting agility. Apply agility to agility. Start with small teams, small slices of value, and small investments. Achieve big through small.

ANTIPATTERN 2.3

Grass Roots Hits a Grass Ceiling

I've found that a lot of organizations view ways of working as something that's only applicable at the team level, often the IT teams or some separate digital entity within the organization. The scaling tends to take place with the product development teams, expanding, or scaling, sideways.

That often misses middle management, the vice presidents, directors, and managers who are responsible for delivering the company's strategic initiatives. Jonathan Byrnes, a senior lecturer at MIT, has described this level of management as the "frozen middle."[11] I prefer the term "pressurized middle." Traditionally, senior leaders set the strategy and delegate execution. It's the pressurized middle who *have* to deliver, at the same time as they are being asked to change *how* they deliver.

Beginning only with IT software development teams in particular risks creating isolated bubbles of agility. The organization ends up with small agile pockets that lack middle and senior support across functions. At best, it's a local optimization, which will have a negligible impact end to end. The new practices have no way to expand out to the rest of the organization. This creates an approach that lacks cohesion. On more than one occasion, I've seen three different approaches compete simultaneously for agility in an organization: one from "the business"; one from IT; and a third from "Digital" that was separate from both business and IT.

Grass roots implies that it's a thing for teams and not for leaders. The term "grass roots" highlights the differences between something at the team level and the more traditional power structures. When there are organizational impediments to unblock, of which there will be lots, this is where grass roots hits a grass ceiling. As well as needing senior leaders' support to prioritize and allocate limited resources to unblock organization-wide impediments, leaders' behaviors may also be impediments. Leadership culture and leaders understanding ways of working may be issues. If it's just for the team, there will be bubbles of agility in a sea of waterfalls, with limited progress on improving outcomes.

From Antipatterns to Patterns

Shrink to Fit

We've seen that the bigger the capital "T" Transformation, the deeper and longer the dip into depression, struggle, unlearning, and in some cases, chaos or giving up. The tenure of a C-suite leader can be shorter than the time it takes for the organization to climb back up out of the hole. Or the organization may revert back to ways of working suited for the mass production of identical widgets in the early 1900s, applying them to the unique emergent knowledge work in the Age of Digital. We also looked at Parkinson's observation that not only does work expand to fill the time available but human organizations also grow naturally at a rate of 5% to 7% a year, irrespective of the amount (or any) work to be done. A large, old, traditional organization that's had a century or more of uncontrolled spread is likely to be at the highest level of inefficiency and bureaucracy that its revenue can support. It is suboptimal to apply a framework or methodology across an entire organization in such a state. The scale itself is an impediment to **Better Value Sooner Safer Happier**. And making it grass roots only, with horizontal scale, risks creating bubbles of agile and excluding support from the pressurized or frozen middle, which the change needs to succeed and grow.

In the patterns that follow, I'll describe how to simplify by starting small. That simplicity is important, and it takes effort. There's a reason that writers from Cicero to Mark Twain are all said to have apologized at one time or another for writing a long letter because they didn't have the time to write a shorter one. Concision requires work, as does simplification, descaling the organization and descaling the flow of work end-to-end before scaling up agility. I will also look at scaling vertically (connected stripes of senior leadership, pressurized middle, and team together, starting small) and then sideways, so that what was only grass roots before becomes a tall, strong tree with access to sunlight at the top of the forest canopy and water from the roots.

In these patterns, I will describe how to move further forward, faster, with less risk by achieving big through small and adopting change with an S-curve profile.

PATTERN 2.1

Achieve Big through Small

As we saw in Antipattern 2.1, the expected outcome when change is introduced in a big-bang manner to a large organization is a big Kübler-Ross curve: a slight initial rise with either excitement or denial, followed by a deep depression when reality hits (see Figure 2.1). I have learned the hard way that people have a *limited velocity to unlearn and relearn*. You cannot force the pace of change, even if you think that you are. The outcome will be new labels on existing behaviors, the robotic maneuvers of Agile, people in an agentic state waiting for the next order, and little actual agility. Change can be given a headwind or a tailwind. Initial progress can feel like walking through molasses—and inviting everyone to go molasses-walking at the same time is outside of my risk appetite.

Instead, apply an agile approach to agility and *achieve big through small*.

Start with small teams, small slices of value, and small investments. The time to value, to learning, to achievement, to improving outcomes (not just activity) is sooner. The dip is considerably shorter and shallower. Impediments are identified earlier, and experiments are safe-to-learn—they are within the risk appetite. A path is being beaten through the organizational jungle. Your context is unique. Your organization is a complex adaptive system and the domain is emergent and unknowable. The only way to determine the optimal course of action is by safe-to-learn doing. Betting the whole farm is not safe-to-learn.

The bigger the transformation, the deeper and longer the dip, represented by the big Kübler-Ross curve in Figure 2.4. In my experience, time, "t2" on the graph, is at least two to three years for a large organization. The squiggly line above the large Kübler-Ross curve represents a series of small Kübler-Ross curves. This is what happens when you take a "big through small" approach. There are still dips, but they are shallower and shorter lived. Failing is learning; there will inevitably be setbacks. New skiers fall over. New musicians hit the wrong note and new language learners struggle to find the right word. A willingness to fail fast and often results in learning sooner. There is no such thing as a failed experiment. There is learning.

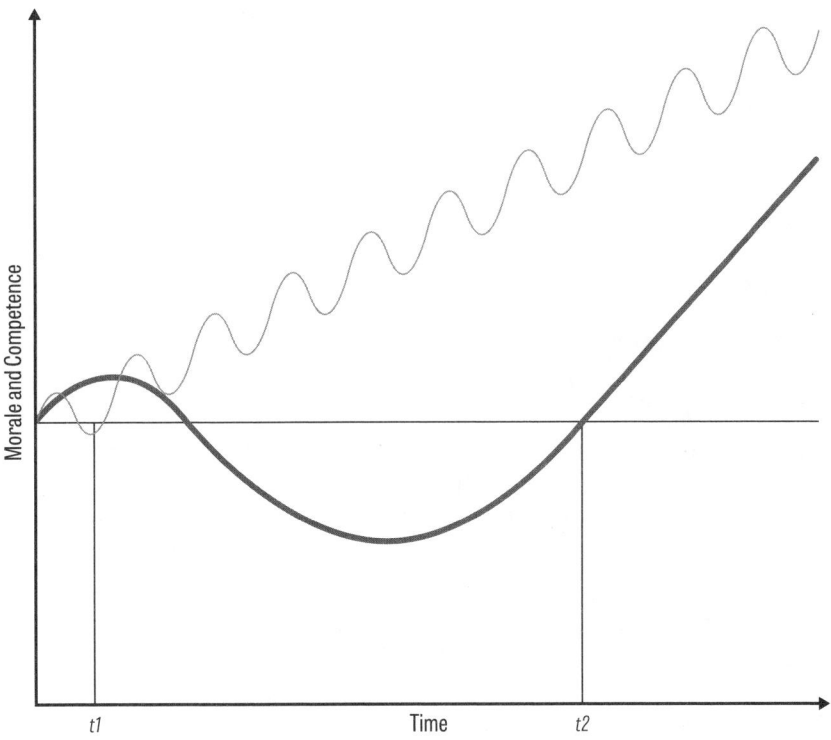

Figure 2.4: Achieve Big through Small to Improve Outcomes Sooner

   Those learnings should happen on a small, safe-to-learn scale. Mountaineers don't start learning to climb by trying to conquer Everest, and new piano players don't play their first concert with the philharmonic. They start by climbing walls and performing short renditions in front of family and friends. Change in complex adaptive systems is messy. There is no "click here to install Agile" command that can be run, like updating an operating system. You can't force the pace of change and you can't predict it. You can nurture it and enable it; you can create a tailwind or a headwind. The **BVSSH** metrics are your feedback loop, your dashboard. With a set of balanced measures you can see if forward progress is being made and then amplify or dampen the experiments. You beat a path through the organizational jungle, making it easier for others to follow. To learn sooner, to get to value sooner, within risk appetite and given that humans have a limited velocity to unlearn and relearn, there should be a

PATTERN **2.1**

series of early, often, and small change curves that link together as the company pursues continuous transformation aligned to outcomes.

Adopt the "Rule of One":

1 experiment

1 customer or team

1 location

in production

Start in areas that are naturally receptive, with the natural champions, the Innovators on the left of the Diffusion of Innovation Curve. They're enthusiastic about employing a better way of working, probably with many years of experience doing it. The dips are not as deep, and the learning and feedback are quicker. There is less risk, and the champions, who are likely to have been trying to implement similar changes in a small way in the past—despite, not because of, the firm—are best placed to forge the trail. They'll have a growth mindset and personal resilience.

It's as though our ski instructor, instead of trying to teach everyone at the same time, had asked who wants to go first. They'd know that the first five students to put up their hands will be the most enthusiastic (the Innovators). They might have skied before. They might have watched the Winter Olympics and hoped that one day they'd do that too. They can't wait to get their skis on and ski.

So the instructor tells everyone else to keep doing what they're doing—drinking hot chocolate in the hotel bar—and he takes those five skiers out onto the nursery slopes. Those skiers are keen. They want to learn. Eventually they're enjoying smooth turns down the piste and sliding to a stop while spraying snow over the hotel bar window. They also make mistakes and fall over, all while having fun at the same time. They're learning. Each time they cross the tips of their skis or catch an edge and fall face-first in the snow, they learn how to ski a little better. There is a feedback loop that modifies actions. Also, they find out more about the environment, the terrain, and are able to advise the fast followers, advising them where to go and where not to go, so that they can learn to ski better, sooner, safer, and happier.

Eventually the next set of people want a go. They've watched the first group make progress and they've seen that skiing is fun. The instructor invites them to join the class. He now has a group of five new students and a second group of five intermediate students who are skiing by themselves. The intermediate students are able to help encourage the new students. Both groups are learning by doing. They're still making mistakes, and they're learning.

Soon more people join the class, and eventually most of the group is on the slopes. The first group of students are already off on the ski lift to some more exciting runs. Other groups have enough knowledge to avoid bumping into each other on the nursery slopes. After enough practice, there are enough people with enough skill to help those who are beginners. Eventually, the people who have spent most of their days in the bar start to feel that they're missing out. More choose to ski because they don't want to feel left out or different and they can see how much others are enjoying it, until only a small handful are left drinking schnapps. Some will eventually choose to stagger home without having picked up the skills needed to ski—and that's okay.

Since humans have a limited velocity to unlearn and relearn, instead of trying to change everyone at the same time, invite the natural champions, the "Hell, yes!" people, the Innovators, to go first. Then nail it before you scale it. Enable safe-to-learn experiments that are within your risk appetite. If an experiment works, amplify it. If it doesn't work, dampen it and repeat. The successful embedding of that change creates social proof. It's now okay to opt in. The knowledge diffuses through the rest of the group. There's no denial and no depression, as it's not a forced frog march.

The Rise of the S-Curve

We've seen in Figure 2.4 that it is preferable to take a series of smaller, safe-to-learn experiments rather than betting the farm. Any dip is shorter and shallower. The outcome is reached sooner, safer, and people are happier. This is applying an agile mindset to agility. Importantly, as we zoom out, the many small curves form an S-curve. As we saw in Figure 1.4, the Diffusion of Innovation curve, which is derived from 508 studies into how large groups of people adopt change over time, is a normal probability distribution. Draw a normal probability distribution as a *cumulative* distribution over time and it's an S-curve. This also matches my personal experience learned the hard way.

This is how groups of humans adopt change, an S-curve over a multi-year time period. The pace of changing human behavior over time cannot be forced. It can be given a headwind or a tailwind.

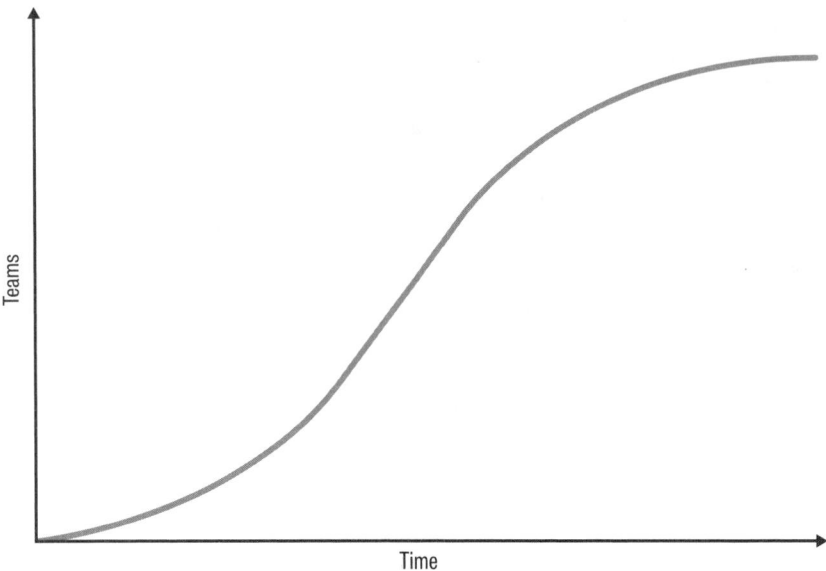

Figure 2.5: The S-Curve of Long-Term Change

There's no quick, steep slope straight to the top. The gradient is low at the beginning. The Innovators go first. They create social proof within their organization's context. It makes it acceptable for the Early Adopters and then the Early Majority to participate. A trail has been blazed. It becomes easier. There's less friction, more understanding, fewer impediments, and crucially the change is taking place within risk appetite. Finance, internal audit, procurement, HR, and so on come along on the same journey too, starting small. The complex adaptive system is adjusting to accept a new normal in a non-threatening manner without triggering corporate antibodies or unacceptable risk or cultural tissue rejection.

The gradient increases over time. At the beginning one team at a time is invited to experiment with new ways of working, within minimal viable guardrails. When it's working, then the next team is invited and so on. When about ten to fifteen teams are experimenting with the new ways of working, and if everything is good, then invite five more teams at a time. When you have about thirty teams working, invite ten more teams at a time and so on. Each time, the impediments will become more systemic and harder to resolve. Don't pass go until they have been alleviated. They don't need to be totally eliminated with a big-bang mentality; they need to be incrementally alleviated

PATTERN **2.1**

so that they are no longer the weakest link in the chain. Keep focusing on the weakest link, which will move.

The pace of change cannot be predicted or forced; it's a case of reading the tea leaves and nurturing it, giving it a tailwind, looking at the **BVSSH** trends. It depends on culture, history, leadership, support, dependencies, understanding, existing processes, and so on. It starts out really hard and gets exponentially easier. As the midpoint is reached and the Late Majority are improving ways of working in line with outcomes, the shift starts to have momentum of its own, especially if internal audit is on board.

I've found that this is the point when positive change begins happening by itself. Teams and business areas optimize for **Better Value Sooner Safer Happier**. Internal audit, when auditing an area, tip people toward the control environment or lifecycle (the context-sensitive minimal viable guardrails) that supports better ways of working. As controls are more effective, there is less risk and this leads to better outcomes. **BVSSH** metrics shine a light on improvement (or not), which leads to action. Business units pivot from temporal projects with role silos and temporal teams to long-lived products on long-lived value streams with long-lived multidisciplinary teams, through pull not push, due to social proof in context and because it demonstrably improves outcomes.

Does this mean everyone is "super-freakin' Agile?" No, of course not. Because "Agile" might not be the answer. But people *are* optimizing for **Better Value Sooner Safer Happier**, and with a control environment that enables it. This could be working on fifty-year-old code on a mainframe computer or it could be a social media advertising campaign.

The S-curve graph doesn't represent teams *doing* Agile or Lean. It is not a count of "Scrum Teams." It represents product teams who have been invited to start experimenting on ways of working within minimal viable guardrails in order to improve on outcomes. From the perspective of Safer, it very explicitly represents teams who were previously governed to a traditional, waterfall, deterministic, not continuously improving, one-size-fits-all, heavyweight, big batch, inspect quality in at the end, control environment to now being governed by a new and iteratively improving lightweight, context-sensitive, continuous everything control environment and lifecycle (i.e., minimal viable guardrails) that enables rather than hinders the delivery of **Better Value Sooner Safer Happier**. (We do a deep dive on this topic in Chapter 6.)

This is an important point from the perspective of risk, control, compliance, internal audit, and external regulators. It is within risk appetite. To the

PATTERN **2.1**

left of the S-curve are the old ways of working and the *existing control environment*; at the beginning, that is the majority. To the right of the S-curve are the new ways of working and the *new and iteratively improving control environment* that is optimized for delivering **Better Value Sooner Safer Happier**. I have found that people in risk, control, compliance, and audit roles have appreciated the clarity that the pace of moving up the S-curve is within risk appetite gives. If there is an issue, adoption is paused and the issue is addressed before progressing again. It's safe-to-learn with the cheapest cost and lowest impact of failure. The implication is that two control environments need to run side by side for some time. The old legacy control environment should not be allowed to evolve to continue to further impede **BVSSH** outcomes; it should be marked as non-strategic and for future decommissioning, with changes kept to a minimum. In the meantime, it clearly needs to continue to be fit for purpose if any new control gaps are identified. Ideally, any changes that have to be made are leveraged from the new continuous control environment (which we look at in Chapters 5 and 6). Eventually, the old control environment, which does not support both speed and control, can be decommissioned, with all changes completed in the new continuous control environment. This domain is emergent; there are unknown-unknowns. A big-bang, overnight pivot in the control environment across a large traditional organization because it's "quicker" is usually outside of risk appetite and in reality is unlikely to be "quicker."

Trying to force the pace of change, ordering change, leads to a different picture, as is illustrated in Figure 2.6.

It leads to new labels on the same old behavior, to cargo cult behavior, and a potentially risky situation. Fragile rather than agile. Or it leads to frustration as a large number of people are requested to adopt new ways of working within an environment that doesn't support it, a Catch-22. I've made this mistake in the past and I've observed, spoken to, and worked with organizations that have the same learning. Even with empowerment in the how, we tried to do too much, too soon. It was a lesson learned; I would not do it again. We pivoted and we went at the pace of change, observing S-curve adoptions in line with the Diffusion of Innovation studies.

Importantly, it doesn't need to be *one* S-curve. A number of S-curves still add up to an S-curve. A success pattern I've found is an S-curve per business unit or top-level value stream and an S-curve per key systemic enabler. Often each business unit has its own subculture, history, and local impediments. Think Big, Start Small, Learn Fast. In the previous chapter, I mentioned a small, central servant-leader Ways of Working Center of Enablement (WoW CoE) team. The Wow CoE should be complemented with a small WoW CoE per business unit, in a federated and fractal manner. Each WoW CoE supports the S-curve per business unit or top-level value stream, bubbling up any systemic impediments.

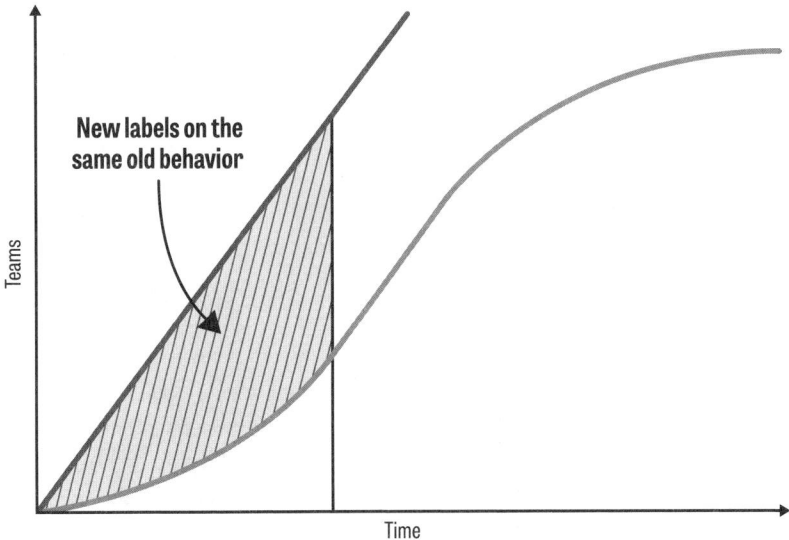

Figure 2.6: #AsYouWere

In my experience, for large traditional organizations, the timeline of getting to the 80/20 rule on the overall S-curve is at least three to five years with a tailwind, and five to seven years with a headwind (if at all). The beginning of the S-curve, where the gradient is low, is twelve to eighteen months. Resist the pressure and temptation to try to do too much too soon. In my experience, with a tailwind, it was after about four years that the old, traditional, stage-gate, change-control environment was decommissioned, with all change being governed through a lifecycle and control environment fit for the Age of Digital.

Your mileage may vary, and you're never done improving. Human systems experience the loss of information and things will start to creep back if your foot is taken off the gas. Unique to your context, there will be new S-curves for new experiments in ways of working in order to further improve on **Better Value Sooner Safer Happier**.

PATTERN **2.1**

PATTERN 2.2

Descale Before You Scale

We saw in Antipattern 2.2 that a large, old, traditional organization is likely now to be at or close to the highest level of inefficiency and bureaucracy that its revenue can (or cannot) support. It will have fattened and spread over the years, with scale itself potentially being an impediment to **Better Value Sooner Safer Happier**. Applying an Agile method or framework on top of the existing organizational dysfunction and expecting magic to happen, leaving a lot of the bureaucracy and culture in place while following the robotic maneuvers of Agile, is unlikely to lead to better outcomes.

"Scaling agile" *should* mean exhibiting agility across the whole organization, rather than doing more Agile. In order to increase agility, in order to optimize for the fast flow of safe value, work and the system of work needs to be *descaled*. Scaling agility *is* descaling.

To quote Dave Snowden, "You don't scale a complex system by aggregation or imitation but by decomposition to an optimal level of granularity followed by recombination in context."[12] That is, for a heterogeneous, diverse, complex organization, instead of applying an agile framework across it (i.e., imitation, sameness), start small with multiple bounded experiments, aiming to keep them as simple as possible and no simpler (descale, less is more).

An organization is a network of interdependent services. Therefore, the descaling efforts should include working to *break* dependencies, not only to manage them. This leads to fewer bottlenecks, less effort required for coordination, higher autonomy, and increased agility.

Within the multiple bounded experiments, aim to descale the flow of work end-to-end. This could be by inviting additional people into the multidisciplinary team to reduce handoffs and time that work is waiting. Nail it before you scale it.

Then, sustainably increase size and scope with one or more S-curves, as we saw in Pattern 2.1. Scale up a way of working that is already "descaled" in your context, to as great an extent as is possible. This is a good time to run safe-to-learn experiments on the new continuous control environment on the right hand side of the S-curve. This control environment contains the context-sensitive and minimal viable compliance guardrails, optimizing for **BVSSH** (more on this in Chapter 6). Progressively over time, it will be increasingly easier to further descale to improve flow.

PATTERN **2.2**

As the organization scales agility by descaling the work and the system of work, it is important to ensure that teams with high autonomy also have *high alignment*. That is, the work is aligned to strategic outcome hypotheses and the decoupled teams are rowing in the same direction. (This topic is covered in Chapter 5.)

It may be that the current size of an organization or team is the biggest impediment to outcomes. For example, one organization I know of had a team of about a hundred people that had failed numerous times over many years to deliver business value in a traditional waterfall manner. The organization had grown fed up. It implemented a solution: it built two teams of a hundred people, both trying to deliver the same business value in a waterfall manner! The definition of insanity is doing the same thing over and over again and expecting different results. I'm sure you can imagine, and maybe empathize with, how this plan worked out.

The organization changed tactics. The focus was on descaling and simplicity. It appointed a leader with a track record of successful delivery with agile principles. The leader created a team of just five. They were the Innovators in the organization working with agile principles and practices. Within twelve weeks, they put a live product in the hands of customers. They solved a customer need, added value, and provided much-needed learning and feedback. From this point on, the team size didn't grow to more than three teams of nine or fewer each, even as the number and scope of the business lines they supported expanded considerably.

Taking the original hundred people, doing en masse mandated training, and applying robotic maneuvers of Agile would not have addressed the inherent bloat. It likely would have resulted in an overly complex solution. The problem was that it just wasn't a hundred-person problem!

Case Study: Building Agility Is Not Bish, Bash—Bosch ■

Bosch, a global supplier of technology and services, had seen that top-down management couldn't keep up with today's business environment. It recognized that its way of working needed to change and accepted that different parts of its business would benefit from different approaches. According to Darrell K. Rigby, Jeff Sutherland, and Andy Noble, writing in a special "Agile at Scale" edition of the *Harvard Business Review* in 2018, the company created a "dual organization." The most dynamic parts of the business were run with agile teams; traditional functions did

PATTERN 2.2

things the old way. Instead of a Big Transformation, it kept agility in the company small and focused.[13]

In 2015, the management board decided to spread agility deeper into the organization. They started by setting a goal, a target date, and a schedule of regular status reports. That was a traditional and non-agile way of working, and they soon found that company divisions were skeptical of another change program that came from the top down.

So the team changed tactics. It spread out and engaged with division leaders—the "frozen middle." It set up small, agile teams and tested different approaches. Soon the team members had personally experienced the satisfaction of increasing speed and effectiveness. Within two years, the company still had a mixture of agile teams and traditionally structured units, but collaboration as a whole had increased across the company and "nearly all areas" had adopted agile values. They had seen and felt the positive outcomes of the new ways of working.

The company's leadership team doesn't plan everything up front. The leaders, say the authors, recognize that they don't know how many agile teams they'll need, the speed with which they should add those teams, or how to address bureaucratic constraints without upending the organization in the way that a big-bang Agile Transformation would do.[14] When Bosch feels a need to increase agility, it launches a new wave of agile teams, gathers data on the value those teams create and the constraints they face, then balances the value of the outcome of the extra agility against the organizational and financial cost of acquiring that agility. If the costs are higher than the benefits, the company stops and looks for ways to increase the value of the agile teams already in place or decrease the costs of change.

PATTERN 2.3

Scale Agility, Not Agile, Vertically Then Sideways

In Antipattern 2.3 we saw that grass roots hits a grass ceiling. Starting at the team level and going sideways does not bring senior leadership or the pressurized middle on the journey. It is a common learning to miss the middle and need to go back later. I have made this mistake in the past, with senior leadership engaged, teams engaged, and not sufficiently engaging or supporting the pressurized middle.

The pressurized middle should be explicitly supported in the move from traditional, waterfall, Taylorist, command-and-control, deterministic ways of working to servant leadership and an emergent mindset. People in the pressurized middle have a very important role, and that role is no longer command and control or detailed order-giver. It is to help ensure that the mission, the desired outcomes, are clear, then listen, coach, and help remove impediments as a servant leader, allowing for the voicing of differing opinions and recognizing improvement through experimentation, even when the experiments are not "successful." For some, this is already default behavior. For others, it may take a long time for ingrained behaviors to change, if at all. How people in these roles are or are not engaged is critical. People have a limited velocity to unlearn and relearn, and change will not be overnight.

I've found that when starting small, it's best to work first with a *vertical slice of an organization*. That first group should have representatives from every level of the company, including—even especially—the Executive Committee. That is, a multidisciplinary team with leaders at all levels, a connected stripe including senior leaders, the pressurized middle, and team level. Everyone learns together, and no one is left behind.

It's not as easy as it sounds. The most enthusiastic group of people willing to adopt new ways of working is usually at the team level. They've benefitted less from command-and-control, us-and-them, cog-in-a-machine ways of working in the past, and in some cases, as one team once mentioned to me, have been "united through a common suffering" as they've struggled with old ways of working! Conversely, there are some leaders who hold the belief that "they got to where they got" by being authoritarian.

If members of a leadership team are not prepared to adopt the principles and practices that they expect their followers to adopt, success will be limited. To quote Fredereick Laloux, author of *Reinventing Organizations*, "the level of consciousness of an organization cannot exceed the level of consciousness of its leader."[15] (More on this in Chapter 4.)

The initial vertical slice is by invitation not imposition. It should contain the Innovators at every level and with as few dependencies on other teams as possible. Preferably the team won't be aligned by role specialization. It will be aligned by value stream (e.g., credit card business) and sub-value streams (e.g., credit card customer servicing). It shouldn't just be a team of engineers. Starting small, it should include people across disciplines so that the new ways of working can be gradually learned and experienced throughout the organiza-

PATTERN **2.3**

tion. Once the early experiments are working, at the beginning of the S-curve, with a vertical slice of the organization (from CEO, through the leadership of nested value streams, to a team), then start to swing out sideways, picking up more nested value streams and more of the pressurized middle over time.

A great role for middle management here is the Coaching Kata, which comes from research by Mike Rother on Toyota's previously uncodified culture of continuous improvement. Rother recommends using two processes, or "kata," the Improvement Kata and the Coaching Kata, which are a way of practicing scientific thinking, avoiding jumping to conclusions with our many cognitive biases.[16] In the Improvement Kata, the learner sets a direction or defines a vision. They understand their current situation and define the next target condition they want to create, which is just beyond the threshold of knowledge. They work toward that condition, running small experiments, tackling impediments that turn up along the way. The second kata is the Coaching Kata, and it is a great way for leaders to coach and support their teams through the Improvement Kata and to improve their BVSSH outcomes. There are five coaching questions, with part of the coaching on how the learner is thinking and approaching the Improvement Kata. It builds a muscle memory of continuous improvement for all.

Summary

Big Things Start Small

This chapter has been about the sustainable, safe, and successful adoption of better ways of working across large organizations. Many old, traditional, not-born-agile organizations have been doing business in much the same way for decades, and sometimes even centuries. We looked at how those organizations are likely functioning close to the limits of inefficiency that their revenues have allowed.

We looked at the antipattern of a big bang, at not applying an agile mindset to agility, at betting the farm, at a capital "T" Transformation approach resulting in a giant Kübler-Ross curve. We looked at the antipattern of applying agile or lean practices or tools across an organization as-is rather than descaling the work to scale agility. It's not about scaling Agile, it's about scaling better ways of working to improve outcomes. And we considered that grass roots hit a grass ceiling. It's preferable to start with vertical slices of the orga-

PATTERN **2.3**

nization in order to not miss the middle and to ensure that impediments can be dealt with.

People have a limited velocity to unlearn and relearn. The pace of change cannot be forced; it can be nurtured. People adopt change in the shape of a normal, cumulative probability distribution (i.e., an S-curve), starting with the natural Innovators. Improving ways of working needs to be safe-to-learn and within risk appetite. Middle management are critical enablers as servant leaders, coaching their teams in continuous improvement alignment to outcomes and being coached.

Think Big, Start Small, Learn Fast.

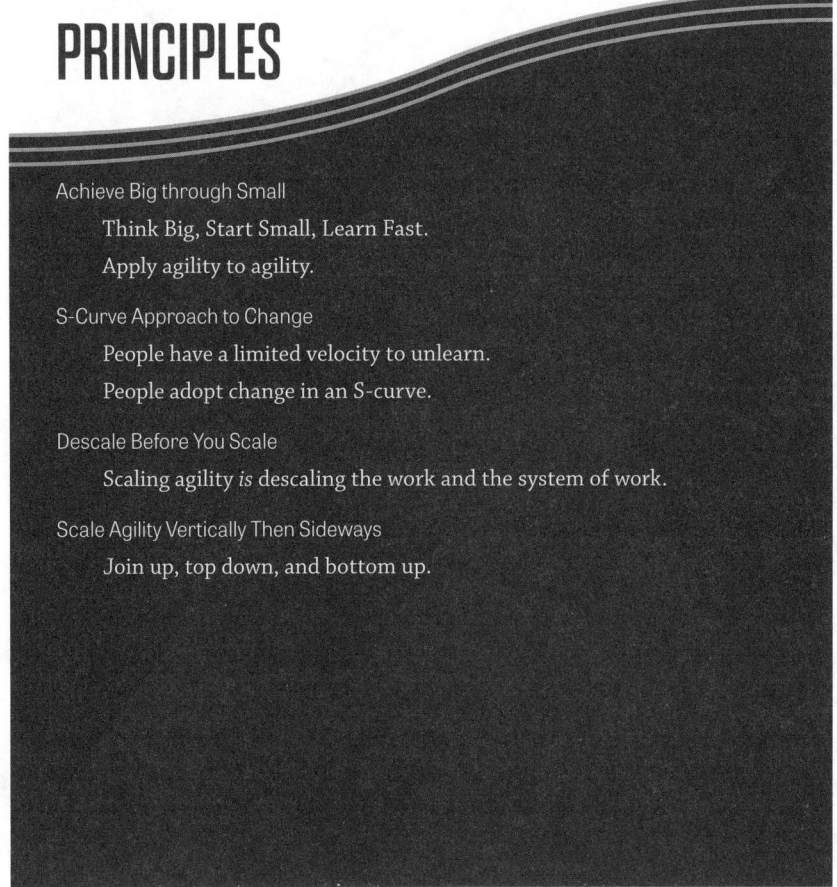

PRINCIPLES

Achieve Big through Small
> Think Big, Start Small, Learn Fast.
> Apply agility to agility.

S-Curve Approach to Change
> People have a limited velocity to unlearn.
> People adopt change in an S-curve.

Descale Before You Scale
> Scaling agility *is* descaling the work and the system of work.

Scale Agility Vertically Then Sideways
> Join up, top down, and bottom up.

3

OPTIMIZATION OVER ONE WAY; INVITE OVER INFLICT

Julie was ready for her job interview. At least, she thought she was. It had been a long time since she had last interviewed for a position and she hadn't planned to look for another role any time soon, let alone interview for her own role at her own company.

She liked the place she had been working at for the last nine years. She was comfortable. Sure, things could be a bit frustrating at times. Deadlines were often unrealistic. Compliance always took forever, and by the time any feedback came in, it was often at the last minute, resulting in unplanned work, missed deadlines, red RAG statuses, re-planning, change control boards, and people involved in political game-playing and finger pointing as to whose "fault" the delay was. Her boss had a fearsome reputation. People went to extreme lengths to provide diversions and bury bad news for as long as possible.

She wasn't surprised that so many of the features her company rolled out had slow take-up by customers, or that they took so long to produce. They were not even fast followers of the new nimble, digital-first disruptors. And it was true that their traditional competitors were doing a better job. The new app that their main rival had rolled out a few months ago was already top of the customer satisfaction reviews, and they had been updating it weekly. It would take her company twenty times as long just to make a decision. And it would take that much time again for the decision to be approved by multiple committees.

So she accepted that there was a case for change. When she'd got the announcement from the board about the transformation, the mandated new roles, the mandated new practices, and the mandated training, she hadn't just rolled her eyes and shaken her head like Albert had done.

"Here we go again, every few years," he'd grumbled. "Last time it was an exercise to make everyone have at least ten direct reports within the existing role hierarchy. A lot of people were let go and the only benefit was for the shareholders, and that didn't last long. We didn't improve customer satisfaction or remove any of the delays to getting work done. We just had less personal development time and a bunch of new, fake, role-based teams. I'll bet you a week of lunches we'll end up with some new jargon and nothing will actually change. The system of work and culture hasn't changed in the twenty-five years I've been here. You watch, it'll be new labels on the same old behavior."

Julie had smiled at that. Already some of their job titles had changed—she was now a "product manager" instead of a "project manager"—but the work itself and everyone's behaviors had remained mostly the same. That last

ANTIPATTERN 3.1

Transformation might have shed visible costs, but it hadn't made the organization any better or faster at delivering value. Nor had it made them or any of their customers happier. In fact, it felt quite the opposite. It felt like a race to the ground.

Albert was probably right. This time didn't look like it would be much different. She wished the articulation of *why* they were doing the Transformation went beyond shareholder gain. That didn't feel like an inspirational purpose. The firm was doing well. Sure, they were losing market share to new and old competitors, but they were still making a healthy profit. If I *were* to be asked, she thought, *I'd say that I don't want to work my colleagues or myself out of a job so that shareholders can enjoy a higher dividend.*

Not that anyone was asking her, or any of the people closest to the customers, even though they probably knew the company's weaknesses and strengths better than most. They were closest to the work, and she was sure they could contribute ideas that would produce better outcomes. Instead, the communication was a statement of fact, a *fait accompli*, with an eighteen-month project plan with milestones, run like any other project. The best survival tactic was to follow the orders and do no more. Don't step out of line. Don't take any risks. *Someone else is taking responsibility for this*, thought Julie, *so I'll do what I'm told. If it doesn't work, it's someone else's problem.*

Julie took a deep breath. She wasn't sure which was worse: the interview she was about to face in order to keep her job, or the months of upheaval that lay on the other side of it. The uncertainty meant that some of her colleagues had already been poached away by competitors. Maybe she'd join them. Surely there had to be a better way of enabling the company to deliver better outcomes.

ANTIPATTERN 3.1

One Size Fits All

There is no one size fits all for organizational agility. There is no silver bullet. There is no One Way, no Agile-in-a-box that optimizes outcomes in all contexts. Your organization, your customers, your value propositions, your environment, your processes, your system of work, your leaders at all levels, your teams, your constraints, your starting point, your behavioral norms, your history, your brand, your team, and you are unique. That's the bottom line of this one-size-fits-all antipattern.

Your Organizational Context Is Unique: There Is No One Way

Organizations are heterogeneous, not homogeneous. Organizations are emergent, not predictive. Organizations are complex adaptive systems. Acting in the space changes the space. The butterfly flaps its wings and either there is no change or there is a tornado a thousand miles away. Small things in a complex system may have no effect or a massive one, and it is almost impossible to know which will turn out to be the case. Interventions are irreversible. Like adding milk to coffee, they cannot be undone. People don't forget.

Increasing agility, improving on **BVSSH** outcomes enterprise-wide, is about leveraging that complexity, diversity, and emergence, treating it as an enabler or as a competitive differentiator. It's not about inflicting sameness on every team. In order to maximize outcomes, the approach to organizational agility cannot be cookie cutter. A one-size-fits-all approach may raise two boats and lower ninety-eight. Within an organization, the levers to pull to improve **Better Value Sooner Safer Happier** outcomes will vary.

Your context is unique and will be made up of a multitude of different factors divided across organization, people, products, process, technology, tools, and data. You can see some of them in Figure 3.1

It is worth noting that the "people" category in Figure 3.1 has the most factors. "Tooling" has the fewest, reinforcing how much this is about people over processes or tools. Yet often organizations start with the tooling because that's easiest. People don't mind playing with new tools. It's easy. It's often done with the existing behavioral norms unchanged. It is harder to start with people, to unlearn existing behaviors and relearn new ones, yet this is the biggest lever for better outcomes.

It didn't take long to brainstorm that list, and it's surprising that as many as ninety different elements can emerge in a short space of time. Together they produce 1.2 octillion unique combinations—assuming that the factors are binary, which they aren't. Clearly, your context is unique, and each large organization contains many unique contexts, each as different as a fingerprint. And your context is changing, not static. And the pace of change is getting faster and faster.

Improving on **Better Value Sooner Safer Happier** outcomes is not optimized by suppressing that uniqueness by dogmatically imposing one set of practices. It means leveraging your uniqueness and optimizing for context within guardrails.

ORGANIZATION	PEOPLE	PRODUCTS
Impediments	Culture (org, business unit, dept., team)	Criticality (life critical)
Starting points	Leader & leadership team buy-in	Cost of delay
Industry volatility & disruption	Prior experience in different ways of working	Rate, predictability, and size
Competitors	Psychological safety	of work entering the system
Urgency	Customer expectations	Level of uncertainty and risk (degree of
Cost of delay of changing	Customer elasticity	knowability)
Organization size	Ease of getting customer feedback	Degree of "scaling" needed
Organization age	Diversity	Degree of coupling
Locations	National cultural norms	Degree of cohesion
Diversity of businesses	Survival anxiety	Type (shared, customer journey aligned,
Purpose, values	Duration that team members have worked together	channel)
History, folklore	Org structure	# handoffs to deliver value
Past mergers & acquisitions	Geographical distribution	Current lead time
Org identity	Permanent vs. outsourced	Current flow efficiency
Safety criticality	Skill level	Current quality
Public vs. private	Knowledge & insight	Amount of regulation
Short-term vs. long-term pressure	Capabilities	**TECHNICAL**
PROCESS	HR processes (promotion, recognition, reward)	Architecture: monolithic vs. microservices
Policies	Tenure	Technologies used
Standards	Orthodoxies & belief	Degree of coupling
Processes	Defined roles	Degree of cohesion
Regulation	Incentivization	Engineering skills
Finance	Training, coaching, support availability	Engineering practices
Hiring	Career paths available	Environment provisioning
Procurement	Working environment	Degree of automation
Degree of framework fundamentalism	Ability to collaborate across boundaries	Branching strategies
Audit	Existence of Communities of Practice	Build & deployment strategy & frequency
Governance, Risk & Compliance	**TOOLS & DATA**	Observability
Product vs. project	Wall space (or tooling) to be able to radiate	Resilience
Environment provisioning	information	Embedded
	Degree of data-led insights being mined	
	Availability of date-led insights	
	Speed of data feedback loop	
	Ability to drill into the data	
	Tools available	
	End-to-end integration of tools	
	No choice, some limited choice, or Wild West	

Figure 3.1 An Incomplete List of Example Criteria

That Make Up Your Unique Context

If the path ahead is clear, you're probably on someone else's.
—Joseph Campbell

There are three contextual criteria in particular that we will take a closer look at. They are Scaling Agile, Culture, and Revolution versus Evolution.

1: Your "Scaling" Context Is Unique: There Is No One Way

I once facilitated a discussion at a conference on the topic of "scaling agile." Everyone who attended had a different mental model of what "scale" meant.

Definitions included:

- A handful of teams (fewer than ten people per team) delivering one product in one context
- Tens or hundreds of teams delivering one product, with teams in a similar context
- Tens or hundreds of teams delivering one product, with teams in differing contexts
- Several teams delivering multiple unrelated products in differing contexts
- Tens, hundreds, or thousands of teams delivering tens, hundreds, or thousands of products in differing contexts
- Agility in a non-IT context such as internal audit, compliance, marketing, or procurement
- Whole organization agility across a small, medium, or large organization with one, several, or thousands of products and value streams

Within each of those differing contexts for "scaling agile" are other key contextual criteria to take into account, such as the degree of dependencies between teams and their products, the level of mastery of modern ways of working, and the cultural norms. If there is a high degree of coupling, a low level of mastery, and a command-and-control culture, the approach will benefit from a focus on a high degree of collaboration, synchronizing work, and identifying and then eliminating or alleviating the dependencies. If there is no coupling, a high level of mastery, and a servant leader culture, then teams, within minimal viable guardrails and with strategy alignment, can be more autonomous.

Unfortunately, more often than not what I observe is one approach across an organization irrespective of context, the application of one set of practices that are rigidly adhered to. This is not applying an agile mindset to agility. One of the *Agile Manifesto* principles states: "At regular intervals, the team reflects on how to become more effective, then tunes and adjusts its behavior accordingly."[1]

When people talk about "scale," there is no single, common definition or scenario. There is no one size fits all. Applying one set of practices is an antipattern. It optimizes for the practices; it does not acknowledge the reality that context is unique and does not optimize for outcomes in context.

2: Your Cultural Context Is Unique: There Is No One Way

The local understanding of "scaling" is related to the second contextual criteria I want to look at: culture, the behavioral norms in an organization. The dominant culture of the business area undergoing change should also inform the approach taken to improve on **Better Value Sooner Safer Happier** outcomes. It is an antipattern to apply one way without taking the behavioral norms of the context into account.

There are a number of possible sources to look to for this, including the Laloux Culture Model, the Schneider Culture Model, or the Westrum typology of organizational culture. We will use the Westrum model.

Ron Westrum, an American sociologist, created a typology of organizational cultures. He argued that the preoccupations of leaders shape a unit's culture. A leader's actions and ability to provide rewards and inflict punishments communicate their preferences, which then become the preoccupation of the organization's workforce. Over time, members of an organization learn how to read the surrounding signs. They engage in behaviors that bring reward and avoid behaviors that bring punishment. In the process, they create the organization's culture: a pattern of response to the problems and opportunities that the culture encounters. Westrum describes three cultural types—pathological, bureaucratic, and generative—that are shaped by the preoccupations of the unit's leaders.

A focus on personal power, needs, and glory creates a pathological environment. A bureaucratic environment is created by leaders who obsess about departmental turf, positions, and rules. And leaders who keep their eye on the mission build a generative style.

Cultures that are pathological or bureaucratic have little psychological safety. A command-and-control culture is prevalent and there may even be a culture of fear with learned helplessness. I have spent time with teams operating in these cultures. They didn't dare to inspect and adapt. They waited for the next order to come down the chain of command. They were frozen rather than having the safety to learn and improve for themselves. In an emergent domain, with a lack of psychological safety, they were never going to experiment to improve on their outcomes for fear of failing.

Table 3.1: Westrum's Three Cultural Types[2]

Pathological	Bureaucratic	Generative
Power oriented	Rule oriented	Performance oriented
Low cooperation	Modest cooperation	High cooperation
Messengers shot	Messengers neglected	Messengers trained
Responsibilities shirked	Narrow responsibilities	Risks are shared
Bridging discouraged	Bridging tolerated	Bridging encouraged
Failure ➡ scapegoating	Failure ➡ justice	Failure ➡ inquiry
Novelty crushed	Novelty ➡ problems	Novelty implemented

In this cultural norm, revolutionary change is less likely to be successful (and ironically, more likely to be inflicted). Evolutionary change, because it is a series of smaller, safer-to-learn experiments, is psychologically safer and more likely to lead to "sticky," long-term improvements in outcomes, in addition to creating new muscle memory of continuous improvement. I have observed a number of times the failure of a revolutionary approach in command-and-control cultures and the success of an evolutionary approach.

A business area with servant leadership, empowerment, a generative cultural norm, and recognition for learning will be much more open to experimentation. This environment is willing to fail fast and often in order to succeed sooner. A more revolutionary approach may be both feasible and optimal, while still inviting change and starting small. The greater the psychological safety and the actual safety (minimal viable guardrails and a risk-aware culture), the more innovative teams can be in their experimentation to improve outcomes.

Within overall cultural norms, there will be variations of cultural norms within different business units, within teams, by historical acquisitions, by geography, by combinations of these, or by intentionally setting up an operation such as an innovation center or a digital hub away from the mothership to allow disruptive new ideas and experiments to take root.

The type of culture predominant in an organization, or in parts of an organization, should inform the approach to change. Taking a one-size-fits-all approach across an organization, ignoring the cultural norms, is an antipattern.

3: Revolution vs. Evolution: There Is No One Way

The third factor that we're taking a look at in this antipattern is revolution versus evolution. A one-size-fits-all approach usually results in revolution without even considering if evolution is better suited to context. This will not optimize for **BVSSH** outcomes.

Evolution and revolution represent two ends of a spectrum for how change is approached. Evolution honors current roles and responsibilities, makes clear the desired outcomes, shines a light on the current system of work, and asks people to pursue continuous improvement with support. Dan Terhorst-North has described this as: "Visualize, Stabilize, Optimize."[3]

Revolution means imposing a fundamentally different system of work and job roles, even if starting small (although today that's usually not the case). For example, going from a traditional way of working, with role-based silos and long lead times to small, multidisciplinary teams, new job roles (e.g., Product Owner, Scrum Master), and an iteration-based approach such as Scrum. There may also be a top-down mandated change to Squads, Tribes, Chapters, and Guilds, the so-called Spotify Model. This is often revolutionary to people experiencing the change.

In my experience, the application of Agile frameworks usually leads to a revolutionary approach. Most frameworks are largely prescriptive and are explicitly described as immutable. When all you have is a hammer, every context will be treated like a nail. And when you've paid a lot of money for a gold-plated hammer, when you've trained a lot of people and are paying renewal fees to use that hammer, people will prefer to use it. The result of the application of the framework, and to some degree the framework itself, may not be an invitation to increase agility in ways that suit the unique context. It is often the imposition of a one-size-fits-all approach that may or may not optimize for outcomes. The focus is on *doing* an immutable framework rather than on improving outcomes.

In some cases, a framework *can* explicitly adapt to context. It can provide a range of options for teams to consider, help to shine a light on problems, and allow the team to work out how to solve them. A framework is adaptable if a team can inspect and change its way of working *entirely*, not just how it's working *within* a set of prescriptive practices.

Frameworks should be treated as a departure point, not a destination. Learn from the bodies of knowledge, then continuously inspect and adapt so that a non-adaptable framework is no longer being used if that optimizes for **Better Value Sooner Safer Happier**. Learn from everyone. Copy everyone. Optimize to context within minimal viable guardrails.

It is an antipattern to take a one-size-fits-all approach, which in most cases results in a revolution in ways of working without actively considering context or whether revolution or evolution will best optimize for outcomes.

ANTIPATTERN 3.2

Inflict over Invite

Mandating specific practices on people and teams is an antipattern. As Martin Fowler, Chief Scientist of ThoughtWorks and *Agile Manifesto* signatory, put it in 2006:

> Imposing a process on a team is completely opposed to the principles of agile, and has been since its inception. A team should choose its own process—one that suits the people and context in which they work. Imposing an agile process from the outside strips the team of the self-determination which is at the heart of agile thinking.[4]

Not only should a team (or team of teams) choose their own process, Fowler continues, the team should also be in control of how that process evolves.[5] Addressing Agile Australia twelve years later, Fowler said, "Our challenge is dealing with what I call faux-agile: agile that's just the name, but none of the values in place."[6] The methods imposed by the "Agile Industrial Complex" are a "travesty," he said.[7] "There is no one size fits all."[8]

The *Agile Manifesto* emphasizes individuals and interactions over processes and tools, collaboration over a contract, motivated individuals who are given support and trusted to get the job done, self-organizing teams regularly reflecting on how to be more effective, and tuning and adjusting behavior, practices, and processes.

Unfortunately, it is common to see prescriptive practices being mandated across teams and across organizations. It is not empowering. It does not show respect for people. It drives fear and resistance, and it is not taking an agile approach to agility. As we saw in Chapter 1, it leads to an agentic state, where people absolve themselves of responsibility for the outcomes. Imposition moves the *locus of control* to be external, reducing psychological ownership. There is *extrinsic motivation* rather than intrinsic motivation. That is, people don't feel that they have control over events or outcomes. People with an external locus of control, with extrinsic motivation, are more likely to have lower levels of job performance and satisfaction.[9]

The imposition of Agile may not be surprising when many leaders at large, traditional firms have an entire career of approaching change or product development work with a reductionist, deterministic, command-and-control mindset. There are people who believe that fixing output at the point of knowing the least, setting a date and "holding people's feet over the fire," leads to them having a reputation for "getting stuff done." However, it comes at a human cost of suffering, and it's unlikely to produce the most valuable "stuff." A deterministic approach to work coming from old, Taylorist ways of working is being applied in a context where organized human endeavor is not about manual laborers with low literacy and repetitive mass production. In the Age of Digital the effort is unique product development, knowledge work, with emergence, in complex adaptive systems, with many unknown-unknowns. In some cases, it may take a new generation of leaders.

From Antipatterns to Patterns

Bespoke Fittings and Invitations for Change

We've looked at how there can be no one-size-fits-all ways of working that optimize for outcomes in all contexts. Your organization, your customers, your value propositions, your environment, your processes, your system of work, your definition of "scale," your leaders at all levels, your teams, your constraints, your starting point, your culture, your history, your brand, your team, and you are unique. There is no one set of practices that can optimize outcomes for every context. As we saw in Chapter 1, there is no "best practice" where the domain of work is emergent. There are patterns and principles that are more likely to lead to successful outcomes and antipatterns that are less likely to.

We've also looked at how inflicting capital "A" Agile is not exhibiting agility. It is counter to the values and principles of agile and lean, with respect for people, empowered teams, and servant leadership. Due to extrinsic motivation rather than intrinsic motivation, it is less likely to lead to successful outcomes and lasting change.

It doesn't have to be this way. Instead recognize that you have a unique VOICE and invite over inflict. This will make it more likely that you will sustainably and successfully deliver **Better Value Sooner Safer Happier**.

PATTERN 3.1

Not One Size Fits All

In Antipattern 3.1, we looked at how taking a one-size-fits-all approach is not going to optimize outcomes for the infinite unique contexts in organized human endeavor.

Instead, it's a case of finding your unique VOICE and using it. In this pattern, we also look at how the level of mastery should be taken into account and consider how cultural norms should inform the approach on the revolution to evolution scale. This includes a comparison of some common frameworks, which are intended as a guide to help you choose in your unique context. A key point is that it's about #AllFrameworks, not #NoFrameworks, using what works best in context and within common minimal viable guardrails (see also Chapters 5 and 6).

1: You Have a Unique VOICE: Use It

The alternative to imposing one set of prescriptive practices across an organization, without considering the many unique contexts, is to apply an agile mindset to organizational agility: to recognize that you have a unique VOICE (see Figure 3.2). It is presented here as a way to approach business agility, as an alternative to imposing a one-size-fits-all set of practices. VOICE stands for Values and Principles, Outcomes and Purpose, Intent-Based Leadership, Coaching and Support, and Experimentation.

PATTERN 3.1

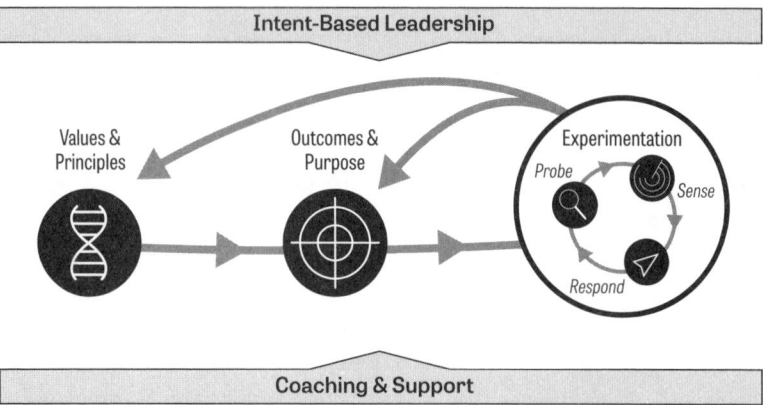

V = Values & Principles O = Outcomes & Purpose I = Intent-Based Leadership C = Coaching & Support E = Experimentation

Figure 3.2: VOICE

Values and Principles: behavioral guardrails that apply across contexts.

Outcomes and Purpose: outcomes such as Better Value Sooner Safer Happier along with a clear articulation of *Why* that is unique to your organization (as we saw in Chapter 1), with measures for the outcomes and fast feedback loops.

Intent-Based Leadership: empowerment that decentralizes decision-making, strives for high autonomy with high alignment, and fosters an environment that leads to teams building a new muscle memory, the ability to continuously improve on outcomes in context. It's not command-and-control, or micro-management, or a culture of fear, or making all the decisions. Leaders go first, role modeling desired behaviors with a clear employee engagement model so that everyone has a way to be heard and a way to influence and shape their own destiny.

Coaching and Support: to unlearn old habits, learn new ones, achieve mastery, and remove organizational impediments. Coaches draw on many bodies of knowledge and employ the practices that are hypothesized to optimize outcomes in context. Leaders at all levels coach and support continuous improvement and technical excellence. It is possible to learn to ski without a ski instructor; however, it leads to bad habits, it takes longer, there's more pain involved, and it increases the risk that the learner will give up. Coaching provides support, guidance, and encouragement; helps others avoid bumps; and reduces fear. Coaching is needed because there is no one way, no cookie-cutter approach that optimizes outcomes in all contexts.

Experimentation: is carried out at all organizational levels with fast feedback, as change is emergent and organizations are complex adaptive systems. We need to minimize the time to learning. Probing, sensing, and responding take place at the team, value stream, business unit, and organizational levels. "Double loop learning" takes learning from the Experimentation loop to create a second learning loop, which is feedback on the overall Values and Principles and Outcomes and Purpose. A goal here is to build a new muscle memory so that everyone is continuously improving on the system of work, being the best at being better.

Let's take a look at each of these in more detail.

V: Values and Principles

An organization's *values and principles* are its behavioral guardrails. They might include "Focus on Outcomes," "Achieve Big through Small," or "Invite over Inflict," for example. They inform every decision and should be repeatedly communicated. Communicate three more times than you think you need to and you're a third of the way there. The values and principles signal intent and allow for behavior that is not in line to be called out. They include teams holding each other to account as well as their leaders' behavior. The values and principles apply across contexts and can help to provide consistency in behaviors and decision-making in a large organization. Amazon, for example, has its fourteen Leadership Principles, a list that includes customer obsession, ownership, thinking big, and bias for action.[10]

Following are at least four sources of values and principles as inspiration in determining what is most applicable for your organization.

The first source is the existing, organization-wide values. In my experience, these are usually so high level—"respect," for example, or "integrity"—that there is still a need for values and principles specific to ways of working.

The second source is the *Agile Manifesto*. These apply as part of an overall agile mindset and are *de facto*. They date back to 2001 and are worded to be specific to software. In my experience, while treating the principles in the manifesto as a given, there is room to emphasize principles that are more up to date and suited to the context of business agility.

The third source is the values and principles that come with an agile framework being used, whether that's Scrum, Kanban, SAFe, Disciplined Agile, or Large Scale Scrum (LeSS), and so on.

And the fourth source is the intentionally long list of principles in this book! The key point is to come up with values and principles that work for you, in your organizational context, and at your current point, taking inspiration from many sources.

While principles apply across contexts, practices differ by context. Practices emerge by applying context to principles and by using coaching and experimentation, leveraging many bodies of knowledge. As Dan Terhorst-North has said:

Practices = Principles + Context[11]

Within guardrails, practices should not be imposed on teams. Teams should be invited and supported to take ownership in order to work out the best way to apply the principles and improve outcomes for themselves. This keeps the locus of control internal. Team members feel that they are masters of their own destinies and can change things for the better without the sky falling in. That sense of control leads to greater intrinsic motivation. Over time, people build a new muscle memory, the ability to continuously improve. With it they build or strengthen an organizational capability for learning and adapting.

O: Outcomes and Purpose

Organizations need to know *why* they are looking to improve ways of working and what their desired *outcomes* are. Outcomes such as **Better Value Sooner Safer Happier**, for example. These outcomes should each have one or more measures. When measuring outcomes, improvement over time is more important than the absolute value; everyone has a different starting point and context. The data should be transparent and timely to increase the ability to determine cause and effect. It should be possible to drill into the data to find outliers, identifying experiments to amplify or dampen. Targets should be avoided when inviting teams to change their ways of working. In my experience, targets drive

PATTERN **3.1**

cargo cult behavior and lead to a gaming of the system. I've found that when organizations remove targets, make the trend over time transparent, and leave each area to decide for themselves and in conversation with their leadership how much they want to improve, the change comes from within rather than from without. It is important that **BVSSH** measures are gathered centrally and by an independent team. This ensures consistent data, algorithms, measures, correlations, and trend comparisons and reduces the prospect of selective gaming of data.

Outcomes and Purpose provide the *What* and *Why* for improving ways of working. They provide high alignment, which enables empowered teams, with support, to inspect and adapt in their context in order to improve. The goal is not Agile for Agile's sake. It's to enable agility to improve outcomes.

I: Intent-Based Leadership

With a high alignment on the outcomes, foster an environment of high autonomy. Adopt *intent-based leadership* (more on this in Pattern 4.3). Empower teams to improve on the outcomes, starting small, with fast feedback and support. Within minimal viable guardrails, move authority to the information, not information to authority. Decentralize decision-making. Do not impose prescription, micro-manage, or make Highest Paid Person's Opinion (HiPPO) decisions. Instead, be a gardener nurturing culture. Make improvement of desired outcomes transparent. Adopt a pull, not push, approach, within guardrails. Be a transformational leader, moving away from the command-and-control management style of the 1900s. It comes as no surprise that *The State of DevOps Report* shows that transformational leadership, in the context of product development, is highly correlated with higher organizational performance.[12]

The leadership team should be team number one in adopting new ways of working. If a leadership team is not willing to role model desired behaviors, it is unrealistic and inauthentic to expect teams to do so. Critically, foster an environment of psychological safety so that people are willing to admit they don't know and are willing to experiment even though they know they might fail. They must be free to inspect and adapt. In order to improve, there has to be a safe environment. Project Aristotle, a study by Google into team performance, found that psychological safety is the number one determinant of high-performing teams.[13]

Autonomy, empowerment, and psychological safety increase intrinsic motivation and engagement as people bring their brains to work.

C: Coaching and Support

Provide *coaching* on agility, on ways of working (not on one framework), optimizing for **Better Value Sooner Safer Happier** outcomes in context, and provide *support* in removing organization-wide impediments.

A success pattern is to start with a small Ways of Working Center of Enablement (WoW CoE) with as broad a scope as possible, ideally across the whole organization. The purpose of the WoW CoE is not to inflict the rollout of one set of prescriptive practices. It's not to saturate the organization with Scrum or to drop everyone into mandated en masse training, or to run an Agile Imposition. The purpose of the WoW CoE is to orchestrate the continual improvement of the system of work and support everyone in the organization to be able to do that on a daily basis, in order to see a positive trend on **Better Value Sooner Safer Happier** measures; to achieve big through small; to coach at the enterprise level; to run experiments to alleviate organizational constraints that bubble up; and to provide clear minimal viable guardrails, so that it's agile, not fragile. The WoW CoE supports teams and plays whack-a-mole on new impediments that pop up, which they will, frequently. It ensures that training in many forms is available on demand, shares learning, collates data on multiple outcome measures, generates insights and feedback loops, and makes sure that desired behavior is recognized and rewarded.

The WoW CoE lead should ideally report to someone on the Executive Committee, either the CEO or COO. This enables organization-wide impediments to have attention from the top table so that alleviating them can be prioritized. Otherwise there will be a bubble of better ways of working restricted to the remit of the most senior leader who is sponsoring it, and a limited ability to resolve the larger firm-wide impediments to **BVSSH** that sit outside of that bubble.

The scope should not be just IT, as that will result in local optimization. Software development cycle time (from starting development to development done but not shipped) could be reduced by 90%; however, that can have little bearing on end-to-end lead time if work is stuck upstream in big-batch portfolio management, or if there is a project-based funding process, or if it takes twelve months to hire people, or if procurement is signing contracts with terms that prevent agility, or if it takes six months to get hardware, or if releases are batched up downstream due to dependencies, or if internal sponsors and stakeholders want to continue with an arms' length, order-giver and order-taker, tell-me-when-it's-done way of working. A key part of better ways of working is

PATTERN 3.1

multidisciplinary teams where it's not about "the business" and "IT." Instead, everyone is "our business." For product development, your primary tribal identity should be your value stream. It should be about what you are producing that is of value, not your job role specialism.

Note that it is a Center of Enablement rather than a Center of Excellence. This is a small, central, servant leadership function, alleviating impediments (servant) and providing enablers (leadership) to improve on the outcomes. As there is no one-size-fits-all approach to optimize outcomes, as the domain of work is emergent, and as it's about serving teams, I believe that it is inappropriate to suggest that it's a Center of Excellence. The Dunning-Kruger Effect has shown that beginners overrate themselves and experts underrate themselves, so if the center is staffed with experts, they will be aware that there is much ongoing learning still to be done.[14]

An approach that I have found works well to provide support at scale, is a fractal pattern of WoW CoEs: one per business unit or value stream, and then if appropriate, also at the next level down of nested value stream. For example: bank → investment bank → equity trading. The lead of each WoW CoE is also a virtual member of the WoW CoE team at the level above. For psychological ownership, the people in the value stream WoW CoEs report into their value stream or business unit, not into the central CoE. This ensures a sense of ownership, a tribal identity, and a collective intrinsic motivation, rather than being viewed as an alien body telling the business unit what to do, resulting in tissue rejection. This results in a scalable network that can deal with impediments at the lowest possible level, aligned to value streams.

The central WoW CoE also coordinates a network of change agents and coaches, ensuring consistent messaging on "Why," and leads a coaches network to share insights, to inspect, and to adapt. Applying the "achieve big through small" mantra, there should not be too many coaches at any one time in any one business area. There are different levels of coaching: at the team level, at the level of a self-contained business unit with a handful of value streams, and at the level of a large global organization of organizations with thousands of value streams. There is technical coaching and ways-of-working coaching. There is no one size coach fits all.

Coaches and change agents should strive to be omnists: they must recognize and respect all bodies of knowledge without framework fundamentalism. They must understand that different contexts suit different practices, within the guardrails of the organization's values and principles. Dan Terhorst-North

PATTERN 3.1

and Katherine Kirk have called this "SWARMing"—Scaling Without a Religious Methodology.[15]

Leaders at all levels should become coaches for their teams on continuous improvement and be coached themselves. This gives a clear role for middle management in particular, giving the pressurized middle a role to play, as per the Toyota Coaching Kata.[16]

E: Experimentation

Once you have high alignment and high autonomy within guardrails, with coaching and support, you can experiment. You can start to run small, safe-to-learn experiments. You can try different approaches and use fast feedback to make progress.

As you are performing unique, complex work within a unique, complex, adaptive system, you will need to *probe*, *sense*, and *respond*. The context here is changing the system of work in order to deliver better outcomes. This is emergent, whether the underlying work is also emergent (unique product development) or more deterministic (repetitive mass production or mass processing). As Edgar Schein has noted: "You cannot understand a system until you try and change it and when you do try to change it, only then will underlying mechanisms maintaining the status quo emerge."[17]

Any experiment is the testing of a hypothesis whose outcome is unknown, as it has not been done before either at all or in this exact context. We can't time travel. Organizations are complex adaptive systems, and we are in an emergent domain. There is no linear cause and effect. Other ways that people have described fast feedback loops and testing hypotheses are W. Edwards Deming's Plan Do Study Act (PDSA), John Boyd's Observe Orient Decide Act (OODA), and Eric Ries's Build, Measure, Learn.

To sense if the experiments are moving you in the right direction, you first need to be able to "see" and measure your current system of work. You need to know your starting points. Here we refer again to Dan Terhorst-North's "visualize, stabilize, optimize."

You first need to be able to *visualize* steps in a value stream from left to right. You need to be able to see the amount of work in the system at each step (the work in progress), how the work is flowing (lead time and throughput), and how long the work has been there (wait time and aging).

You need to "know your flow" and understand your flow efficiency, the percentage of time that work is being worked on during the end-to-end lead time for an item of value. In traditional organizations, flow efficiency is typically 10% or less; work really does wait for 90% of the time. This is where significant improvements can be made. Looking only at resource utilization and busyness tends to further reduce flow efficiency. When resource utilization exceeds 80%, lead time rises exponentially. Instead of busyness or local optimization, look at where the work isn't, the white space between the work, with the items of value waiting like physical inventory stacked up by a machine.

Having shone a light on the system of work, next *stabilize* flow. Apply work in progress (WIP) limits at each stage in the value stream. The fewer cars there are on the road, the faster they can go. Pack the road with cars and everything grinds to a halt. Enable flow in the value stream. If evolution over revolution is culturally preferable, those limits could match the current high WIP levels and then be reduced gradually. Crucially, no work can be started until some work has finished and a slot opens up for it by the work being pulled to the right. The system of work becomes pull-based rather than push-based.

Stop starting, start finishing.

A problem often observed is HiPPO scheduling, where people "start starting." More initiatives are run before completing or stopping others. The organization needs to learn the important ability to say "No," or "Not yet," or "What do we stop in order to do this?" in order to optimize for **BVSSH**. Doing more in parallel is like putting more cars on the road. It moves all of the **BVSSH** measures in the wrong direction.

If the context is one where work entering the system is ad hoc, such as a service desk, different classes of service are useful. For example, the service desk could create an expedited swim lane with prioritization by severity. If work is blocked downstream, people working upstream should swarm on the downstream constraint rather than sit idle or overproduce inventory upstream that will sit and wait in a growing pile of virtual inventory. The goal here is to permanently alleviate the constraint so that it is no longer the primary bottleneck.

Like the tide going down, limiting WIP exposes the rocks that have been there all along, hidden in long lead times. Limiting WIP is an "enabling constraint," surfacing pain points. Glossing over the blockers to flow, going around them, or leaving work waiting will not lead to better end-to-end business—

PATTERN **3.1**

outcomes. It will only leave inefficiencies in the system. Sometimes, depending on context, the pain of the constraint needs to be felt by blocking upstream work so that the complex adaptive system prioritizes its remediation.

Impediments are not in the path;
*impediments **are** the path.*

We're now into the *optimize* part of Experimentation, in order to deliver **Better Value Sooner Safer Happier**. The visualization and measurement of flow will provide clear indications of the biggest impediments. There could be too much work in the system or too much work in progress with considerable task switching, handoffs, and dependencies. There could be starvation, with a lack of flow from upstream or a lack of clear strategic outcomes to work toward. The Theory of Constraints asks that you identify what you believe to be your biggest constraint to flow, focus improvement efforts on alleviating it, and then repeat.

Limiting WIP and focusing on reducing end-to-end lead time will soon shine a light on the impediments. Run one experiment, or probe, then sense the outcome measures while remembering that cause and effect are not linear. Work out what your next improvement experiment will be, amplifying positive experiments and dampening negative experiments. Beware of local optimizations (for example, improving just software development), focusing instead on the end-to-end value stream. The biggest constraint may be upstream in portfolio management rather than downstream in increasing test automation, for example.

The weakest link determines the strength of a chain. Once you've strengthened that link there is no value in strengthening it further. Instead strengthen the new weakest link. Repeat. The Toyota Improvement Kata is a great tool for building a habit of continuous improvement and iterating toward a goal. Ultimately, the goal is for the organization to become a learning organization. We look at this topic further in Chapter 8.

Optimization can be any combination of small change and radical change. The terms for these, with origins in the Toyota Production System, are *kaizen* (continuous improvement) and *kaikaku* (radical change). It can be incremental and evolutionary or radical and revolutionary. Importantly, it is not one size fits all, and it comes from within. It is internally motivated, not imposed.

PATTERN 3.1

Case Study: Nationwide Internal Audit Invites Teams to Focus on BVSSH Outcomes

The internal audit team of the Nationwide Building Society, the world's largest financial services mutual society, started looking at new ways of working in September 2018. Senior leaders wanted to find ways to "do more with less"; however, the Internal Audit team resisted the temptation to focus only on efficiency and looked first at desired outcomes. They prioritized more valuable audits, happy auditors, and shorter lead times. Eleanor Taylor, Internal Auditor and Agile Coach at Nationwide, explains:

The team quickly discovered that its context was very different to IT-centric product development, and that some of the solutions, language, and techniques didn't translate easily. In fact, some of the language is considered cringeworthy and a barrier for some auditors.

The team adapted to context. A previous Scrum-centric approach was replaced with a focus on agility rather than "Agile." The team examined the flow of work, chose an approach based on categorizing the domain of work using the Cynefin framework, and looked for volunteers. The experiment started with one volunteer team responsible for delivering three audits over three months. Keeping it small meant that we were limiting any risks associated with adopting an approach that wasn't right for us and any subsequent fallout with the part of the business we were auditing.

After the first experiment, the team reviewed what worked and what didn't, including from the customer's point of view, and only then invited other teams to experiment. As more volunteers stepped up, they made more adaptations for context and the new ways of working were implemented on a voluntary basis. We have never inflicted new ways of working on any of our audit teams.

As momentum has grown and audit teams have achieved more success, that success was shared with other teams, including senior leadership. As the success was shared, more teams wanted to join in and experiment. Some teams still refuse to join, but they are now the outliers, and I recognize that inflicting change on them will not help them change their mindset.

The result over eighteen months has been a reduction in lead time by two weeks per audit, efficiencies worth the equivalent of eighteen more audits each year, and a rise in satisfaction from 85% to 100%.

PATTERN 3.1

2: Optimize For Mastery: *Shu Ha Ri*

As we know, there is no one size fits all. The level of mastery of the team or business unit or organization is an important factor in an organization's context and hence should inform the unique approach taken to optimize outcomes.

Shu Ha Ri is a Japanese martial arts concept that describes the stages of learning to mastery. It is especially relevant in this context of emergent, complex adaptive systems and to understanding Pattern 3.1.

> *Shu*: Follow the rules (beginner).
> *Ha*: Break the rules (intermediate).
> *Ri*: Make the rules (expert).

The *Shu* stage is for beginners. When people start something new, there is a desire for prescription. People want models to copy and rules to follow in order to learn. New muscle memory needs to be formed and old habits unlearned. A coach saying "it depends" can be frustrating. Beginners want to be told what to do. A team choosing to experiment with a framework can be helpful as a departure point, rather than a destination. Examples of "rote learning" are playing scales when learning to play the piano, snowplowing when learning to ski, or a martial arts *kata*. A *Shu* starting point is not a reason for the imposition of a framework on a team by a leader. The choice to experiment with a given framework (within mandatory minimal viable guardrails), rests with the team, with coaching and support.

The *Ha* stage is intermediate. Learners understand the rules and are ready to break them. There is now some mastery and there are attempts to optimize to context. This can be a dangerous stage due to the Dunning-Kruger Effect, when beginners tend to overrate themselves. They know a little, enough to be dangerous, but they don't yet know what they don't know.

Finally, the *Ri* stage is mastery and transcendence. This is where a team exhibits agility rather than doing capital "A" Agile. Behaviors are in line with Values and Principles, without conscious thought, as practitioners, with an agile mindset. There is fluid adaptation to context. Over time, there may come sufficient mastery to be able to coach and teach others (a skill in itself), along with a recognition of how much more there is still to learn. At the *Ri* stage, someone has sufficient mastery to be able to articulate a complex topic in simple terms.

PATTERN 3.1

Hence, within this pattern, the approach to better ways of working should take the level of mastery into account, optimizing to many unique contexts to increase the likelihood of improving **BVSSH** outcomes.

Shu-stage learners will benefit from coaching from someone who is at the *Ri* stage—who has "skied" for many years—and who has a natural sense for what might optimize outcomes in context. Coaching is something that the WoW CoE should be able to provide as an enabler. It may also be that the team, with advice, decides to experiment with a framework (such as Scrum or Kanban) as their *Kata*. The learners could be at any level in an organization. This includes the coaching of senior leaders, who themselves are at the *Shu* stage in modern ways of working.

Ha-stage learners also benefit from a periodic coaching check-in to ensure that when they're at the top of "Mount Stupid" they are not making sub-optimizations. Also, *Ha*-stage learners benefit from coaches and leaders providing encouragement and recognition in order to continue, to break through, to do the hard yards to reach a more effortless stage of mastery.

Ri-level people are best placed to coach and support the organization, to demonstrate what works in context and in some cases to staff the WoW CoEs. They can be a beacon to the rest of the organization, showing the art of the possible. The last thing you want to do is impose one way of working on people who have mastered adaptation to context and are beating a path through the organizational jungle.

3: Optimize for Your Organizational Context: Revolution vs. Evolution

The antipattern of applying one size fits all tends to result in defaulting to a revolutionary approach, without considering whether revolution or evolution suits the context. This may not optimize for outcomes.

If a pathological or bureaucratic culture is prevalent (see Table 3.1); if the organization or business area is not receptive to upheaval; if there have been failed capital "T" Transformation attempts; if there is little psychological safety; if there is fear; if there are strong vested interests in maintaining the status quo; or if the locus of control is external with learned helplessness and a victim mentality, then inviting evolution is far preferable to revolution. After building confidence with small improvements and having displayed measurable benefits, that evolution creates fertile soil for doing more. It creates social proof in context. It creates safety to continue.

PATTERN 3.1

An advantage of an evolutionary approach is that it builds a culture of constant improvement from the start, as opposed to what can be a cargo cult adoption. There is intrinsic motivation. People are being asked to use their own brains, with support, to improve the system of work. Coaching and a focus on outcome measures can help maintain progress. It's not scary; it's safe to learn.

However, if an organization is facing an existential crisis, if there is a view that survival has a shorter runway than evolutionary improvement, if there is support for a deeper dip in the change curve (even when starting small), if experimentation and learning come with sufficient personal psychological safety, if people are volunteering or requesting a radical change, if there is prior experience of working this way, then revolution, by invitation, *could* be optimal in context. In some cases it's what some teams have wanted to do—despite the firm, not because of the firm—and have been held back by traditional organizational structures and policies. The teams with prior experience can advance quickly to optimize for **BVSSH** outcomes, with support.

In this section, I'll explore some common frameworks or approaches and assess whether they are revolutionary or evolutionary, with the intent that you can consider the optimal approach for your unique contexts in order to deliver **Better Value Sooner Safer Happier**. I'll also look at their degree of process adaptability—whether a team can inspect and adapt its way of working entirely, not just within a fixed set of prescriptive practices.

This assessment is my personal opinion, a perspective, based on practitioner experience since the early 1990s, with insights and shared learning at a wide range of large, traditional organizations across industries.

First, definitions of the column headings:

Revolution: New roles, team structure, ceremonies, artifacts, and cadences.

Evolution: Honor current roles and responsibilities and pursue evolutionary improvement.

Ways of Working Adaptable: Does the framework encourage the adaptation of core ways of working in context? This does not refer to adding more practices when increasing scale.

Enabling Constraint: Is packing work into a limited time period (iteration) or having a pull-based system with limited work in progress (limited WIP) the enabling constraint to shine a light on impediments to **BVSSH**?

The table doesn't list the frameworks by usefulness or priority. It categorizes them to help you choose what might work best in your context.

Table 3.2: Frameworks: Revolution or Evolution and Adaptability

	Revolution Or Evolution	Ways of Working Adaptable?	Enabling Constraint
Scrum	Revolution	No. "Scrum's roles, events, artifacts, and rules are immutable. It's possible to implement parts of Scrum, but the result is not Scrum."[18]	Iteration
Essential SAFe	Revolution	No. Inherits from Scrum.	Iteration
Scrum@Scale	Revolution	No. Inherits from Scrum.	Iteration
Nexus	Revolution	No. Inherits from Scrum,	Iteration
LeSS	Revolution	No. Inherits from Scrum.	Iteration

PATTERN 3.1

	Revolution Or Evolution	Ways of Working Adaptable?	Enabling Constraint
Kanban Method	Evolution	Yes. Kanban states that you "start with what you do now, respect current roles and responsibilities, and pursue evolutionary change."[19]	Limited WIP
Disciplined Agile	Revolution or Evolution	Yes. "DA promotes a goal-based rather than a prescriptive strategy that enables teams to choose their way of working. Start where you are, do the best that you can, always try to get better."[20]	Up to the teams
Spotify Model	Are you a young Swedish one-product org? If not, evolve your own model. The Spotify Model is not Spotify's Model (more on this below.)		Up to the teams
Your Own Model	Either or Both	Yes	Optimize in context for BVSSH

When I'm referring to revolution or evolution by framework, I'm referring to how it is framed and feels for people on teams. I am not referring to the implementation of the framework, such as a big-bang rollout or start small, as we looked at in Chapter 2. Is it new role names, ceremonies, and practices? Is it a case that if you are not adhering directly to them then you are not "doing" the framework? Or is it a case of "start where we are and pursue evolutionary improvement"? Both have pros and cons, depending on your context, which are outlined in this chapter. The only right and wrong is what does and doesn't work best in your many contexts in order to improve outcomes.

Implementing **Scrum** is revolutionary because the implementation of Scrum requires the creation of new roles (such as Product Owner and Scrum Master), new team structures, new artifacts, new events, and new behaviors. It is unadaptable. The official *Scrum Guide* states: "Scrum's roles, events, artifacts, and rules are immutable and although implementing only parts of Scrum is possible, the result is not Scrum. Scrum exists only in its entirety."[21]

In my experience, this often leads to a dialogue along the lines of "Are we doing Scrum right?" or "You're not doing Scrum right" or "How many Scrum teams do we have?" In some cases I've observed Scrum-damentalist behavior, where Scrum is the answer in the absence of knowing the question or context.

The focus should be on improving the outcomes: **BVSSH**. If it helps, great. If not, continue to experiment and optimize. Maybe decoupled cadences and single-piece flow with different service levels (for example, Kanban Method) better suits a context. As it's revolution, perhaps adopting Scrum is not optimal in your context. In some cases, where there is a low-level of psychological safety and emotional scar tissue from previous failed attempts, smaller waterfalls may be a better first approach than inflicting new job roles on people.

The following example is a true story from personal experience. The "Agile" word had baggage, due to previous failed attempts to inflict "doing Agile" rather than increasing agility. It was a headwind, not a tailwind. In this context, the key steppingstone toward a culture of continuously improving outcomes, and eventually to agility, was to start with several smaller waterfalls and less concurrent work. Attempts to change role titles and introduce ceremonies was hindering, not helping. As Peter Senge says, "The harder you push, the harder the system pushes back."[22]

Essential **SAFe** is the building block of a Scrum-based, Agile-at-scale pattern. As it inherits from Scrum, it inherits Scrum's revolution in roles and ceremonies. Additional practices are added to cater to multiple teams working toward a common software deliverable, such as synchronized iterations, nor-malized story points, artifacts, and events. An example, which suits the context it is designed for, is: "PI planning is essential to SAFe: If you are not doing it, you are not doing SAFe."[23] SAFe allows the embedding of a Kanban pull system within a fixed time iteration. For larger IT systems and portfolios of large IT systems, the building block is multiplied with additional roles and practices.

In my experience, SAFe is a great body of knowledge in the context of many software development teams working on one large software product or solution with a high level of dependencies and coupling, with deterministic quarterly commitments, and a relatively low level of mastery of agility, where synchro-nized cadences, normalized story points, and big room planning are beneficial in context. It is a good body of knowledge for coordinating complex human endeavor in such a context (or multiples of that context). In my experience, SAFe clearly can't, and I don't believe is intended to, optimize for outcomes across a diverse, heterogeneous, complex adaptive system such as an entire, large, diverse, organization with thousands of different contexts, products, and product development teams where iterations, normalized story points, quarterly output commitments, and big room planning may be detrimental to optimizing for outcomes. No one set of prescriptive practices can possibly opti-mize for outcomes in all contexts.

Scrum@Scale, as the name suggests, is also Scrum scaled, and there-fore is also revolution over evolution. "Scrum@Scale is designed to saturate an organization with Scrum," according to the *Scrum@Scale Guide*.[24] Better to saturate an organization with agility and context-sensitive continuous improvement.

Nexus is also Scrum scaled. And like Scrum, its approach is all or nothing. "As with the Scrum framework, the Nexus roles, artifacts, events, and rules are immutable," the official guide says. "Although implementing only parts of Nexus is possible, the result is not Nexus."[25]

LeSS too is Scrum scaled. "Large Scale Scrum is Scrum."[26] Therefore, it inherits Scrum's revolutionary and immutable. There are LeSS rules, which are things that the authors consider a must. Like SAFe, LeSS is suited to many teams working on one product, rather than diversity of contexts across a large organization. The authors are articulate about the limitations of prescription. The first two books list "Try" and "Avoid" experiments. "There are no such things as best practices," LeSS's creators, Craig Larman and Bas Vodde, say. "There are only practices that are good within a certain context."[27]

The Kanban Method is evolutionary with a focus on visualizing and optimizing a system of work. Its principles include "start with what you do now," "agree to pursue evolutionary change," "initially, respect current roles, responsibilities and job titles," and "improve collaboratively, evolve experimentally."

It is not a process. It is an approach to improving how you do what you do, with a focus on visualizing and optimizing your system of work. You can use and continuously improve any process with the Kanban Method. It is appropriate in contexts where evolution is preferable to revolution, such as an environment of low psychological safety or where previous failed attempts at inflicting revolutionary approaches have left emotional scar tissue. It is not prescriptive. It shines a light on the system of work, and it results in people using their own brains, with intrinsic motivation to figure out how to deal with impediments that have surfaced, rather than asking whether prescriptive practices are being followed. The "enabling constraint" is limiting work in progress. Like the water level of a tidal river going down, it reveals rocks, impediments to flow that have surfaced and need to be addressed.

Disciplined Agile is a process-decision framework, explicitly with context-sensitive guidance. Its principles include "context counts," "choice is good," and "pragmatism." It is enterprise-aware, designed to cater to many unique contexts, and has organizational guardrails so that it is agile, not fragile. It approaches enterprise-wide agility in a non-prescriptive manner. Teams can start with what they do now and evolve, or they can choose revolutionary change if it suits their context. They can adopt an iteration-based approach or a flow-based approach. Disciplined Agile provides guidance to practices that have worked in different contexts to help teams choose practices in their context.

The **Spotify Model** is not the Spotify Model. In 2012, Henrik Kinberg and Anders Ivarsson wrote in their white paper that articulates Squads, Tribes, Chapters, and Guilds, "We didn't invent this model. Spotify is (like any good agile company) evolving fast. This article is only a snapshot of our current way of working—a journey in progress, not a journey completed. By the time you read this, things have already changed."[28] Spotify employees have spoken at conferences about how the Spotify Model is not the Spotify Model. "Shout it out and I'll tell you how it doesn't quite work that way," said Joakim Sundén, an agile coach at Spotify.[29] "Any aspect was true at the point it was released, but not true everywhere and it's not true in the same form today," said Marcin Floryan.[30]

PATTERN **3.1**

The Spotify Model isn't about a model. What makes Spotify Spotify is its Values and Principles. These include autonomy, collaboration, potential, diversity, long term, and learning.[31] Daniel Ek, Spotify's co-founder, is often quoted as saying: "We aim to make mistakes faster than anyone else."[32] In my experience, when most companies adopt Squads, Tribes, Chapters, and Guilds, they fail to adopt or change their Values and Principles, or their culture, resulting in the placement of new labels on old behaviors, and in some cases, fear and chaos.

The key here is to be an omnist. #AllFrameworks not #NoFrameworks within minimal viable common guardrails (more on this in Chapters 5 and 6). Coaches should, figuratively speaking, have a toolbox with all of the frameworks and bodies of knowledge contained within, with experience of using them, in order to generate the best possible outcomes, with safe-to-learn experiments, and within risk appetite, whilst also recognizing that culture is the biggest lever. Optimize outcomes within context.

PATTERN 3.2

Invite over Inflict

In Chapter 1, I talked about the Diffusion of Innovation curve by Everett Rodgers in 1962 (see Figure 1.4). To invite change as opposed to inflict it, consider the different segments of people on the curve. The Innovators and Early Adopters (the "Hell, yes!" people) will be the first to put their hand up when you invite volunteers to try out new ways of working. They probably are part of a rebel alliance already working with better ways of working despite the firm not because of the firm, with an "ask for forgiveness" rather than permission approach. They have intrinsic motivation. They *want* to do it.

The Innovators will do the hard yards. They believe there is a better way and will have the stronger personal resilience needed at the beginning when the impediments are at their highest. They will beat a path through the organizational jungle for others to follow. A good way to identify the Innovators is via a voluntary Community of Practice (as discussed in Chapter 1). See who attends every time.

As evidence is created within your own organization, the Early Majority will be willing to jump in. It's now starting to become socially acceptable. It's safe to put a toe in the water. It is critical to communicate, communicate, communicate, as well as to recognize and reward the desired behavior. Sufficient social proof and evidence of reward creates what organizational theorist Geoffrey Moore called "crossing the chasm"[36] into the Early Majority and eventually the Late Majority.

Finally, there are the Laggards who are the "Hell, no!" people. They are the last to adopt better ways of working. While the innovators like being different, Laggards do not. Eventually the Laggards will either join in or opt out, choosing to work somewhere else, both of those being a mutual win.

As we saw in Pattern 2.1, people adopt change in an S-curve. You cannot force the gradient, and you cannot force the pace of change. Trying to force a straight line of change leads to the application of new labels on existing behaviors. It leads to an agentic state in which people do as they're told with no thought about *why* they're being told or whether it produces desired outcomes. Humans have a limited velocity to unlearn and relearn. Keep change at a low level initially, the start of the S-curve, and invite over inflict.

In order to increase the likelihood that the invitation to participate is accepted, it is important that improving outcomes, improving **BVSSH**, is communicated as a high priority for the organization from the board or Executive Committee. Clearly, people can only prioritize a limited number of things. Overcoming learning anxiety needs to appeal to the selfish gene. If it's clear that it is a priority and that taking action will lead to recognition, positive appraisal feedback, promotion, and pay, the more likely it is that people will choose to embrace change. Also, the more likely it will be that within the organization doors will open when knocked on. For example, this could be when looking to alleviate impediments in the supporting functions, such as finance, HR, or procurement.

In addition to inviting change, and for teams to optimize their own ways of working within guardrails, a pattern for success is to have clear colleague engagement mechanisms. Provide additional ways in which people closest to the customers and the work can contribute and shape their own destiny, beyond their sphere of control. This can include approaches such as Dan Mezick's OpenSpaceAgility, Mike Burrow's Agendashift, a Ways of Working Community of Practice (WoW CoP), and regular reach-outs to colleagues requesting ideas and suggestions with voting, which can be done either virtually or in person and so on. In the past, I created a voluntary Agile Community of Practice, which grew to over 2,500 colleagues (as discussed in Chapter 1). It was a great way to identify the Innovators, seek input, and share learnings. With all colleagues, we ran regular surveys, requesting ideas and feedback, and

PATTERN **3.2**

held four internal conferences a year with Ways of Working Awards. The feedback from the surveys and events informed our approach on a regular basis. In addition, a network of WoW CoEs and change agents also provided a scalable mechanism to engage with colleagues.

To help amplify learning and to better overcome impediments, I've also found it helpful to create an Exemplar Community. Membership is entirely voluntary. You don't have to be an "exemplary" team already in order to join the voluntary community. You just have to be curious and enthusiastic to learn, with an agreement to seek to *become exemplary*, jumping in with both feet. The "what's in it for me" appeal is that members of the Exemplar Community get benefits of membership, such as smaller group access to external speakers and experts, and first access to try new approaches or tools. It helps to keep the Innovators on the "bleeding edge," which is where they want to be.

I've consistently found that these teams who psychologically sign up to become exemplary exhibit far superior outcomes. I've observed that this group had twentyfold improvements on most measures on average: shorter lead time, faster throughput, fewer incidents, and the highest engagement scores. They provide hard data as a beacon of what is possible, for others to follow. They provide engaging storytelling for the emotional buy-in. And through a corporate cellular mitosis, they are able to spread better ways of working—and all of it without using a cookie-cutter approach or inflicting change. Teams develop their VOICE and rise toward *Ri*.

Summary

You Have a Unique VOICE and Invite over Inflict

In this chapter, I've shown that there are almost infinite contexts and that one set of practices cannot possibly best fit them all and optimize for outcomes. We've looked at how the word "scale" means different things depending on context; we've seen that cultural contexts, such as pathological, bureaucratic, and generative cultural norms need to be taken into account and to not *de facto* take a revolutionary approach to ways of working. One size cannot possibly fit all, and it should not be inflicted top down with a lack of empowerment and without building a muscle of continuous improvement.

Instead, you have a unique VOICE: focus on Values and Principles, Outcomes and Purpose, Intent-Based Leadership, Coaching and Support, and Experimentation.

It is through that VOICE that teams can find the "how" for themselves, improving **BVSSH** outcomes in their own context and within guardrails. Teams can rise through the levels of *Shu Ha Ri*, gaining knowledge and expertise, unlearning and relearning at the pace that they can, with a tailwind not a headwind, avoiding an agentic state, and finding no need for cargo cult behavior.

In addition, change should be pull over push, invite over inflict (with incentivization and support), an appeal to intrinsic motivation, which increases colleague engagement. People like Julie and the team that she is a part of should be engaged and invited to use their own brains, with support, to improve on outcomes.

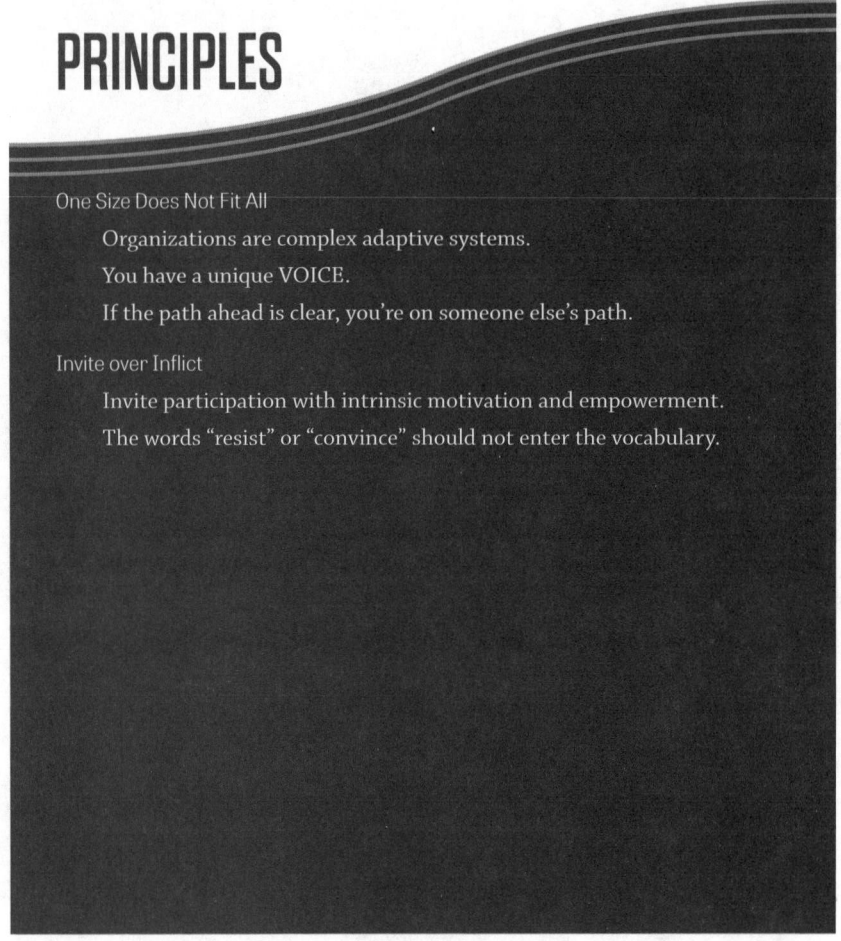

PRINCIPLES

One Size Does Not Fit All

Organizations are complex adaptive systems.

You have a unique VOICE.

If the path ahead is clear, you're on someone else's path.

Invite over Inflict

Invite participation with intrinsic motivation and empowerment.

The words "resist" or "convince" should not enter the vocabulary.

4 LEADERSHIP WILL MAKE IT OR BREAK IT

It was 9:15 in the morning, and the pupils at Pantglas Junior School had just finished singing "All Things Bright and Beautiful" at the school assembly. Mr. Davis, the math teacher, had walked up to the chalkboard and written the sums. The half-term holiday was less than three hours away, and his pupils were busy, bent over their work.

That was when the rumbling started. Survivors described it as loud as a jet plane. Work in Mr. Davis's math class stopped. The room fell silent. Everyone froze in their seats except for eight-year-old Gaynor Minett, who stood up and reached the end of the desk just as the sound grew louder and nearer, and all that was visible outside the window was darkness.

The disaster at the Welsh village of Aberfan, where 116 children and twenty-eight adults were killed in the collapse of a colliery spoil tip, a giant heap of waste material produced by a local coal mine, was entirely preventable. Tip 7 hadn't just been built on the side of a mountain overlooking the village. It had also been built over a natural spring, and its instability was known to both colliery management and to tip workers.

The tribunal into the disaster, which published its findings in 1967, stated:

> The report which follows tells of ignorance, ineptitude and a failure in communication. Failure on the part of those having knowledge of the factors which affect tip safety to communicate that knowledge and see that it was applied.[1]

In a 1976 study, sociologist Barry Turner identified several factors that led to the disaster. They included:[2]

- Years of rigid and unrealistic disregard for the importance of the safety of the above-ground tips;
- A flawed decision-making process that ignored or minimized the likelihood and the scale of the emergent danger;
- A dismissive attitude toward the complaints from Aberfan residents, discounting the validity of their concerns; and
- An incomplete and inadequate response to conditions that caused those complaints.

This disaster, like other disasters such as Chernobyl and the Deepwater Horizon oil spill, saw the worst possible outcome due to an insufficient culture of safety, both physical and psychological. In such an environment, *if* people speak up, the dialogue is dismissed, given a lower priority to other factors such as cost or time pressure, outranked with a view that seniority equates to knowing better, or is actively put down with an unchallenged command-and-control behavioral norm.

More often, people will *not* speak up, due to fear of being shot down, belittled, or blamed. People will not point out problems, warn of potential dangers, voice a concern that something doesn't feel quite right, challenge authority, or suggest improvements. In this cultural norm, people become conditioned to exhibit *learned helplessness*, waiting for the next order and obeying it with little sense of agency, control, or ownership. In this culture, "bad news" (learning) is buried until it's too late, until it is firmly in the jaws of defeat.

Although few outcomes are as terrible as these, from mines in the hills of Glamorgan to nuclear power stations in Ukraine to oil rigs in the Gulf of Mexico, organizations need behavioral norms where, at a minimum, everyone feels confident enough to speak out, challenge authority, voice concerns, and be listened to when they do. People should be encouraged and inspired to challenge the status quo in a safe-to-fail environment without fear of reprisal.

Before we get into the antipatterns and patterns, let's take a closer look at what we mean by "leader" and "leadership."

Leader

Leader comes from Old English *laedere* meaning *"one who leads,"* from *laedan* meaning *"to guide, accompany, bring forth,"* which itself has roots in Proto-Germanic *laidjan* meaning *"to travel."*[3] It is pleasing to see that the origins of leadership are related to guiding on a journey. "Leadership" as a word is more recent, with the first known use dating from 1821, when leader was combined with the suffix "ship" to denote the position of a leader.[4] There is nothing in the etymology of lead, leader, or leadership to do with order, command, direct, commit, or control. The meaning of "command" from the fifteenth century means *"control, right or authority to order or compel obedience,"* with Latin and Old English origins involving words such as "commit," "mandate," "order" and "forbid."[5] Issuing orders, commanding people, telling people what to do and when to do it, is being a commander (*"one who has the authority or power to command or order"*).[6] It is not being a leader.

Table 4.1: Commander versus Leader

Commander	Leader
A position	A behavior and mindset
For a few	For all
Orders	Listens, inspires, informs
Obeying is mandatory	Following is voluntary
Extrinsic motivation	Intrinsic motivation
Power is positional	Power is given by followers
e.g., "commander in chief"	e.g., Greta Thunberg

Commander is a position. It is for a few. A commander orders. Obeying is mandatory. Power is positional. For example, "commander in chief."

Leader is not a position. Anyone can lead. A leader inspires. Following is voluntary. Power is given by followers. For example, climate change activist Greta Thunberg.

They are not mutually exclusive. A *commander* can exhibit leadership, create and inspire followers (rather than have minions), and create *new* leaders at every level, without using the threat of positional power. Equally, when there is a lack of consensus, a *leader* may adopt more of a command style, especially if it is to get out of danger or to prompt action due to a lack of consensus. For example, a principle of "disagree and commit," seeking input and intent from leaders at all levels, so that everyone's voice has been heard. Not a HiPPO decision made in isolation. And then a bias to action, with "strong opinions loosely held," and ability to pivot based on new learning from acting. Given that a group of people is a complex adaptive system, action, any action, ideally small and safe to learn, is needed in order to have a feedback loop, to be able to determine what to do next in order to more optimally achieve an outcome.

Greta Thunberg's campaign on climate change is an example of leadership. Her first school strike was August 2018 when she was just fifteen years old. Only three months later, in December 2018, more than 20,000 students held strikes in at least 270 cities.[7] Thunberg went on to speak at the UN Climate Change Conference, the World Economic Forum, and the UN Climate Action Summit. She addressed several European parliaments, met with Pope Francis, and attracted the sometimes critical attention of many world leaders.[8] She has a very clear purpose, mission, and meaning.

Anyone can be a leader. A leader is not defined by seniority or role. There are leaders at all levels. Being a leader requires, amongst other attributes, self-awareness, humility, and the ability to listen. Being a commander doesn't require any of these.

"Guiding on a journey," the origins of the word *lead*, nicely encapsulates modern leadership. In developed countries, the world of work has shifted from industrial to informational, from repetitive labor to unique knowledge work. Behaviors have needed to shift from order, mandate, and fear to guide, bring forth, and inspire.

In order to maximize positive outcomes, everyone, especially those in senior roles who have a disproportionate impact on organizational culture, need to (1) be more leader and less commander, (2) foster psychological safety, and (3) leverage the fact that product development and organizational change is emergent, not deterministic. There is a need to be able to challenge the status quo, to be supported, and to be able to run safe-to-learn experiments to improve on balanced outcomes. We will look at these topics in more detail in the following antipatterns and patterns.

ANTIPATTERN 4.1

Do as I Say, Not as I Do

The CEO asks the audience: "Who wants change?" Everyone's hands go up.

She then asks: "Who wants *to* change?" No one's hands go up.

Finally, she asks: "Who wants to lead the change?" The room is empty.

A commonly observed antipattern is people in senior roles not exhibiting the behaviors that they are asking or expecting from people within their remit. There is a request for others to change without that change "starting at home." It is a case of do as I say, not do as I do. The lack of role modeling and incongruent behavior is clear to see. One thing is being said and another thing is being done. Actions do not match the words. That is not being a leader. Leaders go on the same journey.

With a charitable intent, a senior team decides that in the Age of Digital, with a new means of production, there are better ways of working that lead to better outcomes.

However, adopting better ways of working is viewed as something for other people to do. In some cases, it's treated as being the same as updating the operating system on a device. Download the latest update, install it, and job done. Or it is viewed as a methodology to adopt or as an org chart change to make, in all cases without a behavioral shift.

For example, as we saw in Chapter 3, it is an installation of the so-called Spotify Model without a focus on principles, continuous improvement, experimentation, emergence, or culture. The ways of working in Spotify are more about *culture*, such as failing fast, autonomy, and experimentation, than about an org chart construct. As a one-product and, at the time, small company, the not-Spotify Spotify-Model may have suited that context, at that time.

I've seen people in senior roles figuratively cross their arms, effectively saying to the people they are managing: "Go on, transform, and tell me when you're done," followed by "Are you done yet?" with no attempt to role model the behaviors being asked of subordinates within their control (I use those words intentionally). Those may be the behaviors that were historically rewarded in some organizations. However, this approach is not congruent with modern ways of working, with agility, with emergence and empowerment to maximize outcomes via fast learning. It is not an optimal approach. *The State of DevOps Report 2017*, with input from 3,200 people globally, found that low-performing teams had leaders with the lowest transformational leader scores (more on transformational leadership in Pattern 6.1).[9]

The biggest lever for better ways of working, leading to better outcomes, is behavioral. Change is a social activity. It is how people are inspired, how people are empowered, how people work together, how people are aligned to a shared purpose with autonomy and agency, how people can run safe-to-learn experiments, how people are recognized and rewarded, how people behave both when under stress and when not under stress. I have often observed in organizations people being managers or commanders rather than leaders, leading from the front.

Leading requires courage. It requires exhibiting vulnerability; in some cases it requires being a beginner again, trying something new, learning about flow and emergence, and experimenting, which will generate learning through sometimes failing and sometimes succeeding. It also requires self-awareness, seeking feedback on the impact of one's own behavior on others. The irony being that the less psychological safety there is, the less likely it is that feedback will be offered or will be accurate. It can be hard for a leopard to change its spots. And a leopard has to want to change. Coaching can help; however, it has to be pulled. It cannot be inflicted.

When a manager sits back with their arms crossed and demands that everyone changes but them, a clear cognitive dissonance is created. Change that happens at the grass roots quickly hits a grass ceiling. A culture of learning, of improvement, of delivering **Better Value Sooner Safer Happier**, cannot be installed like a server, or with the rollout of a framework and tooling alone. It's about people, a compelling vision, a purpose, how people behave with each other. It's about whether people are treated as minions with the thinking done for them or whether they are expected to bring their brains to work. It's about who they work with, how they are incentivized to behave, the role of the relationship, and how the system of work that they are in does or does not enable this change, creating either a headwind or a tailwind. The system of work is itself a human and behavioral construct. Some organizations over-interpret regulation, putting policies into place that are more stringent than necessary, create even more handoffs, reduce flow efficiency, reduce value realization, and are one size fits all, making everyone cater to the lowest common denominator, the riskiest case.

As I write, we are in the midst of the COVID-19 pandemic, and it has been remarkable to see how large, traditional organizations swarmed on challenges and responded incredibly quickly, with people pulling together irrespective of tribal alignment. A commonly heard observation from large traditional firms is that people are at their best during periods of chaos. This could be a pandemic, an IT system outage, or a cyberattack. In the face of chaos, people come together; they rally around a common shared mission and address it. This is without the usual three-month wait for a seventeen-step gated approval process. The right thing is done to respond to the situation at hand. In a crisis, people generally use their initiative and don't wait to be given step-by-step orders. The trick is to maintain this without the chaos. To maintain the swarming and working together with autonomy, with a clear mission, and with a minimal viable process within risk appetite all of the time, being directionally led and supported from the front.

Better ways of working are about creating leaders at all levels with high alignment on desired outcomes. If those in senior roles behave as managers or commanders rather than leaders, they will not optimize outcomes. They will not unleash the full human potential of their employees. Improvement in outcomes will be limited to a bubble anchored at the top by the most senior person who is a *leader*.

ANTIPATTERN 4.2

Psychologically Unsafe

One of the most remarkable accounts of the Aberfan disaster is described by Iain McLean and Martin Johnes in their book *Aberfan: Government and Disaster*. It comes from a tip gang chargehand who had seen that the pile of coal and earth was sinking. It had fallen about eighteen to twenty feet, and the crane rails had dropped into the hole. The chargehand told his team that they would bring the rails back up: "I said before we start, we'll have a cup of tea, and we went back into the shack."[10] The chargehand had become so conditioned to managers with a dismissive attitude and a lack of acting on feedback, that the first thought wasn't to respond with urgency, but rather to have the usual morning cup of tea.

The collapse started less than five minutes later, and while the chargehand's habit of starting the day with a cup of tea might have saved his life and the lives of his teammates, if instead there had been a culture of physical and psychological safety, with leaders who listen and act on feedback, rather than managers with a "dismissive attitude," the chargehand would have escalated the emergence of the sinkhole, which could have led to an evacuation downstream of the spoil tip. Or the issue would not have arisen in the first place, as the spoil tip was known to be sited on top of a stream that was clearly marked on maps.

1: Boeing

787 Dreamliner Factory, North Charleston, South Carolina

Cynthia Kitchens was a quality manager at the Boeing North Charleston factory, which makes the 787 Dreamliner. According to an investigation by the *New York Times* in 2019, Kitchens said that her superiors penalized her in performance reviews and berated her on the factory floor after she flagged wire bundles rife with metal shavings and defective metal parts that had been installed on planes. "It was intimidation," she said. "Every time I started finding stuff, I was harassed." The *Times* found that in order to meet deadlines, managers sometimes played down or ignored problems, according to current and former workers.[11]

Several former employees said high-level managers pushed internal quality inspectors to stop recording defects. Some employees said they had been punished or fired when they voiced concerns. Workers filed nearly a dozen whistleblower claims and safety complaints with federal regulators, describing issues like defective manufacturing, debris left on planes, and pressure to not report violations. Others resorted to litigation, saying they were retaliated against for flagging manufacturing mistakes.[12]

Another quality manager, William Hobek, filed a suit in 2016 claiming that he'd been fired after repeatedly reporting defects up the chain of command. When he complained, a supervisor replied, "Bill, you know we can't find all defects." Hobek called over an inspector, who quickly found forty problems, the suit claimed. Boeing settled the case out of court.[13]

737 Factory, Renton, Washington

In December 2019, Ed Pierson presented testimony to the US House of Representatives committee looking at the 737 MAX. Mr. Pierson was a senior manager at the factory and a thirty-year-veteran of the US Navy. In June 2018, four months before the fatal Lion Air 737 MAX crash, he emailed the 737 program head, raising concerns over excess schedule pressure, workers fatigued due to too much overtime, and managers not role modeling desired behaviors. Pierson said, "Frankly right now all my internal warning bells are going off. And for the first time in my life, I'm sorry to say that I'm hesitant about putting my family on a Boeing airplane."[14] He recommended that production pause to safely finish the unfinished planes.

This didn't happen. In fact, according to a Boeing press release, in the middle of 2018, production of 737s *increased* from forty-seven to fifty-two planes a month.[15]

Not satisfied with the response and two months after the first 737 MAX crash, Pierson wrote to the then CEO Dennis Muilenburg, the Boeing Board of Directors, the NTSB, the FAA, and eventually the media to flag his concerns.[16] In the subsequent dialogue with senior management, in February 2019, just one month before the second fatal 737 MAX crash, Pierson wrote:

. . . manufacturing managers were peppered with schedule-related questions and publicly criticized (berated) during daily status meetings . . . in front of 100+ colleagues. Executives routinely disregarded, bypassed, and/or ignored the technical advice of experienced senior managers. There were concerns that less experienced managers might model this type of leadership and communication style. . . .

There appeared to be absolutely no interest at the executive level in slowing or stopping the production line to give employees and our suppliers the chance to catch up. I recommended to the 737 GM to stop the production line. In a dismissive manner he told me "we can't do that; I can't do that." I responded by asking "why not, I've seen larger operations shut down for far less safety issues." He challenged me asking "like where?" I responded, "in the military and those organizations have national security responsibilities." His response, "Well, the military isn't a profit making organization."[17]

Tragedy struck again one month later in March 2019 with the fatal Ethiopian Airlines crash. While there is no direct link with the working conditions in the factory, it paints a picture of the culture and environment in the Renton factory where the 737 planes are built. In a statement, Boeing said:

Importantly, the suggestion by Mr. Pierson of a link between his concerns and the recent MAX accidents is completely unfounded. Mr. Pierson raises issues about the production of the 737 MAX, yet none of the authorities investigating these accidents have found that production conditions in the 737 factory contributed in any way to these accidents.[18]

Fear

In an interview with *Bloomberg*, Adam Dickson, who worked at Boeing for almost thirty years and was a manager of fuel systems engineering for the 737 MAX, said that managers felt heat to hit ambitious cost targets.[19]

The sales team would sell planes for delivery four years out at prices the company couldn't yet hit from an engineering standpoint—creating immense pressure throughout the organization to drive down costs. In 2016, Boeing started asking for specific time and cost reductions as part of managers' performance evaluations.[20]

And by 2018, Dickson says his superiors warned in "very directly and threatening ways" that pay was at risk if the targets weren't met.[21]

"It was a climate that didn't reward people willing to challenge managers," said Mark Rabin, who worked at Boeing for seventeen years in a flight test group that supported the 737 MAX and who was laid off in 2015. "It was pretty intense low morale because of all the layoffs—constant, grinding layoffs, year after year," he says. "So you really watched your step and were careful about what you said."[22]

In an ethics complaint filed seven weeks after the second fatal crash of a 737 MAX, which was reviewed by *The Seattle Times*, a Boeing engineer whose job involved studying past crashes and using that information to make new planes safer said, "I was willing to stand up for safety and quality, but was unable to actually have an effect in those areas."[23] The engineer describes management as:

> . . . more concerned with cost and schedule than safety and quality. . . . Given the nature of this complaint, the fear of retaliation is high, despite all official assurances that this should not be the case. . . . There is a suppressive cultural attitude toward criticism of corporate policy— especially if that criticism comes as a result of fatal accidents.[24]

He wrote that co-workers told him in private they are afraid to speak up about similar safety concerns out of "fear for their jobs."[25]

In all of these reported cases, there is a lack of psychological safety, people are fearful for their jobs and afraid to speak up. It takes extreme courage to speak up in an environment of fear of retaliation. On January 9, 2020, 117 pages of emails and instant messages were made available as part of the US House Committee investigation. Sara Nelson, the president of the Association of Flight Attendants union, said the messages revealed a "sick" culture at Boeing, noting that "the trust level was already in the toilet."[26]

Boeing said of the messages on the same day as their release:

> We regret the content of these communications, and apologize to the FAA, Congress, our airline customers, and to the flying public for them. We have made significant changes as a company to enhance our safety processes, organizations, and culture. . . . The language used in these communications, and some of the sentiments they express, are inconsistent with

Boeing values, and the company is taking appropriate action in response. This will ultimately include disciplinary or other personnel action, once the necessary reviews are completed.[27]

I find the last sentence interesting. Rather than a humble reflection of the organizational culture and the cost and schedule pressure that incentivized and led people to behave how they behaved, there is a threat of disciplinary or other personnel action.

Issues

Even before the COVID-19 coronavirus pandemic, Boeing had been facing a number of issues, spanning commercial, military, and space. There were the two tragic 737 MAX crashes within five months of each other in which 346 people lost their lives. The aircraft had an undocumented system (MCAS) that repeatedly took control of the plane with a single point of failure reading from one angle-of-attack sensor. It was undocumented due to a desire to minimize cost and to keep pilot training requirements to a minimum. Boeing had offered Southwest Airlines a rebate of $1 million per aircraft on an order of almost three hundred aircraft if flight simulator training was required.[28] This rebate would have covered the cost to Southwest Airlines had expensive pilot flight simulation training been required. However, Boeing had created further financial pressure to minimize pilot training, in addition to competing with the Airbus A320neo. Unfortunately it took two fatal crashes before all planes of that type were subsequently grounded, with Boeing and the FAA still asserting that the aircraft were safe, even after the second crash and after most of the rest of the world had grounded the plane.[29]

The 787 Dreamliner production also had issues. It was late by three years and was billions over budget, costing an estimated $32 billion on an original approved budget of $7 billion.[30] An investigation by *The New York Times* in April 2019 showed that workers on the 787 in North Charleston were pushed to maintain an overly ambitious production schedule, and they were fearful of losing their jobs if they raised concerns.[31] The 787 Dreamliner was grounded by the FAA in 2013 due to battery fires. Boeing had two airplane models grounded within six years. The last time that the FAA grounded an aircraft was the McDonnell Douglas DC-10 in 1979.

There have been issues with Boeing delivering a KC-46 Pegasus mid-air refueling tanker to the US military, $3 billion over budget, three years behind schedule and beset with technical issues, including lack of visibility for the last ten feet of the refueling boom, cargo fasteners coming undone during a flight, and chronic leaks in the aircraft's fuel system, a problem especially bad for a plane that is supposed to perform aerial refueling.[32]

In December 2019, Boeing's Starliner crew space capsule failed an unmanned test flight due to an eleven-hour offset in the mission clock on board, plus additional potentially catastrophic software errors were detected after the launch and fixed from the ground. NASA labeled this aborted mission, during which the spacecraft was nearly lost two times, a "high-visibility close call."[33]

Culture

In March 2020, the US House Transportation and Infrastructure Committee in its preliminary investigative findings stated, "Cost, schedule, and production pressures undermined safety of the 737 MAX."[34]

The report continues:

> A Boeing internal survey conducted in 2016 at the height of the 737 MAX's certification activities, and provided to the Committee from a whistleblower, found that 39 percent of Boeing employees that responded perceived "undue pressure" and 29 percent were concerned about consequences if they reported potential undue pressure, painting a disturbing picture of cultural issues at Boeing that can undermine safety and oversight.[35]

"We've all seen this movie before, in places like Enron," Chesley B. Sullenberger III, the pilot who safely landed a plane on the Hudson River in 2009, said in an interview. "It's not surprising that before a crisis, there are indications of real deep problems that have their roots in leadership."[36]

The origins of a profound pivot in corporate culture at Boeing can be traced back to 1997 and the acquisition of McDonnell Douglas. Or as some have called it, a "reverse takeover," as it was McDonnell executives who ended up in charge of the firm. "McDonnell Douglas bought Boeing with Boeing's money," went the joke around Seattle.[37]

Founded in 1916, Boeing was engineering-led. Its executives held patents, designed wings, and had engineering and safety in their DNA. Finance wasn't a primary language. As late as the mid-'90s, the company's chief financial officer had minimal contact with Wall Street and answered colleagues' requests for basic financial data with, "Tell them not to worry."[38]

Bill Allen, Boeing's legendary leader from 1945 to 1968, described his company's ethos as: "To eat, breathe, and sleep the world of aeronautics." By 1998, the then-CEO saw it differently: "We are going into a value based environment where unit cost, return on investment, and shareholder return are the measures by which you'll be judged. That's a big shift," said Phil Condit.[39]

"The important thing is not to get overly focused on the box," the Boeing CFO said in an interview with *Bloomberg* in 2000. "The box"—the plane itself— "is obviously important, but customers are assuming the box is of great quality."[40] This was heresy to engineers, to whom the box was everything. It was enough to drive the white-collar engineering union, which had historically functioned as a professional debating society, into acting more like organized labor. "We weren't fighting against Boeing," one union leader said of the forty-day strike that shut down production in 2000. "We were fighting to save Boeing."[41]

In 2001, Boeing moved its head office from Seattle to Chicago, 1,700 miles away from their nearest assembly line. The isolation was deliberate. "When the headquarters is located in proximity to a principal business—as ours was in Seattle—the corporate center is inevitably drawn into day-to-day business operations," Condit explained.[42] This was a very visible signal of the change in corporate culture, the opposite of "go see" or a Gemba Walk ("management by walking around") as practiced at firms like Toyota.

The company that once didn't speak finance was now, at the top, losing its ability to talk engineering. It wasn't just technical knowledge that was lost. As aerospace analyst Richard Aboulafia said:

> It was the ability to comfortably interact with an engineer who in turn feels comfortable telling you their reservations, versus calling a manager 1,700 miles away who you know has a reputation for wanting to take your pension away. It's a very different dynamic. As a recipe for disempowering engineers in particular, you couldn't come up with a better format.[43]

Top engineers reported primarily to business leaders for each airplane model, and secondarily to the company's chief engineer. With this structure, engineers who reported concerns faced resistance from executives whose jobs revolved around meeting production deadlines.[44] Employees in interviews described the old Boeing as a "democracy" that valued debate and a group approach to problem-solving. "In those days, 'people were treated as people, not numbers,'" one worker is quoted as saying.[45] After the merger, Boeing had become more authoritarian.[46]

In 2000, Jim Collins, author of *Good to Great and Built to Last*, said:

> If in fact there's a reverse takeover, with the McDonnell ethos permeating Boeing, then Boeing is doomed to mediocrity. There's one thing that made Boeing really great all the way along. They always understood that they were an engineering-driven company, not a financially driven company. If they're no longer honoring that as their central mission, then over time they'll just become another company.[47]

At Boeing, "cost, schedule, and production pressures undermined safety of the 737 MAX" and there is a "culture of concealment."[48] People are fearful to speak up. There is a lack of psychological safety. The pivot in corporate culture in 1997 took the firm from being engineering-led and democratic to finance-led and autocratic, treating the plane as a commodity. Between 2013 and 2019, Boeing diverted 92% of operating cash flow to dividends and share buybacks to benefit investors and increase the share price. Since 1998, share buybacks have consumed $70 billion, adjusted for inflation.[49] That could have financed several new airplane models. Meanwhile the production deficit on the 787 Dreamliner, as of the end of 2019, eight years after the first commercial flight, is $20 billion.[50] The vast majority of employees undoubtedly want to do the right thing, but many appear to feel powerless.[51]

In order to optimize for outcomes, organizations need to listen to employees at all levels, creating an environment free of fear and capable of acting on feedback. There should be a focus and incentivization on a balanced set of outcomes (over output), including quality, the flow of work, safety, happiness of colleagues and customers, as well as value. With a positive trend in quality, flow, safety, and employee engagement, such that improvements are sustainable (not through allegedly working eight weeks without a day off[52]), cost and schedule will come down.

There should not, however, be a primary focus on cost and schedule. As the Boeing story has illustrated, the consequences can be disastrous. In addition to the tragic loss of life, and prior to the COVID-19 pandemic, the consequences for Boeing included their first annual loss in more than twenty years and the worst annual sales figures in decades, with more cancellations than new orders in 2019. An overt focus on cost has had the opposite outcome than desired.

Boeing's chief executive, Dennis A. Muilenburg, who was fired on December 23, 2019, said in a speech in October 2019 that "it is critical we take a step back to humbly look at our culture."[53]

2: Organizational Culture

In Antipattern 3.1: One Size Fits All, I mentioned Ron Westrum's typology of organizational culture. To recap, Westrum articulated three cultural types, pathological, bureaucratic, and generative, which are shaped by the preoccupations of leaders. Leaders' actions and ability to provide or withhold rewards communicate their preferences, which then become the preoccupation of the organization's workforce (see Table 3.1).

Not surprisingly, it's in a pathological culture that the strongest antipatterns are exhibited. Information is withheld to be used for personal gain. When things go wrong, a scapegoat is sought to take the blame, rather than trying to discover problems with the system of work that people are working within. Alignment is typically to a person or clique rather than to a mission and purpose, and there is a tendency to avoid taking responsibility, due to fear of retribution and scapegoating, with problems being concealed.

In this organizational culture, team members develop *learned helplessness*, not stepping out of line, not thinking for themselves, not continuously improving, keeping their head down, and waiting for the next order. They fear doing the wrong thing.

I observed the leadership of one business area at an organization that lead with a culture of fear. Two-week iterations were mandated for everyone. The intent was positive; the implementation of the intent was not. There was no articulation of why, no vision, no purpose, no desired outcome for everyone to get behind. It appeared to be two-week iterations for the sake of two-week iterations, Agile for the sake of Agile.

The result was dysfunction: existing waterfall behaviors with the word "sprint" used many times, five iterations of analysis, five iterations of development, five iterations of testing. Agile labels; same old behavior. And yet even though this way of working clearly wasn't producing the desired outcomes, no one dared improve or experiment due to the fear of getting something wrong.

I met with about fifty people in a group session and did a floor walk. I don't think I've ever experienced so much learned helplessness. There was a lot of shrugging. Initiative had been drilled out of the teams. No one was willing to take responsibility. Everyone was waiting for the next order, like statues.

At its worst, this creates a behavior that psychologist Stanley Milgram has described as an "agentic state,"[54] as we looked at in Antipattern 1.2. A person no longer sees themselves as responsible for their own actions but as an instrument for carrying out someone else's wishes. Their role is to obey, to do as they're told, if the person commanding it is in a position of authority and takes responsibility for the outcomes. This can include concealing information and putting to one side safety considerations or even ethics. Leaders operating in or fostering a pathological culture, with employees in an agentic state, hear no complaints and misinterpret the silence as a sign that everything is fine. Bad news is buried until it's too late.

Silence is unhealthy. In *The Fearless Organization*, Amy Edmondson describes how she discovered a correlation between the number of reported errors in hospitals and surveys on hospital team effectiveness. Some teams, she noted, were stronger than others, with higher levels of mutual respect, collaboration, satisfaction, and confidence in their ability to deliver results. What surprised her was that the correlation ran in the opposite direction to the one she had expected. The more errors a team reported, the more effective it was. She understood that better teams don't make more mistakes, *they're more willing to report the mistakes they do make.*[55]

Other studies, such as Professor Sidney Dekker's work on Safety Differently have also shown a *strong negative correlation* between incident reports and fatalities. Construction sites that fail to report incidents suffer more serious accidents. Airlines with the highest reported incident rates have the lowest mortalities.[56]

The more effective teams exhibit more psychological safety. Rather than concealing fear and blame, there is openness, dialogue, and inquiry.

ANTIPATTERN 4.3

Deterministic Mindset

In the previous age, the Age of Oil & Mass Production, organized human endeavor was on the whole repetitive. This age saw the creation of the moving assembly line in the Ford plant in Detroit and lean production in Japan at Toyota. Fueled on an abundance of cheap oil, we covered the ground with highways, crowded the skies with jets, and filled our houses with appliances. We created mass production, mass media, mass transit, mass tourism, and mass consumerism. The advance in ways of working was centered around how to do the same thing many times, more efficiently. It is expensive to retool an assembly line to build a stream of unique physical products, hence commonality, standardized work, and standard parts. The focus was on *output*, shareholder returns, and productivity (defined as the number of units of output per unit of input).

Repetitive work is *knowable*. It's been done many times before. Whether it's building 100,000 cars or processing millions of currency trades a day, there are *known-unknowns*. We know if the car has been built and we know if a trade has settled. We usually know what to do if something goes wrong. It is *deterministic*.

In the current age, the Age of Digital, organized human endeavor is increasingly *emergent*. Product development is unique, it's not been done before, either at all or in context, and there are *unknown-unknowns*. We don't know what we don't know. Due to the new means of production, with instant and vast compute power, storage, and communication, change is continuous rather than staccato. With software, it's not a case of writing the same code 100,000 times. Code is written *once* and run 100,000 times.

The same applies for non-software product development (e.g., an internal audit report or the design of an entirely new model of car). Organized human endeavor is then working out how to continuously add the most value, based on fast feedback. There is a stream of innovation, an evolving service, a meta-level capability, an experience that customers are buying, not only a point-in-time product. The "assembly line" *is* a stream of unique, evolving products. For knowledge work the assembly line does not need to be retooled for each unique product iteration. Even if a modification is needed, the cost is close to zero as the assembly line itself is software.

All non-trivial change and product development in organizations is *emergent*. There is a need to focus on *outcome hypotheses* and fast feedback in order to maintain optionality and pivot to optimally achieve desired outcomes. Or to realize that the hypothesis was not correct, change the bet mid-race, and move on to the next one, with the cheapest cost of learning.

The notion that we can predict what's going to happen in an emergent context is an important, wasteful, demoralizing, and potentially dangerous antipattern. In order to get the best outcomes, there is a need to optimize ways of working in order to leverage the advantages of emergence. This is instead of trying to force a deterministic approach in an emergent domain, effectively

ANTIPATTERN 4.3

assuming that the future can be predicted or that the tide can be commanded to not come in, delaying real learning to "the end" when there is no time to respond, the most pressure (e.g., to prioritize spending or schedule over safety), and the highest cost of failure.

In Chapter 0, I described Cynefin, a framework by Dave Snowden that categorizes different domains in which work takes place. (See Figure 0.2.) It is a useful tool to aid decision-making and to take an optimal approach in context, such as agile, lean, or neither. To recap, there are five domains:

> Within the **Clear** domain, there are *known-knowns*. There is best practice. The relationship between cause and effect is clear. This has been done many times before and specialist expertise is not required (e.g., paying for goods in a store, commuting to work, riding a bike).

> In the **Complicated** domain, there are *known-unknowns*. There is good practice, not best practice. The relationship between cause and effect requires analysis or expertise. There is a range of right answers. This has been done many times before and specialist expertise is required (e.g., installing a server in a datacenter, processing payments, building a million Toyota Priuses). This is the sweet spot for lean.

> The **Complex** domain has *unknown-unknowns*. There is emergence. There is no such thing as best practice. Cause and effect can only be determined in retrospect. Acting in the space changes the space. There is a need to experiment, get fast feedback, and respond to it. This is the domain of unique product development. It's not been done before. We don't quite know how we're going to do it or what people want. This is the sweet spot for agile.

> When in the **Chaos** domain, cause and effect are unknown. Quick action is the only way to respond. If you smell smoke and see flames, you don't design experiments; you get out of the way of danger. Act, sense, and then respond.

> If you cannot tell which domain you are in, you are in the **Confusion** domain, so you seek more information or try to break the situation down into constituent parts.

As we have advanced to the Age of Digital, we have gone from being more focused in the *Complicated* domain (repetitive, predictable, and knowable) to more people being more focused in the *Complex* domain (emergent and unknowable, needing outcome hypotheses and fast learning). We are producing new iterations of products and responding to feedback at a faster rate in order to delight customers.

If the type of work is repetitive (operations such as processing payments, customer onboarding, customer servicing, or onboarding new joiners), then *Complicated* is the appropriate domain and the focus should be primarily on Lean (see Chapter 0 for the definition of Lean).

Work moves around the domains. A new product is created (*Complex*). It becomes a mass-market product (*Complicated*). There is a dip into *Chaos* when something unforeseen happens, such as an IT outage or an issue leading to a product recall. In some cases that leads to a new good practice in the *Complicated* domain.

In Taylorist workplaces of the 1900s, and in some workplaces today, workers in the factory or at the bottom of a coal mine knew exactly what they would be doing all day: the same thing they did yesterday and the same thing they will do tomorrow. Very little changed. With Fordism, there was more micro-specialism. For example, all you did all day was add spokes to wheels. When you know exactly how many identical widgets you can mass produce in an hour, you can state with reasonable confidence how many widgets you can expect to produce by the end of the month.

In the Age of Digital, for product development, each iteration of the product is new and unique and has never been done in that context with those people before. This also applies to package software, such as ERP or CRM systems, as well as bespoke development. It's not been used in that context, with those unique people or the same processes, data, culture, organizational history, and memory before. In a context that is emergent and adaptive, predetermined solution-based deadlines and milestones are an antipattern. Milestones are fixed and deterministic. As the domain is unknowable and acting in the space changes the space, the focus should be on *outcome hypotheses*, a breadcrumb trail of North Star outcomes with nested cadences, experimentation, and fast feedback within guardrails in a safe-to-learn environment, as we will see in Chapter 5.

A culture with a deterministic mindset in the context of product development focuses on the wrong things: on milestones, predetermined detailed plans, velocity, output, and busyness. Often there is a focus on resource utilization, which increases lead time exponentially and slows flow, as we will see in Antipattern 5.3. This mindset often comes with a focus on cost rather than value. Reducing visible costs nearly always ends up increasing hidden costs due to a reduction in flow efficiency, in a double whammy reduction in value generation. There is less value generated and the rate of value generation has reduced, with more wait time and handoffs. It's a mindset that doesn't lead to high levels of colleague engagement and satisfaction at work.

An insistence on a predetermined and fixed solution and set of tasks (output) for unique product development is misapplying a way of working from two technology revolutions ago that suits manual, repetitive, knowable work, to unique, knowledge-based endeavors. It prohibits a business advantage of being nimble, it prevents optionality, it wastes time up front trying to perfectly analyze the future and it is demoralizing for colleagues. It also does not optimize for customer delight with the slow flow of "now that I can use it, I know what I don't want that I asked for, and I know what I want that I didn't ask for" value. That does not mean that there is no planning and no fixed dates. Quite the opposite. More on this in the next chapter.

In some cases, this is a leadership maturity step. Some people are uncomfortable exhibiting vulnerability, preferring to maintain a comfortable status quo. Often, with a charitable intent, it's a lack of understanding of alternative approaches. Sometimes, a deterministic mindset is driven by a lack of trust in others, a desire to micro-manage or a view that a detailed project plan is needed to hold people's "feet to the fire," to hold people accountable to activity and output, to make sure that they are not slacking. In extreme cases, some people are bullies and have a belief that getting stuff done at almost any human cost is acceptable because someone did that to them in their past or they are copying a more senior manager. Some people in leadership positions are insecure and don't want to say that they don't know or that they don't have all the answers. They can't say "Let's try it and find out" or "I don't know" or "Tell me what you intend to do, rather than ask me what to do." With some people there is a self-imposed view that as a leader there is a need to know it all and have all the answers. This is not the case. Be clear on the vision, the purpose, and the desired outcome hypotheses, invite experimentation and empowerment within guardrails. Celebrate safe, fast learning. Leverage emergence and maintain optionality to the last responsible moment in order to optimize outcomes.

From Antipatterns to Patterns

Guide on a Journey, Lead from the Front

These antipatterns are common. It's not unusual to find workplaces in which people expect others to change while they stay the same, with the infliction of an org design and process leaving culture unchanged, commands being barked, activities being doled out.

It's not unusual to find workplaces in which people have learned never to do more than they're told to do, not to speak up, not to run safe-to-learn experiments in order to improve for fear of reprisal. In some organizations it's safer to do nothing than to do something.

It's also not unusual to find people taking false comfort in having plotted the future in detail in the context of unique work and then proverbially holding people's feet over the fire for a nigh-on impossible task, with rallying cries of "Have fun!" and team-building exercises while constrained by a system of work and incentivization that cannot lead to high levels of engagement.

The recognition that product development work is emergent led to improvements in manufacturing in the 1980s in Japan. This led to "lightweight processes" for software development in the early 1990s and the *Agile Manifesto* in 2001, as we explored in Chapter 0. This is not new. As we've passed the tipping point in the Age of Digital, this is now table stakes to survive and thrive.

Instead, leaders should guide people on a journey from the front, role modeling desired behaviors, exhibiting vulnerability, and learning in the process. There needs to be psychological safety, the number one determinant of high-performing teams.[57] And, in order to optimize outcomes, there needs to be an emergent mindset with servant leadership. Instead of "reporting lines," there are "supporting lines." Ensure that there is high alignment, that the desired outcomes are clear, then allow people to use their own brains to work out how to optimally get there within minimal viable guardrails. Use emergence to your advantage to significantly reduce delivery risk, to raise morale by regularly seeing the fruits of your labor add value, and for survival.

PATTERN 4.1

Leaders Go First

Leaders lead from the front, guiding and accompanying people on a journey as per the origins of the word. The same trials, tribulations, and triumphs are felt.

PATTERN **4.1**

It's not a case of saying "Go ahead, I'm staying here. Off you go. Let me know when you get there." It requires courage, the role modeling of desired behaviors and attracting followers. It's easy to say and hard to do. Change starts at the top. Behavioral norms exhibited by those in senior roles, that is, the tone from the top, has a disproportionate impact on culture, on recognition, on reward, on reinforced behaviors, on purpose, on motivation, on "who we are" and "how we are" as a company.

The leadership team (as senior as possible, ideally the board) is team number one. To quote Frederick Laloux, author of *Reinventing Organizations*, "The consciousness of an organization cannot exceed the consciousness of its leader."[58] There will be a bubble of better ways of working around the most senior leader who is supporting and encouraging improvement. For successful organization-wide change, that bubble needs to be anchored at the top table. If not, there will likely be organizational impediments or culture outside of the bubble that will remain a blocker.

There should be incentivization and invitation (see Chapter 3) from the top for people to improve ways of working with support to deliver **Better Value Sooner Safer Happier**. That is, improving on **BVSSH** outcomes should be articulated as one of a limited number of priorities, firm-wide, for which people will be recognized and rewarded. The "how" is not mandated. There is an expectation of a positive trend on **BVSSH** outcomes over time. There are no targets (as targets can drive cargo cult or in some cases, with agentic state, unethical behavior). Support is provided and there is role model behavior from leaders.

For people in leadership positions, they may have got to their position via traditional ways of working, exhibiting behaviors such as those in the antipatterns. What led to personal success in the past won't necessarily bring ongoing success. In order to optimize outcomes, there is a need to exhibit courage and vulnerability, to break through learning anxiety, to experiment, to encourage others to experiment safely, to be more leader and less commander, to role model desired behavior, to ensure that the outcome hypotheses are clear, then allow teams to get on with it within minimal viable guardrails. Seek coaching, limit work in progress, visualize and radiate information, run short and often standups rather than wading through sixty-page committee decks, do "Gemba walks" (go see), swarm as a leadership team on organizational blockers, run regular retrospectives, pivot based on regular feedback, and focus on a balanced set of outcome hypotheses not on activity or output. Humans have a limited velocity to unlearn and relearn; there are no quick fixes. In my experience, some people in leadership roles, especially if close to retirement, just want a quiet life. They don't want to rock the boat. If that is the case, as we saw in Pattern 3.2, start with those who have responded to the invitation.

Leaders at every level have a role in fostering, coaching, and supporting better ways of working throughout an organization. Grass roots only will soon hit a grass ceiling. Top down only is inflict over invite. Instead, as we saw in Pattern 2.3, engage a vertical slice of the organization, including the pressurized middle. Start with the natural innovators, and apply the Rule of One. Get the new way of working going in a small group, then go sideways. There is a role for everyone, including middle management who can coach their teams as servant leaders. Mike Rother's Toyota Improvement Kata includes a Coaching Kata in which leaders at all levels have a vital role as servant leader coaches.[59] This is coaching teams on how they are thinking and how they are problem-solving, avoiding giving direct advice on the issue or improvement. It's coaching on the thinking process.

1: Transformational Leadership

The notion of transformational leadership was made popular in James Burns's 1978 book, *Leadership*.[60] The alternative is transactional leadership, which is management rather than leadership; it is managing people with a task focus with financial rewards offered or denied, more akin to ways of working from the early 1900s in factories. In 1985, Bernard Bass further expanded the concept, saying transformational leaders are those who inspire followers to achieve extraordinary outcomes and, in the process, develop their own leadership capabilities.[61]

There are four components to transformational leadership:[62]

Role Model: the leader is a role model, embodying the qualities that are desired, and "walks the talk." Followers identify with the leader, who is respected and trusted. The leader is consistent and can be counted on to do the right thing, demonstrating high standards of ethical and moral conduct. Also known as Idealized Influence.

Vision: a clear vision is articulated that inspires and motivates followers. There is a clear and shared view of aspirational future states, which provide a higher level purpose and meaning to work. There is

PATTERN **4.1**

a higher-level cause, which is energizing. Communication is inspiring and motivating even in an uncertain environment. Also known as Inspirational Motivation.

Intellectual Stimulation: the leader challenges followers to think about problems in new ways, challenges the status quo, and questions assumptions. Experimentation and new ideas are encouraged. Ideas are not criticized (initially there is no such thing as a bad idea) and failed experiments lead to learning and inquiry, not personal blame. There is psychological safety.

Coach: the leader coaches and develops people. There is a recognition and support of each follower's unique needs, strengths, motivators, and aspirations. The leader seeks first to understand then be understood, practicing active listening. The follower feels they are learning and being supported by the leader as an individual. Also known as Individualized Consideration.

The *State of DevOps Report 2017* found that high-performing teams have leaders with the strongest transformational leadership behaviors.[62] Transformational leadership, not surprisingly, is also strongly correlated with employee engagement. People are happier, more loyal, and more engaged. This in turn correlates to higher organizational performance.[63]

Transformational leadership is an enabler for better organizational outcomes. Interestingly, *The State of DevOps Report* found that while transformational leadership is critical for high performance, alone it is insufficient. There may be other systemic impediments beyond the sphere of influence of a transformational leader that prevent high performance. Hence the importance of the whole organization being in scope and having support from the top table rather than a collection of local optimizations in order to deliver **Better Value Sooner Safer Happier**.

2: Communicate, Communicate, Communicate

Leadership behavior is a culture amplifier. Behavior change requires incentivization, safety, recognition, and social proof, which requires communication. To enable lasting behavioral change, communicate three more times than you think you need and you're a third of the way there. Leaders at all levels should communicate frequently, recognizing desired behavior and learning, and using a range of mechanisms, including internal social media, internal conferences, Communities of Practice, meetups, show-and-tell demo sessions, internal awards, enterprise visibility rooms (virtual and physical), and so on.

The pattern for better outcomes is to be the change that you wish to see. The leadership team is team number one. Be a leader rather than a manager or commander. Leaders at all levels lead from the front; role model desired behaviors; walk the talk; are authentic; can articulate a clear, purposeful, and aspirational picture of the future; encourage experimentation; and coach followers as individuals. Leaders "bring forth" and accompany people on a journey, unchanged since the earliest known origins of the word 2,500 years ago.

PATTERN 4.2

Psychological Safety

We saw in Antipattern 4.2 the potentially tragic consequences of a culture where people fear to speak up or receive a dismissive attitude when they do. We saw that with a lack of psychological safety, people become conditioned to exhibit learned helplessness, waiting for an order and exhibiting an "agentic state," with extrinsic rather than intrinsic motivation. In some cases people have described being "united through a common suffering." Feedback is suppressed. Information does not make its way to where it needs to be. Clearly this is not going to optimize outcomes.

Whether it's unique product development or repetitive work, in order to have continuous improvement, in order to optimize outcomes, people need to be able to experiment safely. People need to be able to feel that it is safe to learn, safe to challenge the status quo, safe to question someone in a more senior role, safe to run improvement experiments, to test a value hypothesis that might fail. More than that, people need to be actively recognized for the lowest cost and quickest time to failure, avoiding a sunk cost fallacy. Some organizations have a virtual or physical "Failure Wall" to celebrate and remove stigma from failure. In reality there is no such thing as a failed experiment. There is only learning. The only failure is assuming that the future can be predicted and that organizations are reductionist, like the workings of a mechanical watch.

As we've passed the tipping point in the Age of Digital, as the pace of change today is faster than yesterday, psychological safety is not nice to have,

PATTERN **4.2**

it is essential in order to unleash human potential and to deliver **Better Value Sooner Safer Happier**. This is something that Toyota has known for a long time, with a *kaizen* process of continuous improvement. In Toyota factories there is an Andon cord or Andon button that when pulled or pressed leads to a team lead, who used to do the job on the line, to come running over and ask how they can help. There might be an issue or a suggestion for improvement, enabling quality and safety to be built in rather than inspected in later. There is a process for people to speak up. The team leader exhibits servant leadership and thanks the employee for flagging a potential quality issue. If it cannot be taken care of in the "takt time," the assembly line will stop with complete personal psychological safety.

In one factory alone, the Andon cord is pulled 5,000 times a day.[64] Compare this to General Motors where there was one cardinal rule: the line did not stop. To quote an ex-GM worker, "If you stopped the line, you were fired."[65] There are stories of cars being dragged off the line with the engine in backward.[66] In 2006, Toyota became the number one automobile manufacturer.[67] In 2009, General Motors became the largest industrial bankruptcy in US history, costing taxpayers more than $50 billion.

1: Generative Culture

In Ron Westrum's typology of organizational culture (see Antipattern 4.2), psychological safety is a characteristic of a generative culture. People are encouraged to speak up and think outside of the box. Information gets to where it needs to be irrespective of tribal alignment or hierarchy. When things go wrong, the focus is on understanding what it is in the system of work or culture that needs to be addressed rather than personal blame. For example, consider the scenario of an unintended systems outage due to an electrical engineer disconnecting power in a datacenter. A generative culture would look at it as a systemic issue where greater safeguards and resiliency are needed, not look at it as an error by the electrical engineer. A generative culture also fosters transparency, taking deliberate efforts to keep people informed and to make data available rather than concealing information. Transformational leadership and a generative culture go hand in hand.

In 2012, Google embarked on an initiative called Project Aristotle to examine what factors lead to high-performing teams. The research found that the number one factor is psychological safety. "In a team with high psychological safety, teammates feel safe to take risks around their team members," Google's guide states.

"They feel confident that no one on the team will embarrass or punish anyone else for admitting a mistake, asking a question, or offering a new idea."[68] It matters less about who is on the team and more about how the team works together.

Another Alphabet company, X, is focused on "moonshots." The X stands for 10 with a goal of 10x impact on the world's most intractable problems. Here, failure is actively rewarded. "One of our most valuable cultural habits is our willingness to kill our ideas. Our teams start each day assuming failure is the norm,"[69] writes Astro Teller, captain of Moonshots at X. "We keep people brave by rewarding teams that kill their projects. Last year we killed over 100 ideas. Not long ago a team of 30 engineers killed a project they'd been working on for 2 years. I announced they were getting a bonus for killing their project."[70] Astro goes on to say that "psychological safety is free. That means any company, any group of leaders, can choose to make being audacious their path of least resistance. So if your leadership team says, 'We don't have time for feelings' or 'We don't have the money that X has,' they're missing the point: the secret ingredient you need for moonshots doesn't cost a thing."[71]

Pixar has produced twenty-two computer animated feature films, all of which have debuted with positive critical acclaim. Four films are in the top fifty highest-grossing films of all time, whether animated or not.[72] According to Ed Catmull, former president of Pixar, "A hallmark of a healthy culture is that its people feel free to share ideas, opinions, and criticisms."[73] Pixar has a mechanism called the "Braintrust," which encourages candor in the process of making a film. On a regular basis the Braintrust meets to assess movies that are being made. Directors, writers, and storyboard artists look at each other's work and provide candid feedback. Catmull explains, "Candor could not be more crucial to our creative process. Why? Because early on all of our movies suck. At Pixar, we try to create an environment where people want to hear each other's notes (even when those notes are challenging) and where everyone has a vested interest in one another's success."[74] This is opposed to the traditional Hollywood approach where directors are micro-managed through "mandatory notes" from development executives ranking above the producers.[75]

2: Creating Psychological Safety

Creating a psychologically safe workplace requires a lot of conscious effort. Deep-seated and entrenched organizational norms, beliefs, and behaviors need to change. It won't happen overnight. As the saying goes, "The best time to

PATTERN **4.2**

plant a tree is twenty years ago. The second best time is now." According to Amy Edmondson, author of *The Fearless Organization*, there are three steps to take in order to build psychological safety in an organization.[76]

> First, **set the stage**. This is about reframing the context so that it's not about personal incompetence, it's about the system of work. It is about reframing failure, viewing intelligent failure as learning, and approaching unintentional failure with blame-free inquiry. Safe-to-fail experiments are to be celebrated. It is also about ensuring that there is purpose and meaning, be that rallying around zero accidents or being the world's most trusted brand.

> Second, **invite participation**. People may be conditioned to not speak up. Proactive steps should be taken to solicit input from everyone regularly. This is in addition to anyone being able to speak to anyone else without fear of retribution or hierarchy. Leaders need to be humble, actively listen, and ask questions, challenging the 300+ cognitive biases that we have, seeking diverse opinions that otherwise might not have been voiced. The greater the perceived power distance, the greater the need for the leader to solicit feedback.

> Third, **respond productively**. Express appreciation for the feedback or for the learning. Celebrate fast, intelligent failure. Equally, there are minimal viable guardrails, both procedural and behavioral that are non-negotiable. These need to be clearly communicated.

3: Safety I and Safety II

Professor Erik Hollnagel, a specialist in safety issues, coined the terms Safety I and Safety II.[77] Safety I focuses on ensuring that nothing went wrong and looks at the circumstances that arose when things did go wrong: an emphasis on root cause analysis. The focus is on avoiding failure altogether. However, with complex systems there rarely is one root cause. And looking for a root cause can result in missing the broader, cultural environment. Safety II looks at why things go right and tries to build a culture in which those things occur more often. Psychological safety—the confidence to speak up and take the initiative—is an important part of this approach.

PATTERN **4.2**

From the work of Sydney Dekker (which we will look at in more detail in Chapter 6), the difference between things going wrong and things going right is not the absence of negatives, it is the presence of positives. Those positives are:

- The ability to challenge the status quo; to say stop.
- Past success is not taken as an indicator of future success.
- There is diversity of opinion.
- Conversations about risk and potentially "bad news" are kept alive.

All of these require active psychological safety.

To summarize, in order to improve, in order to deliver **Better Value Sooner Safer Happier**, in order to create a more humane, engaging, and rewarding working environment, people need to feel safe and be encouraged to offer their ideas, to ask potentially stupid questions, and in some cases to pull a real or virtual Andon cord to stop the line. People need to be able to run safe-to-learn experiments, to feel safe delivering news that the recipient might not want to hear, to express diverse opinions, and to ask for help. It needs to be safe to have a *bias to action*, rather than doing or saying nothing being the safest behavior. Organized human endeavor should not be run as a benevolent dictatorship; rather, leaders should be helping people bring their full selves to work.

Case Study: How Bank of Ireland's Auditors Raised Their Agility[77]

Bank of Ireland is the oldest bank in continuous operation in Ireland, founded in 1783. It is one of the "Big Four" Irish banks, with over 10,000 employees. Steve Saunders, Chief Internal Auditor, shares the internal audit ways of working story so far:

The journey in the Group Internal Audit (GIA) team at Bank of Ireland toward better ways of working started in 2017. We could see that the existing ways of working were not setting teams up for success.

The first move toward agility was a move toward servant leadership. Everyone in the function is considered a leader, be it a leader for a particular skill set, risk type, or for a particular business division. We very much adopted a philosophy of "leaders at all levels." Senior people within the function are encouraged to support and coach their colleagues to achieve their goals rather than telling them *how* to do their job. The change was cultural rather than focused on mechanics and process, and it proved to be the bedrock for our journey.

The culture we sought to build has been founded in the twelve principles of the *Agile Manifesto*. For example, customers and team members working together. The highest priority being satisfying customer needs through early and continuous delivery. We've also been striving to foster a culture of self-directed teams, minimal organizational hierarchy, putting the power to make decisions where the knowledge is (with the teams), and being comfortable that we can fail fast, learn, and get better.

To support the change, teams took part in training sessions and workshops, enabling the leadership team to endorse and promote agile auditing. The training was then rolled out to all audit teams. Some auditors stepped up to become champions of agility within the audit function, allowing GIA to contribute toward the bank's move to greater agility and be seen as a leader in the field.

May 2018 saw a GIA Town Hall dedicated to agility. Only then did the group begin looking at process. Champions began the experimentation of an iteration-based process using Scrum. Stakeholders had iterative value early, continuously, and frequently. Instead of only receiving conclusions at the end of audits that were known to last for months, they received assurance every two weeks.

What we noticed is that with our servant leadership approach, providing value every two weeks, and holding retrospective sessions often, staff morale and engagement very quickly shot up. Teams adopting these approaches and ways of working quickly became the highest engaged teams when surveyed.

Linking up with a small set of like-minded colleagues from peer organizations, we established the "Agile in Audit" meetup group. Through this we began inviting colleagues from across our profession to get together regularly and compare notes on working with increased agility. So popular have these sessions become that they are now massively oversubscribed. Quite simply the flames have been lit. And what we have achieved is a profession-wide shift from agility being an interesting extra "thing," to an industry EXPECTATION. Indeed, firms performing independent quality assessment of audit teams now test and probe a department's agility! The world for an auditor has quite simply been changed.

PATTERN **4.2**

PATTERN 4.3

Emergent Mindset with Servant Leadership

If there's one place where you would expect to find a strong adherence to hierarchies and the kind of deterministic mindset described in Antipattern 4.3, it's in the military, a place with clear ranks, a firm pecking order, and where orders *must* be obeyed.

1: Intent-Based Leadership

In 1998 with just two weeks' notice, having spent a year preparing to take command of the US Navy submarine *Olympia*, David Marquet was unexpectedly asked to take command of a different sub, the *Santa Fe*. It had the worst track record in the fleet with only three of its crew asking to remain with the ship during the previous twelve months, the lowest retention rate in the Navy.[78]

Usually, captains are know-all, tell-all commanders, with their orders being followed. Decisions would bubble up to the top. However, in this case Captain Marquet could not be the all-knowing commander, as he had not trained on this type of submarine, as was brought to light one day while performing a test simulating the sub running on electric power. Marquet suggested that they speed up. The navigator ordered, "Helm, ahead two thirds." Nothing happened. Eventually Marquet asked the helmsman what was going on. He said, "Captain, on this submarine there's only one third on the electric motor." Marquet asked the navigator, "Did you know that?" "Yes, sir." "Well, why did you order it?" "Because you told me to, sir."[79]

Following that incident, Captain Marquet made a deal with the crew that he would never give another order. In return, the crew would have to say what they *intended to do*. This shifted ownership to each crew member and created leaders at all levels. Each leader resisted telling people what to do and instead communicated intent. In addition, authority was moved to where the information was rather than information being moved to authority.[80]

Twelve months later the *Santa Fe* had the highest rating of any US Navy submarine ever, and 100% of sailors re-enlisted.[81] The captain's job was no longer to tell everyone else what to do; it was to ensure that the intent, the mission, was clear, and then to listen to team members and their thinking process as to how they intended to go about the mission.

PATTERN **4.3**

A group of humans working together is a complex adaptive system (CAS). A CAS is emergent, not deterministic. How people react to input is not knowable and will not be the same each time, as CASs have memory. Whether it's 160 people locked up in a metal tube for up to six months at a time in the depths of an ocean or a large, traditional organization, change is emergent, not deterministic. There are unknown-unknowns. To maximize outcomes, intent-based leadership harnesses everyone's brains to create the smartest possible group of humans who are able to make the smartest possible decisions. This is with a check (intent is communicated), with an ability to coach ("What do you intend to do if . . . ?"), rather than people having a lack of ownership of their own actions ("You told me to, Captain.") and rather than relying on one brain to give all the orders.

2: Servant Leadership

The idea of servant leadership was proposed by Robert Greenleaf in a 1970 essay, "The Servant as Leader." Greenleaf distinguished between leaders who are motivated by leadership and leaders who see their role as helping others to achieve their potential. The best test of leadership, he argued, is whether those served grow as persons, whether they become healthier, wiser, freer, more autonomous, and more likely themselves to become servant leaders.[82]

Case Study: Journey to the East

Robert Greenleaf has attributed his idea of servant leadership to the short novel by Herman Hesse, *Journey to the East*. That book, itself inspired by the Chinese classic *Journey to the West*, tells of a branch of a religious sect called "the League" that travels to the East in search of an "ultimate truth." The party journeys with a servant called Leo, who helps to carry the luggage, works happily in a simple and natural manner, and ensures that no one is left behind. He is described as "an ideal servant."

When the party reaches the mountain gorge Morbio Inferiore, Leo disappears. Shortly afterward, the party breaks down. The members argue and blame Leo for the failure of the journey. Later, it becomes clear that Leo wasn't just the party's servant. He was also the head of the League. He had become the glue that held the group together.

"You can imagine what Hesse was trying to say when he wrote this story," says Greenleaf. "To me, this story clearly says that the great

PATTERN 4.3

leader is seen as servant first, and that simple fact is the key to his greatness. Leo was actually the leader all of the time, but he was servant first because that was what he was, deep down inside."[82]

Servant leaders, says Greenleaf, listen and exhibit empathy. They acknowledge other people's perspectives, give people support to be able to meet their goals, involve them in decisions, and build a sense of community.[83]

It is important not to focus too heavily on "servant" and forget the "leader" part. Too much servant and not enough leader will result in Brownian motion, with teams behaving like the random motion of particles suspended in fluid. As a leader there is a need to ensure that the outcome hypothesis, the mission, the North Star, the purpose and meaning, is clearly articulated and understood. This provides high alignment. People are aligned toward a common goal. Then, as a servant, get out of the team's way. Provide high autonomy and support to remove impediments that are preventing the team from optimally achieving the desired outcome. The Andon cord or button at Toyota is a great example of servant leadership in action. The Andon is pulled or pushed, a team lead comes over and says, "Thank you for flagging a possible issue or improvement. How can I help you, dear team member?"

This is especially important where the context is emergent. In a deterministic, knowable environment, it is more feasible, if unempowering, to be a commanding manager telling people what to do and when to do it. In an emergent domain, it's distinctly sub-optimal to try to take this approach, as the link between cause and effect is not knowable in advance. Rather than have a team of subservient order-takers, be both a servant and a leader and enable everyone to bring their brains to work and experiment in order to deliver **Better Value Sooner Safer Happier**.

3: Emergent Mindset

Adopting an emergent mindset in place of a deterministic mindset places a new value on continuous learning. Change, improvement and the future are not predictable, and the way a complex adaptive system responds is also not predictable. In order to optimize outcomes, as we will see in Chapter 5, when the nature of work is emergent there is a shift from output (fixed path, slow learning) to outcomes (wiggly path, fast learning), from predetermined solutions (sunk cost) to testing hypotheses (learn fast and cheap). The way to test

PATTERN **4.3**

a hypothesis is to probe, sense, and respond. People need to feel safe to experiment, learn, and adapt. Over time organizations who want to survive and thrive need to build a new muscle memory, becoming a (re)learning organization, with everyone striving for constant improvement, as per *kaizen* at Toyota.

The role of leader at all levels is to build a humane, engaging, rewarding workplace with purpose and meaning, where people can realize their potential, bring their full selves to work, and at the same time, as per the "H" in **BVSSH**, add value not only to institutional investors, pension funds, hedge funds, and other shareholders but also to society and to the planet.

Summary

Lead with Safety and Experimentation

Disasters like those at Aberfan and at Boeing are often due to organizational culture, the behavioral norms, rather than a surface-level root cause, such as creating a spoil tip on a stream or only reading from one angle-of-attack sensor. Usually the "root cause" is a symptom of a deeper cultural issue. If that is not addressed, it's likely that the same outcome will happen again.

There are parallels here with the *Challenger* and *Columbia* space shuttle disasters. In the *Challenger* accident, engineers were warning not to launch but were overruled, outranked, and gave up. In the *Columbia* accident, engineers were trying to raise the problem but were told not to email more senior people, found repeated resistance, and gave up.[84] Engineers were overruled by managers, seniority was a blocker to both psychological and ultimately physical safety, schedule pressure took precedence, and past success was incorrectly viewed as an indicator of future success with tragic consequences. Greater psychological safety, greater ability to challenge the status quo, to say stop, to have a virtual Andon cord to pull, might have led to a better outcome.

Those in leadership positions have the biggest influence on culture, setting the tone from the top, able to give out or withhold incentives, to reward or intimidate, and effectively create a self-selection effect where people will, if they can, choose to leave if the organization's values do not match their own (consider the *Santa Fe* attrition rates before and after).

Desirable outcomes are more likely to take place when leaders have created the psychological safety that provides room for everyone to speak up and to bring their brains to work, rather than just follow orders. They're also more likely when everyone feels a sense of responsibility for what happens

PATTERN **4.3**

around them, when they feel agency and control, when they regard themselves as leaders, and when they are provided with the support and coaching needed to grow.

Instead of "do as I say, not as I do," leaders go first. Rather than be a commander, be a transformational leader, role model desired behaviors, and exhibit humbleness and vulnerability. The leadership team is team number one.

Instead of a culture of fear, of learned helplessness, of short-term shareholder returns or schedule pressure taking precedence, create a psychologically safe organization where the status quo can be challenged, where someone can say stop, where past success is not taken as an indicator of future success, where information is shared, where feedback is actively solicited and acted on.

Instead of treating product development, change, and improvement as a deterministic, knowable activity—trying to command a square peg into an irregular and regularly changing shaped hole—acknowledge that it is not knowable, that the domain of work is emergent, which requires experimentation and fast feedback. To optimize outcomes, intent-based leadership increases the collective problem-solving capability and collective ownership by everyone in the group. And with a servant leader stance, there is a recognition that, like Leo, a leader is there to serve followers, to act as the glue that keeps people together, and to help remove blockers in the path. They are supporting lines rather than reporting lines.

These are the most impactful and most sustainable levers to enable everyone to deliver **Better Value Sooner Safer Happier**. They are also the hardest and take the longest. The best time to plant a tree was twenty years ago. The second best time is now.

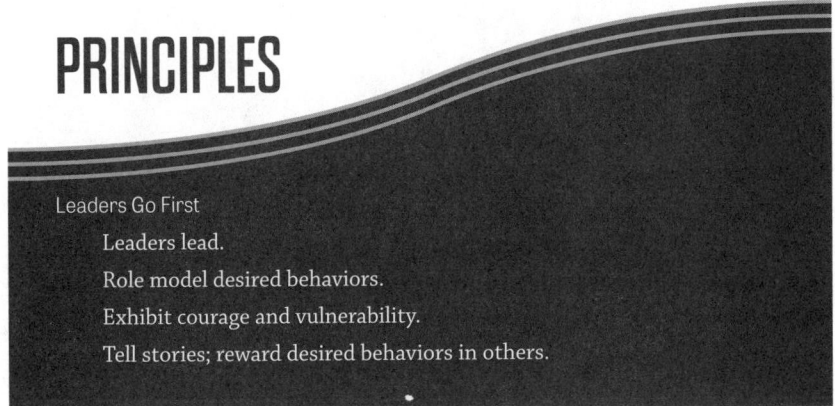

PRINCIPLES

Leaders Go First

Leaders lead.

Role model desired behaviors.

Exhibit courage and vulnerability.

Tell stories; reward desired behaviors in others.

Foster Psychological Safety

    Invite participation.

    Foster an open culture of learning through intelligent failure.

    Listen and act.

    Foster a blame-free culture.

Leverage Emergence

    Leverage emergence to maximize outcomes.

    Adopt an emergent mindset.

    Move authority to the information, with transparency.

    Coach and support; supporting lines over reporting lines.

5
BUILD THE RIGHT THING;
INTELLIGENT FLOW

Workplaces in industrialized countries have largely moved on from Fordism. Even in car factories, the place that pioneered conveyor belt manufacturing, robots now largely perform the tasks that are simple and repetitive. The human employees on the factory floor do work that is specialized and in harmony with the machines. Toyota calls this "autonomation" or *jidoka* in Japanese, which can be roughly translated as automation with a human touch. Not even Ford practices Fordism anymore.

There is one place where you can still see that old way of working. You can see it in many independent coffee shops.

When you arrive at a coffee shop, there's one till, and you join the end of the line. The line rolls forward. It stops. It moves forward again. It stops again. When you're close enough to the counter to read the menu and see the cakes, you stop. The person at the counter asks you what you want. You look at the options. You order your almond milk, flat white, extra strong coffee, and point at a Danish. The person at the counter asks your name. You tell them. You correct them . . . then correct them again. Eventually, you give up and watch them write your name with two "k"s and a silent "p" on the side of a cup. They pass the order to the barista, you hand over your money and take your change or tap to pay, move further down the line, and . . . wait. Finally, after a few more minutes, constrained by one barista and one espresso machine, the café's process is complete: a customer with a need is transformed into a customer with a coffee, a pastry, and a cup with an interestingly spelled version of their name.

There are all sorts of constraints in that system. Customers can't always see what's available until they reach the counter, which means the line has to stop moving while they make up their mind. Communication between the customer and the clerk can introduce requests that need to be clarified and errors that need to be corrected. That stops the line too. Those errors can be compounded when the information is passed to the barista, who can make mistakes of their own as they handcraft the product. There is one cashier, one till, one barista, and one coffee machine. The clerk won't know how much change to give until the customer has paid, if paying with cash, stopping the line again, and the customer has to hang around until their order is ready. They also have to be able to recognize their own misspelled name.

Flow is limited to the slowest part of the process of ordering and delivering coffee. Every time the line stops and customers have to wait for someone to scan the glass shelves and ask whether there's gluten in the *pain au chocolat*, flow is interrupted.

So cafés have room to improve their flow. They have space to become more efficient and perhaps more lean and agile. Some try. They make sure that the menu above the counter is big enough to be seen from the back of the line. They might offer table service to take the pressure off the takeout line. They might have someone walk down the line taking orders to alleviate the bottleneck that is the cashier (moving it to the barista), or they might enable customers to place their orders on an app. For example, Starbucks has made customer flow measurable and visible through technology installed in the stores, including the ability to notify customers when their order is ready. As Courtney Kissler explained at the 2018 DevOps Enterprise Summit, the "speed of service" is a measure of transactions across stores. It is the lead time, from order placed to order received. With this insight, it is possible to visualize the impact of changes in operational processes or menu items and optimize for flow and for customer experience.[1] More usually, though, customers stand in line, strain to see whether their favorite muffins are sold out and wait while constraints in the flow extend their time to value.

In this chapter, we're going to focus on value and time to value. We'll focus specifically on how organizations choose (implicitly or explicitly) what work to do and how they approach that work in the context of product development, with a view to delivering **Better Value Sooner Safer Happier**.

A scenario often observed is that processes upstream of product development teams become the primary constraint to valuable flow, especially as the product development teams increase their agility. Done badly (and anything can be done badly), the result is fragile rather than agile. As empowerment and autonomy are increased, the system of work can become chaotic and disconnected. Teams become a self-fulfilling prophecy, with Product Owners replenishing a backlog and forgetting to speak to the customer. A coffee shop can have the world's fastest, most agile baristas, but if they are churning out hazelnut soy macchiatos that no one wants and if customers don't know what they can order until they reach the counter and are stuck in a long line behind one person at the till, it will still be a long time from customer need identified to customer need met. And a waste of hazelnut soy macchiatos.

Another scenario often observed is Water-Scrum-Fall, sometimes referred to as "Hybrid Agile." It consists of a predictive, deterministic-mindset project plan that attempts to predict the future at the point of knowing the least, with the traditional big, up-front planning, analysis, design, and solutioning, then the word "sprint" ten times in the middle of a Gantt chart, followed by a testing phase and a big-bang go live. The requirements . . . sorry, "stories" . . . are predictively planned into each sprint.

With a charitable intent, it is intended to be Agile; however, there is nothing agile about it. There is still a deterministic mindset being misapplied to an emergent domain of work. There is still a focus on predictively planned output, not outcomes. There is no optimizing for the fast flow of safe value. Predicted work has been packed into traditional Gantt chart work breakdown structures by a project manager and called a "sprint." There are no thin slices of value regularly going into a production or production-like environment catering to emergence and fast learning. It is still Think Big, Start Big, Learn Slow, and there is little evidence of agile values or principles being lived.

So how do large, traditional organizations make sure that their teams are working on the most valuable things as agility increases? How do they maintain their flow of value? This chapter will explore the antipatterns around a lack of flow of value and describe the corresponding patterns that can keep a business moving in the right direction toward the outcomes it actually wants to achieve—and give customers the coffee they want quickly, smoothly, and with their name spelled right.

ANTIPATTERN 5.1

Local Optimization

I once met with a software development team that was rightly proud of the progress it had made in increasing its agility. The Team Outcome Lead, or Scrum Master, showed me the improvement the team had made in the software development cycle time—the time between pulling work off the backlog to the end of development. The difference was impressive. Feedback and learning were much faster, and the team had roughly halved their average cycle time in the past year. They were twice as productive!

However, something wasn't right. The recipients of the change were complaining that they weren't seeing the claimed benefits. As far as they were concerned, the team's increased agility had made no difference. Things were taking just as long as before. Value wasn't being realized more often. By the time any new features arrived, the world had moved on. And getting any new ideas implemented was measured in years rather than months or weeks.

I was surprised, so I asked the Team Outcome Lead what happened after development and testing was complete.

"Well, we need to wait for integration testing," she told me, "because we've got lots of dependencies. Then there's the user acceptance testing, and then we have to wait for IT Ops to do the release."

I asked about the cadence, the frequency of each of these stages.

"Integration testing is monthly," the Team Outcome Lead said. "Acceptance testing and releasing is quarterly."

So the production timeline for those agile development teams looked look this (see Figure 5.1):

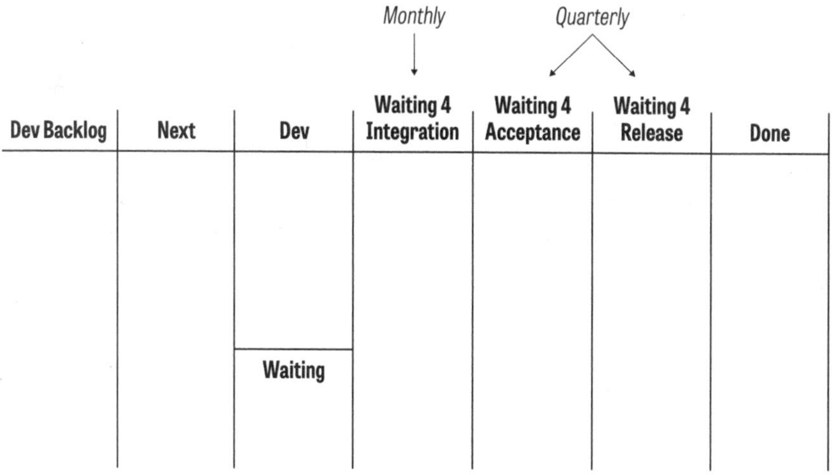

Dev Backlog	Next	Dev	Waiting 4 Integration	Waiting 4 Acceptance	Waiting 4 Release	Done
		Waiting				

Figure 5.1: Bottleneck at Acceptance Testing and Release

The team would pull an item of value from the backlog on the left, implement it, and then it would sit and wait. And wait some more. And wait yet again. At least three months would pass between the software development team completing their work and value and learning being realized.

That was just the bottleneck that followed the development team's work. I asked what happens before the work reaches the dev team.

"Well, before that, there's a product backlog with bigger chunks of work or bigger outcome hypotheses, which need to be broken down into experiments and smaller items of value to get fast feedback in order to test the hypothesis. In some teams that work is pulled and refined just in time, in order to pivot and maximize value. In other teams it is predictively planned into multiple iterations over a quarter, with more of a focus on committed output for that quarter rather than outcomes. I guess it depends on context," the Team Outcome Lead said.

"Right," I said. "And there's nothing before that?"

"Well, of course, a detailed design has to be drawn up and reviewed by the Technical Design Authority. That's an organization-wide team. And before that, there's a Detailed Business Case that has to be completed. They have to agree to funding and seek approval from a business line steering committee. Before that is an Outline Business Case approval step."

"An Outline Business . . . ?"

"Outline Business Case approval step. That filters the business cases that go into the Detailed Business Case review. And before that is Idea Triage."

"And how often does all this happen?" I asked—and braced myself for the answer.

"It's monthly for the Idea Triage, quarterly for the Outline Business Case, and an annual planning process that takes about six months to complete using the Detailed Business Cases. We start planning in September. Around March, we'll know our level of funding. So by the end of the year, the plans are about eighteen months old. Oh, and there are twenty mandatory artifacts we have to produce."

So the actual end-to-end lead time lasted at least eighteen months and looked like this (see Figure 5.2):

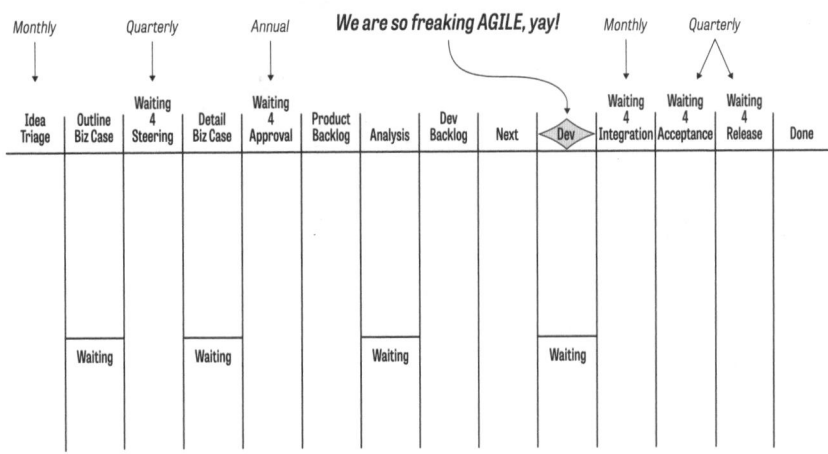

Figure 5.2: We're So Freaking Agile!

Adapted from Leopold, *Rethinking Agile.*

This kind of flow leads to what Don Reinertsen and Preston Smith have called an "urgency paradox."[2] Valuable ideas sit in twelve to eighteen months of big, up-front planning with no sense of urgency, waiting for the next big batch of prioritization. By the time they reach the product development team, they're suddenly urgent. By then the market opportunity may have passed. The time to learn early and often has passed. There is a cost of delay. Product development teams are then under pressure and are more likely to incur technical debt and cut corners, leading to lower quality and unhappier customers and colleagues.

Software development teams can improve all they like, but if the time from customer need identified to need met hasn't changed because of bottlenecks in the flow, any local optimization of agility in IT will make little or no difference in the end-to-end time to value.

Compounding the lack of end-to-end flow is a way of working from two technology revolutions ago, suited to repetitive manual labor, and people organized into role-based silos. With a tribal identity by role, rather than by value and customer, there are multiple handoffs, queuing, and an us-and-them, "throw it over the wall" culture. The concept of "team" is a local optimization. People "see" only one stage, not needing to know the flow. There is little to no end-to-end ownership or accountability aligned to the flow of value. It's a series of local optimizations.

Time to learning, time to value, time to delighting customers, and the flow itself will have not materially changed. This was a lesson learned in manufacturing a long time ago: improving the performance of a non-bottleneck will only stack up more inventory at the bottleneck itself. It won't improve the end-to-end flow of value. A coffee shop can take orders on a tablet from people waiting in line, but if there's still only one barista, there's still going to be a bottleneck. There may be a local human benefit in the local optimization: the working lives of members of teams may become more humane and rewarding with small, multidisciplinary teams within the local optimization; however, the overall human endeavor won't generate broader benefits.

The result of that lack of end-to-end flow and inability to learn early and pivot reduces the probability that teams are working on the most valuable thing. There will likely be a perceived lack of responsiveness to customer feedback or to meeting needs. Traditional competitors or non-traditional disruptors may have first-mover advantage and be better able to create customer advocates.

One way that traditional organizations try to push flow faster is through the use of deadlines and milestones. That's an antipattern too.

ANTIPATTERN 5.2

Milestone-Driven Predicted Solutions

"We are united through a common suffering."

That was the answer I received once from an employee at a large organization when I asked why more people hadn't left.

The work itself was meaningful. The company was venerable and respectable. However, the way of working in at least one area was leading to a form of organizational Stockholm Syndrome.

Project managers would set deadlines at the start of the work when the least was known, without consulting those doing the work. Work was one big batch, making its way sequentially and slowly through job roles, from analysis to design to development and then testing, which, for the people involved, was a feast-to-famine way of working. There would be finger pointing when deadlines weren't met. And the plan never changed. During the feast phase when the big batch of work was with a given role, people would work unsustainably long hours and over weekends. When people realized they were going to miss a milestone, they'd feel fear and shame. Instead of a cycle of work, review, and learn, employees went through cycles of rush, handover, and hide.

With a tribal alignment by job role, people would relax if "the hole was on someone else's side of the boat," even if the boat was sinking. There was a lack of shared ownership. If they'd thrown their work over the wall, the next stage of the journey was someone else's problem, someone else's milestone to meet.

Milestones do not exhibit agility. They're made of stone. They are hard to move, and when moved, they are no longer valid. They're more like tombstones than measures of progress. People also refer to them as "deadlines" or "drop dead" dates. They don't convey any expectations about *why* you want to get to where you're going, *how* you might get there, *how else* you might get there, *whether* you'll make it there at all, or the level of safety on the journey. They say nothing about the quality and experience of the journey, nor whether it's even the right destination given your intent. They are one-dimensional. The distance between two fixed points along one fixed route. Originating 2,300 years ago in the Roman Empire, milestones were set more than two feet into the ground, stood five feet tall, and weighed more than two tons. They measured 1,000 paces.[3] They personify a rigid immovability.

You don't know *when* you're going to reach a milestone. The last 20% of the journey might take 80% of the time. There might be roadworks, an accident, a flooded river crossing, or a major design flaw that requires a significant refactor of the product. You only know you've reached a milestone when you reach a milestone. And even then, given your intent, you might find that it's not the optimal place to be.

Milestones are a sub-optimal mental construct to use for unique change in a rapidly changing terrain.

The word "deadline" is also an inappropriate metaphor for complex, unique, emergent change. The word originated in 1864 from Camp Sumpter in the US Civil War. The deadline was a light wooden railing beyond which transgressors were shot.[4] Obviously an analogy of death—"drop dead date" is another one—is not optimizing for high levels of colleague engagement.

On a Gantt chart, milestones focus on activity completion—on *output*—a static business case, and a fixed route. They don't allow for continual thought about how to maximize *outcomes* based on strategic intent and ever-increasing knowledge of the landscape. They're about whether the activity has been achieved rather than what might be optimal to do next, given fast feedback. The former is "order-giver" and "order-taker," with thinking put on hold. The latter requires everyone to use their brains.

Milestones with a RAG status—marked red, amber, or green depending on perceived status—are usually even more culturally toxic. In my experience, in an organization with a command-and-control, pathological culture, a red RAG status is not viewed as a call for help or an opportunity for servant leadership. In practice, it's usually viewed as failure with shame and reprisal. There is typically a lack of psychological safety. This results in burying bad news, withholding learning, cutting corners, working harder not smarter, lower quality, lower engagement, lower satisfaction, and a lower likelihood of achieving the desired outcome. Anything to avoid the dreaded red RAG status against the deterministic output, which was fixed when knowing the least.

Milestones are an unsuitable metaphor to use for unique product development (which is emergent) within organizations (which are emergent) to continually delight customers (who are emergent) in a landscape (which, you guessed it, is emergent) in which everything is changing faster than ever. The milestone metaphor, in this context, traditionally has been overloaded to predict distance (work done), the quality of the destination, and time. Add in managers versus workers; business versus IT; low psychological safety with fear, blame, and reprisals; individual incentivization over team incentivization; and tribal identity by task-based job role, and it shouldn't be too surprising that one study put success in traditional software projects as low at 29%.[5] Another study found that US employee engagement, while rising, is low, with 34% of people actively engaged, 53% not engaged, and 13% actively disengaged.[6]

Importantly, this is not to say that fixed dates don't exist in the workplace. They do. For example, compliance to new regulation or planning backward from the launch of a new model of car in a few years' time. More on this in Pattern 5.2. The antipattern here is that continuing with the "milestone" metaphor fails to optimize for outcomes. It perpetuates old behaviors and outdated ways of thinking for unique change. It enables a deterministic mindset to continue in an emergent domain, inhibiting agility. The focus is on hitting a predetermined plan over maximizing outcomes.

People don't know what they want until they have it. And they don't know how they're going to build something unique until they've built it. In the process, there is learning. Learning about what not to do next time, if there is a next time. Learning about what actually ends up being valuable and what is not valuable. And yet the conventional wisdom that the majority of large organizations have been practicing, reinforced by the use of project management methods applied to software such as PRINCE2, is a fallacy of treating complex, emergent, unique knowledge work as if it's predictable, inhibiting optionality and delaying learning to when there is the least time to respond and highest sunk cost. Change is treated as if it's five miles from here to the next village, as if unique change never done before is knowable with milestones in Gantt charts.

Which brings us to Gantt charts. In Chapter 0, I gave an overview of the Gantt chart. Created by Henry Gantt, who worked with Frederick Taylor in the early 1900s, it was originally called a Man Record Chart. A line represented whether a worker had shoveled enough coal or moved enough crude iron for the day, as determined by the "foreman." The "short line" man was incompetent; the "long line" man was to be encouraged.

The Gantt chart is a tool of manager versus worker oppression. It is deterministic. It was a step forward in the early 1900s for manual, repetitive labor. It is totally unsuited to emergent, knowledge-based product development.

In the Age of Digital, with a new means of production in a rapidly changing terrain, there are better ways of working if an organization wants better outcomes. This includes work with a fixed date and fixed scope, such as mandatory regulatory initiatives. It is about emergence over determinism. Better business outcomes are of course optional. Surviving and thriving are not mandatory.

ANTIPATTERN 5.3

Headless Chickens

Imagine that product development teams have adopted agile ways of working suitable for the Age of Digital. However, they have become a "feature factory." They keep adding new features to products; however, the features are disconnected from customer needs and company strategy. Teams are typically incentivized by *output*. They're measured by velocity—by activity—instead of outcomes. Activity should not be mistaken for achievement. The teams become a self-fulfilling prophecy of backlog replenishment. This is a scenario I often see.

Sometimes, the cause is a lack of clear strategic alignment, the absence of a "North Star" to guide outcomes and link the work being done to strategic goals. When there is low alignment and high autonomy, the result is often something that looks like Brownian motion: there's plenty of movement in random directions without a shared purpose. Sometimes, the cause is personal. Businesses can suffer from a HiPPO approach—the highest paid person's opinion carries the highest priority, even when that opinion is disconnected from customer feedback.

A common behavior I see is Product Owners (especially new Product Owners who used to be Project Managers) becoming so focused on the notion that they "own" a product that they, still with a command-and-control behavioral norm, decide what to build, don't seek broader team input, and fail to seek feedback from customers to understand what might be most valuable for them. There is a product myopic focus. There is an unlearning and relearning journey for people to go on, which does not happen overnight.

This antipattern of teams churning out stuff disconnected from strategy, feedback, or value can also result from a traditional mindset around resource utilization, with a view that people need to always be busy. There is a focus on the worker rather than the system of work. This leads to overproduction in siloes rather than coming together, swarming, and helping to alleviate constraints to flow. A system of work in which everyone is working all of the time is very inefficient, a lesson learned in manufacturing. A focus on individual busyness has the opposite effect to that desired, in that lead time rises exponentially as utilization increases (see Figure 5.3).

In this situation, there is no time for continuous improvement, for resolving impediments, for reflecting, for pivoting, or for swarming. The system of work goes slower. People are fully occupied pushing the square wheels.

Or to use a different metaphor, they run around like headless chickens.

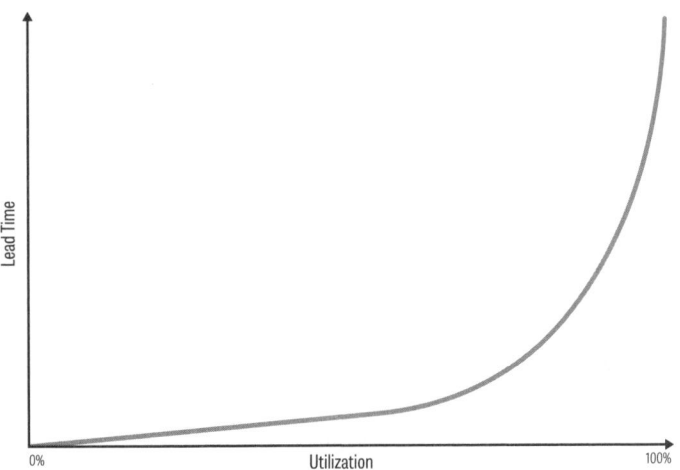

Figure 5.3: The Rise of Lead Time

ANTIPATTERN 5.4

Start Starting

Imagine a junction on a multilane road. The cars on the road are moving at a steady rate. At the next junction, a long line of new cars are coming down the ramp to join the traffic. In fact, they're joining the road at a faster rate than cars are leaving. What do you think will happen?

The more cars on a road, the slower they go.

The fewer the cars, the faster they can go.

The same process happens in companies. Blissfully unaware of the capacity of the system of work and treating it as a push-based rather than pull-based system, organizations continue to start initiatives, launch projects, and agree to customer or stakeholder demands.

More cars that are put on the road, the more congestion builds. Or to put it another way, the coffee shop's marketing attracts more coffee drinkers without adding more baristas or espresso machines. The more work that is in progress concurrently, the slower it all goes.

On an individual level, task switching is one of the most expensive neurological activities. According to the American Psychological Association, "even brief mental blocks created by shifting between tasks can cost as much as 40 percent of someone's productive time."[7]

Queueing theory also applies here. Little's Law states:

$$\text{Lead Time} = \text{Work in Progress/Throughput.}$$

Reducing work in progress (WIP) reduces end-to-end lead time, time to learning, time to pivot, time to realizing and maximizing value. It increases agility. It increases the chances of being able to identify causality, to be able to correlate actions to outcomes. There is a faster feedback loop on strategy.

Increasing WIP increases end-to-end lead time. Organizations that "start starting" are increasing the time to value and to learning, decreasing agility, making it harder to respond, harder to react, and harder to correlate actions to outcomes.

I once saw part of an organization continuously commit to double the number of work requests than the natural capacity of the system of work could handle. This was being done with a positive intent of trying to be responsive, and it was done in absence of any insight of the flow of work end to end. Unfortunately it has the opposite outcome to the desired one, resulting in work taking longer. Measures such as lead time, throughput, aging, WIP, or flow efficiency were not being measured. The majority of people didn't know the end-to-end process, as people were organized in role-based silos. Each month the work in progress, the backlog of committed work, grew by another month without awareness and, even worse, with an expectation that it was all going to get done.

Applying traditional thinking, the focus was on the service level agreement (SLA) at each stage in the sequential workflow. People were incentivized to work harder to meet the SLAs as a series of local optimizations. In one example, the SLA was two days, yet the empirical evidence showed it took on average fifteen days. However, the SLA remained, with an implicit assumption that people needed to work harder. Work was being pushed rather than pulled, building up bigger queues at each stage and further increasing the end-to-end lead time. There was effectively unlimited WIP. Once every twelve to eighteen months, the system of work was reset.

The result was an acceptance by stakeholders that things took a long time to get done. This created a vicious circle: the desire to start *more* things, otherwise they would never get done and grow into piles of invisible inventory and an "us and them" behavioral norm. The result was low quality, as people tried to work harder rather than smarter, and low engagement. It was a no-win situation due to a lack of awareness of the system of work.

From Antipatterns to Patterns

"Valuetivity"

The antipatterns described here stand in the way of delivering **Better Value Sooner Safer Happier**.

A local optimization doesn't necessarily deliver better end-to-end outcomes. It just moves the bottleneck, if indeed it was the bottleneck to start with. If it's not the weakest link in the chain, there is no value in continuing to strengthen it.

Milestones are a suboptimal metaphor to use, inhibiting agility and usually coming with a culture of fear, with learning being buried, until the endeavor is firmly in the jaws of defeat. The green watermelon explodes with a cascade of red. It is not optimizing for employee engagement.

Some organizations that have set their agile hares running are finding that they have metamorphosized into agile headless chickens, disconnected from company strategic intent or the voice of the customer.

And most large organizations have too much work in progress concurrently, slowing down time to value and learning. "Surely the sooner I start it, the sooner it's done?" is an often heard vague question. No, not if 6,000 initiatives are all in play concurrently. Starting more will further slow everything down, like adding more cars to the road on the Friday evening of a holiday weekend. It hides the impediments to flow; it hides the rocks under the high tide of concurrent initiatives and waiting work. It builds up queues and reduces flow efficiency. Instead of "start starting," stop starting and start finishing.

These antipatterns are all fairly common, as organizations go through the cycles of unlearning and relearning. For each of these antipatterns, there are patterns that help to optimize for the fast flow of safe value and **BVSSH** outcomes.

It's a mindset shift from a focus on local "productivity," the number of units of output per unit of input, to end-to-end "valuetivity," the soonest realization of the most value with the least output. Producing the wrong thing faster isn't going to improve outcomes if there is no recognition that it's the wrong thing.

This is the pivot from a deterministic mindset to an emergent mindset, from project to product, from output to outcomes. In my experience, this is fundamental to enabling better quality, optimal value, sooner time to learning, safer control environment, and happier colleagues, customers, citizens, and climate.

PATTERN 5.1

Optimize for Fast End-to-End Flow

Local optimization, increasing agility in just one part of the end-to-end flow, in IT alone, does not optimize for outcomes. Instead, focus on and optimize for the fast flow of safe value end to end with long-lived value streams, long-lived products, long-lived teams, and funding the flow of value.

1: Long-Lived Value Streams

First, identify the long-lived **value streams**. A value stream has a flow of value creation, from needs-identified coming in on the left to needs-met emerging on the right. There are one or more value consumers, and the value stream has a value proposition. It is likely that the organizational structure of your business is already set up as value streams. For example, mortgages, savings, investment advice, luxury bags, groceries, shipping, customer onboarding, helicopter engines, passport applications, immigration services, and so on. It's the rationale behind the organized human endeavor, the reason your organization is operating, whether commercial, public, or charitable. Value streams have long-lived products (e.g., a mortgage or the generation of renewable energy), some of which are IT products or are supported by one or more IT products (e.g., a mortgage processing system or near real-time display of energy generation). Some of the value streams (typically 20% of the organization) are internal "shared service value streams," such as HR, finance, internal audit, real estate, and legal. The value consumers are internal, and these value streams are needed to support the external, customer-facing activities. (See Figure 5.4 for an illustration of delivery via value streams.)

Value Stream Nesting

A value stream should be genuinely end to end and ideally have as few dependencies as possible. It should have high cohesion (does one thing well) and low coupling (has minimal dependencies on other value streams in order to enable agility).

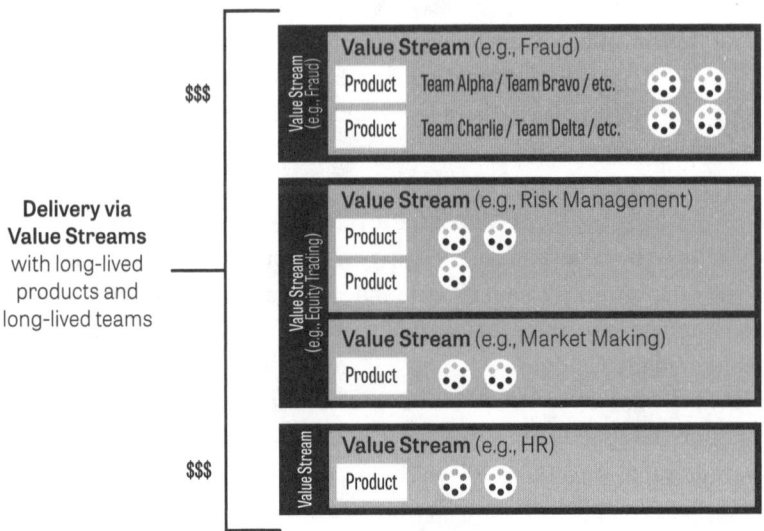

Figure 5.4: Delivery via Value Streams

Importantly, value streams are nested, as you can see in Figure 5.4. For example, Bank → Investment Bank → Capital Markets → Trading → Equity Trading → Market Making. At the lowest level, a value stream is a team-of-teams. This should be no more than 150 people (based on Dunbar's Number, a cognitive limit to the size of a group who can maintain stable social relationships). The so-called Spotify Model uses the term "Tribe" for its team-of-teams. The next level up is the team-of-teams-of-teams and so on, always organized by logical value creation. (Note that the so-called Spotify Model never got big enough or complex enough, with one product, to need nested value streams, or nested "Tribes." Hence, this is often missed when large, complex organizations of many business units and hundreds or thousands of products try to adopt the so-called Spotify Model.)

Again, in my experience, the business is usually already set up as value streams: it's usually the org structure of people in Information Technology that is partially or not at all aligned to business value streams. It's often organized by job role (such as a group of PMs, or BAs, or Dev or Test).

A lesson learned the hard way is to not worry about getting the value stream identification right at the beginning. Don't spend too long on it. It won't be right. Start, inspect, and adapt. Go in with an expectation that there will

PATTERN **5.1**

be change. There is no right and wrong; it's whatever works in your context. An indicator for value stream identification is being neither too coarse-grained (a few value streams with lots of products) nor too fine-grained (lots of value streams with one product each, unless your landscape has little duplication and a low level of dependencies).

Value Stream Naming

I prefer the term *value stream*, as language is important, and this makes it clear that the orientation is around *value* (and hence a value proposition and customers), and *stream* makes it clear that there is a flow of work. Also, this term is common in manufacturing.

I was fortunate enough to do a tour of a jet engine turbine blade factory. Giant signs hung from the roof saying "Commercial airline value stream," "Private jet value stream," and so on. The work was physically laid out with processing going from left to right. The factory was built for the raw materials to enter on the left and the finished turbine blades to be loaded and transported out on the right. It was designed to enable an extension to be built out (into the parking lot!) to accommodate more value streams if demand increased. We are late in applying learning from modern manufacturing to knowledge work. Ultimately, there is no one size fits all, no best practice. As an organization you should use whatever language you think will work best in your context and be prepared to inspect and adapt.

Value Stream Orientation

The primary orientation is around these business value streams. It's no longer "the business" and "IT." If you find yourself saying "the business," instead say "our business." Everyone in an organization is in "our business." Having a tribal identity around value and the customer brings together "business" and "IT," moving away from an order-giver and order-taker relationship to one where we are all the business and will succeed and learn together.

For example, in the context of a financial services firm, there is a credit card value stream that enables people to buy goods now and pay later (with interest). To provide this, it requires multiple specializations optimized for the fast flow of safe value. Referring to Cynefin (Chapter 0), within the value stream work will exist in and move around the domains, from Complex, to Complicated, to Chaos, back to Complex, and so on. Apply agility for unique continuous product development change and a lean approach for repetitive knowable work (e.g., customer onboarding, payments). Both cases optimize for **BVSSH** outcomes.

Importantly, value streams are usually *not* oriented around customer personas (for example, "retired couple," "student," "young professional," and so on). The same is true of customer journeys. Each persona or journey may *use* services from multiple value streams. Organizing by personas, as I saw one organization do, results in duplication of the actual value streams and an increase in dependencies, which inhibits agility. For example, duplicating customer onboarding, customer servicing, loan provisioning, etc.

If you think of value streams as layers of a cake, personas, delivery channels, and journeys are the candles on the cake. They stitch together and serve up the value streams in a persona-friendly manner. In the Age of Digital, technically those value streams can be served up via APIs. Effectively, it's bringing the business, people, and technology architectures all into alignment, with high cohesion (doing one thing well) and low coupling (minimizing dependencies, maximizing flow and agility). Ultimately you have a *value stream network* with interdependent services.

Product Development

As we saw, long-lived value streams have long-lived products (e.g., a mortgage, the generation of renewable energy), some of which are themselves IT products (e.g., social media software) or are supported by IT products (e.g., a mortgage processing system). In the Age of Digital, there are few products that do not involve IT in some way. Products (with or without IT and treating business and IT as one, "our business") have a value stream for change, in order to safely turn innovative ideas into features that should add customer and business value.

For example, there may be a hypothesis that implementing a one-click online application for a credit card will increase market share. The implementation of this feature in the mobile phone app follows the product development value stream, turning the idea into reality so that the hypothesis could be tested. As product development is unique and emergent, this is the sweet spot for agility, for fast feedback loops, for safe-to-learn experimentation. Do customers trust a one-click credit card application process? Is there an underserved market or not? With agility, it is possible to have the quickest and cheapest cost of learning in order to maximize value. This is not just an IT task, it is an "our business" experiment including marketing and legal.

PATTERN **5.1**

The credit card IT application is itself not a value stream around which people orient themselves. Unless the organization is in the business of selling credit card IT applications to other financial services firms. More likely, the credit card IT application is an IT product that supports the credit card product. It is a long-lived product, mapped to the credit card value stream. Within the credit card value stream there are multiple domains of work (see Cynefin), from continuous unique change to repetitive operations. As mentioned, products have a value stream for change.

In my experience, in large, old, regulated organizations, product development value streams are usually articulated via a Policy and Standard with formal controls. This is the formal control environment for change in an organization. Internal Audit will use the standard when auditing teams; therefore, it's important that Internal Audit are on the better ways of working journey too.

As a formal standard, it usually also leads to mandatory commonality in the product development value streams. The goal here is to ensure that it is *minimal* viable compliance (#MVC) and not one-size-fits-all catering to the lowest common denominator. This topic is explored in considerably more depth in Chapter 6.

Often, this formal standard is one of the top impediments to **BVSSH**, where the standard can trace its lineage back to the 1970s and is inherently waterfall in its construct. I know of one organization where the formal standard had a minimum of twenty-two mandatory artifacts and up to forty-five artifacts adding in the optional ones. It took about three months to shepherd a change through this lifecycle, and that was *per release!* Clearly it was not fit for purpose in the Age of Digital.

Value Stream Flow Efficiency

Leveraging learning from manufacturing again, value stream mapping is a valuable technique for visualizing and understanding the steps involved in the horizontal, left-to-right value creation flow. It shines a light on the health of the system of work. It's a great exercise to do with people who represent each part of the end-to-end flow. Usually the people in the virtual room have never met each other before, even though they are part of the same value creation process. As people map the process virtually or physically, including estimates for "value add time" and "wait time," there are always a number of lightbulb moments.

By looking at the "value add time" as a percentage of the total elapsed time end to end, it's possible to estimate the flow efficiency, which is the time that work is being worked on versus the time that work is waiting. As we saw in Chapter 1, at most large organizations the flow efficiency for knowledge work is rarely more than 10%; work is waiting 90% of the time, which is frankly shocking. Even more shocking is that most organizations are oblivious to this, not even looking at flow efficiency.

2: Long-Lived Products

Having identified the value streams that enable the organization to serve its purpose economically, socially, and environmentally, next map long-lived products to the long-lived value streams. The products may not be IT products, be supported by IT products, or involve IT at all. For example, a financial organization might have an equities trading system IT product that enables the equities market-making value stream where the product is an exchange-traded equity. All large firms will have an HR system that supports the onboarding of new employees. A FinTech firm might have a smartphone app that enables the management of personal finances, a retailer has an app for online shopping, and a social media firm has an app that enables you to publish a photo of your lunch. Or your dog. Or your dog eating your lunch.

You will likely also have products that are non-IT products. For example, an internal audit report, a research report, a press release, a sponsor's booth at a conference, a marketing campaign, and so on are all uniquely created products and would benefit from an agile approach, with fast feedback and cheapest cost of learning. If it's been done before lots of times, and there are known-unknowns, then it's in the sweet spot for a lean approach.

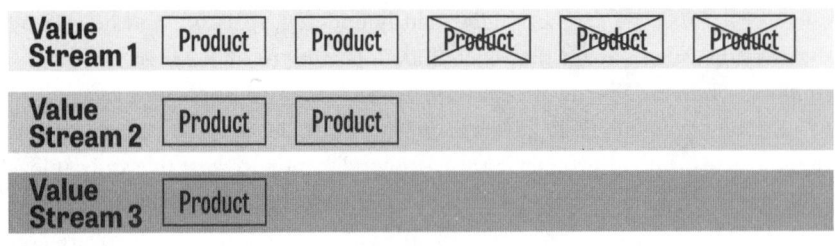

X = Not Strategic

Figure 5.5: Long-Lived Products on Long-Lived Value Streams

In the Age of Digital, the mapping of IT products to the value stream, as shown in Figure 5.5, shines a light on the duplication of systems and eases simplification of the IT landscape. In my experience, this provides a clear alignment, which was lacking from previous efforts to simplify the IT landscape. Where it was clear that there was duplication, an invest-or-divest decision was made per IT product. The goal is to make the environment as simple as possible, and no simpler. In some cases, the mapping of products to value streams leads to an organization actually having an IT product inventory for the first time.

On the term "long-lived," the goal here is "evergreen." IT products should be continually refactored so that they are always up to date. Systems naturally entropy if left untouched. The weeds grow. Instead, continuously upgrade the plane little and often mid-flight, turning it from a biplane into a jet plane into a spaceship. For example, from monolith to microservices to serverless. In old ways of working, with a project-based approach, the "not invented here" syndrome was a common occurrence, with each project leading to a new software build and a ballooning in the number of IT products. Applications would then be left until the weeds had grown so large that the only approach was to slash and burn with yet another big-budget, big-bang build.

The mapping of IT products to value streams also reveals the big, monolithic IT systems that straddle multiple value streams and inhibit agility due to built-in hard dependencies, where it's a case of deploying everything or nothing. These are often referred to as a "monolithic ball of mud." This is where IT architecture can be an impediment to agility.

If the business has a monolithic IT product that spans multiple value streams, put that product in its own temporary, shared service value stream. Then, over time, work on breaking it down into smaller components (such as microservices). They can be independently updated, released, and housed by the relevant value stream that isn't shared, leading to high cohesion and low coupling. There will be fewer dependencies and improved agility.

Initially, you will likely have a lot of dependencies across IT products and value streams, with IT products that are not independently testable and deployable. Spend time *breaking* those dependencies rather than just *managing* them. Ways to do this for software products, in addition to the point just covered on componentization, includes shared code ownership, internal open source, service virtualization, and dedicating developers to a customer facing value stream from the shared service value stream.

An important point in the context of IT products is that all software development is unique, as the same code is not written many times; compiled code is run many times. It is unique product development. It's not been done before in that context and with those people. It is emergent, not predictable, including the installation of third-party software that has never been installed in that same context with the same integrations, data migrations, data, surrounding systems, processes, or people before.

3: Long-Lived Teams

Long-lived value streams, with long-lived products, should have long-lived, small (ideally less than ten people), multidisciplinary teams in order to optimize for **BVSSH** in the context of change. Teams pass through Bruce Tuckman's description of group development: they can form, storm, norm, and perform[8] and then, crucially, they stay together. This is unlike project teams who disband and reform on every project, are time-sliced over multiple projects and have a role-based tribal identity.

The long-lived teams come to understand the unarticulated needs of the customer. Their multidisciplinary nature means they have the skills needed to deliver end-to-end value, and it brings together "the business" and "IT" into "our business." People have "T"-shaped skills—they are generalizing specialists with a deep expertise in a skill set and an expectation and willingness to help out broadly on the team where help is needed. The so-called Spotify Model uses the term "Squad." Personally I prefer the term "team." In practice, teams name themselves, which adds individuality, identity, and social bonding. Again, as with value streams, there is no right or wrong on naming. Use what works for your organization. And be prepared to inspect and adapt.

The multidisciplinary nature of the teams minimizes handoffs and dependencies on other teams, enabling flow, fast feedback, learning, and agility. Teams should be "full stack" and able to independently deliver and deploy value. The teams are ideally genuinely multidisciplinary with, depending on context, participation from business, UX, marketing, IT, operations, compliance, and so on.

A smaller number of specialist teams may be needed to provide more niche skills for the product teams. For example, a team in Financial Services might need low latency network specialists for on-exchange electronic trading. (The engagement model with compliance is covered in depth in Chapter 6.)

PATTERN **5.1**

Small Centers of Excellence (also known as Practices or Guilds) help to foster the craft, a concept especially common in Europe with medieval craft guilds, such as the guild of blacksmiths, goldsmiths, leatherworkers, bakers, and so on. The CoEs are there to advance the state of the craft; to share innovation, learning, and understanding; to determine principles and standards; and to clear impediments and provide assistance in a servant leadership capacity. A rising tide raises all boats. An organization might have an Architecture CoE, a Quality CoE, or an Engineering CoE, for example. The CoEs are small and are not a centralization of people. The vast majority of people are primarily aligned to their value stream's small, long-lived teams. Their tribal identity is to the business value stream. People are secondarily aligned to a CoE, relevant to the vertical part of their "T"-shaped skill set, their specialism.

In order to share learnings across value streams and across the small CoEs, the addition of voluntary, open invite, Communities of Practice (CoPs) is incredibly useful and powerful. Here, the Law of Mobility applies: attendance is voluntary. They are Darwinian in that they are not artificially kept alive. They are run as a regular meetup to help share learning, understanding, social proof, and to innovate across teams.

For example, in a past role I founded and provided servant leadership for thirty-seven CoPs, some of them dormant and all of them voluntary. To illustrate the benefits in addition to the CoEs, in the Technical Architecture CoP more than half of the attendees were not architecture specialists. This was a great sign of interest and shared learning more broadly.

The alignment of long-lived teams to long-lived value streams creates a tribal identity focused on the value stream. Instead of people thinking "I'm Business" or "I'm IT," team members think "we are Mortgages" or "we are Luxury Bags" or "we are Helicopter Engines." The nature of the organization has people working *together* daily toward shared business outcomes.

Roles

Within long-lived teams, an approach that has been observed to work well in the context of unique product development is to have a *triumvirate* of roles (that is, three key roles) within each team, and importantly at every level in the nested value streams. This is in addition to team members with "T"-shaped skill sets and some specialist niche skills. These three roles are a Value Outcome Lead, Team Outcome Lead, and Architecture Outcome Lead.

PATTERN **5.1**

The **Value Outcome Lead** focuses on the *what*, with an outward view toward the customer, the stakeholders, and the economic, human, and environmental outcomes. Value should not come at any cost to society or the planet. The focus is on the **Value** of **Better Value Sooner Safer Happier**. This role is also known as a "Product Owner"; however, that term is from the early 1990s, and in the spirit of inspect and adapt, I feel that times have moved on. The role is more about value and outcomes; therefore, I believe that there is a better identity. Language, as well as the system of work, is important. The title encourages self-identity around value and outcomes, instead of, as we saw in Antipattern 5.3, an often-observed, product-myopic focus of "I *OWN* this damn product," forgetting to speak to the customer, and a self-fulfilling prophecy of backlog replenishment. The value outcomes themselves are articulated as quarterly outcome hypotheses with leading and lagging metrics, as I will explore further in Pattern 5.2. While everyone is "our business," the person in this role is the primary business person. Business architecture and Product Management, building the right thing, have a primary accountability with this role.

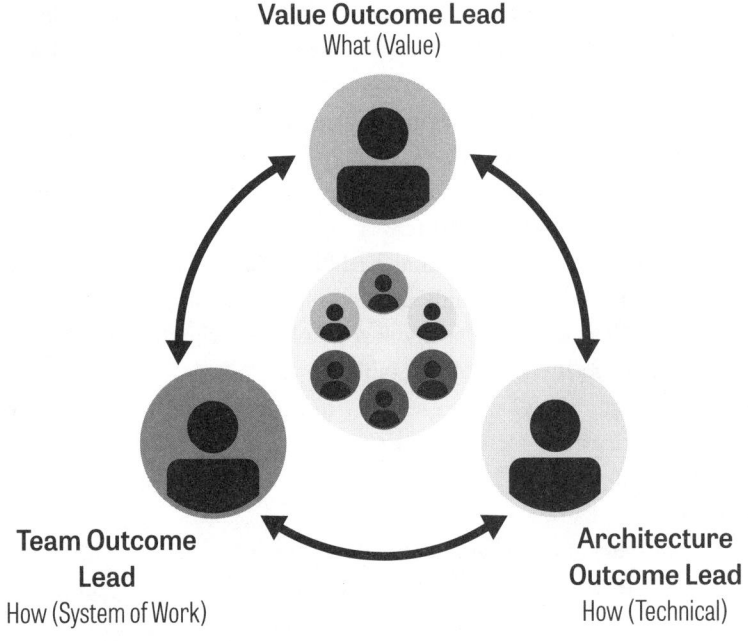

Value Outcome Lead
What (Value)

Team Outcome Lead
How (System of Work)

Architecture Outcome Lead
How (Technical)

Figure 5.6: Three Key Roles

PATTERN **5.1**

The **Team Outcome Lead** focuses on the *how* for the system of work and people. The Team Outcome Lead supports and facilitates the team to have a positive trend on **Better Sooner Safer Happier** and hence having a positive impact on **Value**. This is a servant leader role with an inward focus, helping the team—or teams of teams—deliver successfully. The person in this role helps alleviate impediments, builds continuous improvement as a daily habit practiced by everyone, and acts as a coach to the team. If a team has adopted Scrum, this role may be called "Scrum Master." However, in large organizations, as I covered earlier, applying one size fits all is not optimizing for outcomes. Some teams may take an iteration-based approach (such as Scrum), while others take a flow-based WIP-limit approach. Some teams, due to history and culture, may even take an approach of smaller waterfalls initially. The title "Team Outcome Lead" emphasizes that this role exists to support the team or team-of-teams to have a positive trend on **Better Value Sooner Safer Happier**.

The Architecture Outcome Lead focuses on the how of the technical implementation within the organization's broader technical architecture and engineering principles and standards. (Credit to Scott Ambler for inspiration on this role in an agile team.[9]) The behavioral stance in this role should be one of coaching and servant leadership. At the team level, this does not need to be a dedicated role; it can be a hat that someone wears, typically a senior developer in an IT product development context. At the value stream level, in the team-of-teams, this is a full-time role. This is "transparent box" or "solution" architecture, with a focus on how the long-lived IT products are developed within the horizontal value stream scope of the role. (It's called "transparent box" as the architect specialist has the lid off and is responsible for and working on the internals.) For example, does the software comply with architecture principles, such as high cohesion and low coupling? Is the software well written or is it a spaghetti mess of unmaintainable code? How resilient is it? Can it handle failure gracefully? (We cover this topic in more depth in Chapter 7.) The vast majority of architects (who are hands-on "player-coaches") sit in the horizontal, value-stream aligned teams and at every nested value stream level, as illustrated in Figure 5.7.

A small percentage of architects are Enterprise Architects (EA). This is "opaque box" architecture looking vertically over the horizontal value streams, providing governance, standards, support, and guidance to the majority of architects in the value stream aligned teams. This small group is the Architecture Center of Excellence (or Practice or Guild), as described earlier. (In my experience, a pattern that works is one Architecture CoE per business unit and an overall central Architecture CoE.)

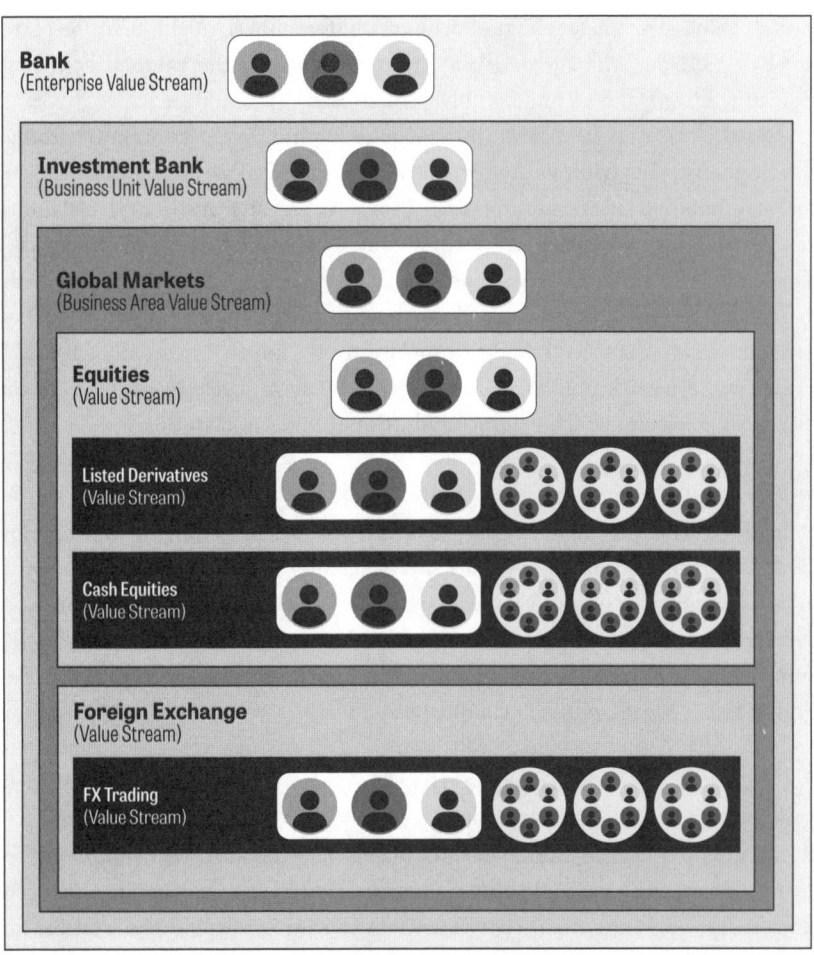

Figure 5.7: Triumvirate of Roles at Every Level

Here, the EA focus is on organization-wide architectural principles, minimal viable standards, how the opaque boxes talk to each other across value streams, and architectural agility and resilience. The term "opaque box" is used, as the lid is not lifted to look inside. The focus is on the architectural patterns between the opaque boxes. For example, the Architecture CoE focuses on how inevitable failure can be handled gracefully. EA have mandatory risk stories and are part of the Safety team construct. More on this in Chapter 6.

This triumvirate of roles (VOL, TOL, AOL) exists at every level in the nested value streams (see Figure 5.7): at the team level; at the team-of-teams level (e.g., Order Management); at the next level up the value stream (e.g., Equity Trading); and so on (e.g., Investment Bank ➙ Bank).

At the business unit level in the Age of Digital, in the context of product development, this triumvirate becomes the CEO (what), CIO (how, the system of work, change delivery), and CTO (how, technically, resilience, scalability, the "ilities"). For a large firm, it's the Group CEO, Group CIO, and Group CTO. These three roles need to work as one at every level. Are we working on the right outcome hypotheses (value)? Are we improving the system of work (better sooner safer happier)? And technically are we improving on all of **BVSSH**? For example, just shipping new features and incurring technical debt is an "our business" decision, which will incur additional costs at a later date.

Coaching

Behavior in these roles should be servant-leader and coaching in stance. "How can I help?" rather than "Do what I say." Coaching is something that leaders at all levels should be doing. This, in particular, is a clear responsibility for those referred to as the pressurized middle. As Mike Rother notes in the Toyota Improvement Kata and Coaching Kata, it is highly recommended that this be a daily habit.[10] More on this in Chapter 6.

4: Funding the Flow of Value

Funding is aligned to value streams. Each value stream, with its long-lived teams, is capacity funded. *Funding is a constraint on which to maximize value.* For knowledge work, the main cost in a value stream is people. This cost cannot (and should not) be easily turned on or off. This is the pivot from project to product, from output to outcomes.

Projects are not funded. Value streams are. Outcome hypotheses are pulled to maximize "valuetivity." If value tails off or doesn't materialize, there is the ability to pivot early and quickly by pulling the next business outcome hypothesis from the prioritized backlog. As we will see in the next section, business outcomes have value measures (i.e., business case) built in. Typically there is a lightweight governance check done by a reinvented PMO (more on this later) to

PATTERN 5.1

ensure that business outcomes are well written and have lineage to the annual portfolio outcomes at the next level up, ensuring strategic alignment. This optimizes for the fast flow of value and enables the lowest cost of learning. Bets can be changed mid-race with a high degree of insight.

No longer is it a case of trying to predict the future at the point of knowing the least, having to prematurely solutionize, in order to ask for one-off project funding (might as well add the kitchen sink as it'll be years before we see value, and let's add a 30% buffer as we'll know we'll be knocked back and we know we can't predict the future). This leads to trying to treat emergent unique knowledge work as deterministic. It leads to predicting the solution, the tasks, and the benefit, and then focuses on the plan rather than on outcomes. It's like placing a fixed bet with the least insight while having your eyes closed during the race, when alternatively you could change your bet multiple times mid-race.

The funding of long-lived teams on long-lived products in long-lived value streams is a constraint on which to maximize value with fast feedback. This results in seeking out the "golden bricks" in order to maximize the value curve. When the value curve starts flattening (or if it doesn't rise at all), "cut the tail" (i.e., stop work on that business outcome and pull the next one) and repeat (see Figure 5.8). The golden bricks are articulated as quarterly outcome hypotheses, the bets that are considered to be the most valuable for customers, colleagues, citizens, and the climate. There is frequent deployment of value to customers in order to get as close to real-time feedback on value, on the bets, as possible, which enables agility.

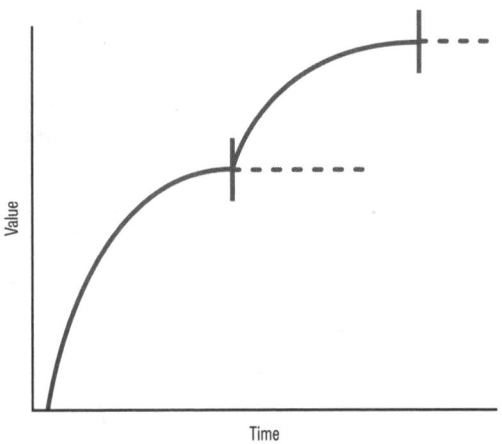

Figure 5.8: Maximize the Value Curve; Cut the Tail

If there is a macro economic change or opportunity, and there is a desire to change the funding across value streams, the pattern is to change funding no more frequently than quarterly, unless it's an unexpected event. Redirecting funding for knowledge-based work means moving people from one value stream to another. It takes time for people to get up to speed on a new domain, and it will slow velocity for those already in that value stream. It also assumes that technical skills are fungible.

What I've observed is that rather than people moving, any new demand changes the prioritization of the work that the teams are doing. For example, more time on regulatory outcomes and less time on discretionary outcomes. In rare cases, such as Brexit, I've experienced increasing spend on change overall, which was then distributed across value streams where the work needed to be done, with a small, central team sitting in a group center value stream with oversight of the nested outcomes.

As the multidisciplinary teams take more of a "you build it, you run it" approach, with "continuous everything," the coming together of "major works" and "minor works" into one prioritized backlog and a thinner IT Ops catch-and-dispatch layer, it's no longer about some people only doing capitalizable work (CapEx, building an asset) and others only doing operational work (OpEx). People are increasingly doing a little of both. One way to capture this where time sheeting is in place, is to have two line items: "CapEx" and "OpEx." The approximate balance is entered: for example, three days building an asset and two days to support the asset. Over time, in a stable environment with steady-state "continuous everything," it may be possible to determine the empirical balance for teams or teams-of-teams, such as 80/20, and use that balance without time sheeting.

To recap, in order to optimize for the fast flow of safe value end-to-end, have multidisciplinary long-lived teams on long-lived products on long-lived value streams.

Optimizing for the fast flow of safe value is critical. The most important factors for investing in product development according to Douglas Hubbard, author of *How to Measure Anything*, is first whether a product or feature will be used at all and second how quickly it will be used.[11] These are more important factors than all other data including cost. If it's not used, it's binary; the investment has been wasted. Therefore, it is important to optimize for time to value, even if it's a sliver of value. Another way to think about it is the Cost of Delay, the value not realized, due to a long time to market. How soon can you sustainably and repeatedly get an innovative idea from concept to customer?

Case Study: U.S. Bank's Transformation Journey ■

U.S. Bank, with over 18 million customers, 70,000 employees, and a history dating back to 1863, recognized the need to improve ways of working in the face of several new challenges: Fintech encroachment into its traditional markets, changes in customer demographics and a surging customer desire to embrace digital channels. Werner Loots, leading on ways of working, explains:

Starting in late 2017, three key business focus areas were identified and teams assembled to tackle the opportunities with more agile ways of working. One of the priorities was aimed at dramatically improving the small business lending process. At the time, a loan required a great deal of effort on the customer's part—trips to the branch, providing more than 120 fields of data, and taking eleven days on average to complete. The bold vision was to be able to complete a loan digitally in under fifteen minutes, from time of application to funds in the customer's account, with a primary desired outcome of increased customer satisfaction and secondarily an increased efficiency of business as usual.

The first order of business, in January 2018, was to assemble a cross-functional team from all areas of the organization (Business, IT, Compliance, Risk, Legal, Design, etc.), with a Product Owner, Scrum Master, and an Agile Coach. The context was not trivial, since the team was going to have to navigate twenty-one different IT systems to accomplish their business outcome.

Everyone agreed to a set of core working principles. Customer obsession anchored those principles and was accompanied by empowerment, co-location, dedicated people, time-boxed phases, and a focus on outcomes. The idea of being dedicated and face-to-face was new to everyone, and sitting without cube/office walls was new and a bit frightening to many.

With the guidance of an experienced agile coach, the team conducted an agile mindset kickoff, then jumped into a design sprint to create a story map and build personas. U.S. Bank traditionally did a lot of research/analytics up front, and bringing customers in routinely for design sessions and co-creation/feedback was not a well-developed muscle. The team quickly realized they were embarking on something completely different than they had ever done before. Business leaders and techs sitting together, designers leading the discussion with customers, risk being involved early versus after decisions had been made, and

PATTERN **5.1**

everyone having a voice throughout—there was early proof that this was indeed different.

Customers coming into the office became a normal thing. They were up on the floor every two weeks. On off weeks, business bankers were brought in. I can't emphasize enough how powerful it was to have co-creation and feedback sessions happening every week and how it redefined what being customer obsessed really meant.

While working with small business owners, our business team was very focused on the speed of getting the money in their account. Fast was the drumbeat until at one point the customers said, "You keep saying the word 'fast,' but I can't get to fast if it isn't easy." That was a big pivot point for the team, and it allowed them to change their focus to intuitiveness and simplicity. Speed became a benefit of those two focus areas. Customers also guided the team to another significant shift—while getting the money in their account quickly was nice, the most important thing was to get the decision quickly. Once the decision was made, they could start planning while the money made its way into the account.

The team delivered the first digital small business loan in under fifteen minutes within four months of starting as a new team and with a new way of working. In a follow-up presentation, the IT leader was asked how long this would have taken in the "old" way of working. He said "At least two years." When the business leader was asked the same question, he said, "Oh, that's easy, we would have never delivered it. We would have scrapped it before we got to done." As a long-lived, high-performing team, the team is together today, tackling one new business outcome opportunity after another. They can't imagine going back to the old way of working in their physical job role and process-based silos.

PATTERN 5.2

Outcome Hypotheses

In the Age of Digital, with a new means of production, emergent work, and rapidly changing terrain milestones, a deterministic mindset and big, up-front, detailed solutioning is an antipattern. The environment changes and the two-ton milestones become millstones holding you back. It is not an optimal metaphor for emergent work.

In order to optimize for the fast flow of safe value in the context of product development, there needs to be a shift from deterministic, fixed, big, up-front designed solutions to outcome hypotheses with experimentation. There is a pivot from output to outcomes, from following a fixed plan to maximizing value. We'll break this pattern down into five sections: emergence, nested outcomes, business outcome, rolling roadmaps and fixed dates, and moving from PMO to VET.

1: Emergence

As discussed, product development is emergent; the work is unique and unknowable. Organizations are complex adaptive systems; they are not predictable. We can't accurately predict what people want, how to build it, the obstacles we'll come across on the way, or how external market forces will change over time. We cannot travel in time and see the full path ahead.

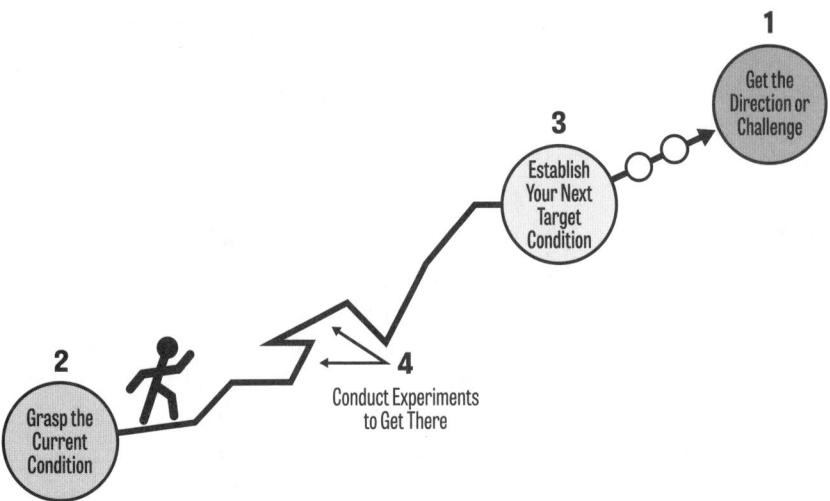

Figure 5.9: The Journey from A to B
Adapted from Rother, *Toyota Kata*.

That said, there should be a clear North Star, a clear mission. This is the "Think Big" in Think Big, Start Small, Learn Fast. It provides high alignment and clear direction for empowered teams. For this type of knowledge work, that North Star should not be articulated as a fixed solution or output by a date with predetermined tasks. There is no knowable straight path from A (current condition) to B (desired outcome). The bigger the distance from A to B, the less knowable the journey; it is beyond our knowledge threshold.

Instead, as per Figure 5.9, the reality is that the journey is an unknown wiggly line from A to B, overcoming obstacles and surfacing unknown-unknowns along the way in order to maximize the business outcome (the "**V**" in **BVSSH**). A business outcome is an articulation of business value in the form of a *hypothesis*, a bet, as no one knows for sure what's going to happen. Data insights can be gathered; however, the only way to know is by doing. The system of work should be optimized for fast feedback, safe-to-fail experiments, and psychological safety in order to test the business outcome hypothesis early and often.

For unique work, we want to maximize variability and, in some cases, might choose to run multiple experiments to maximize learning and de-risk delivery. For example, getting feedback on multiple prototypes from a small set of representative customers. This approach allows us to change our bet while the race is running or even to decide, based on fast feedback, that we don't want to bet on this race at all—we want to pivot to another race entirely.

2: Nested Outcomes

Nested outcomes provide strategy alignment and built-in benefits realization. Instead of milestones, there are nested hypotheses and feedback loops at multiple cadences: daily, weekly, monthly, quarterly, yearly, and multi-year. The key focus is not on a predetermined deadline but on *quarterly outcome hypotheses*: business outcomes (OKRs). Outcomes have dates (more on fixed dates later); that said, the focus is not on the activity, it's on the *outcomes*, how the leading and lagging value measures (the key results of OKRs) are doing in terms of putting potential value into the hands of customers early and often. It's about maximizing the value curve, as per Figure 5.8. It's not a conversation about being halfway through User Acceptance Testing; rather, the conversation is along the lines of "Have we achieved a Net Promoter Score of +50 from customers on the pilot of the new service?"

A quarterly time period is neither too close nor too far. It is just beyond our knowledge threshold and yet not too far away. Each quarterly business outcome consists of monthly "experiments" to test the outcome hypothesis.

These are in turn broken down into "stories" (the smallest item of potential value), which are daily and optionally turned into hourly "tasks." Ideally, there are frequent (daily or weekly) releases of value into the hands of customers. It should not be a case of the first deployment being at the end of the quarter. This provides the fast feedback loop that enables learning, insight, and the ability to pivot. It provides fast feedback on multi-year strategic intent, enabling increased business agility.

Traversing up the outcome hierarchy, the quarterly business outcomes are grouped into a handful of annual *portfolio epics* for each value stream. These portfolio epics are also articulated as outcome hypotheses. This is starting to get into strategy alignment. The annual portfolio epics are grouped into multi-year *portfolio objectives*, which are business-unit level strategic items. For larger firms, these are contained within a handful of *strategic objectives*, a top-level, strategic intent that spans the organization.

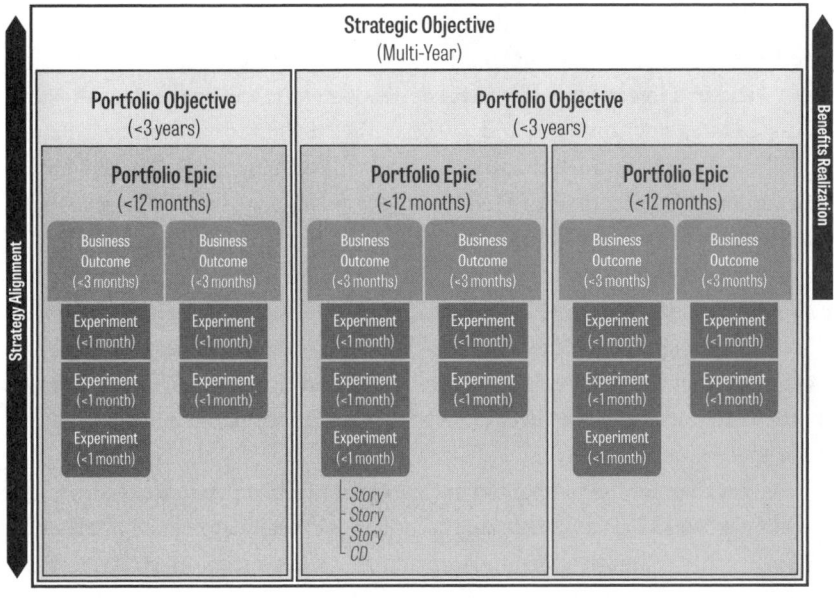

Figure 5.10: Strategic Objectives

This structure of nested outcomes (as seen in Figure 5.10) is incredibly powerful. With tooling to visualize and make the nested outcomes transparent, someone can be working on a two-hour task and click up the outcome hierarchy

PATTERN **5.2**

to see how their task aligns to one of a few strategic outcomes. Those closest to the work are best placed to innovate to achieve the desired outcomes. There is strategic alignment.

The nested outcomes are represented vertically, from multi-year strategic intent down to daily stories. Each level should have its own physical and virtual board to visualize the system of work, with WIP limited at all levels in the outcome hierarchy so it's pull-based at every level and optimized for flow. There should be no more than three to five business outcomes in progress concurrently, and be wary of having too many leading and lagging measures to avoid metrics hell. Less is more.

For example, a multi-year portfolio objective at a credit card provider might have a desired outcome be to be in the top three for market share in order to reverse a decline, to increase profitability, to enable continued gainful employment, and to help more people with responsible financial liquidity. An in-year portfolio epic might be a hypothesis to launch a partner card with an airline. A quarterly business outcome might be a hypothesis that issuing one partner credit card to at least one customer and using it for at least one transaction end-to-end in a live environment will de-risk delivery, will enable fast learning in a safe-to-fail environment, and will result in a delighted customer with more air miles or cash back, such that there is likely to be an increase in market share. The approach is outcome-oriented, in business language (not IT jargon), with real feedback, learning, and the ability to pivot in response to measures.

As can be seen from the example, the outcomes do not *cascade*; they are not passed down, unchanged, in a traditional order-giver, order-taker manner. Instead they *align*. They have a shorter time horizon and are mapped to a lower level in the nested value stream, as we will see in the next pattern. They are written and "owned" by the people, in particular the triumvirate at each level in the nested value streams.

Rather than eat the elephant in one go, aim for elephant carpaccio. Aim to get the thinnest vertical slice of real value in the hands of real customers. This de-risks delivery and maximizes learning, providing fast feedback on strategic bets.

3: A Business Outcome

Articulating unique product development work as *outcome hypotheses* creates a clear expectation that it *is* a hypothesis and may be invalid, and that there are unknown-unknowns that will only be uncovered when the work takes place. It also creates a clear expectation that experimentation is required, with people empowered to use their own brains to discover how to best achieve or even if the outcome hypothesis is worth continuing trying to achieve.

You can write an outcome hypothesis like this:

Due to <this insight>
We believe that <this bet>
Will result in <this outcome>.
We will know that we're on the right track when <leading behavioral value measures (such as the number of call center calls or app downloads) and lagging behavioral value measures (such as volume sold, market share, customer NPS or carbon emissions)>:
> Measure 1: quantified and measurable leading or lagging indicator
> Measure 2:
> Measure 3:

For example:

Due to *declining customer NPS scores and a reduction in new account applications*
We believe *that enabling online applications in under five minutes, instead of requiring in-store new account applications*
Will result in *happier customers.*
We will know we're on the right track when:
> Measure 1 (leading): Customer focus group NPS score is +50 or higher within this quarter.
> Measure 2 (leading): Mobile app downloads increase by 5% this quarter versus the previous quarter.
> Measure 3 (lagging): Online new account applications increase by 5% each month for six months.
> Measure 4 (lagging): Customer NPS increases by ten points by the end of Q3.

Importantly, to reiterate, this is a hypothesis, and the value is articulated with the leading and lagging measures that are relevant to customer behavior, citizens, and/or the climate so that it's not at any cost to society or the planet. The business outcome measures are not the completion of testing or the imple-

PATTERN 5.2

mentation of an IT system, which is a means to an end. They are the definition of business value.

Over time, as mastery increases, consider writing business outcomes as moonshots, as stretch goals. Traditional objective setting tends to lead to mediocrity, to under promising in order to over achieve the goal. Instead, achieving 60% to 70% of a business outcome is doing well. Achieving 100% regularly is not thinking big enough. To quote Google's "Ten Things That We Know to Be True": "We set ourselves goals that we know we can't reach yet, because we know that by stretching to meet them we can get further than we expected."[12]

To aid the writing of OKRs a canvas could be used, such as the example in Figure 5.11. This business outcome canvas contains strategic alignment to the twelve-month portfolio epic outcome and contains a view of the customer personas along with the potential customer problem, opportunity, and benefits; the outcome hypothesis; the leading indicators; and finally the lagging impact measures.

Business Outcome (OKR <3m)
North Star: <Portfolio Epic (<12m)>

Problem Statement, Insight, Drivers	Outcome Hypotheses (Data > Insight > Belief > Bet)
Due to <*this insight, feedback, or belief*> e.g., • **Due to** <fewer branch visits>	**We believe** <*this bet*> **Will result in** <*this outcome*> **We'll know we're successful when** . . . <*see below*> e.g., • **We believe that** <piloting online ID verification) • **Will result in** <delighting our customers and maintaining our market share> • **We'll know we're successful when** . . .

Who Is the Customer/ Customer Segment?

What are the behavioral changes, patterns you expect?

e.g., • Young people
• Young professionals
• First-time home buyers
• Rural unbanked
• Busy, always online, or remote from a branch
• Ease, security, insights into my spending

Key Results Leading Indicators Tree	Key Results Impact Metrics
Indicators of performance that may predict future success e.g., • 5k visits to the microsites • 1k downloads of the app • 100 online applications • 90% right first time • Takes less than 5 minutes	**Value based lagging measures of positive impact to customers, colleagues, society, and business.** e.g., • Improved NPS from 25 to 35 • Enabled 2% more first-time home buyers to own property • Increased mkt share from 55% to 65% • Increased diversity by 5% • Increased flow efficiency by 5% • Customer complaints down 8%

Figure 5.11: Business Outcome Canvas

4: Rolling Roadmaps and Fixed Dates

To recap, quarterly business outcomes inherently have a date built in, which is once a quarter. Within that, there are monthly experiments and daily stories, ideally with daily releases of value into the hands of a customer. Here the focus shifts from a date in a plan to the ongoing outcomes and what to do next. Planning is done continuously at the multiple nested cadences. To quote Eisenhower, "Planning is indispensable and plans are useless."

A successful pattern here is a twelve-month rolling roadmap of quarterly outcomes, working backward from the multi-year and annual outcomes. The near term is more fine-grained; outcomes for future quarters are more coarse-grained, as the further into the future the more uncertainty there is. When the British government was planning its GOV.UK online services development, a curved glass partition was intentionally picked to roadmap their work. The future was always out of view; they literally couldn't see what was around the corner.[13]

Don't artificially lock in a fixed date if the date doesn't need to be fixed. Don't back yourself into a corner unnecessarily. I've seen many cases of leaders insisting on fixed output with fixed dates, limiting the organization's ability to respond to learning and thus limiting value. Instead focus on early and often value and learning.

There are cases that need fixed scope and fixed dates, such as mandatory regulatory change like GDPR and the Dodd-Frank legislation after the 2008 credit crisis. I have implemented many mandatory regulatory initiatives. All were fixed date and fixed scope and had a high *cost of delay*, in that business activities would need to stop if they were not implemented. All of them were implemented with agile principles, and all were completed early. I have found that even if you think the scope is fixed, legislation is usually written in a way that enables near-infinite ways to implement it. Also, even if you think the rule-writing is fixed, it may not be.

For example, around 2012, within a value stream I was leading we implemented the riskiest, least-understood bit of the UK version of the US Dodd-Frank financial legislation. The team tested it with production data and picked up insights within the first month that showed that the legislation would have put the UK at a competitive disadvantage to other financial centers globally. We took those insights to the Bank of England, which updated the legislation.

A waterfall approach with learning and value delayed to the very end, with a focus on the milestone and the output instead of the outcome, is far too risky

PATTERN **5.2**

an approach for fixed-date, fixed-scope work where the implications are stopping business activities. Everything should be done to remove ignorance, to minimize time to learning, and with the most time to act that learning.

5: From PMO to VET

The role of the traditional Project Management Office (PMO) changes when we pivot from temporal projects to long-lived products with long-lived teams on long-lived value streams and a rolling cadence of outcome hypotheses, pivoting to a servant leader team with a focus on the **Value** part of **Better Value Sooner Safer Happier**. To make the change in identity clear, it can help to rename the team. For example, it could become the "Value Enablement Team" (VET) or "Value Realization Office" (VRO).

The VET coaches and supports teams in articulating and measuring business outcomes, assists with prioritization of business outcomes in the backlog, coaches the limiting of WIP at every level, ensures alignment in the nested outcome hierarchy, helps to gather the leading and lagging measure data, and provides consolidated data for a monthly cadence with value stream teams to inspect and adapt on quarterly and annual outcome hypotheses. For more on this topic, please see my DevOps Enterprise Summit 2018 presentation "The PMO is Dead, Long Live the PMO."[14]

On the topic of prioritization of business outcomes, it is worth looking at Cost of Delay (COD). That is, the cost of inaction. It is a forecast view of the difference in benefit (revenue increase or cost avoidance) over time by starting now versus starting at a later date. For example, being late to market for a new product might mean that there is little market share left, hence either do it now or don't bother. The cost of delay will be high.

Regulatory work also has a high cost of delay, if there is a need to cease business operations or receive a large fine if the regulations are not implemented. A recommended prioritization approach is cost of delay divided by duration (CD3), which is a form of weighted shortest job first (WSJF) prioritization. That is, it's the highest forecast cost of delay per unit of time and a strong indicator for prioritization.

In Pattern 5.2, swapping fixed milestones on fixed solutions for outcome hypotheses changes the question. Instead of constantly asking, "Is it done yet?" we ask, "What value have we observed, what have we learned, and what steps shall we take next to get closer to the desired outcomes?"

PATTERN 5.3

Intelligent Flow

To avoid falling into the antipattern of headless chickens, there is a need to focus on alignment. Bring together the horizontal nested value streams with the vertical nested outcome hierarchy. Each long-lived team on a long-lived value stream with long-lived products has clear business outcome hypotheses to work on.

With clear nested North Star outcomes, *alignment* is high. Because the multidisciplinary teams are empowered to use their own brains and possess the mastery needed to decide (within guardrails) how to best achieve those nested North Stars, there's also high *autonomy*. Strategy is aligned from the top of the house all the way to a daily story, and the quarterly business outcome metrics articulate the realization of value.

When the horizontal value streams are aligned with the vertical outcome hierarchy (see Figure 5.12), the multidisciplinary teams have a shared purpose and a shared mission to experiment on. This starts to remove the behavioral boundary that divides "business" and "IT" in traditionally organized companies. Instead of a relationship of order-giver/order-taker, people work together to achieve and experiment toward desired outcomes. The "tribe" becomes the value stream rather than the job role.

No longer are agile teams headless chickens disconnected from strategic intent. They stop being self-fulfilling feature factories. Instead, there is clear strategic alignment with two-way strategy—down and back up—and rapid testing and learning.

As a rule of thumb, while quarterly business outcomes may need to straddle multiple value streams, monthly experiments do not. A monthly experiment, as a slice of a business outcome, is aligned to only one value stream with fast learning via daily stories being frequently deployed into production. Functionality in other value streams can be emulated with service virtualization. Ideally, over time, dependencies are eliminated so that each value stream can deploy changes independently and on its own cadence. This could be through re-architecting, shared code ownership, internal open source, feature toggling, and so on. Depending on context, there may be integration testing needed across value streams. Preferably this is little and often, even daily.

To summarize, in the context of product development, this pattern of bringing together people working in long-lived, multidisciplinary teams ("our

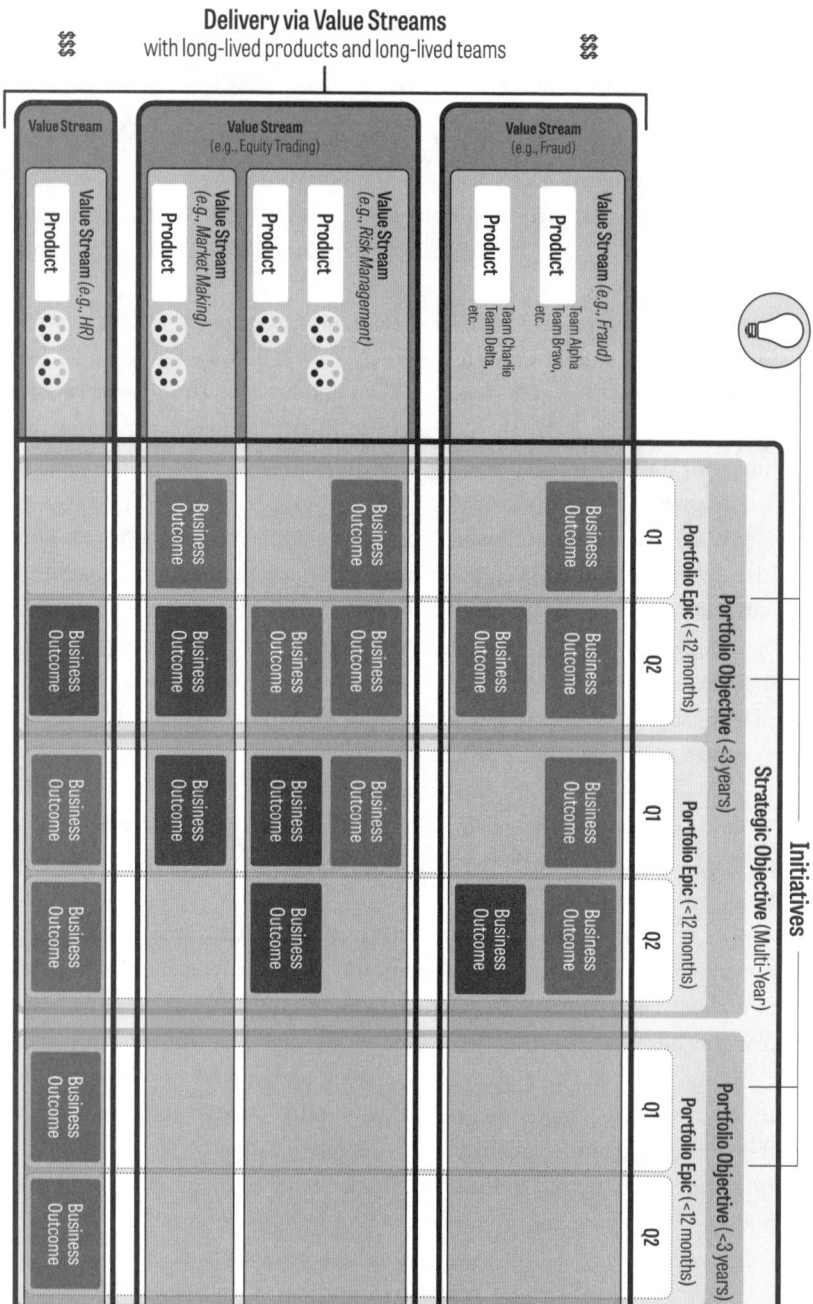

Figure 5.12: Intelligent Flow

PATTERN **5.3**

business") on long-lived products and on long-lived value streams, horizontally, with clear nested outcome hypotheses at multiple cadences, vertically, is optimizing for **Better Value Sooner Safer Happier**.

PATTERN 5.4

Stop Starting, Start Finishing

The pattern to the antipattern of Start Starting, in order to optimize for the fast flow of value and the ability to pivot, is to *Stop Starting and Start Finishing*! The fewer cars you have on the road, the faster they can travel. Reducing WIP, as we saw in Little's Law in Antipattern 5.4, reduces lead time. Time to value and time to learning is sooner. This de-risks delivery, enables pivoting, and maximizes value.

In addition, limiting WIP by pulling work rather than pushing it is an "enabling constraint" to improving agility. It is a forcing function. When a work item is blocked due to an impediment, the team does not pull another work item. This shines a light on the impediment to flow. It leads to swarming, as team members, irrespective of specialism, help to alleviate the impediment. In a pull-based system a new item cannot be pulled until one is done or stopped, leading to the potential for some people to sit idle. Instead of sitting idle, effort goes into alleviating the bottlenecks, permanently improving flow, reducing time to value and learning. The system of work is improved.

Reducing WIP is like watching a tidal river go down; it reveals the rocks and shopping trolleys, the impediments to flow efficiency that were always there but invisible beneath the surface of the previous long lead times and high levels of concurrent work.

Visualize

In order to stop starting and start finishing, information on the system of work should be radiated. Ideally, there is a virtual and physical enterprise visibility room (EVR) where the system of work is made visible. Very quickly, too much WIP and blocked items become apparent. The previously invisible system of work for knowledge work becomes clear. Often, it's the first time people have actually seen the full end-to-end value stream. There may be multiple Kanban boards representing multiple cadences (multi-year, year, quarter, month, daily) along with cumulative flow diagrams, which are an incredibly insightful visualization to show cycle times, lead time, and throughput over

PATTERN 5.4

time. Very quickly you can get an idea of the health of the system of work and areas that benefit from attention.

Pull, Don't Push

Part of the "Stop Starting, Start Finishing" pattern is ensuring that an outcome, experiment, or story is not pulled until another is finished. This results in the system of work becoming a pull-based system rather than a push-based system at every level. Every system of work has a natural capacity, a natural throughput, determined by the bottleneck. By making the system of work pull-based, the work flows at the capacity of the system, revealing the capacity itself which can then be improved.

Case Study: How Moonpig Iterated toward Business Agility

Moonpig is a digital business selling personalized greeting cards, flowers, and gifts in the UK, US, and Australia. In 2007 the company was responsible for 90% of the online greeting card market in the UK. Amanda Colpoys, previously Head of Agile Coaching, explains:

In 2015, Moonpig's newly appointed Product Director, Jane Honey, observed a lack of alignment between the Product & Tech (P&T) function and the rest of the organization. P&T were treated broadly as a service delivery capability, and digital product initiatives tended to be tactical, reactive, and opinion driven. She successfully argued for a more strategic approach aligned around outcomes. She proposed cross-functional teams be formed around key missions.

We called them "honeycombs." They brought together groups of product, tech, and business partners aligned around strategic outcomes with autonomy as to how those outcomes were achieved, within guardrails. Thanks to the honeycomb model, the concept of cross-functional working became mainstream beyond P&T, and the benefits of high alignment to a mission, high autonomy, and high collaboration were recognized.

While honeycombs dramatically improved digital product development, the same was not necessarily true elsewhere in the organization. A lack of shared objectives and a gated waterfall process caused frustration. P&T had an experiment-based approach; however, much of the rest of the organization was still output-focused and heavily "big bang" oriented. Digital product experiments had short delivery

PATTERN 5.4

cycles, while an email for a campaign could take up to four months to produce. Engagement rates were also substantially different—in some cases engagement within P&T was double that of other areas in the organization.

In short, P&T was delivering better value, sooner, and happier. This led Managing Director James Sturrock to consider a broader adoption of agile ways of working across the wider organization. This led to the next iteration of the honeycomb model. Having proved the benefits within our local context, next all customer-facing functions were reorganized into multidisciplinary teams aligned around missions. These we decided to call "squads." A principle of squads was that each must strive to have a clear mission that can be achieved independently of another squad, as this enables agility. Over time, this means breaking dependencies. Squads bring together the skills needed to achieve the goal and have the autonomy to decide how to achieve that goal within minimal guardrails.

The functions themselves continued with their role shifting to one of skills communities, fostering excellence within a particular discipline. Functions no longer had objectives or dictated what would be done, but instead focused on how it would be done to a high standard. We continued to iterate the squad structure as part of continuous improvement. We also invested in preparing people for change from the start—the message we communicated was one of *evolution*. We expected to be continuously iterating as we identified impediments and as our business evolved and scaled.

While the journey is never done, the change was overwhelmingly positive. Outcomes were met and frequently exceeded. Squads delivered healthy incremental revenue growth, creating more value. Delivery times improved dramatically—from months to days—meaning that value was delivered sooner. Happiness, engagement, also improved. In employee surveys people reported that they felt better aligned and significantly more enabled to meet their outcomes successfully. Evolving our operating model allowed Moonpig to continue to grow and retain its dominance in the online card and gifting space.

I've learned that there is no one size fits all. You have to optimize to your context. It's a long journey, and it is rewarding and hugely beneficial. Start small and start now.

PATTERN 5.4

≋ Summary ≋

Value Sooner

Flow isn't something you can usually see. Few, in fact, can see the end-to-end flow in their own value streams any more than they can see the end of the line in their local coffee shop on a Monday morning. So people tend to create a local optimization within their role-based silos, not improving end-to-end flow.

Don't focus on local optimizations but on the end-to-end flow of long-lived products developed by long-lived teams working in long-lived value streams. Milestones, fixed and immovable, should be replaced by outcome hypotheses with regular cadences that optimize for Value Sooner, where some of those outcomes may have fixed dates. However, the path from A to B is still a hypothesis that needs to be tested early and often. Alignment turns headless chickens into flocks with aim and direction, while "Stop Starting, Start Finishing" ensures the flow of work is sustainable and brings value sooner.

These patterns might not get your name spelled right in your local coffee shop, but you can expect them to produce a better flow of value in an emergent domain.

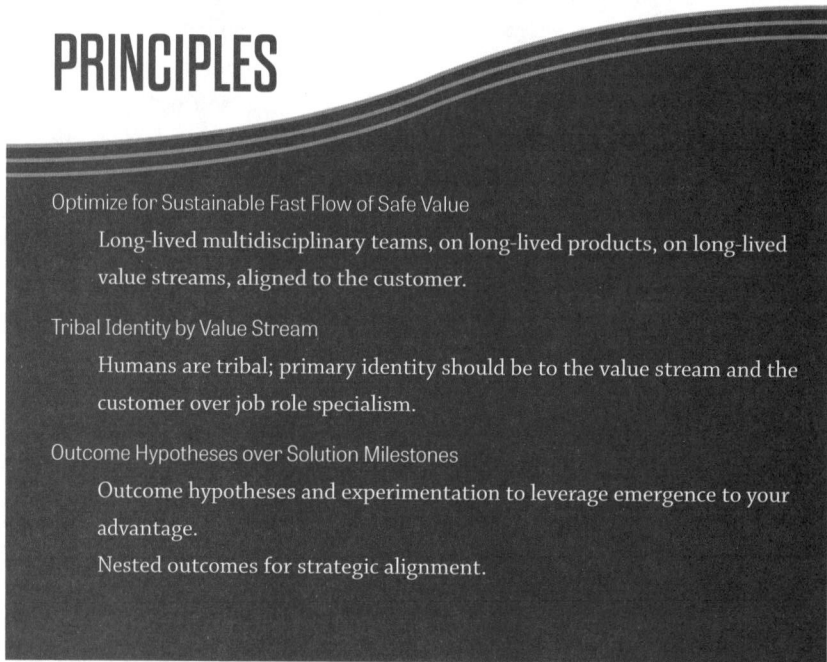

PRINCIPLES

Optimize for Sustainable Fast Flow of Safe Value
> Long-lived multidisciplinary teams, on long-lived products, on long-lived value streams, aligned to the customer.

Tribal Identity by Value Stream
> Humans are tribal; primary identity should be to the value stream and the customer over job role specialism.

Outcome Hypotheses over Solution Milestones
> Outcome hypotheses and experimentation to leverage emergence to your advantage.
>
> Nested outcomes for strategic alignment.

Stop Starting, Start Finishing

Limit WIP at every level.

The fewer cars on the road, the faster they go.

Pull Work, Don't Push It

Pulling work shines a light on the natural capacity of the system and impediments to flow.

Impediments are not in the path, impediments ARE the path.

6 BUILD THE THING RIGHT;
INTELLIGENT CONTROL

It was a June afternoon in Copenhagen in 2017 when employees at A.P. Moller Maersk, a global shipping and services conglomerate, started to notice unusual behavior on their laptops. Computers turned themselves off, then rebooted. Some flashed warnings in black and red lettering: "repairing file system." Others declared "Oops, your important files are encrypted" as though they had been hacked individually and demanded $300 worth of bitcoin to decrypt them.

None of the 88,000 global employees could have imagined what was about to follow. As row after row of PC screens across the organization turned black, the IT organization slowly woke up to what was happening. The entire global enterprise, with a revenue of $35 billion and spanning 130 countries, was about to be stopped dead in the water. Over the next two hours, laptops, workstations, and the entire telephone and operational control systems were brought to a halt. Impacting organizations around the world, the 20% of global trade handled by Maersk was plunged into the dark as dockside control equipment and container manifests were erased. Maersk had been infected by the NotPetya virus.

Maersk Chairman Jim Hagemann Snabe subsequently explained to a cyber panel at the World Economic Forum in Davos that Maersk had not been targeted and was simply "collateral damage" from what was probably a state-sponsored cyberattack on Ukraine.[1] While the international community continues to debate how to maintain security in the commons of cyberspace, enterprises cannot afford to wait. The rebuild effort at Maersk was immense. Damage was estimated at $300 million or 3% of the total global $10 billion of damages caused by NotPetya.[2] The worm had spread indiscriminately, affecting companies, utilities, bus stations, gas stations, airports, banks, and hospitals around the world.[3]

Snabe observed that Maersk was able to maintain 80% of its volume during its crisis only through human resilience and operationally falling back to paper systems, supported by customers. However, looking ahead to a digital future where "more and more and more is automated" and ships themselves are becoming autonomous, Maersk's chairman worried that "this wake-up call [came] only just in time" as human resilience will be inadequate to offset our increasing digital dependency.[4] Strong cybersecurity is now a competitive advantage with implications for individuals, economies, and society that stretch far beyond localized short-term losses.

This chapter addresses the **Safer** aspect of **Better Value Sooner Safer Happier**. It reveals the antipatterns and patterns that are associated with risk management and controls as product development accelerates and agility improves. The chapter is focused on operational risk categories (as described by the Basel II framework), including types of risk such as fraud, workplace, business practice, legal, regulatory, continuity, and resilience, and execution risk such as enterprise architecture and data governance. Specifically not covered in this chapter is strategic risk—the risk of a loss arising from a poor strategic business decision—which was addressed in Chapter 5.

One CIO I met recently said at our initial meeting: "You agilists are all very well, but when you hit the risk and control gates you all slow down; show me the agilist who is prepared to own the risk and control agenda." It was the perfect cue. In a previous role I led the redrafting of the standard for risk and control for product development. This required a reimagining of intent and a fundamentally leaner approach than a traditional, one-size-fits-all, multi-gated and multi-artifacted approval model. Partnering with teams from across the risk and compliance community this approach has now been adopted successfully by tens of thousands of staff. Risk outcomes and control innovation have been improved and continuous delivery has been enabled. By applying agile and lean concepts (in manners congruent with the other patterns in this book), it has proved possible to introduce the kind of behavioral nudges that lead to improvement in **Better Value Sooner Safer Happier**.

Every company relies on trust with customers. Data leaks are the new oil spills. Data leaks may be software-enabled, but the issues are not software issues; they are commercial imperatives. The frequency and magnitude of data breaches has been growing steadily over the past decade, as has the size of the fines issued by regulators. In the European Union, the GDPR regulation of 2018 increased the potential size of fines issued to up to 4% of annual turnover.[5] In the month of July 2019 alone, it was reported that British Airways faced a record fine of £183 million for a data breach; Marriot was fined £99 million for a data issue inherited through a corporate acquisition; Equifax agreed to pay $700 million to settle a data breach dating to 2017; and following a data breach at Capital One, Chairman Richard Fairbanks issued a public apology: "I am deeply sorry for what has happened,"[6] he said. Is your organization on the brink of an oil spill?

No one is exempt from cyberattacks, especially with the emergence of state actors. The WannaCry ransomware virus infected 230,000 computer systems across 150 countries and cost an approximate $4 billion in global financial losses. It caused widespread disruption in Britain's National Health Service hospitals, leading to the cancellation of 20,000 medical appointments.[7] That came only months before the release of the NotPetya virus that caused $10 billion of losses worldwide and nearly destroyed major multinational organizations such as Maersk and Merck, a pharmaceutical giant.[8]

As the cadence of product delivery goes up, operational risk mitigations need to be built in, not inspected in later. To quote W. Edwards Deming, "If applied to making toast, [this] would be expressed as 'you burn and I'll scrape.'"[9] Anything can be done badly; new ways of working done well offer considerably more control than traditional approaches, with small and frequent changes made to loosely coupled technical components as described in Pattern 7.3, leading to complexity that fits in your head, and de-risking delivery.

ANTIPATTERN 6.1

Lack of Safety within Safety

The governance, risk, and compliance community (which I refer to as "Safety") understands that it's on the front line. It has to design systems and processes that will defend the organization against attacks that may have the resources of a state behind them, while balancing this need with the existential commercial pressure to allow freedom to innovate.

This antipattern refers to a lack of safety within Safety domains in large, traditional organizations.

People in Safety domains are in a difficult position. A statement regularly heard from Safety practitioners is "There is too much work and not enough people. We simply cannot review everything that everybody does." However, the leadership antipatterns described in detail in Chapter 4 remain all too real, a fact of life in the traditional enterprise. Whether its Aberfan in 1966, whistleblowing at Boeing, or at an organization closer to you—if people are fearful for their jobs and afraid to speak up, the result will be an unhealthy silence. Problems will be covered up. Lack of psychological safety in Safety domains prevents organizational learning and increases operational risk.

Sidney Dekker, who runs the Safety Science Innovation Lab at Griffith University in Brisbane, Australia, coined the term "Safety Differently" in 2012. While speaking at the DevOps Enterprise Summit in 2017, Dekker reported:

. . . that there is this inverse correlation between the number of incidents reported, the honesty, the willingness to take on that conversation about what might go wrong, and things actually going wrong. The airlines that report more incidents, have a lower passenger mortality risk. If you're going to fly back from San Francisco, find the airline that's got the most incidents, and you get to the other end alive, okay. That's the lesson.[9]

Dekker's example above is based on statistics published by MIT based on 100,000 departures for major air carriers over five years, and he reports that the same inverse correlation between number of incidents reported and serious events actually occurring has been replicated across multiple industries, including construction and retail.[10]

A regulatory compliance colleague in a large organization recently described their own experience of working in a traditional Safety domain:

When there is a failure, this leads to a witch hunt for who to blame. It's never the process. Even though the ISO9000 series says we should treat exceptions as learning events, this doesn't happen. The consequence is that every person in Risk has to have their own personal protection, so that every question presented to them is offset to someone else—a subject matter expert, a manager, another department. This risk offset happens at every stage so everyone is covered. I have seen the most extraordinarily long approval trails that are utterly meaningless. There is no collective objective, and no incentive to say yes to innovation.[11]

Ron Westrum's bureaucratic and pathological culture models are apparent within many organizations today. The meaning of compliance is "the act of obeying a rule" (Cambridge Dictionary); however, rule makers need to beware of creating an agentic state (see Chapter 1). While adherence to external legal and regulatory rules is of course essential, these are too easily augmented by internal Safety domains within the organization using overly narrow interpretations, leading to a myriad of one-size-fits-all internal process and control guidelines. Whilst the additions are well intended, without psychological safety the challenge and feedback loops to create genuine organizational learning and improvement will not occur.

Case Study: Deepwater Horizon: Blame Culture, Safety ■ Culture, and Control

On April 20, 2010, the Deepwater Horizon oil rig exploded, killing eleven workers, injuring seventeen others, and spilling almost five million barrels of oil into the Gulf of Mexico. It was the largest accidental oil spill in history.[12]

Soon after, President Barack Obama appointed a seven-member commission to investigate the disaster and recommend reforms. In its final report, published in January 2011, the commission concluded that the well blowout could be traced to a series of mistakes by numerous parties "that reveal such systemic failures in risk management that they place in doubt the safety culture of the entire industry."[13] The report went on to say, "Absent major crises, and given the remarkable financial returns available from deepwater reserves, the business culture succumbed to a false sense of security. The Deepwater Horizon disaster exhibits the costs of a culture of complacency," and "that complacency affected government as well as industry."[14]

Although the owner of the oil platform, Transocean, was reported to be responsible for three out of every four incidents in the Gulf of Mexico that triggered federal safety investigations between 2008 and 2010, the company had still been honored by regulators for its safety record.[15] On the day the rig exploded, company executives were on the platform celebrating seven years without a serious accident.[16]

In fact, in a survey of the Transocean crew conducted just weeks before the accident hints at the organizational roots of the problem. The research involving hundreds of employees onshore and on four rigs, including Deepwater Horizon, found a culture of fear. Only about half the workforce said they thought they could report actions that could raise risk without fear of reprisal.[17] Some workers would submit false data, distorting the perception of safety on the rig.[18]

Complex systems fail in complex ways. "It is critical that companies maintain a pervasive top-down safety culture that rewards employees and contractors who take action when there is a safety concern even though such action costs the company time and money."[19]

There was an absence of an adequate safety culture and a fear of reprisal, with tragic consequences.

In a group with psychological safety, trust enables motivated individuals to share their ideas and hold honest and open debates. Terms like "witch hunt" and "personal protection" convey the opposite, suggesting a climate in which individuals may be reluctant to speak up to improve their team or their organization because they fear they will be harshly judged or ignored. As Amy Edmondson, a professor of leadership at Harvard Business School, has put it: "Psychological safety is . . . a climate in which people are comfortable expressing and being themselves."[20]

Organizations reporting the fewest incidents showed the most devastating accidents. The Deepwater Horizon story is one such example: the drilling rig had a "perfect" safety record for several years until the day of the explosion. When honesty and openness are replaced by fear of reprisal, bad news is buried, problems are hidden, risks go unreported or misreported, and learning doesn't happen, resulting in the worse possible outcome.

ANTIPATTERN 6.2

Role-Based Safety Silos

Large traditional organizations often structure themselves by role specialization: Sales, Marketing, IT, etc. The Safety domain's functions are no exception: Information Security, Fraud, Anti-Money Laundering, Data Privacy, IT Operations, Data Governance, and Enterprise Architecture are organized as role-based silos. The tribal identity is by job role. As we discussed in Chapter 2: "Policies, Standards, and Controls expand with the number of control staff employed," and also is related to Antipattern 4.1: Local Optimization.

Organizing by functional, role-based silos is an impediment to the fast flow of safe value, and in the Safety context generates a number of specific issues.

1: Subject Matter Experts (SMEs) Rule Their Niches… and Only Their Niches

As a Chief Controls Office employee recently described the issue:

> There are many regulations and they can conflict with each other—for example credit risk reporting versus data privacy. This leads to conflict between different risk communities. Issues get escalated but there can be a lack of transparency: resolution tends to be slow, closed door,

without process traceability, a smokescreen. This creates stress for risk teams. I do think behaviors can reach extreme personal conflict and shift us from partners to combative.[21]

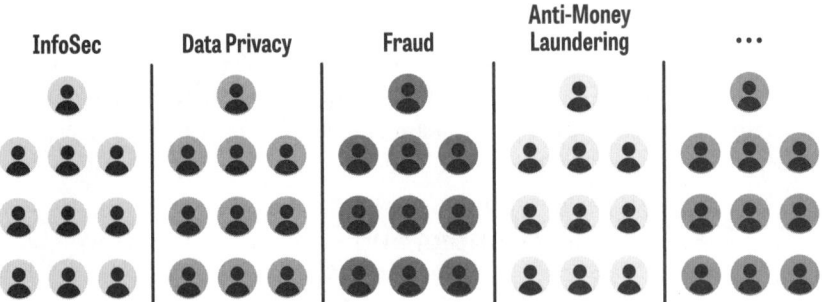

| **InfoSec** | **Data Privacy** | **Fraud** | **Anti-Money Laundering** | **...** |

Figure 6.1: "There Is No Collective Objective"

Specialization by job role is a fractal pattern with subdivision within a role family. There are specialists for data privacy, for data lineage, for data models. There are many architectural disciplines. People in value streams who seek help need to know how to navigate the full range of Safety silos, to find the right individuals, to collect disparate, ambiguous, and sometimes conflicting guidance. This can be challenging, and it's usually a different person each time who may lack of understanding of context.

From the perspective of the Safety SME (subject matter expert), there are a myriad of incoming support requests from across all value streams, which leads to being time-sliced across many initiatives. These Safety silos are not in a position to prioritize across the value stream and thus individuals must fall back on personal intuition, a way of working that is not optimized for the fast flow of safe value.

At one organization in order to quantify the compliance overhead of passing work between many role-based silos, a simple "Hello World" application was created. This type of application is the simplest possible, just one line of code that displays "Hello World" onto your screen. We measured the time for the traditional governance across processes and all Safety silos to approve production deployment of the application. A project manager was needed to complete the extensive risk review forms required by each Safety domain and (acting as expeditor) to chase the standard workflow processes operated by each Safety domain. In all, it took three months, one month of which was pure project management effort. There was absolutely no connection between the effort required and the risk represented. When scaled across perhaps 1,000 concurrent projects with multiple releases, this is a level of waste that traditional enterprises can ill afford.

Following this process leads to control and no speed. The alternative is teams choose to not follow the process, which is "fragile"—speed without control. The problem is widespread and amusingly represented in a YouTube animation published in 2011 by Carson and Julian Holmes, titled "I Want to Run an Agile Project."[22]

2: Hierarchies Control and Limit Organization

Safety silos are physically and organizationally separated from Value Streams. The justification for this arrangement is typically based on segregation of duties (SoD) requirements that emerge from a number of different regulatory bodies. For example, the UK Financial Conduct Authority states that:

> The effective segregation of duties . . . helps to ensure that no one individual is completely free to commit a firm's assets or incur liabilities on its behalf. Segregation can also help to ensure that a firm's governing body receives objective and accurate information on financial performance, the risks faced by the firm, and the adequacy of its systems.[23]

The intent here is laudable—to improve transparency and accuracy and to reduce the potential impact of internal bad actors. There are many ways to achieve the intent. In this case the working is not *prescriptive* about organizational design, location of staff, and how work needs to flow. Segregation of duties can occur *within* multidisciplinary teams, for example.

When a Safety silo has different objectives to the customer-aligned value streams of the organization, when the "what" and the "how" of the Safety team's work is directed from within the silo, combative behavior can arise in the silo, creating tension between those whose goal is risk avoidance versus those whose goal is delivering value within a context-sensitive risk appetite. Although "constructive tension" can be a force for creative progress, this needs to be appropriately placed, as described by Matthew Dixon and Brent Adamson in *The Challenger Sale*.[24] In a low-trust environment or one without shared objectives, tension can rapidly become "destructive" or "unproductive."

The accelerating frequency and volume of change from the value streams leads to Safety SMEs slicing their time thinner and thinner as concurrent with Work in Progress (WIP) rises. As we know, this is not good for flow. As context switching slows down the flow, so the control-related work queues build up—with associated handoffs, multitasking, long lead times, and stress.

3: Template and Process Zombies Eat Brain Work

In order to manage requests into a support department, it is common to establish an engagement process. The familiar premise being "please fill in your details here and wait to be served." Each department devises a process that works for them, perhaps using Excel and email. This will include IT Operations, Enterprise Architecture, Data Governance, IT Security, Data Privacy, Fraud, and other Safety silos. As time passes, well-intentioned improvements are made in response to risk events, regulatory changes, and organizational changes, with questions added and the process slightly extended. Now consider the consumer of this process attempting to navigate multiple Safety silos. There are different engagement processes and timelines published on a myriad of intranet portals and with multiple different ways of engaging, each with their own jargon requiring an enterprise archeological dig each time. Or alternatively, the process can be navigated by contacting Mary, who has been hired by the value stream specifically to deal with all the bureaucracy. A crazy but common solution to a poor system of work is to hire your way through it, adding to cost, handoffs, queuing, and not improving on **BVSSH** outcomes, leaving the impediments firmly in place.

Each Safety silo builds growing work queues where misunderstanding of process can become a reason to be sent to the back of the queue at any time. "Governance gridlock" is a familiar refrain from project and product teams alike.

I was working for an organization that wished to improve their experience of client onboarding. The Head of Client Onboarding commented:

> Some of our clients have to bring in a sack trolley to carry all the documents we require them to sign, created by different teams within the legal department, the compliance department, the product department, the marketing department. Every department has its priorities and the

situation has evolved over a long period of time. However, the data is mostly duplicative; it is not productive for anyone and the experience is no longer sustainable for our clients.[25]

This approach is not optimized for Safer or Happier outcomes.

The same behaviors are true with governance of the internal product development process, and it is no longer acceptable for organizations that wish to survive and thrive in the Age of Digital. As Safety silos specialize and subdivide over time, their engagement templates spawn and duplicate requirements from other silos. This is all lowest common denominator, forcing all teams to answer questions for the riskiest, lowest-risk-appetite scenario with the added benefit of 100+ years of audit points. Entropy, as discussed in Chapter 7, and constant attention to simplification is as important in the context of governance process as it is for technical excellence. In one organization, governance templates required nearly 800 questions for each release! Clearly, not something suited to continuous delivery.

4: Control Tools Optimize Reporting... and Duplicate Actions

In order to improve the effectiveness of Safety domains, staff in the silo establish tracking systems to manage workflow, capture exceptions, and assign responsibilities. These workflows may include expediting for priority items with risk dispensations and policing of remediation plans. Safety domain tooling is designed to optimize reporting and workflow for the Safety domain itself and not to optimize for the fast flow of safe value end to end. Worse, the separation of control tooling (containing risks, control actions, and remediation plans) from the day-to-day tooling used by value streams to manage other types of work requires records to be translated and duplicated from multiple other locations and formats. This lack of transparency and connection with value stream systems of work is a source of friction and risks creating gaps, both in understanding and action.

5: Information Bubbles

The flow of information in an environment with many dependencies and handoffs across silos can be a challenge. People are less inclined to share across boundaries. Language, terminology, and tools may differ, with no explicit attempt to optimize learning in line with the customer and value streams. Safety areas such as information security, data privacy, and fraud can be represented as a Venn diagram of overlapping concerns. We have observed substantial duplications between different Safety standards, with inconsistent controls, mitigations, risk appetites, and update frequencies. Each domain response will seem entirely rational within the domain, but taken together from the perspective of the value stream, the information bubbles create confusion and delay. Often there is no one with oversight across all the Safety silos with a focus on the end-to-end system of work. This duplicative and siloed approach is a significant impediment to **BVSSH**. (This will be discussed in more detail in Chapter 8.)

ANTIPATTERN 6.3

Fixed Mindset to Risk

Risk and compliance are different disciplines and can pull against each other. Risk management involves assessing realistic threats and discovering suitable responses, whereas a compliance discipline involves adherence to predetermined requirements. The two relate in that having discovered a risk mitigation that works in one context, there may be the temptation to keep applying the same mitigation in other contexts. However, measuring compliance to historical check lists as a proxy for risk management is a fixed mindset to risk. Safety SMEs often note that a "compliance mentality to risk" can increase risk levels. As one advised me: "As the pace of change increases, the past is an unreliable indicator of what future risks could happen."[26]

As per the Cynefin framework introduced in Chapter 0, in the "Clear" and "Complicated" quadrants work is predictable and a fixed, standard approach to mitigating risks may be appropriate. However, "Complex" quadrant product development is unique. It has not been done before, either at all or in context, and there are unknown-unknowns. There is a need to focus on outcome hypotheses and fast feedback in order to maintain optionality and pivot to achieve desired outcomes—the same applies when understanding and mitigating risks. I find the Cynefin framework useful when working with Risk colleagues, allowing us to have the conversations about what learning is needed to get greater confidence about the risk and to allow us to stay safe and secure.

ANTIPATTERN 6.3

1: Conflicts Grow between Risk and Compliance

A Security SME recently explained to me that "maintaining security means studying your adversaries, pre-empting their next move. Security leaders have a well of academic competence, but they don't think like hackers. An [internal] compliance mentality is dangerous if it means we lose sight of why we are doing this."[27]

The mismatch can become apparent in traditional organizations attempting to adopt public cloud infrastructure. The context of running applications in a public network environment using compute on demand is quite different to a traditional "walled garden" corporate network where perimeter security is paramount and physical servers may persist for many years. The new context raises new risks and requires new mitigations.

During a recent public cloud implementation, one organization attempted to apply existing risk management standards to the cloud environment. The standards had been established over many years, with one, for example, intended to mitigate operational risk such as licensing, malware, and patching. To remain compliant with this standard, the cloud platform team was constrained to use a one-size-fits-all approach for provisioning servers on the cloud. This ignored the fact that servers on the cloud might last for minutes (not years) leading to different mitigations. Although the old standard *could* be implemented on cloud servers, it added out-of-context complexity and actually *increased* the attack surface available to bad actors! The compliance approach resulted in a service that, while compliant with legacy standards, failed to deliver most of the benefits of public cloud and was riskier. Clearly this is not optimizing for Safer.

2: One Size Really Doesn't Fit All

One reading of the above example could be to conclude that a one-time update is needed to the standard to support "cloud," but that isn't as straightforward as it sounds. An increasingly wide range of cloud enabled innovative services (FinTech, LegalTech, RegTech, etc.) offer high-value capabilities, and the underlying software, hardware, and service offerings vary greatly. Amazon Web Services alone releases hundreds of new and changed services every year, including custom-modified hardware and software with constantly upgraded security features. A key question is whether a resource-constrained, centralized control organization can learn fast enough on its own about emerging technologies and emerging threats to pre-emptively identify and document detailed control solutions appropriate for all contexts and scenarios.

Rather than attempting highly prescriptive control standards with maximum possible compliance, organizations need to explore alternative options. The challenge is fundamental and arises due to a fixed mindset to risk. At one large, traditional, global organization, Safety domains operated around 300 policy and standards documents. A total of 5,000 pages of documentation, some highly prescriptive. As the pace of technology change accelerates, this prescriptive approach becomes counterproductive. Context varies widely across an enterprise. The risks inherent in a payment platform, for example, are fundamentally different to those in a staff cafeteria menu application. The traditional approach leads to ever-growing compliance functions but does not always lead to improvement in outcomes, a problem found across organizations and disciplines.

In a 2015 lecture, Sidney Dekker noted that Australia had seen a growth in compliance workers from 5% in the early 2000s to almost 10% of the total national workforce by 2015. During the same period, he said, industrial fatality rates were largely unchanged.[28] Throwing more bureaucracy at the problem does not necessarily reduce risk, and it can be counterproductive.

3: Big, Up-Front Risk Planning

Big, up-front risk planning occurs when a project or large, complex initiative is estimated and predictively planned early, at a time when the least information is known. Early stage risk assessment aims to identify all the project risks in advance in order to predict the cost and effort of mitigating activities, and it is rarely revisited during the lifecycle.

The behavior of fixing risk requirements at the start of a project is usually correlated with late lifecycle testing and sign-offs by Safety SMEs, typically just before a large, big-bang release goes live. Due to the long duration of traditional projects, the control environment is likely to have changed since initiation, with new controls to implement. For this to be discovered late in the lifecycle leads to unplanned work, delays, and the dreaded red RAG status. Or the project might have to seek dispensation and incur a control debt, increasing risk. Bureaucracy, organizational barriers, and big-batch, sequential, left-to-right delivery planning get in the way of building in control rather than inspecting it in at the end. This is not optimizing for fast flow of safe value.

ANTIPATTERN 6.3

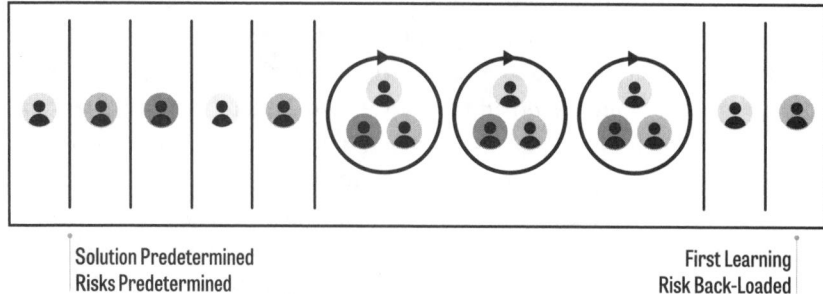

Solution Predetermined
Risks Predetermined

First Learning
Risk Back-Loaded

Figure 6.2: Big, Up-Front Risk Planning

Organizations need a more incremental and iterative approach to discussing risk. In fairness, this is noted by traditional project management frameworks such as Prince2; however, all too often, as the *Prince2 Handbook* admits, "it seems to get forgotten about as soon as the project starts up."[29]

An organization is a complex adaptive system with many internal moving parts. Those parts change simultaneously in response to external opportunities, pressures, and threats. In a complex adaptive system, risk will also change in ways that cannot be predicted. Companies should take note of the warning of Adam Banks, Maersk's CIO: "You need a perimeter to keep criminals out and you need to think wider. You need to assume that the increasing number of state-level attacks are all going to be 100% successful."[30]

From Antipatterns to Patterns

Escape the Zombies!

This chapter began with a real-life horror story: a cyber viral attack that spread rapidly around the world, compromising vital systems and causing billions of dollars' worth of damage. Its rapid spread highlights the escalating importance of a safe product development process to enable organizational survival in a world in which software viruses like NotPetya and WannaCry circulate. The antipatterns described show the reality of life inside many large, traditional enterprises today as they attempt to do the right thing: reduce risk, apply controls, and increase compliance. But in any organization as complex as today's large companies, actions have unforeseen and sometimes negative consequences. All too frequently, management culture uses fear as a motivational tool, and this in itself may increase risk levels. It's worth frequently asking "What are we optimizing for?" Is it one-size-fits-all compliance to the lowest common denominator? Control without speed? Is it local optimization within role-based Safety silos leading to duplication? Or is it optimizing for the fast flow of safe value in a context-sensitive manner, enabling both speed AND control?

The patterns below offer a transformational approach. When adopted with the right culture and mindset, they allow safe delivery at speed with higher levels of human engagement and increased "value-tivity." They enable the delivery of **Better Value Sooner Safer Happier**.

PATTERN 6.1

Safety within Safety

Given that data leaks are the new oil spills, leading to a lack of trust with customers and growing fines, and given that cybercrime is relentlessly increasing and that an accelerating pace of technological change presents new risks, there has to be safety within Safety. Psychological safety (see also Chapter 4) is critical in the context of the Safety functions of an organization. In Antipattern 6.1 we looked at the implications of a lack of safety within Safety.

An organization needs to stay ahead of external bad actors. Maintaining a high level of staff engagement in the workplace and creating conditions for rapid learning (see also Chapter 8) are safety critical considerations. Amy Edmondson and Zhike Lei have noted that psychological safety is "the underpinning" for organizational learning and that individuals who experience greater psychological safety are more likely to speak up at work.[31] A Gallup poll found that only three in ten people agreed "very strongly" that their opinions count at work. Gallup calculated that if this level could be increased to six in ten, then a 40% reduction in safety incidents would arise.[32]

Edmonson, a leader in the study of psychological safety, has described psychological safety's four dimensions as:[33]

1. **Attitude to risk and failure:** the degree to which it is permissible to make mistakes.
2. **Open conversation:** the degree to which sensitive and difficult topics can be discussed openly.

3. **Willingness to help:** the degree to which people are willing to help each other.
4. **Inclusivity and diversity:** the degree to which you can be yourself and welcomed.

Example of specific actions that can be used to improve psychological safety in a Safety context include:

- Conduct regular, whole-team debriefs, after-action reviews, pre-mortems, and *blameless* post-mortems on a regular cadence after successful events as wells as failures or near misses. Proven across industries, including the US military, these ceremonies have the specific goal of focusing on improving the system of work, not the worker.
- Consider "bad actor" use cases as well as customer journeys when designing solutions.
- Establish a partnership between Safety SMEs and product teams to create common goals and, where necessary, innovate new control patterns that meet control objectives.

In a 2017 presentation, Sidney Dekker describes a review of safety outcomes within a hospital. Investigations of root causes of failure included human errors, procedural violations, and miscalculations. However, investigations of successful outcomes identified exactly the same root causes of success: human errors, procedural violations, miscalculations. This led to the conclusion that "the difference between success and failure is not the absence of negatives; it is the presence of positives."[34] Specifically, the positives are:

- The ability to say "stop"—if there are people who say this is not a good idea, stop even in the face of acute production pressures.
- Past success not taken as a guarantee—in a dynamic, complex system, past success is not predictive of success today.
- Diversity of opinion, dissent—is there a willingness to accommodate dissent when people say "I disagree"?
- Keeping the discussion on risk alive—is there an ability to listen to that diversity of opinion?

All four of these factors are behavioral. Not one is process or tooling.

It is hard to overstate just how important a culture of psychological safety is in sustaining a safe environment. It manifests as transparency, openness, support, learning, a focus on how the system of work can be improved, shared ownership, and a safety-first culture. Psychological safety is critical in order to deliver **Better Value Sooner Safer Happier**.

PATTERN 6.2

Organize Safety by Value Stream

Organizing by role-based silos in the context of product development inhibits the delivery of **Better Value Sooner Safer Happier**. The corresponding pattern is to optimize for the fast flow of safe value by applying the same approach for Safety functions as with product development teams as outlined in Chapter 5.

1: The Cross-Functional, Long-Lived Safety Team

Applying a pattern for unique product development that has been known about since the 1970s in firms such as Xerox and Honda in Japan, Safety SMEs deploy as long-lived, cross-functional Safety teams aligned to a long-lived value stream.[35] This optimizes for the fast flow of safe value aligned to the customer. The tribal identity shifts from being a role-based silo, time-sliced on many contexts and projects, to a multidisciplinary, long-lived Safety team aligned to value and customers. This enables Safety teams to go through forming, storming, norming, and performing, and then stay together with a common tribal identity aligned to the customer and aligned to the value stream product development teams.

Over time this enables the Safety team to deeply understand the value stream context and build an appreciation of the customer's unarticulated needs. There is considerably less context switching. Also, long-term relationships are built, with early-and-often risk conversations optimizing for the fast flow of safe value. Rather than risk management being an overlay to normal product development activities, the presence of a Safety team supports a continuous conversation that becomes part of the normal flow of work. Over time, we have observed a shift for Safety SMEs from 80% of time being reactive, to the opposite—80% of time being spent proactively, minimizing the amount of time being spent reacting and fire-fighting. Instead of being incentivized to say no, the Safety SME is now incentivized to lean in with the value stream to find a safe way to yes.

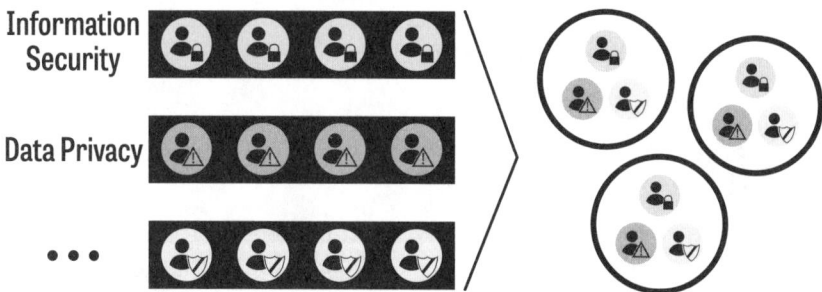

Figure 6.3: From Safety Silos to Cross-Functional, Long-Lived Safety Teams

A cross-functional Safety team (as seen in Figure 6.3) works because, once aligned to value, the Safety SMEs have more in common with each other than they might typically realize. Safety SMEs share the overhead of engaging with stakeholders to understand new business initiatives and to understand where risk is arising. They require business context and can learn from and help each other build this understanding. They need an understanding of the people, data, and technologies involved. They need to understand the business outcome hypotheses being worked on and the nature of the high cadence of product releases, which is the moment when risk typically materializes. Safety SMEs are a core part of the fabric of the value stream; they can achieve more together than they can individually as silo specialists. They can resolve duplication or inconsistency between control standards, eliminate the traditional gaps between niche SME specialisms, and be more productive.

2: Safety Teams Are Aligned to Value Streams

Organizing Safety teams by value stream (see Figure 6.4) creates clarity for colleagues in the value stream. Product teams now have consistent, long-term points of contact for all Safety matters. Relationships and trust can develop, optimized for the fast flow of safe value. Individual Safety SMEs in each Safety team represent their Safety domain to the value stream. If there are gaps in personal knowledge, the Safety SMEs can call in help from their colleagues

PATTERN **6.2**

elsewhere, learning and broadening their own knowledge in the process and across the Safety community and increasing the resilience of the organization by reducing key person SME dependencies. Information bubbles are no longer siloed by role-based specialism. This approach is equivalent to the "T"-shaped skills of the cross-functional product delivery teams.

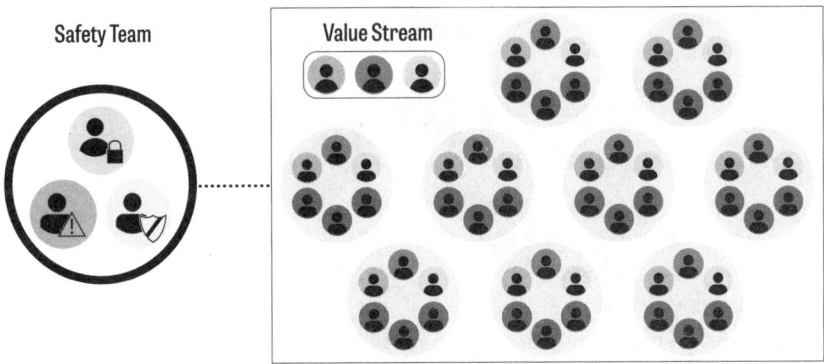

Figure 6.4: The Safety Team and Value Streams

Both the Safety team and the value stream to which it is aligned have the same goal: the fast flow of safe value to customers. There is a shared purpose via the value stream business outcomes (as seen in Chapter 5), and it fosters a shared accountability for safety. Partnering with value stream leadership allows Safety teams to educate and coach the organization to increase risk awareness. On "Risk Game Days," for example, functional work stops and staff focus on Safety improvements, demonstrating their results at the end.

By understanding the customer, business, and technical context of the value stream, the Safety team can communicate better with delivery staff, increase trust, and offer better risk advice sooner. With a "continuous everything" way of working, it is much simpler for Safety SMEs with the same value stream, tribe, and identity as the product development teams to identify risks and mitigations early and often, understanding the customer, the people, and the context deeply. There is a common North Star, there is high alignment, and people are incentivized with the same outcomes. It is optimizing for the fast flow of safe value.

■ **Case Study: A Big Data Research Project in a Large Financial Institution**

A research team member at a large organization contacted me with an innovative idea. "We want to use the new cloud platform to experiment with advanced analytics," he said.

This was a great opportunity to showcase the new cloud service recently built using Amazon Web Services. The team member advised, "The initial data set is 90TB plus about 1TB more per day. The vendor stores their data on AWS, so it should be easy."

After initial discussions with Safety colleagues, it became clear that this data import raised a malware risk. There were two allowed controls available to mitigate the risk:

1. **Secure download to on-premise servers**. Early analysis indicated this would take *several months* due to bandwidth limits and put the internet link under stress!

2. **Physical transfer via encrypted 1TB disks**. The recommended approach. However, the logistics of exchanging many physical disks between datacenters were substantial. A large number of people would be involved, with daily repeats. This was a manual and costly approach, not sustainable.

The cloud platform team proposed an alternative. A button on AWS allows the vendor to automatically dispatch a big data payload. "Why don't we just use that?" they asked. The Safety team explained that the service wasn't security-assessed and it would take six months to schedule and conduct such an investigation. The cloud team proposed a second idea. "Can we copy the data directly from the vendor's AWS account and run approved malware scans in the cloud?" The Safety team explained that the approved enterprise scanning solution was not available in the cloud. At this point, having exhausted all cost-effective options, the traditional next step would have been to halt. *#NoInnovation*.

However, in this institution a ways of working transformation had been underway. A Safety team had aligned with the cloud platform team for a substantial period. The Safety team wanted to enable business value as much as the cloud platform team. The group agreed to head to the whiteboard to explore options. By looking closely at the detailed business context, the file types in question, and detailed technical options, it proved possible to identify a lightweight, cloud-native malware-beating solution. A short time later, under the watchful eye of the Safety team, an enthusiastic pair of application developers linked to the research team were able to complete the AWS re-configuration. The data import routine was established. The research experiments got underway.

This outcome would not have been possible with a traditional, one-size-fits-all, centrally mandated controls model and fixed mindset. The institution was subsequently invited to present this work at the cloud vendor's industry conference, including the novel use of massively parallel technology. This was a career-enhancing moment for the team and an example of the virtuous circle that results from focusing on **Better Value Sooner Safer Happier** outcomes.

3: Safety Authorities

When functional, role-based silos pivot into Safety teams, Safety authorities are the communities of Safety SMEs who share a common discipline and are the accountable advisory experts within the organization (hence authority). They work as a unit to support knowledge management, career paths, and line management within the authority. This is a similar construct to the small, craft-aligned Centers of Excellence described in Chapter 5. The Safety SME role is matrixed. Their primary value stream alignment determines what business outcomes the Safety SMEs need to engage with at any one time; the Safety authority they are part of determines *how* their work is professionally undertaken, the business process of risk management and assurance. The Safety authority shares learning and innovation in their craft.

In this pattern, the Safety authority continues to be responsible for clearly articulating control objectives within the organization's policies and standards, as well as articulating risk appetite suited to context. Prescriptive, one-size-fits-all, lowest common denominator approaches should be avoided, allowing the value stream aligned Safety team to "right-size" the controls suited to context (minimal viable compliance [MVC]). The Safety authority collaborates to produce a common risk catalog that helps to create consistency of language and approach across the organization. The Safety SMEs in

PATTERN 6.2

the value-stream-aligned Safety teams are empowered to determine which controls apply in context.

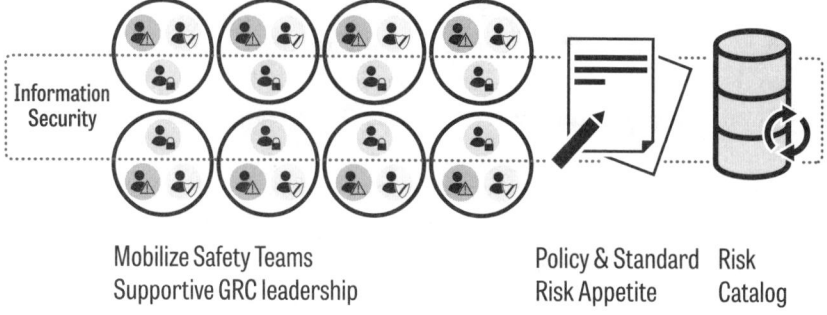

Mobilize Safety Teams
Supportive GRC leadership

Policy & Standard   Risk
Risk Appetite   Catalog

Figure 6.5: Safety Authorities

Safety authority leadership adopts a servant-leader stance, providing direction and standards, liaising with regulators and industry bodies, sharing innovation and insights from across value streams, and advancing the craft while supporting the value stream aligned Safety SMEs. This includes Safety SME recruitment, ensuring that specialist learning and development is available, and ensuring that there is a focus on continuous improvement and safe experimentation in order to deliver **Better Value Sooner Safer Happier**.

4: The Risk Catalog

One of the knowledge management tools of the Safety authority is the risk catalog. Safety SMEs in a Safety authority collaborate with the Ways of Working team to translate risk statements from policies and standards into risk story templates that explain the risks, the control objectives, the acceptance criteria, and the common risk mitigations. Risk story templates communicate the control objectives and controls of the organization to the product team. Where different policy areas overlap (e.g., Data Privacy, Information Security), the risk story translation process de-duplicates to provide a consistent and clear position. Risk stories are articulated using language that delivery teams can understand and evidence. The translation can be difficult for both sides to achieve, and in my experience it requires a significant investment of effort by Safety SMEs and the Ways of Working team. Inherent in this work is coaching to the Safety organization. Rather than highly prescriptive technical instructions—which risk becoming one size fits all, catering to the lowest common denominator—it is preferable to describe the intent and allow teams as much flexibility as possible to decide how to meet the acceptance criteria. This allows for greater innovation.

For example, for a malware risk story template it is better to use language that describes identification, isolation, and alerting principles that must be applied in all cases than to specify a technical solution such as "each server must contain a Symantec Antivirus agent that can be the basis for one recommended control pattern; however, it is automatically updated with new definitions every week." The latter statement is needlessly restrictive for some technical contexts (e.g., certain cloud technologies).

The risk catalog enables consistency in language and approach across Safety teams and helps product development teams to understand control patterns applied elsewhere. Risk story templates are timesavers to be customized to reflect the business and technical context for each specific use case.

Figure 6.6 is an example of a risk story that has been used to mitigate a risk associated with public cloud adoption.

PATTERN 6.3

Intelligent Control

In Antipattern 6.3, we looked at how a fixed mindset to risk fails to optimize for the fast flow of safe value. A fixed mindset to risk in a complex and changing environment actually increases risk levels. Slavish adherence to fixed, prescriptive standards does not suit a digital era of fast-paced, complex change.

Instead create an environment where the value stream aligned product teams and Safety team collaborate daily as part of the normal flow of work, where people feel safe to speak up and have an active debate about context-specific solutions that meet control objectives within risk appetite. This creates an environment that supports the delivery of **Better Value Sooner Safer Happier**.

For such collaboration and conversation to replace classic, fixed-mindset compliance processes at scale across a large enterprise, a minimal process is necessary, bearing in mind that it's people, process, tooling in that order. Having a lightweight process allows a level of automation to be introduced, enabling

PATTERN 6.3

RiskID-60 Logical Access Management Using
Public Cloud Database

Level 3 Risk: Failure to protect the confidentiality or integrity or availability of information assets

Link to relevant policies & standards:

<document link 1>

<document link 2>

GIVEN the context of application teams using public cloud native database without automated infrastructure layer database logical assess controls

I WANT TO ensure application owners understand their responsibilities for adhering to data retention, password complexity rules, daily reporting of database logins, and permissions

SO THAT the organization is able to:

a) maintain a central record of which staff have access to what data at what time, allowing reporting and remediation of unauthorized access combinations

b) investigate and recover from any accidental or deliberate database deletions

c) ensure that data access for staff moving roles or leaving is proactively managed

d) mitigate the risk of unapproved data access through password hacking

Mitigations:

1. Establish local automated daily detective reports of logins and permissions to all active database instances in the cloud resource container (aka AWS account).

2. Ensure each login is identifiable to an accountable active member of staff.

Figure 6.6: Risk Story Example

Safety teams and authorities to visualize areas of heightened risk. A minimum viable process enables both speed AND control.

The pattern starts with the operating model described above. Safety teams are established and aligned to long-lived value streams and products (see also Chapter 5).

The product team engages with their Safety team about a short-term business outcome. The engagement results in a conversation about potential risks and relevant policies. Through discussion, the risks are explored and mitigation hypotheses proposed, leading to the creation of risk stories in the product backlog. Safety governance can then operate at the risk story level, with the Safety SME empowered to validate when ready without extensive approval chains.

At the time of product increment release—providing all required risk stories have been validated by the Safety SME and closed—then the Value Outcome Lead is empowered to issue a certificate of release readiness. This self-service approach allows the product team to adopt any release cadence their system of work can sustain—hourly, daily, weekly. Since risk story validation and closure is decoupled from the release process, there is no requirement for any additional release-specific Safety domain approvals.

This pattern has evolved and iterated over a number of years in an environment with a high level of regulation and has been proven in the context of all change across tens of thousands of people. The following sections discuss each stage in a little more detail.

1: Continuous Engagement

Product Teams engage with their Safety team on a continuous basis (see Figure 6.7). A key event arises when there is a new quarterly business outcome. A short engagement questionnaire may support this process, to indicate the nature of the business outcome, such as any impact on personal data. A wiki page is used to describe the intent—such as a product vision delta, architecture vision delta, or key features. Up-front elaboration is not expected or required. There is just enough information to have a meaningful conversation, no more.

2: Set the Safety Engagement Level

In the light of the new business outcome, each member of the Safety team reassesses how frequently they feel it is necessary to engage with the product team (e.g., daily, weekly, monthly). The lowest risk products—an internal holiday app, for example—may not require any engagement at all. By setting the engagement level, the Safety SMEs acknowledge awareness of the business outcome being iteratively worked on. The product team remains accountable at all times for the safety of the product they release. Their Safety team understands external regulatory framework, cyber threats, and enterprise control objectives, and together the teams identify the potential risk areas, the learning needed, and the mitigation hypothesis. This engagement can be treated as a formal control point.

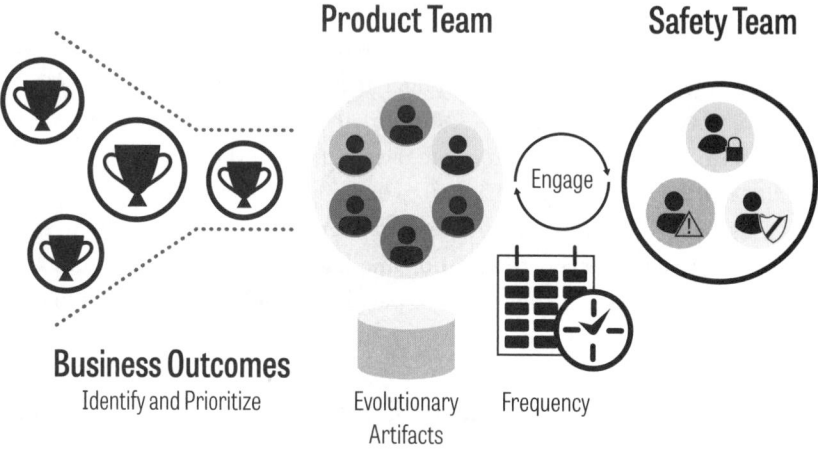

Product Team   **Safety Team**

Business Outcomes
Identify and Prioritize

Evolutionary
Artifacts

Frequency

Figure 6.7: Continuous Engagement

3: Risk Stories and Continuous Testing

The Safety and product teams meet at the agreed frequency to discuss the business outcome, review learnings, and refine their joint understanding of any risks presented. The exact nature of controls that needs to be implemented will vary based on the control objective and the business and technical context. This includes the risk appetite of the business unit. Control requirements are not fixed:

$$\text{Control Requirement} = \text{Control Objective} + \text{Context}$$

For change in the "Complex" quadrant of Cynefin, the control requirement cannot be fully predetermined—as we've seen, there needs not to be a fixed mindset for controls. While risk story templates are available from the risk catalog, these accelerators can be adjusted to suit the context through discussion and agreement between the Safety and product teams.

Risk stories are a type of work in the backlog, alongside other types of work such as user stories. Once in the product backlog, the risk stories are handled in much the same way as other forms of learning and work required, with evidence through automated tests where possible. Depending on the level of trust between the product and Safety teams, the completed risk stories (which are being completed early and often) may require validation by the Safety team before closure, or the Value Outcome Lead may be fully empowered to validate risk story completion (see Figure 6.8).

Figure 6.8: Risk Stories and Continuous Testing

For novel risks or where established risk mitigations are unsuitable, the risk story may be expressed as a hypothesis that takes the form of: "Given the risk of X, we believe that activity Y will be an effective mitigation. We will know this is true when we observe key result Z." Figure 6.9 is an example of a risk story used to achieve a novel risk mitigation.

PATTERN **6.3**

Risk of Malware

Level 3 Risk: Failure to protect the confidentiality or integrity or availability of information assets

---

Link to relevant policies & standards:

<document link 1>

<document link 2>

GIVEN the context of malware risk resulting from copying data from a 3rd party public cloud account into an enterprise public cloud account

WE BELIEVE THAT it will be possible to mitigate this risk using automated scanning in an "airlock" public cloud account that effectively isolates malware and notifies the cyber team

WE WILL KNOW THIS IS TRUE WHEN exceptions can be injected into the 3rd party data set and successfully detected and isolated

Mitigations:

A malware detection pattern will be designed to ensure that:

a) only verified clean files can be copied to the enterprise cloud account

b) files where exceptions are detected are held in isolation within the airlock for investigation

c) an alerting process exists for the cyber operations team to be alerted to exceptions

d) an assurance process is established to periodically inject exceptions into the 3rd party data stream and confirm positive detection in enterprise monitoring tools.

Acceptance Criteria for Risk Story closure:

Acceptance Criteria 1: The pattern is agreed with the Safety team and documented here.

Acceptance Criteria 2: Code passes an automated test suite to validate each design element.

Acceptance Criteria 3: The code has been reviewed by a member of InfoSec architecture.

Acceptance Criteria 4: The alerting process is agreed with the InfoSec representative.

Acceptance Criteria 5: The assurance process is agreed with the InfoSec representative.

Figure 6.9: Novel Risk Mitigation Story

PATTERN **6.3**

Case Study: Control Innovation at Auto Trader ■

Auto Trader was founded in 1977 and is the UK's largest digital automotive marketplace, serving 13,200 customers, with 800 employees. Auto Trader has gone on a transformational journey from paper to digital. Here, Dave Whyte, Operations Lead, and Russ Warman, Head of Infrastructure and Operations, share a story of safety in Safety and a not-one-size-fits-all mindset in order to optimize for the delivery of Better Value Sooner Safer Happier.

Auto Trader had built a private cloud platform, which had proven very successful in enabling developers to build self-contained applications and carry out their own releases, embracing a DevOps culture. We planned to scale this platform across the enterprise.

One of our business customers had a requirement for their end-user personally identifiable information (PII data) to be fully encrypted, end to end. This was not something that we had yet tackled with our delivery platform. The engineering team felt that this was achievable, probably within about six weeks, by using a technical solution to handle encryption separately from the main application. After about twelve weeks it became clear that the technical challenges and complexity meant we were not going to meet customer expectations. We also acknowledged that the ongoing effort for our engineers to maintain it was going to be a significant burden.

With time running out, a couple of engineers decided to try a different method using some standard *public* cloud services to test a theory that it would be inherently quicker and easier to achieve the same result this way due to the features available on the vendor platform. Within a matter of days they had successfully created a proof of concept that met the control acceptance criteria. Due to the success of the proof of concept, we completely pivoted from running a private cloud within our datacenters to beginning a wholesale public cloud migration with a view to being fully in the public cloud within two years. Currently, we're three quarters of the way into that journey and the benefits have been enormous, as the public cloud has enabled us to adopt continuous delivery. Due to safety in Safety and not having a fixed mindset, we've been able to deliver **Better Value Sooner Safer Happier**.

Figure 6.10 shows how our adoption of public cloud in has transformed our ability to release more frequently using continual delivery.

PATTERN 6.3

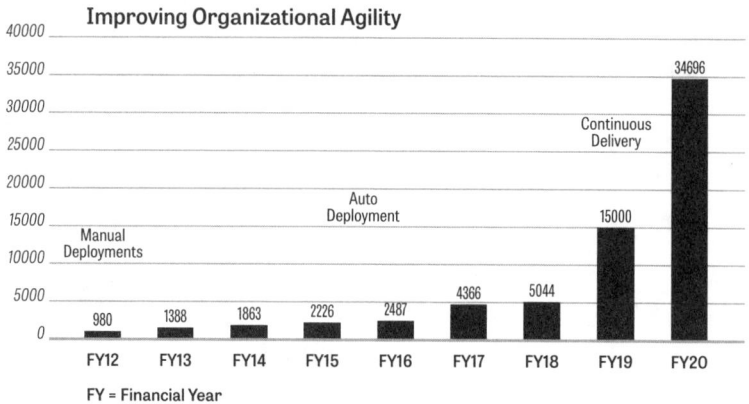

Figure 6.10: AutoTrader Cloud Adoption 2019/2020

What Did We Learn?

The customer need pushed us to think differently in order to keep our customer safe. The first solution we imagine is not always the right one. Having flexibility about how to mitigate the risk allowed us to experiment and learn, rather than being precious or tied to an approach when we recognize something is not working. We have also learned that being truly cloud native gives us the ability to experiment faster with less effort, risk, and cost.

In effect, the impact of a flexible approach to risk mitigation for one customer has had a positive impact across our entire business, enabling us to deliver **Better Value Sooner Safer Happier**.

4: Risk Awareness

A key contribution of the Safety team lies outside a structured process related to standards. This is the broad opportunity to raise risk awareness levels across the value stream(s). The greater the risk awareness, the better the Safety teams will be able to triage and focus scarce SME resources on the highest risk areas. This can involve the use of simulated attacks as described by CREST International for Simulated Target Attack and Response (CBEST), an accrediting body, and by thought leaders in the DevSecOps movement such as Shannon Leitz.[36]

In cybersecurity defense games, the attacking team is typically known as the Red team and the defending is the Blue team. Within an Intelligent Control operating model, these defense games are a responsibility of the InfoSec/Cyber Safety authority and can be extended into the daily operation of Safety teams. Louis Cremen, in *Introducing the InfoSec Color Wheel*, describes the need for the development team to be a close partner in these games: "Only having Red and Blue Security Teams is not enough. The people building what must be defended need to be included. Introducing Yellow Team—The Builders . . . need to be included as a part of Information Security."[37]

5: Evolutionary Artifacts

As with a traditional SDLC, some artifacts are useful to give context to the conversation. The absence of these artifacts can indicate heightened product risk from a Safety team perspective. The product is long-lived and constantly upgraded, and the Intelligent Control pattern (see Figure 6.10) is to use the existing operational documentation of the product as the key information source for risk assessment. Artifacts will naturally improve and evolve over time and do not require duplication for every outcome or OKR. Relevant artifacts typically include:

- product vision
- architecture vision
- architecture wiki
- product roadmap
- threat model
- lean test strategy
- operations run book

6: Candidate Release Validation

The validation of release candidates (i.e., potentially releasable code) is the second of two control points in the Intelligent Control pattern as in Figure 6.11. Unlike a traditional SDLC requiring multiple stage-gated approvals, if the risk stories associated with the release have had appropriate closure, then the Value Outcome Lead for the product has the authority to approve the release. If any mandatory risk stories are not closed, then release validation is not authorized, preventing any further product release from proceeding.

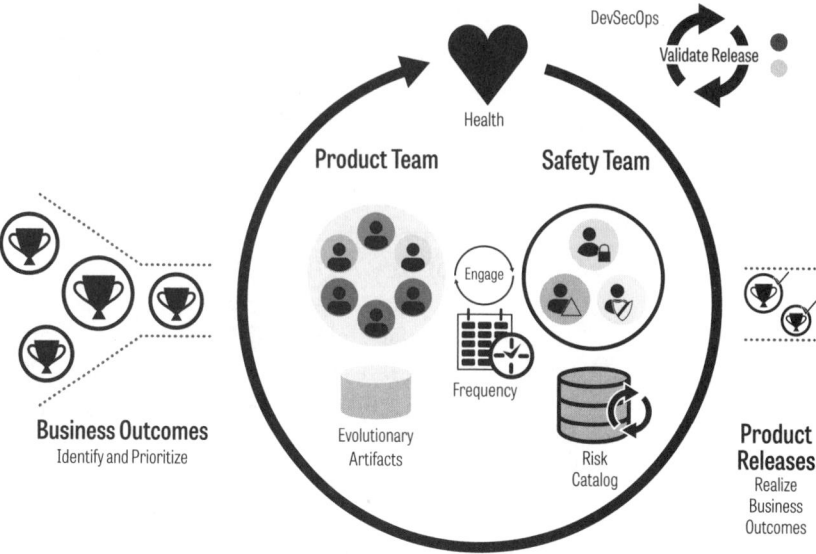

Figure 6.11: Intelligent Control

A virtual IT change request (CR) process at the point of actual release may still be applied to address IT management objectives such as technical dependency notifications. CRs supported by an Intelligent Control "validated release" certificate are able to follow an accelerated and in some cases automated approval flow into a production environment on a regular cadence.

As the maturity of DecSecOps processes increase in the organization, process traceability improves to connect stories, releases, CI reports, artifacts, and change requests. The processes provide automated vulnerability checks and library scans as standard for every software build, making sure that safety is built in rather than inspected in later. Building security into the product development pipeline is part of the Safety team engagement via Intelligent Control.

Virtual Andon Cord

If at any time there are issues that require servant leadership attention to resolve, such as poor engagement between the Safety team and the product teams (e.g., staff absence, lack of responsiveness, or inadequate minimal artifacts), then either party is able to call for help. Like Andon cords on the Toyota production lines, a virtual Andon cord pull can be used to notify Safety authority and value stream leads that their help is needed, in a servant leadership style. For this process to work, culture is all-important. Leaders should approach this with a "Dear team, how can I help you?" stance. As with a blameless post-mortem, the support focuses on improvements to the system of work. This helps to encourage a culture of continuous improvement.

7: Active Leadership Support

The Intelligent Control pattern allows governance, risk, and compliance priorities to be injected into the "continuous everything" product development cycle without the need for big, up-front blueprints or sequential governance control stage gates.

Value stream leadership has a key role to play in maximizing the value from this pattern, including:

- Taking responsibility for risk and actively promoting the risk agenda across teams
- Partnering with Safety authority leadership to ensure Safety teams have capacity, including potentially co-funding, if that is the best way to deliver **Better Value Sooner Safer Happier** (remember: impediments are not in the path, impediments ARE the path)
- Partnering with the Safety team as part of the value stream extended leadership to focus on the presence of positives: to keep the discussion on risk alive

8: Risk Metrics

Data captured from the intelligent control process allows value stream leadership to visualize areas of relative risk, allowing more support to be given where there is elevated risk. Safety authority leadership may require a different view. Everyone needs access to the same data.

Understanding elevated risk level is a more nuanced view than process compliance. There are a number of data points that can be used as key risk indicators, allowing blameless questions to be asked from the involved teams

PATTERN 6.3

about what the drivers are so that the system of work can be improved. Examples of key risk indicators in the delivery process include:

- Total products in the value stream with inflight business outcomes. Are there any persistently not engaging with Safety teams? Why is this?
- Products in the value stream that are any persistently flagging low health with Safety teams? Why is this?
- Products in the value stream with risk stories persistently left unresolved for an extended period? Why is this?
- Products in the value stream with implemented change requests (CRs) in a period—how many CRs were uncorrelated to a validated release certificate? Why is this?

9: Tooling

When an enterprise has a large number of value streams, hundreds of products in development, and a large number of Safety teams, I have found that a level of tooling integration and automation is essential ahead of scaling so teams can operate efficiently and to create transparency or process.

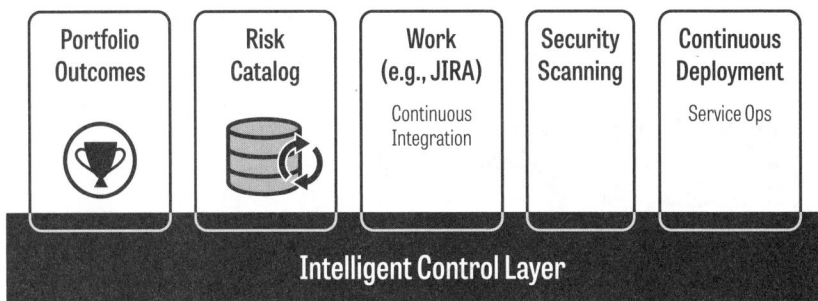

Figure 6.12: Intelligent Control Layer

The principle of minimum viable tooling is to minimize data duplication by using the core delivery tooling of the product teams. It is typical in many large enterprises for tooling to be disconnected across portfolio management, standards and policies, work management, continuous delivery, and service operations. Intelligent control tooling connects these domains to provide

Safety teams with visibility across the product development value stream with access to simple dashboards to visualize the system of work specifically around risk. (See Figure 6.12.)

Summary

Putting the Safer in Better Value Sooner Safer Happier

In this chapter, I've identified a number of antipatterns that increase risk when accelerating the cadence of product development. Building new and emergent products right is primarily a people challenge. It is people, process, tools, in that order. Throughout this chapter, the human and psychological safety aspects in effective risk management have been emphasized, with a shift from a compliance mindset against fixed, centrally determined policy to an empowered growth mindset with substantial accountability delegated to Safety teams and product teams. The more likely an organization is to keep the discussion on risk alive, the safer that organization is likely to be.

The DevSecOps movement has long advocated "developing security as code,"[37] and the patterns discussed in this chapter advocate extending this practice beyond security and across governance risk and compliance domains, which we broadly refer to as "Safety." The patterns highlight the importance of shifting left on all these Safety conversations, building them into the normal system of work of the value stream. A context-sensitive engagement approach ensures risk mitigations are always relevant and allows product teams to move fast and stay within risk appetite:

Control Requirement = Control objective + Context

Finally, the patterns acknowledge the critical role of Red, Blue, and Yellow teaming approaches to continuously raise risk awareness and "test exploits over relying on scans and theoretical vulnerabilities."[38] With this shifting both left and right of risk awareness along the product development lifecycle, we might say the intent behind DevSecOps could be expressed as:

RiskDevRiskOpsRisk

Getting Maersk back online after the destruction caused by the NotPetya virus required 600 recovery staff working in a rescue center in Maidenhead in England. At first, it appeared nothing could be recovered. Every one of the company's network controllers needed to enable data recovery appeared to have been wiped by the virus. In fact, one remained. A power cut in Ghana had disconnected one network controller in a remote office. It hadn't been infected by the virus. With no time to lose, a nervous Maersk employee was tasked with flying from Ghana to Nigeria to hand over the hard drive in the airport to another employee who had the necessary visa to fly with it to London.[39]

While the patterns in this chapter won't prevent states from building destructive and costly viruses, the improved safety they foster might just lower the risk of team members having to hand over an organization's entire data in a Nigerian airport.

In the next chapter, we're going to talk about leadership in an agile environment.

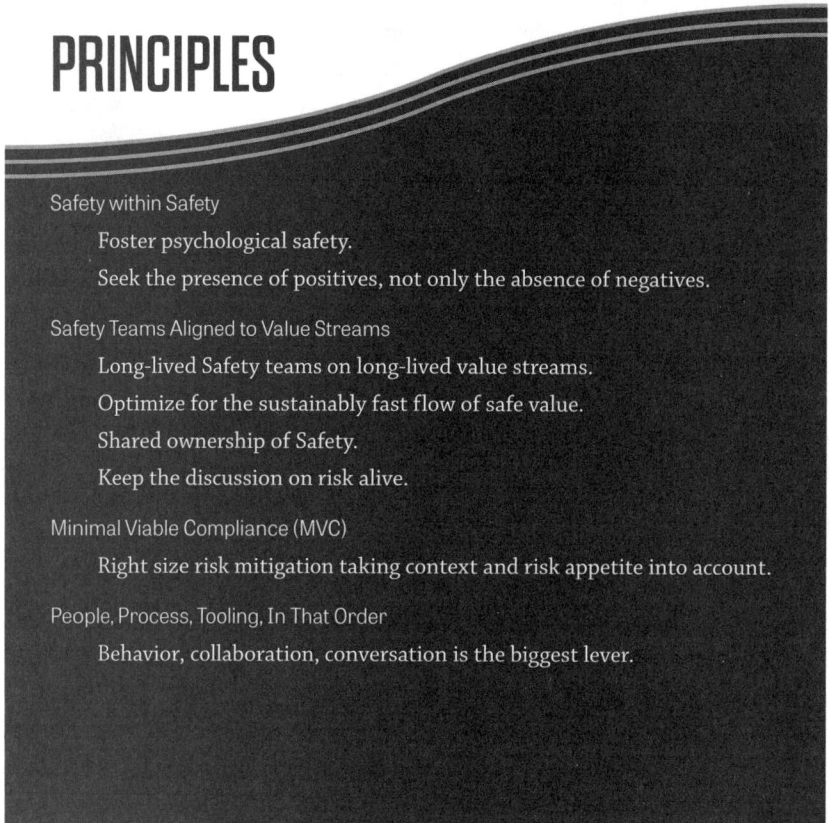

PRINCIPLES

Safety within Safety

> Foster psychological safety.
>
> Seek the presence of positives, not only the absence of negatives.

Safety Teams Aligned to Value Streams

> Long-lived Safety teams on long-lived value streams.
>
> Optimize for the sustainably fast flow of safe value.
>
> Shared ownership of Safety.
>
> Keep the discussion on risk alive.

Minimal Viable Compliance (MVC)

> Right size risk mitigation taking context and risk appetite into account.

People, Process, Tooling, In That Order

> Behavior, collaboration, conversation is the biggest lever.

7
CONTINUOUS ATTENTION TO TECHNICAL EXCELLENCE

In 1938 Marjorie Courtenay-Latimer, a curator at the East London museum in South Africa, received a phone call from the local docks. A fisherman had landed a strange-looking fish. He knew that Courtenay-Latimer was always interested in seeing unusual specimens and thought she might like to come down and view the catch.

Reaching the quay, Courtenay-Latimer opened the net and picked away at the layers of detritus. What she found, she said, was the "most beautiful fish" she had ever seen.[1]

Courtenay-Latimer should, perhaps, have seen more fish. The specimen was five feet long, "a pale, mauvy blue with faint flecks of whitish spots [with] an iridescent silver-blue-green sheen all over."[2] It had four "limb-like" fins and a raggedy tail that she compared to a puppy dog's. Perhaps she should have seen more puppy dogs too.

Courtenay-Latimer had the fish stuffed and showed it to ichthyologist J.L.B. Smith. He immediately identified it as a coelacanth, a fish that was believed to have been extinct for 65 million years. Courtenay-Latimer had found a "living fossil," a living part of the evolutionary record.[3]

Biological evolutionary theorists used to separate into two schools: those who believed that evolution proceeded gradually over time, and those who believed that species change suddenly after long periods of calm, triggered by significant geological events. Those two schools have now largely reconciled. Change happens both gradually and with occasional step changes.

The same is true in organizations. Change is gradual, not staccato, occasionally punctuated with disruptive changes that may come from new innovation, regulation, or market events. Terms for this include exploit (existing business models) and explore (new ones). Also, *kaizen* (continuous improvement) and *kaikaku* (radical change), as in lean. In evolutionary biology the term is "Punctuated Gradualism." (See Figure 7.1.)

And the "gradualism" is getting steeper, the pace of continuous change is getting faster. Occasionally, relics are left behind. For example, a Compaq PC from 1993 with parts being scavenged from eBay keeping a critical manufacturing production line running. A number of Visual Basic applications, which have been out of support since 2008, keeping day-to-day business operations running. A few fossils somehow survive and surface occasionally, caught in a developer's Integrated Development Environment.

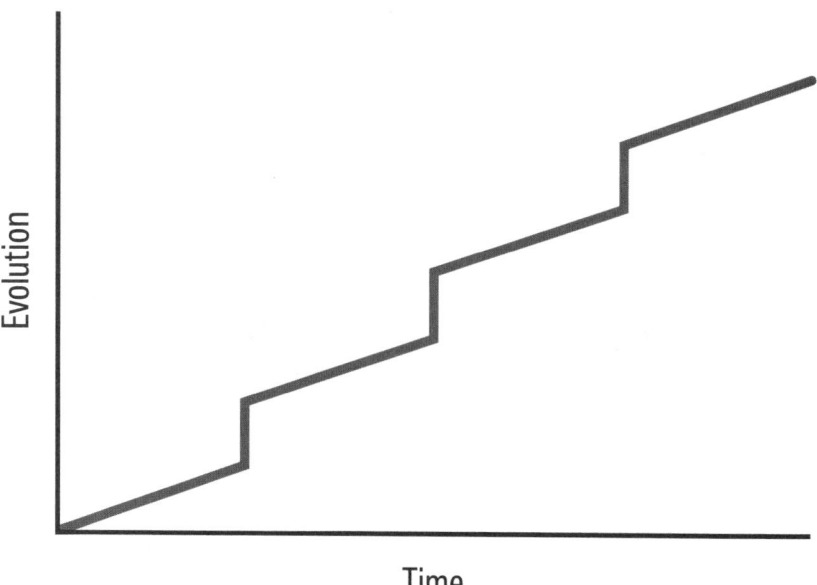

Figure 7.1: Punctuated Gradualism

Product development teams rarely uncover long-forgotten fish; however, they often find themselves dealing with the detritus of legacy enterprise applications and tripping over layers of fossilized but still-living code that's been left behind.

Even in the Age of Digital, living software fossils are still evolving in many older companies. Some companies teach COBOL to new graduates so they can continue developing mainframe software written in the 1960s and 1970s. Other companies maintain massive, monolithic databases built for client-server architectures from the 1990s and 2000s. At many organizations, critical processing takes place on thick client desktop interfaces even as much of the industry now builds browser front ends by default.

In organizations with traditional ways of working, change (in the context of unique product development) is staccato. In evolutionary biology terms it's "Punctuated Equilibrium" rather than "Punctuated Gradualism." There are long periods of *stasis*, then a burst of disruptive (often negatively disruptive) change. There is a lack of ongoing continuous improvement. There is a comfortable status quo, punctuated with a big budget, big timeline, big overrun, big bang.

With a project-centric mentality, where the future is predicted at the point where least is known, and a financial process that encourages premature solutioning and a deterministic mindset, the "punctuated" tends to be yet another new IT product (application) being deployed. As previous projects have disbanded and the original knowledge has dispersed, applications are generally left in stasis. They are running in lights-on mode, and with each new application, the percentage of spend on "run" increases. There is less spend available for discretionary work, a commonly observed issue. Akin to gardening, the weeds are left to grow. Operating systems, compilers, third-party libraries are no longer supported and patched. Eventually the garden is so overgrown, a point of no return has been passed, such that the only approach is to slash-and-burn and do yet another big-budget, big-bang, greenfield, replacement software system. And so the madness continues. This is *not* optimizing for **Better Value Sooner Safer Happier**—quite the opposite.

Applications and puppies have something in common: "An application is for life. Not just for Christmas."

The antipatterns here illustrate how failing to recognize the importance of continuous attention to technical excellence, how staccato change, how "Punctuated Equilibrium" does not optimize for outcomes.

The patterns show how tending the garden, upgrading the plane midflight, continuously evolving, taking a "Punctuated Gradualism" approach optimizes for the delivery of Better Value Sooner Safer Happier.

ANTIPATTERN 7.

Going Faster Leads to Going Slower

In this common antipattern, teams are a feature factory churning out *stuff*. There is a focus on output. Words like "velocity" and "say do ratio" (don't ask . . .) are used a lot. The production of *stuff* is prioritized over anything else. And it needs to be done yesterday. There is no time for continuous improvement, for refactoring, for making code more maintainable, more scalable, more resilient, or increasing the level of automation.

Each new feature adds more manual testing overhead. Supportability is not built in, so the IT Ops cost rises. The code has become a tangled mess, like a three-year-old eating a bowl of spaghetti. The code is hard to read, hard to maintain, and hard to add to. Corners are cut to meet the relentless pressure to ship features. Code changes take twice as long as they did a year ago. The cost of development keeps on rising. The lead time, time from concept to cash, time to learning, time to respond to customer feedback is taking longer. Incidents are increasing and the team has a high turnover.

Only Priya, the longest-serving team member, understands how the most complex part of the system works, and she's always on call for every outage. Due to the pressure to ship, ship, ship, the code has become bloated with lots of hands on it. Breaking it into separate components has not been prioritized. Everyone has to coordinate testing and shipping at the same time. It's become a monolithic ball of mud.

As progress slows, there's even more pressure from stakeholders. "I thought you said you were Agile?!" they say. "But we're delivering more story points," the Team Outcome Lead says, which is taken like a red rag to a bull. More corners are cut. Eventually someone says, "Stop! We need to pitch for investment to rebuild this app from scratch, as this is now legacy." And so the merry-go-round continues, the quickest route to building legacy code.

If you don't schedule maintenance time to exercise, to service your car, to clean and tidy your house, to have machines serviced in a factory then you, your car, your house, your machines, will degrade—sometimes unexpectedly and in a catastrophic manner, which is not what anyone wants. You incur debt, with compound interest. Fitness debt, maintenance debt, being-able-to-find-the-remote-control debt, technical debt. By not paying down that debt, everything goes slower.

This is why it's "Sooner," not "Faster," in **Better Value Sooner Safer Happier**. It is about reducing time to learning, to being able respond, to shortening lead time in order to maximize outcomes, to being able to innovate, to being able to spend time talking to the customer. It's not about churning out *output* at the expense of continuously improving IT products or the system of work.

This antipattern can manifest itself in partnership with Antipatterns 4.3, 5.2, and 5.3. There is an unrealistic, predetermined plan, a "commitment" to activities, a "drop-dead date" or "deadline" milestone with an analogy of death if not met, rather than optimized business outcomes with nested learning loops. Technical excellence, refactoring, goes out the window, as does pride and colleague engagement. Technical debt is increased. Progress slows. It becomes a vicious cycle and can be broken into three parts: lack of partnership, emergence demands continuous improvement, and systems entropy.

1: Lack of Partnership

A common statement is "the business just wants more features." Sometimes it's a group-think assumption, a victim mentality, the absence of a conversation about the importance of continuous refactoring. Sometimes stakeholders lack understanding and take (or continue with) a dictatorial stance. And sometimes the decision to add new features is valid and entrepreneurial, as there is a first mover advantage, where it's worth incurring short-term technical debt.

The decisions should be intentional and made *together* by the Value Outcome Lead, Team Outcome Lead, and Architecture Outcome Lead. The "us and them," order-giver/order-taker, dictatorial, command-and-control, old way of working is at the heart of this antipattern.

The traditional split between business and technology, with an us-and-them behavioral norm, with a tribal identity by job role rather than value stream, doesn't help to alleviate any misunderstanding of the nature of software development work. Increasingly people need to be "T"-shaped. Not just in IT. Across "our business." Non-technology specialists will be able to add more value if there is an appreciation of technology. Technology specialists should have a strong grasp of the business value stream they are in. Where this is not the case, it is often observed that some people, often adopting an "order-giver" stance, feel that only work spent directly on implementing business features has value.

In some cases, where stakeholders or partners have not valued refactoring and technical excellence at all over the long term and have had a more dictatorial and micro-management behavioral style, I've seen teams actually *hide* technical improvement work, with a belief that it's essential to maintain or increase flow, that their efforts will reduce the effort, cost, and time to value for future work.

It is crazy that in the Age of Digital, due to a long-term lack of improvement work being prioritized, people feel the need to *hide* it from colleagues, with a view that it's good for the organization and the outcomes. There's ownership needed all round here, both to seek to understand technology patterns, and for technology-specialists to not exhibit a victim mentality, and to make the business case that "valuetivity" declines over time with a lack of focus on paying down technical debt.

This lack of partnership can also manifest itself in what is measured and how it is measured. It is an antipattern to measure the *worker not the work*.

I've often seen attempts to measure individual developer productivity. It is a Taylorist, command-and-control, lack-of-psychological-safety approach to attempt to measure individuals on technical excellence. It drives a big brother, lack-of-trust culture and will not help engagement. Worse, it leads to gaming the system if the measure includes "productive hours" or lines of code. It will lead to verbose, bloated, cut-and-paste code to game a metric that shouldn't be being measured. It will suppress innovation and time spent talking to customers and stakeholders.

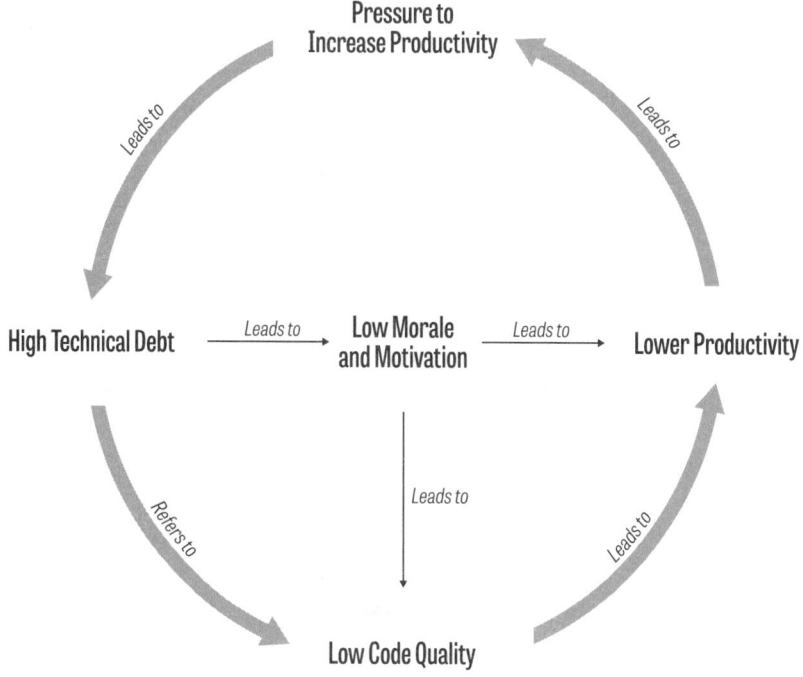

Figure 7.2: Technical Debt's Vicious Cycle

2: Emergence Demands Continuous Improvement

In this antipattern, there is a lack of ongoing refactoring and continuous improvement that is needed when work is unique and has unknown-unknowns, which leads to **BVSSH** outcomes heading in the wrong direction.

Product development is emergent. People don't know what they want or exactly how they are going to develop the software because it's never been done before. Identical software is not written thousands of times. It's written once (and then needs to be re-written a few times) and it runs lots of times. Therefore, as it is a unique endeavor, every time that software is developed lessons will be learned. Hindsight is a wonderful thing.

If lessons are learned and acted on, if there is retrospection and an ability to continuously improve, then by going slower to go faster, all future software product development can be done Sooner. As an emergent activity, one which is intellectual, scientific, artistic, and collaborative, there is a need to regularly refactor code. This is needed to improve its maintainability and extensibility, to make it more readable, less complex, easier to fix defects, easier to make a change, possibly breaking up a monolith into components. It takes longer to write simpler code.

Putting those lessons learned to one side to move quickly onto the next feature doesn't allow the benefits of the insights to be implemented. That said, there may be exceptional cases where being first to market makes it worth incurring technical debt. However, that debt will eventually need to be paid down. If it is not, going faster results in eventually going slower.

In addition to refactoring code, engineering benefits from continuous improvement in order to be "fit-for-purpose." A human equivalent is to sleep well, eat well, move well. Much like investing time in personal wellness, time needs to be invested in engineering wellness. The gym equivalent includes things such as test-first development, automated testing, static code analysis, trunk based development, non-functional testability, scalability, supportability, observability, and resilience. Failing to invest time in these will eventually lead to lower quality and slower, riskier, and unhappier delivery of less value.

It is essential that there is dedicated time for refactoring and continuous improvement to be able to deliver **Better Value Sooner Safer Happier**.

3: Systems Entropy

All systems experience entropy over time. Due to entropy, doing nothing is worse than standing still: it's actually going backward. This is the Second Law of Thermodynamics, which says any closed system will tend toward disorder.

The environment around an IT system is constantly changing. The format, type, and timeliness of data, the business activities, the hardware, operating system, compiler, third-party software libraries, security vulnerabilities, people, and processes are all changing.

At one organization, there was a mission critical system that, due to a lack of continuous attention to technical excellence was on an unsupported compiler, that in turn required an unsupported operating system, that then required unsupported hardware. It also required developers willing to continue to develop code on this unsupported combination. It had gone beyond the point of no return. It was not possible to process new business. There was no option but to slash and burn. It had been allowed to entropy into a dead-end and at a *far higher* cost and risk to the organization than continuous attention to technical excellence.

"Evergreening" is needed to keep entropy at bay, to keep applications on supported technology and with the latest security patches. Otherwise, the result can be wide open vulnerabilities with severe consequences, such as the impact of the NotPetya and WannaCry viruses as we saw in Chapter 6.

Attention to technical excellence must be continuous, not occasional. With a "continuous everything" approach it should be little and often, with a regular larger refactor, such as going from monolith to microservice, from on-prem to cloud and so on. Like evolution, software should evolve through Punctuated Gradualism in order to optimize for outcomes.

Teams that have operated with technical "good enough" rather than technical *excellence* for many years—something I've seen time after time—will need to schedule time to get their practices up to scratch if there is a desire to deliver **Better Value Sooner Safer Happier**. They don't have to stop working on business features entirely. Schedule a few hours or days every week or month to focus on improving work: architecture, testing, deployments, and more. Eventually improvements will become routine, a part of daily practice. Failing to prioritize continuous technical excellence over the long run is failing to optimize for **BVSSH**.

ANTIPATTERN 7.2

Agile Hollow Shell

In this antipattern, even if there is not a relentless pressure for features, there is an "agile hollow shell": an agile approach to work, such as Scrum, without any focus on technical excellence. This is Agile *work management* only, often in an environment that also has big, up-front architectural design and review.

There is an agile shell, lacking technical excellence in the core, which does not optimize for outcomes.

The *Agile Manifesto* is explicit: "Continuous attention to technical excellence and good design enhances agility" is one of the twelve principles.[4] Note the use of the word *continuous*.

Scrum or the Kanban Method, as approaches to ways of working, don't explicitly cover technical excellence principles and practices. They are designed to be applied in a broader context than just software development. This often results in organizations whose primary activity is software development focusing on the mechanics of Scrum or Kanban, on work management, and not paying enough or any attention to technical excellence. After a while, progress slows as the code base becomes less maintainable. The poor internal quality in the software makes it harder to add new features. Over time, total cost of ownership increases and flow decreases. This results in less for more, not the outcome that anyone is looking for. Martin Fowler, an *Agile Manifesto* signatory, has called this "Flaccid Scrum."[5]

1: Wagile Solution Architecture

Worse, there is often still a traditional, big, up-front solution architecture and design stage before an iteration-based approach, in a Water-Scrum-Fall manner. This results in the technical design being detailed and deterministic rather than just-enough and intentionally emergent, with change inhibited and too much time spent designing in a bubble, and with no real learning or feedback loop through doing. With this "Wagile" approach there is no "continuous attention to technical excellence and design," which is not optimizing for outcomes. There should be just enough technical architecture envisaging, no more and not none. It should be done continuously, matching the daily, weekly, monthly, quarterly nested outcome cadences on long-lived IT Products.

2: Traditional Enterprise Architecture

In addition, above the level of projects and solution architecture, often the enterprise architecture processes are not lean or agile and do not support *continuous attention to technical excellence and good design*.

In my experience, enterprise architecture functions are typically concerned with some form of technology governance and reduction of duplication. There is a focus on technical standards, software, and infrastructure development policy. Enterprise architects in a traditional way of working are typically only involved in software development initiatives in the early stages of a significant new build or refactor, when design documents are reviewed for adherence to policies or standards, with another big, up-front, stage-gate approval. And then that's it.

Even when teams take months rather than minutes to deliver features, big, up-front design reviews are close to useless. Application delivery teams nearly always discover complexities during actual software construction that mean designs that were presented to a Design Authority or Architecture Board rarely resemble the final delivered software. It is a theater of control, unsuited to the context of the fast flow of safe value.

There is no continuous, and typically there is insufficient focus on, *technical excellence*, which is an impediment to the delivery of **Better Value Sooner Safer Happier**.

ANTIPATTERN 7.3

Misalignment of Teams and Architecture

In this antipattern, the technical architecture and the people architecture are not optimized or are not in alignment. When left unchecked, this is failing to pay attention to technical excellence and fails to optimize for outcomes. Another related scenario is organizing people by technology *layer*. This inhibits technical excellence practices as well as flow.

In 1967, computer scientist Mel Conway wrote an article whose thesis became known as Conway's Law. "Organizations which design systems are constrained to produce designs which are copies of the communication structures of those organizations."[6]

That is, if people are organized into large, role-based teams, such as a project team of a hundred, of which thirty are developers, they are more likely to produce software that is monolithic. If people are organized into small, multidisciplinary teams, they are more likely to produce software that is componentized. In 2008, Harvard Business School published a study confirming this hypothesis.[7]

A more componentized technical architecture, with high cohesion and low coupling, results in greater agility, as it is complexity that fits in your head, it's within the cognitive load of the team and there are fewer dependencies. Teams have more ability to release value at their own cadence. Hence, it is preferable to have many small, multidisciplinary teams, in addition to the human communication benefits.

A corollary of Conway's Law is that an organization's structures themselves can be constrained by the architectures that they designed many years earlier. And without intentional action, it's a Catch-22. "We cannot solve our problems with the same level of thinking we used when we created them," Einstein said.

An example of this antipattern is a misapplication of an operating model where the technical architecture has not been considered, which can lead to additional dependencies and handoffs. A naive reorganization of people from monolithic, role-based, large teams into small, multidisciplinary teams aligned to value streams without attention to how the technical architecture landscape will also evolve will lead to suboptimal improvements at best.

At worst, the reorganization adds another layer of coordination and dependency management. The new teams could be working with an application architecture in which features require changes across a number of components and demand coordination with other value streams, slowing lead time and reducing flow efficiency.

1: Organizing the Enterprise by Technology Layer

Another scenario is organizations that have structured both people and architecture by technology layers, as per Figure 7.3, rather than by the ability to deliver end-to-end flow. For example, a layered technical architecture across an organization, business unit, or value stream. And within an application development role silo, this is the same as having all front-end developers in one pool and database developers in another pool, often with a view that fewer will be needed and hence it's cheaper. Perversely, it ends up costing the organization more via more handoffs, dependencies, and work queuing; a reduction in flow efficiency; lower flow; unhappier people; more time-slicing; and the delivery of less value more slowly.

As people are confined to their layer, without a view over the application, a significant part of the design of valuable features is performed outside the teams by yet another role sub-specialism, solution architects, before the teams are able to work on the features. The teams have little autonomy, having to estimate and commit to time frames in order to support synchronized delivery. Some of the simplest features need many teams to cooperate to deliver value. With localized knowledge by layer, it's super hard to estimate, design, build,

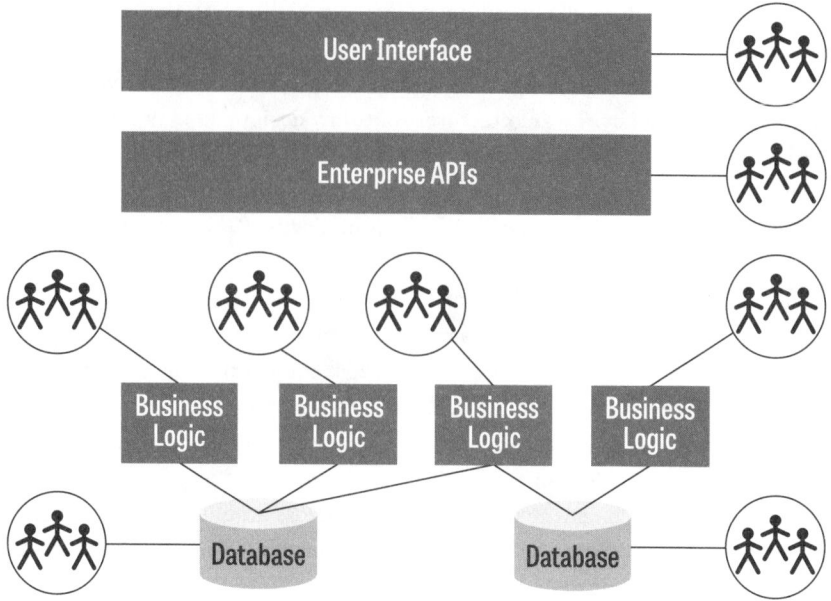

Figure 7.3: Organization by Technology Layer

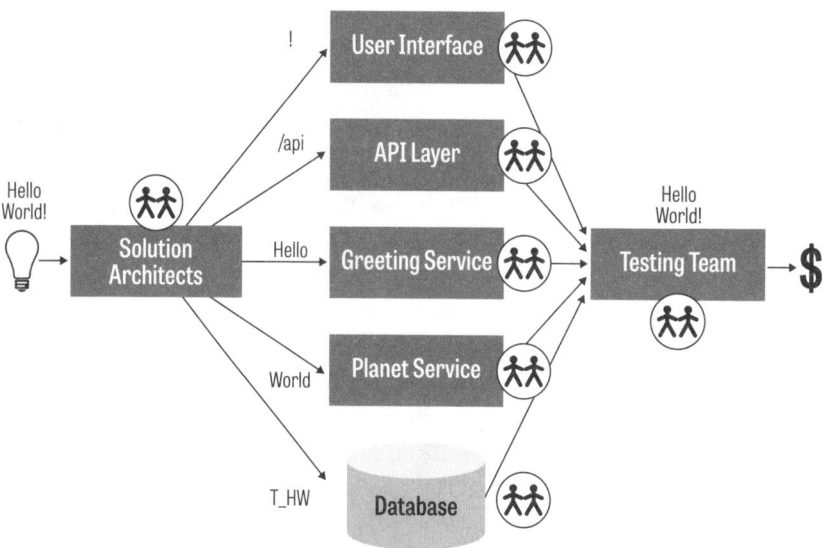

Figure 7.4: Solution Architecture Funnel and Organization by Layer

test, debug, and support. There is little to no shared ownership for outcomes. In order to deliver value, there is no one team with everything it needs.

The State of DevOps Report and the book *Accelerate* correlate technical excellence with high-performing organizations.[8] If we look at some of the technical practices in use by high-performing teams and organizations, we can see that they lose significant effectiveness when the people architecture and enterprise architecture are organized by technology layer.

As described by Matthew Skelton and Manuel Pais in *Team Topologies*, "Organization design and software design are two sides of the same coin, and both need to be undertaken by the same informed group of people."[9]

ANTIPATTERN 7.4

Tools over People

Another common antipattern on the topic of continuous attention to technical excellence is to focus on tools over people. Install Jira and Jenkins and you're agile! Also often observed is a lack of career path for technical specialists and an over-reliance on automation.

A focus only on tooling will have little improvement on outcomes if processes, the system of work, and behavioral norms, how people are organized and incentivized, are not changing. Rather than tooling first, it should be People → Process → Tooling in that order.

1: DevOps Transformations Focus on Tooling

A commonly observed scenario in particular is an organization embarking on a DevOps transformation, which is predominately a tool transformation.

Tooling, such as build and release automation, source code control, and binary artifact repositories, provides a must-have foundation for much of the collaboration and flow efficiency that underlies DevOps, agile, and lean software development. Too often, the belief is that installing a modern development toolchain is the DevOps journey. In reality, it's a bit like a tennis ball machine, firing the software binaries over the net to IT Ops at an ever-faster rate. For example, enterprises often focus on the tools that support automated build and deployment, often mislabeled as "CI/CD," when most teams using it are practicing neither continuous integration nor continuous delivery, and certainly not continuous deployment.

Table 7.1: Technical Excellence Practices and Organization by Technology Layer

Technical Practice	Impediment in Organization by Technology Layer
Test automation/ continuous testing	Tight coupling means teams are unable to gain confidence without significant numbers of integrated tests, which often require waiting for other teams.
Deployment automation	Automated deployments of individual components require team or sophisticated automated orchestration in which many teams' contributions come together to implement a business feature.
Loosely coupled architecture	Loose coupling is challenging, if not impossible, when multiple layers come together to implement a single business feature. Feature changes typically require coordinated changes across multiple teams.
Continuous integration	Continuous integration across teams is challenging but possible, e.g., using a "monorepo" (one code repository) approach, but requires significant investment in non-standard tooling and processes.
Frequent or continuous refactoring	Refactoring across team boundaries is a significant challenge, again requiring tooling and process changes.

A "narrow DevOps" focus on tooling over people and as a local optimization in IT is not optimizing for outcomes. The foundations of DevOps, continuous integration, and continuous delivery (or even continuous deployment) are based on a culture focused on cooperation and collaboration across role specializations in order to optimize for the fast flow of safe value. Tools can only hope to support the skills, culture, and flow, and at best encourage them. They cannot replace them. As Patrick Debois, godfather of the DevOps movement, has often stated, "DevOps is a human problem."[10]

2: No Technical Career Path for Hands-On Software Developers

Often there is a failure to provide a career path—recognition, impact, pay, safety, interesting work, management if you want it or individual contribution if you don't—for technology specialists. Offering this is second nature for IT organizations; however, it's not for traditional, non-IT organizations, despite having large numbers (tens of thousands) of engineers.

Many enterprises fail to recognize individual (non-manager) contributors at senior levels, at least ones with hands-on software engineering roles. In traditional organizations outside of the IT industry, software developers often have to stop coding and take up either line management or PowerPoint to progress in seniority.

Progressing to manage people whose job you used to perform is a well-worn path to seniority and an aspiration for some. But for those with a software engineering mindset in particular, the transition from hands-on engineer to managing engineers can be a challenge. Personnel management isn't for everyone, and it shouldn't be the only choice for engineers who want to further their career.

Alternatively, moving "upwards" from hands-on coding to "design" or "architecture" roles where the output is PowerPoint or Visio or similar is also something we continue to observe in many organizations. Given the continuing rapid advances in technology, there's often a significant danger having those who don't develop or operate software, or haven't for a number of years, giving command-and-control instructions in the form of architecture and design artifacts to those who do.

3: Robots Replace Testers

Sometimes the balance can tip too far on automation, in particular test automation. People are still needed for the human touch, for "unhappy path" testing, for the scenarios that automation was never considered for. Also, automation cannot currently continuously improve itself, an issue observed at Tesla where, according to Elon Musk, they went too far on automation, which led to not being able to meet expected production volumes.[11]

Automated testing and test-first development are key practices of modern software engineering. Automated functional tests protect against new functionality causing defects in existing features. They run repeatedly as small changes are introduced to software and are essential for the move to small batch work and continuous delivery. None of the practices in agile software development, DevOps, and continuous delivery have a fraction of their effect without comprehensive, automated functional testing.

Test-Driven Design—or Behavior Driven-Design or Example-Guided Design—is a core practice for driving simple, maintainable, agile software that can grow over time. Software consultant Michael Feathers has made it clear that testing and design are complementary, the former informing the latter: "If it's difficult to write a test for a code change, your code could be more modular, and the modules should be relatively small. . . . Bugs are a symptom of misunderstanding. With modularity, quality follows."[12]

Organizations, however, often "throw out the baby with the bathwater," going too far in thinking that testing specialists are no longer needed due to automated tests written by developers. By no longer including testers on teams, they miss people who excel at finding the "unhappy path."

Michael Bolton and James Bach, proponents of the Context-Driven school of testing, warn against the dangers of this approach. They distinguish *testing*, which they describe as an essentially human activity like programming, from *checking*, the potentially repetitive task of setting up, acting, and asserting behavior that is often performed by manual testers and that can be automated in software.[13]

Bolton and Bach assert that the human element of testing is exploring a built product or feature in its operating context in order to assess its quality through experimentation. They reject the need repetition of "exploratory testing" (it's just "testing") and make use of Herb Simon's concept of "satisficing,"[14] a portmanteau combining "satisfy" and "suffice," to argue that testing activities can never completely prove that a product or feature is entirely defect-free. The process of testing—no matter how automated—can only communicate to people what exploration and assessment has been performed and advise on the risk of releasing the feature to users.

From Antipatterns to Patterns

Be Excellent

The common factor in the antipatterns of this chapter is not paying enough *continuous attention to technical excellence*.

There might be an over-indexing on the word "velocity," where over the medium to long term there is too much focus on being a feature factory and not enough focus on paying off technical debt, or even continuously improving to build up technical credit, which leads to future work being done Sooner. It may be that there is a focus on agile *work management* alone, with insufficient attention to technical agility. The technical architecture and the people architecture may be misaligned, or the focus might be on tooling while forgetting about people.

Of course, there are patterns to counter these antipatterns. They leverage many decades of experience in both manufacturing and software development in the context of product development.

For example, go slower to go faster. Prioritize a percentage of capacity in order to continuously improve. Avoid compound interest on your technical debt. Move from a vicious cycle to a virtuous circle. Second, have agility with a solid technical core, prioritize technical principles and practices. Third, architect and organize for flow, designing for team cognitive load and breaking dependencies. And fourth, focus on smart people with robot friends. As Toyota calls it, "autonomation," which is automation with a human touch.

These patterns, applied in context, optimize for delivery of **Better Value Sooner Safer Happier**.

Go Slower to Go Faster

High-performing organizations recognize that they need to go slower to go faster. In the same way as training for physical endurance events, such as a marathon or a cyclo-sportive, the recovery days are just as important as the training days, as that is when the body adapts and becomes stronger. Failing to schedule in enough recovery leads to overtraining, fatigue, and eventually illness or injury. We saw the product development equivalent of this in Antipattern 7.1, where a relentless focus on going faster incurs technical debt, which leads to going slower.

Organizations optimizing for **Better Value Sooner Safer Happier** recognize that a portion of all software development effort, week by week and even hour by hour, must be dedicated to a *continuous attention to technical excellence* instead of solely focusing on feature delivery. Granted there will be exceptions, such as intentionally incurring technical debt in order to capture an early mover opportunity. However, it's done intentionally, knowing that the debt needs to be paid down and that it will slow down future work. We will look at four key points: visualize, visualize, visualize; prioritize improvement of daily work over daily work; coaching technical excellence; and measuring and feedback loops.

1: Visualize, Visualize, Visualize

A "behavioral ninja move" is to visually represent the count of different types of items of value being completed for each iteration or over time. To quote Dominica DeGrandis, "make work visible."[15] There are at least four types of work: (1) new features, (2) failure demand (fixing defects), (3) risk stories (as per Chapter 5), and, most importantly to this chapter, (4) improvement stories. Mik Kersten uses the words Features, Defects, Risks, and Debts to refer to these four types of work in his Flow Framework.[16] These items of value are typically at the "story" level in agile terminology; each one should be small.

By visualizing the count over time of each of these types of work (see Figure 7.5), it's like switching on a light in a dark room. Let's say that features are represented in blue, defects in red, risks in yellow, and debts in green. If it's a sea of blue (a feature factory), it's a strong indicator that at some point in the future time will end up being a sea of red (defects) and green (debts), squeezing out capacity for blue (new features).

If there is a healthy balance between the work types, with a little of all of them all of the time, with a sustainable and *continuous* attention to technical excellence, that yo-yo from features to remediation is considerably less likely to happen. And it improves outcomes for future delivery. This can be a great visualization to enable teams to inspect and adapt.

The improvement work (either paying debt down or doing work proactively to prevent it occurring in the first place) is mostly *kaizen*, or continuous improvement. This is at the heart of both agile and lean, a constant process of reflection and action to improve based on insights. At Toyota, knowledge workers are expected to spend as much as 40% of their time on *kaizen* activities![17]

Occasionally the improvement work is *kaikaku* or radical change: rewriting rather than just refactoring applications; moving to cloud; or other significant architectural changes that need planning, funding, and time. As with the balance between work types, balance between *kaizen* and *kaikaku* in improvement work is needed too.

PATTERN 7.1

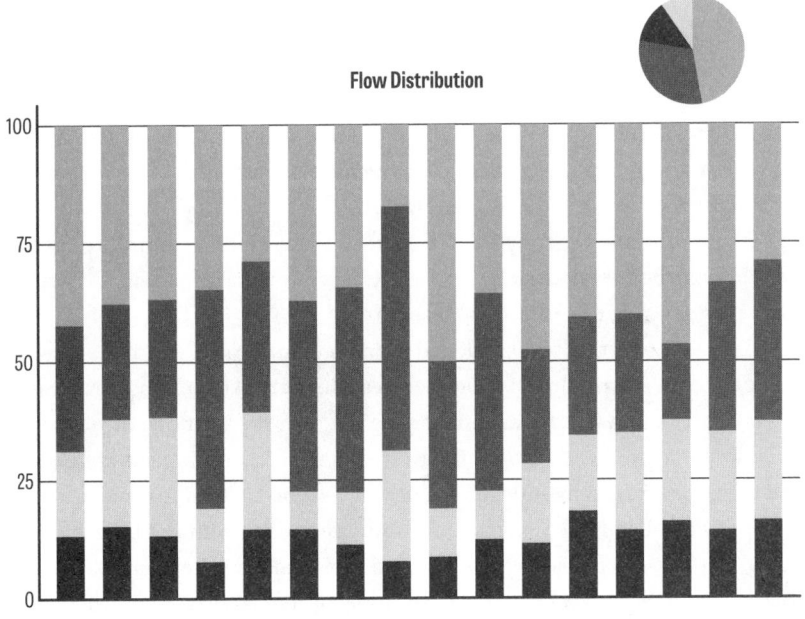

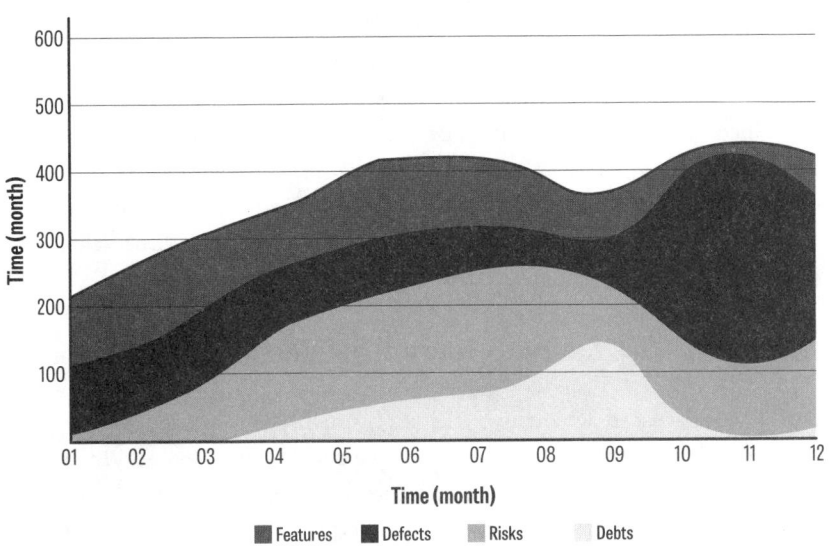

Figure 7.5: Flow Distribution

2: Prioritize Improvement of Daily Work over Daily Work

In *The Unicorn Project*, Gene Kim writes, "The Third Ideal is Improvement of Daily Work. Reflect upon what the Toyota Andon cord teaches us about how we must *elevate improvement of daily work over daily work itself.*"[18] This is the second part of the Go Slower to Go Faster pattern.

At a minimum, organizations as well as teams should commit to reserving a portion of their work backlog for technical improvement activity. In our experience, a good rule of thumb is at least 20%.

This balance of feature work and improvement work should be agreed over the long term. If one time period requires a higher focus on business features, the proportion of work types should even out over the next one or two periods.

I've seen this work most effectively when it's been agreed at the senior level of an organization—ideally the CXO level—so that there's understanding, support, and encouragement that the short-term commitment to features, features, features will be balanced with continuous improvement, allowing for any intentionally incurred short-term debt for commercial reasons, such as capturing a market opportunity.

As we saw in Antipattern 7.1, ongoing refactoring in an emergent domain is needed, as there are many unknown-unknowns. In addition, we saw how closed systems entropy over time. Both of these require that we have a *continuous attention to technical excellence and design*.

A focus and incentivization on **Better Value Sooner Safer Happier** influences desired behaviors, as constant technical improvement is needed for a positive trend on each of the **BVSSH** measures. It requires good cooperation, coordination, and partnership between the triumvirate of roles: the Value Outcome Lead, Team Outcome Lead, and Architecture Outcome Lead.

3: Coaching Technical Excellence

Pattern 2.1 discussed achieving big through small. The same approach applies to the adoption of technical practices by application delivery teams. While good practices exist, given that we're in an emergent domain of work, there are no *best* practices. Most of the practices that embody technical excellence and good design require tuning to context. And most are best adopted by teams with the help of software development professionals who have experience using them. This could be a coaching engagement across teams in an organization or it could be a "dojo"—a separate learning environment, as adopted by Target, Verizon, Walmart, and others.

As per Antipattern 7.4, it should not be a case of tools over people. Tooling by itself cannot perform or lead most good practices for highly maintainable software. Some tooling elements, though, used alongside human guidance, can help teams steer toward technical excellence. Table 7.1 lists key technical practices, along with the degree to which they are supported by tooling.

Table 7.2 Technical Practices Require Human Coaching, Not Tool-Only Outsourcing

Technical Practice	Tooling Supported?	Human Element	Tooling Element
Test-Driven (or Behavior-Driven, or Example-Guided) Design/ Development	Supported	Understanding the interplay between testing, modularity, and judicious use of test doubles. Understanding the nested levels of behavior and example—from customer or user behavior at feature injection level down to method or function behavior. Using BDD without any automation to explore scenarios augmented with feature injection.	Testing/BDD and mocking frameworks. Mutation testing frameworks to check the quality of tests themselves.
Domain-Driven Design	No	Appropriate application of DDD social and design patterns such as Ubiquitous Language or Bounded Context.	n/a

PATTERN 7.1

Technical Practice	Tooling Supported?	Human Element	Tooling Element
Simple Design; Clean Coding	No	YAGNI (You Aren't Gonna Need It); deciding on simplicity; good naming; right sized classes and methods..	n/a
Collective Code Ownership & Coding Standards	Supported	A high degree of cultural change from individuals owning areas of code.	Modern source code control supports collective code ownership strongly. Modern coding standards are typically highly automated.
SOLID principles	Slightly	Appropriate application.	Dependency injection frameworks for statically typed languages, if appropriate. (Though only if appropriate.)
Refactoring	Heavily supported	Refactoring's purpose is to aid human-to-human communication.	Most modern IDEs support a significant number of refactorings.
Continuous Delivery	Slightly supported	Involves the judgement of multiple stakeholders in a delivery team on continuous confidence in delivery quality through the pipeline.	Requires CI/TBD capabilities as above, extended to one-click deployment through to production systems.

PATTERN 7.1

Technical Practice	Tooling Supported?	Human Element	Tooling Element
Trunk-Based Development (TBD)/Continuous Integration	Supported	Continuous integration/TBDs aim for a fully integrated and working codebase on master/trunk available continuously to aid collaboration. Stop and fix practices—e.g., everyone focuses on fixing a broken build—as well as use of either pair programming or rapid review of small pull requests to ensure smooth flow are often significant cultural changes.	Requires a combination of source code control system, build server, and test automation. Some tooling can help with broken build fixes.
Observability	Heavily supported	Requires Development/Operations teams to prioritize the information they need to rapidly diagnose production issues.	Modern structured logging, monitoring, visualization, querying, and alerting capabilities.

PATTERN 7.1

Technical Practice	Tooling Supported?	Human Element	Tooling Element
Testing in Production	Heavily supported	Testing in production requires deep stake-holder confidence in a limited and highly controlled impact radius of novel features. It is *in addition* to all usual forms of testing, not instead of; therefore, it is Safer. It reduces risk significantly by acknowledging the real difference between pre-production and pro-duction environments and allows small incremental steps of production release rather than big bang.	Infrastructure to support blue/green deployment, canary/ring deployment, feature flagging, etc.

Teams and organizations should either take advantage of internal exper-tise and experience or bring in external, specialized agile software development coaching. These coaching skills are much rarer than "Agile process coaches." The split between agile-as-work-management, or at best agile-as-product-development, and agile-as-software-development is evident. The coaches should be used to up-skilling people and helping them understand how soft-ware engineering practices differ from those they might have used before when working in an agile way.

The pattern of design coaching used by Extreme Programming (XP) is for the team to continuously coach itself on appropriate technical practices with "promiscuous" pair programming. We'll discuss this more in Pattern 8.2. XP has an explicit role: a "Coach" who seeds the team with experience. It's a collab-orative rather than command-and-control approach to design quality.

The Toyota Kata techniques discussed in Chapter 8 are also highly applicable here. They allow teams to learn by doing, with the team lead typically adopting a coaching stance.

4: Measuring and Feedback Loops

The fourth part of the "Go Slower to Go Faster" pattern is to measure what matters. If you can't measure it, you can't improve it. Also, not everything that counts can be counted, and not everything that can be counted counts. In the context of continuous attention to technical excellence, all of the **BVSSH** measures matter, as they balance each other out. That said, the top two measures are Sooner (cycle time) and Better (quality). Improve these and they will have a virtuous effect on Happier, Safer, and Value.

Sooner measures the sustainable speed of delivery. An easy-to-measure metric is release cadence, the frequency of software releases. However, release cadence is also the easiest metric to game; thus, it is the least useful. For example, I've seen six "projects" running concurrently, each with a six-month lead time and each staggered by one month, giving the impression that the team was running monthly iterations. In reality there was a lot of context switching, the flow efficiency remained low, and the six-month lead time allowed a lack of technical excellence to remain, with impediments to flow remaining unresolved.

The State of DevOps Report and the book *Accelerate* concentrate on a subsection of the concept-to-cash value stream: the time taken from code check-in to production. It's a good metric to focus on for technical excellence as one part of the end-to-end flow. Optimizing this, getting it as fast as possible, including its component elements such as build time, where radically fast builds including automated test execution are possible, is a worthy endeavor as it will drive the need for technical excellence and provides a fast feedback loop. That said, take an end-to-end view and be wary of local optimizations. If it's not the weakest link in the chain for **BVSSH** outcomes, stop strengthening it and move to the weakest link.

Considering the broader end-to-end lead time, from concept to cash, and the "urgency paradox" described in Antipattern 4.1, we will see in Pattern 7.2 how enterprise architecture history, decisions, and design can have a significant impact on Sooner beyond the improvements that individual product development teams can make.

The other metric to look at—one that will also have an impact on speed—is Better, which is quality. Quality should be continuous and built in, not inspected in later. A lagging measure of Better is "incidents in production." This is a primary measure, as the proof of the pudding is in the eating. Defects that are not in production are not a measure of quality; they're just unfinished work.

There are also leading measures of quality, such as static code analysis metrics. Tools such as SonarQube allow a high-quality data visualization of at least some aspects of code level design quality. They can also spot security vulnerabilities, potential bugs, test code coverage, cut and paste duplicated code, coding standard breaches, code complexity, and so on—and tools like this plugged into the developer's Integrated Development Environment (IDE) shift these quality checks far left (e.g., SonarLint, the IDE plugin for SonarQube, or language specific tools like FXCop, Checkstyle, ESLint, and a plethora of others).

Maintainability of code is key in order to optimize for outcomes—understanding code from individual lines, to methods or functions, up through the nested modules of the design. Static code analysis can help indicate areas that may be more complex than they need to be.

Significant success has been seen in implementing these in a phased approach. Start by visualizing code quality and surfacing it to teams, then have teams hold themselves to a quality bar. SonarQube, for example, distinguishes the stock (old) and flow (new) code and allows teams to set a quality bar on the flow of code so that continuous improvement is supported.

Regardless of what is being measured, measure the *work not the worker* and focus on the trend over time rather than the absolute, as contexts vary. As we saw in Antipattern 7.1, measuring the worker does not optimize for outcomes. A team succeeds and learns together. The atomic unit for the work is either the IT product, or the team. If there is a desire to compare outliers, to see what's working well, compare teams. Then it is up to the team to continuously improve and/or to coach others. If there are individuals in teams who are generating low-quality code, the team is best at resolving that.

PATTERN 7.2

Continuous Technical Excellence

In Antipattern 7.2, I explained how agile work management alone creates a "Agile Hollow Shell" without necessarily improving technical practices. The counter pattern to that focuses on the technology ecosystem, at the team level and at the enterprise level, that supports continuous technical excellence. This enables agility with a solid technical core.

When Diana Larsen and James Shore introduced the Agile Fluency model in 2012, they offered an evolutionary approach for teams and organizations to adopt layers of agile approaches. The model is neither a maturity model nor the basis for targets for teams or organizations. Kelsey Hunter notes that in the model, "[i]t is even possible for teams to go backwards deliberately, if a lower level of fluency makes sense for your context."[19]

Fluency Level 1, *Focusing*, is solely concerned with agile work management: "agile fundamentals" as Larsen and Shore describe it; "it's a great way to demonstrate success and create buy-in for further investment."[20]

Level 2, *Delivering*, is where significant benefits start to accrue. Larsen and Shore describe how the technical practices in Extreme Programming and some of the technical aspects of DevOps go beyond the initial "focusing" benefits of pure work management delivered by Scrum to create work with "low defects and high productivity." They note that Level 2 "is the most technically intensive fluency zone."[21]

However, Level 1 is where we have seen most agile adoptions or transformations stall—it's where many agile coaches feel most comfortable and where, for example, most process training focuses. But "low defects and high productivity"—as *Accelerate* demonstrates—are correlated with the technical practices of Agile Fluency Level 2 and beyond, which need coaching too.[22]

1: Technical Excellence throughout Everyday Work

This pattern asks us not to treat technical work and feature work in software delivery as two separate concerns. There should be no "Agile hollow shell." Overall technical excellence principles and context-specific practices should be well defined and part of the process. There should be a solid technical excellence core to build with.

Extreme Programming and its advocates understand that to deliver software agility, you need to fold lightweight software practices throughout the system of work. Many of the practices described above need to be applied together continuously, from high-level definitions of a concept to delivering value. Technical excellence practices need to be part of everyday work.

PATTERN 7.2

These technical practices are largely focused at the team and individual application levels. We also need to look at how these individual teams and single applications change together to build valuable business outcomes.

2: Provide Craft Servant Leadership

Providing servant leadership support for technology engineering should cover both software engineering as well as infrastructure engineering (which is turning into software engineering in modern cloud environments).

In order to have agility with a solid technical core, a small, shared Software Engineering Center of Excellence (CoE) (aka Guild or Practice) and a voluntary, open-to-all Community of Practice (CoP) work well, per Pattern 4.1. The CoE is not a Center of Employment—quite the opposite. It is a small team that is there to support the engineering specialists in the organization who are aligned to value streams, own the software engineering principles for the firm, advise on practices, determine the minimum viable guardrails, catch bubbled up impediments, remove those impediments from the teams, connect people, improve processes, provide tooling, share, connect the learning bubbles, foster a technical career path, attract and retain engineers, and ultimately enable the delivery of Better Value Sooner Safer Happier.

3: Enterprise-Level Architecture Development Excellence

We've seen that existing enterprise architecture design, and especially heavily layered architectures and their organizational structures, can be a significant impediment to flow. It can significantly impact the effectiveness of team-level technical practices. Instead, focus not only on team-level or application architecture but also on enterprise-level architectural excellence.

Enterprise architecture practices should be like the business outcome–driven approaches described in Chapter 5, and their strategies should evolve to optimize for the fast flow of safe value across the enterprise application estate. There should be a focus on architecting for flow and autonomy (as well as the "-ilities")—not only for individual applications but also for the interplay of the enterprise application ecosystem, which is often counterintuitive for traditional EA functions. Teams may have quarterly business outcomes that are focused on enterprise architecture refactoring, which go on the portfolio roadmap. The beauty of this approach is that it also forces a business value articulation of the refactoring, which can help with partnering as an "our business" team.

As we saw in Chapter 5, the way EA interacts with value stream teams needs to be optimized for the fast flow of safe value, with an EA member being part of a value stream Safety team, with frequent and lightweight interaction and in context, rather than just up front.

The *kaizen* continuous improvement activities on long-lived IT products, as discussed in Pattern 5.1, should also be attached to business outcomes. Teams should feel that when they deliver this set of experiments this quarter, they'll do them the right way and they will evolve the enterprise architecture toward a structure that better supports team autonomy.

PATTERN 7.3

Architect and Organize for Flow

In Antipattern 7.3 we saw a failure to pay heed to Conway's Law. We saw a model where teams and technologies were organized around component layers and the implications of a mismatch in the people architecture and the technical architecture. This can come about via a transformation attempt to change the team model without changing the technology architecture or vice versa.

Organizations orienting around value streams are optimizing for the fast flow of value, as we saw in Pattern 4.1. And in order to maximize outcomes and avoid introducing additional dependencies, it is important that this is done with the essential technical nature of software work in mind where the value streams include IT.

The implications of Conway's law and its reverse need to be taken into account. The architecture of technology in enterprises with large legacy technology estates will continue to constrain the most efficient structure of the organization unless deliberate efforts are made to improve both together. (See Figure 7.6.)

1: Temporary Shared Service Value Streams

A "ball of mud" IT system is monolithic. It does many things for many value streams. It is tightly coupled, and because it is not componentized, it struggles to exhibit agility. It has lots of hands on it and generally has complexity that does not fit into one person's head. It usually requires everyone to test and release at the same time, whether they want to or not. It is a living, technical bottleneck to flow and quality and should not exist in its current form in order to optimize for BVSSH.

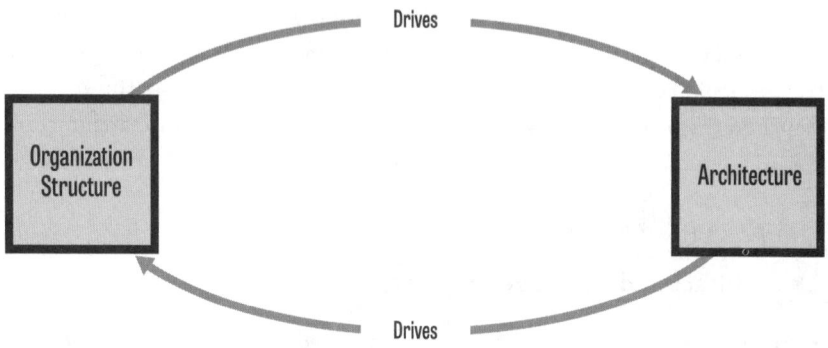

Figure 7.6: Organization Structure Drives Architecture, Drives Organization Structure

To architect and organize for flow, house it in a *temporary shared service value stream*, as we saw in Pattern 4.1. Then, over the course of potentially multiple years, work on breaking it up into many small, independently testable and deployable components, with a people architecture to suit, such as a small agile team and small agile components. A "Strangler Pattern" can be applied. The Strangler Patter was first described by Martin Fowler in 2004, named after the Australian strangler fig. Fowler says:

> An alternative route [to huge rewrites] is to gradually create a new system around the edges of the old, letting it grow slowly over several years until the old system is strangled. Doing this sounds hard, but increasingly I think it's one of those things that isn't tried enough.[23]

The components should sit over time in the proper long-lived value streams. Eventually, you can decommission the temporary value stream, with the monolithic "ball of mud" no longer existing. This takes time. There is no quick fix. Therefore, the best time to start is now.

2: Design for Team Cognitive Load

In their book, *Team Topologies*, Matthew Skelton and Manuel Pais write about the intersection of architecture and organization with reference to Conway's Law. They argue that independently deployable software components should be about the size that a single agile team of around nine people with T-shaped skills (see Chapter 8) can develop and operate. Most of those components, they add, should deliver independent business value with a minority of specialized components and a thin layer of infrastructure.[24]

Skelton and Pais make clear that this approach does not necessarily imply the use of a microservices architecture. That said, the nature of a well-designed landscape of modern "big" microservices (beware of making them *too* micro) fits this pattern. Those microservices should own their own data, holding it in a single, logical data store or database that only the service can access directly. They should have their own business logic, may be based around a "bounded context," and may own their own front end in a micro-front end pattern. They should also be loosely coupled to other services via events or messages with limited reliance on API calls and be independently testable, deployable, and scalable.

When architecting and organizing for flow it is advisable to design for what Skelton and Pais call "Team Cognitive Load,"[25] or as Dan Terhorst-North says, "software that fits in your head."[26]

This requires a very intentional focus on continuous improvement, on upgrading planes mid-flight, and a broad recognition from everyone that "evergreening" and continuous technical improvement is a first-class category of work. As we've seen throughout this chapter, it's a daily process of constant improvement (*kaizen*) and occasional step changes (*kaikaku*). It's Punctuated Gradualism.

A principle that I've used successfully in the past is "Multiple Speeds in Parallel." There may be daily deployments of slivers of value, generating fast feedback and fast value. There could be monthly refactoring, such as the first small experiment with a new technology or the splitting of a microservice that was starting to lack high cohesion. And there may be larger, quarterly improvements (still with a start small, learn fast, de-risk approach), which could be going from on-prem to cloud for the first time or running an experiment with a new technology for the streaming of data.

PATTERN 7.3

3: Don't Only Manage Dependencies, Break Them

Effort must be put into breaking dependencies between technical components and teams, not only in managing them. Breaking dependencies enables agility and BVSSH.

A mistake I have seen made in the past is spending too long managing dependencies rather than breaking them. There was then a pivot to put a lot of effort into breaking dependencies. There are many ways to break dependencies, including, as above, moving from a monolith to independently testable and deployable components, service virtualization (to mimic the work having been done on a dependent service), feature toggling (so that the work can be shipped, toggled off), shared code ownership, and in some cases seeding developers onto other teams (alleviating human dependencies). Your choice will be unique to your context. Most important is the capability to inspect and adapt and continuously improve. Habitual behaviors and the support you have is important in building meta-level capability.

These approaches increase high cohesion and loose coupling in enterprise architecture, which increases agility. In particular, they allow many of the work-management aspects of enterprise agile frameworks to fall away. As dependencies are broken, as teams have high autonomy, high alignment, and the technical ability to release customer value independently to production, there is less need to spend time on coordination, on synchronizing releases, on big-batch integration testing, or on dependency coordination.

Most of the scaling practices of these frameworks are about the scaled management of hard dependencies across teams. Because enterprises have traditionally optimized their architectures for factors other than the fast flow of safe value, starting with some of the practices used to scale frameworks can be useful, and they shouldn't be viewed as the destination. They'll give an incremental improvement in efficiency as opposed to the radical, exponential improvements possible with autonomous teams and architecture.

Case Study: CSG Pivots From One-Size-Fits-All Agile to a Focus on Outcomes and Behavior

In 2007, CSG International, a provider of software and services to the telecommunications industry, decided to move away from a more than twenty-year-old waterfall practice to an all-in Agile methodology. This methodology, adopted in a big-bang manner, implemented the same practices and roles across the entire portfolio of 600+ people across fifty teams. After two years, the effort was abandoned. Scott Prught, SVP Software Engineering, explains:

In lieu of a one-size-fits-all approach, our teams stepped back and, in the context of software development, initially focused on technical practices on a few teams. These practices "paved the way to production" in a similar way across teams. There was a Think Big, Start Small, Learn Fast approach. This accelerated feedback and hence learning greatly, which was critical in changing the way people worked and behaved.

In 2009, the lead time for features were still very long, and customers were frustrated. We realized that overall lead time would not improve unless we continued to improve our agility. Specifically, we found that the wait time from handoffs and queues dominated a significant amount of our end-to-end time to value. We had a low flow efficiency, with large batches of work (200+ features) and a time to market in excess of 430 days. Quality remained problematic. With many role-based handoffs, we had the "there's no hole in my side of the boat" problem.

We wouldn't get to the next level unless we addressed these handoffs and lack of end-to-end accountability with role-based silos reminiscent of Taylorism from the early 1900s. In 2012 we reorganized from role silos to product aligned groups with multidisciplinary teams. Our teams doubled their release cadence, going from twice a year to one a quarter. This cut our batch size in half and enabled sooner delivery of value to customers.

The next impediment that surfaced was IT Operations struggling with the faster pace. To improve this, we launched "Shared Operations Teams" who "owned" both non-production and production environments and who deployed daily to the non-production environment. At first this change in behavior was very difficult. It took many months for the team to rationalize the differences between environments and automate many of the manual tasks required to get to daily deploys. The results of this experiment were amazing though. By practicing deployments daily, the Operations teams were able to learn about upcoming features and changes as well as to continually improve their deployments and the operational environment. With this new habit, releasing became a non-issue and our Operations engineers were able to play video games as the release was deployed!

PATTERN 7.3

We found that release quality was very good but that 98% of the issues in production were occurring outside the release, and 92% of those were quick fixes by IT Operations. We discovered that although we were going fast, there was a lot of rework on the other side of the operational wall. There were still many manual processes to get the software into production. Worse yet, the developers understood very little about the production realities and pressure the IT Operations teams were under to "get things right" with difficult to run software.

We decided to design a team topology such that accountability and understanding of both the software and how it runs live on the same team. "You build it, you run it." To do that we merged the development and operations teams together to form cross-functional "DevOps Teams." These teams own the full lifecycle from design to operations of a product. We also provided more self-service provisioning to further remove hand-offs and wait time.

Our overall improvement journey to this point took many years, and we will never be done. The results have been amazing. Overall quality (Better) has improved about 80% while increasing transactions (Value) over 700%. Our time to market and time to learning (Sooner) to deliver features is almost at a five times improvement, with a reduction from 249 days to fifty-six days. And the most amazing part is that our people are happier! Our overall employee net promoter score has increased over 400% in this time frame! We are delivering **Better Value Sooner Safer Happier** with more improvement still to come.

PATTERN 7.4

Smart People and Smart Teams with Robot Friends

In Antipattern 7.4 we looked at how taking a tool-first approach without taking the human factor into account does not optimize for outcomes. All the advances in using technology to build and operate software have not removed the need for skilled and talented people. On the contrary, they've helped provide a foundation for skilled and talented people to focus on creative knowledge work rather than repetitive drudgery. Matching smart people in smart teams with robot friends, what Toyota calls *jidoka*, or autonomation, leads to **Better Value Sooner Safer Happier**. There are four parts to this pattern: change culture through behavior: start small and experiment; develop technical careers; autonomation: quality specialists with robot friends; and build resilience.

1: Change Culture through Behavior: Start Small and Experiment

The first thing to remember is people first. Adopting continuous attention to technical excellence and good design requires *cultural change*—not a new process or shiny tools. "No matter how it looks at first, it's always a people problem."[27] Tools can help, but cultural change patterns such as unlearning and relearning, safe-to-learn experiments, inviting innovators per the Diffusion of Innovation curve, and generating social proof are needed to bring lasting success. The focus is people → process → tooling, in that order.

John Shook, chairman of the Lean Global Network, has argued that you don't change culture or mindset before behavior; you change behavior first, typically in a small way—"act your way to a new way of thinking," and the mindset will follow.[28] You lead by example—not by mandating a process, but by sharing or suggesting a practice in the context of the people.

I've had great success using this in coaching technical excellence—for example, working with a team to experiment with adopting Trunk-Based Development practices, sharing how things could be done differently, asking a team what blocks they would have to working this way, sharing why it might be better, and then leaving the team alone for a few weeks to experiment with it, with an option of continuing or reverting to their old ways of working.

As we saw in Pattern 2.1, it is usually optimal for that shift to take the form of "Achieve Big through Small" and an S-curve adoption in which cultural change happens at the pace that people unlearn and relearn, which cannot be forced, only given a headwind or a tailwind. It avoids new labels on the same old behaviors. Breaking down barriers between Dev and Ops, between Dev and Test, between Business Analysis and Dev, between customers and Business Analysis doesn't happen overnight in any large enterprise. As per Pattern 3.2, invite over inflict. Start with your natural champions, your Innovators.

Often, changes to formal processes can catalyze changes in behavior, as observed by John Shook. We typically don't want to mandate processes on people. That said, every medium and large organization will have documented policies, standards, controls, and processes for change delivery and for service management, as part of the control environment.

PATTERN 7.4

I have seen in a number of organizations how a ways-of-working team takes ownership of such processes—such as a formal software delivery lifecycle (SDLC) or Release Management process—and updates the processes to allow and incentivize teams to behave more like they actually own their applications. This is done with the rationale that given that these formal processes are needed for clarity of controls and consistency, they should be updated to optimize for continuous delivery, for the fast flow of safe value. This is done with the formal backing of senior management and internal audit.

The increase in team autonomy can lead to an increase in technical excellence and quality through the greater sense of shared ownership of outcomes. In addition, the team becomes value stream–aligned and multidisciplinary. From a partnering perspective, there should be no "us and them." There should be no role-based handoffs. The tribal identity is within the value stream and the team succeeds or learns together. Done well, a virtuous circle results.

Of course, some modern tooling can help out, as we have seen earlier. And typically this again needs to be done in the context of people—the pace of their learning and their ability to absorb change.

2: Develop Technical Careers

A technical career path to the highest levels in an organization must be paved and supported. A number of traditional organizations, late to the game compared to IT firms, have started to formalize a technical specialist career path for software engineers, providing an option beyond managing other engineers or producing PowerPoints.

Distinguished Engineer Programs

Technology firms including IBM have long had the role of Distinguished Engineer. Other enterprises, particularly in the financial services industry, have initiated similar programs to recognize and reward outstanding individual contributors. Depending on the organization, it can represent the pinnacle of a technical specialist career path.

A standalone recognition for a few distinguished individuals—typically numbering in double digits in organizations of tens or hundreds of thousands—is worthwhile; however, it is not sufficient to motivate, retain, and reward skilled developers as they progress through their career. A feeder program can bring more junior and highly recognized expert or enterprise engineers to a level below the Distinguished Engineer track, such as Expert Engineer.

Some industries both in and out of IT have a clear managerial "M" track and a technical specialist "S" track. However it's built, the career structure of an organization should be clearly marked as a path to promotion and recognition for software and infrastructure engineers who want to remain hands-on, although this should be done while avoiding a "hero" or "rock star" culture, and ensuring that their experience is used to coach and act as a beacon to the next generation of talented technologists.

UK Government Digital Service Technology Career Framework

One great example of a framework for career development in technology, and one that has been an inspiration for a number of other enterprises, comes from the UK Government Digital Service.[29]

The framework describes roles, with a set of skills and expected skill levels, at differing levels of seniority. For example, the Software Developer role passes through six levels, from apprentice to principal developer, and has two tracks with differing skill expectations: management and technical specialist, which remains a hands-on role up to the highest level of seniority.

3: Autonomation: Quality Specialists with Robot Friends

The third part of this pattern is to focus on "autonomation"—automation with a human touch. In the antipattern, we looked at how automation alone is not optimizing for **BVSSH**.

Within the umbrella of quality, the value that testers bring is finding the "unhappy path." Human testers can, usually, find flaws in features that developers think are delivered perfectly. A modern testing approach shifts quality left. It automates as many repetitive checks as possible, with test-first (happy path) development, and leaves space for human interaction when a distinctive testing mindset and skill set are needed, in scenarios that perhaps the developer did not or could not consider with three hundred cognitive biases at play. Those instances might include spotting unconsidered defects or unhappy paths prior to development starting on a new feature or story. Human testing can also take place during construction as developers build small, valuable slices in minutes or hours. The test specialists on the teamwork closely with the developers at their desktops or over chat software rather than waiting for formal handoffs.

PATTERN 7.4

Testing can take place after construction when a feature is close to release and the testers can spot final, unpredictable "unfinished work" in user experience and business functionality. They can also track down defects in production for teams who are closer to operating in a "you build it, you run it" manner.

The trick for organizations is training and nurturing talent in testing specialist roles within a product development team. This quality assurance work should be focused on people using their creative mind, not performing repetitive tasks that a robot can and should undertake. Humans should not be completing a spreadsheet of several hundred predetermined manual tests.

4: Build Resilience

As there is a shift left in testing and an increasing focus on quality over testing—as quality is built in (for example, with test-first development) rather than tested in later—there should also be a shift in focus in the team toward resilience. This means assuming failure will happen and handling it gracefully rather than seeking to avoid failure and then failing catastrophically when it happens, as has been the focus in the past. This is a focus on mean time to recovery over mean time between failure.

Resilience is a part of technical excellence and needs to be factored in continuously. It needs to be designed in and tested and improved over time based on learnings. It needs a proactive approach. One approach to building in resilience is Chaos Engineering, injecting deliberate failure into a production environment, similar to Red Team testing in a cyber context. This enables a fast feedback loop, identifying deficiencies with a limited "impact radius" ahead of an actual outage. It helps developers better consider failure patterns in the wild and how to architect the system to be fault tolerant. This is a combination of human "unhappy path" testing, supported by tools to inject failure in order to build resilience.

Summary

Go Slower to Go Faster, or You Will Go Slower

Technical excellence antipatterns such as a relentless focus on new features build up technical debt, create a lack of partnership, fail to deal with entropy, develop "agile hollow shells" with no focus on a solid technical excellence core, misalign people architecture and technical architecture, and prioritize tools over people.

Challenges with software delivery speed and quality come from a lack of a *continuous attention to technical excellence and design*. Systems experience entropy, unless attended to on an ongoing basis. Ongoing simplicity in software is hard.

There is an old programmers' joke: a junior developer writes code; a senior developer deletes code; an expert developer avoids writing the code in the first place. Simplicity and technical excellence at the enterprise level requires intention and prioritization. It requires deliberate practice.

Going slower allows you to go faster by visualizing work types, prioritizing improvement, coaching, measuring, making technical excellence part of everyday work, providing craft servant leadership, aligning people architecture and technical architecture, breaking dependencies, and utilizing smart people and smart teams with robot friends.

Together, over time, these patterns optimize for the delivery of **Better Value Sooner Safer and Happier**.

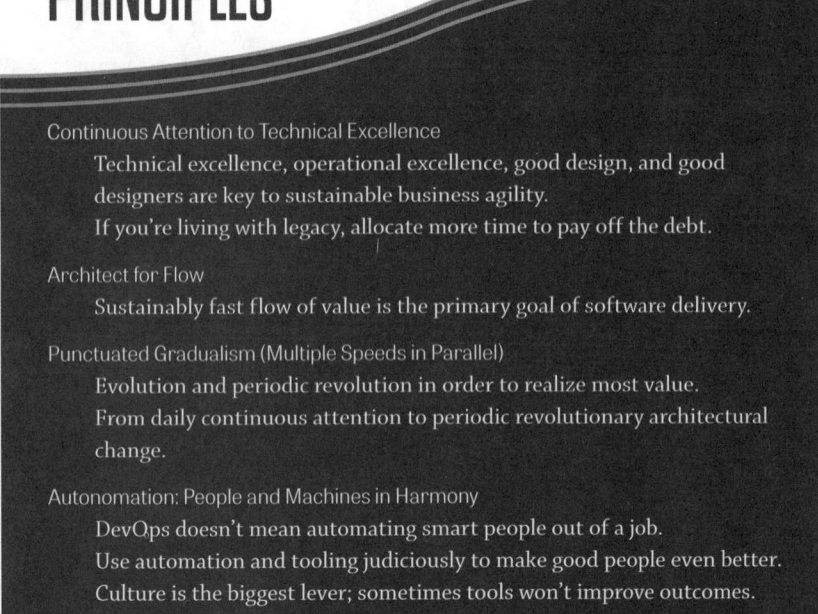

PRINCIPLES

Continuous Attention to Technical Excellence
> Technical excellence, operational excellence, good design, and good designers are key to sustainable business agility.
> If you're living with legacy, allocate more time to pay off the debt.

Architect for Flow
> Sustainably fast flow of value is the primary goal of software delivery.

Punctuated Gradualism (Multiple Speeds in Parallel)
> Evolution and periodic revolution in order to realize most value.
> From daily continuous attention to periodic revolutionary architectural change.

Autonomation: People and Machines in Harmony
> DevOps doesn't mean automating smart people out of a job.
> Use automation and tooling judiciously to make good people even better.
> Culture is the biggest lever; sometimes tools won't improve outcomes.

8
CREATE A LEARNING ECOSYSTEM

Between 1910 and 1920, the population of Detroit doubled, reaching a million
people. Most of that growth came from the arrival of immigrants looking for
jobs in the new automobile industry. They came from Austria-Hungary, Italy,
Russia, and countries across eastern Europe. A 1915 survey found that the workforce in Ford's Highland Park plant, which built the Model T, spoke more than
fifty languages.[1] So how did so many workers without fluency in a common language work together to assemble such a complex masterpiece of engineering?

In the days of Taylorism and then Fordism, workers didn't need to talk to
each other. The assemblers on the factory line had a division of labor. The first
screwed a screw. The second tightened a bolt. The third examined the screw
and the bolt and checked a box. Each person knew exactly what they had to
do—it was simple enough—so they had no need to speak to the person next to
them on the line. They didn't need to plan or share information or swap learnings. They just had to screw or tighten or check. It didn't matter that people
spoke fifty different languages in the same factory, with few able to speak one
common language. Communication was unnecessary. People were machines.

Today, a hundred years later, workforces are made up of knowledge workers, often scattered around the world. Microsoft, for example, has business
activity in 190 countries.[2] Teams working in the same value stream may speak
multiple languages; however, in the Age of Digital where product development
is unique, lack of collaboration and shared learnings has a direct negative
impact on productivity and organizational outcomes. Teams *must* be able to
communicate, collaborate, co-create, reflect, share what they're discovering,
and build a learning ecosystem irrespective of location or mother tongue.

This chapter focuses on learning and how knowledge is shared inside organizations so individuals, teams, and the enterprises themselves are able to be
the fastest learning organizations and continuously deliver **Better Value Sooner
Safer Happier**.

ANTIPATTERN 8.1

Information and Learning Silos

When you were a child, you might have played a game called "Gossip" or "Tele-
phone" or "Secret Message." In the game, everyone lines up or sits in a circle.
The first player whispers a message to the second person. That person whispers
the message to the third person, and so on until the message reaches the end
of the line or comes back to the start of the circle. The last person repeats the

message aloud, and everyone laughs at how the message changed as it moved from person to person. It is the simplest example of how quickly information can be lost because of cumulative, unintentional errors.

This same information loss occurs in business environments. Every time an analyst hands work off to a designer who then hands it off to a developer who then hands it off to a tester, some information about the work is lost. Each handoff might come with documentation, but each interaction with the work also generates "tacit knowledge," experience that cannot be written and is difficult to share. Michael Polanyi stated in his book *The Tacit Dimension*, "I shall reconsider human knowledge by starting from the fact the we can know more than we can tell."[3]

Lean software pioneers Mary and Tom Poppendieck have estimated that as much as 50% of information is lost in every handoff.[4] That means that by the time the work has undergone just four handoffs, that recipient is getting just 6% of the knowledge associated with the work.

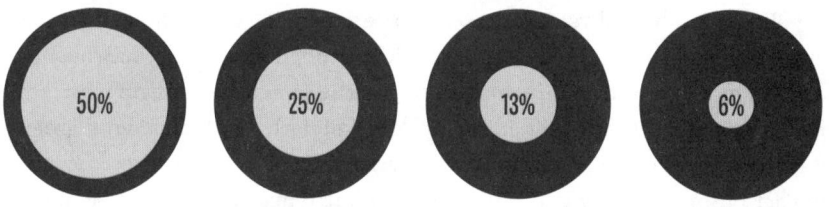

Figure 8.1: Information Loss on Handoffs

Back in the 2000s I was working for a major healthcare software company that was building hospital information systems. The company employed clinical analysts—physicians, registered nurses, dosimetrists, and so on—all SMEs in their fields with many years of hands-on experience. The SMEs were tasked with writing the requirement documents. They would describe when and what the system had to show to the hospital staff in different medical situations so the developers could plan the features. During an operating room procedure, for example, the software would need to show patient records, vital signs, and so on.

The requirement documents were long, often more than fifty pages. They rarely contained information that could be considered requirements even in the traditional sense. They didn't supply business logic or describe inputs and testable expected outputs. A developer might get to read an interesting account of how gamma knife surgeries are conducted. They would, however, come away little wiser about what exactly the gamma knife surgery software needed to do.

To its credit, the company recognized the problem and employed "systems analysts." Their role was to translate these lengthy documents created by SMEs into a language that developers could understand. They received the whispers from the SMEs and whispered them on to the developers who whispered them on to the testers and so on.

Like a game of Gossip, the process produced no winners, but it wasn't fun. Information was lost in each handoff, which produced cumulative errors. Because these big, up-front requirement documents took such a long time to write—often months, followed by several more months of translations, design, coding, and testing—comparing the original ideas with the end results in user acceptance testing took place twelve to fifteen months later! That is a long time from concept to learning. It's also a very long game of Gossip. The response to the difference between the intention in the original documents and the end result wasn't laughter. It was heated discussions, arguments, finger pointing, and blame.

The problem was that the structure at the company was made up of silos whose walls were guarded by quality gates. Information had to pass infrequently, in a fixed format, between silos. Incentivization was within silo.

That structure isn't unusual. Companies often create role-based information and learning silos. Others build temporary teams. They use projects as temporary vehicles to forge groups of people to conduct a mission. Once the project is over or during the ramping down phase, the teams are dissolved and its members are assigned to other projects. The learning that the team has built up throughout the project is lost. And there is an additional cost as every new team formation has to go through Tuckman's stages of forming, storming, norming, and performing all over again.[5] They lose the learning, cohesion, and social bonds that the team has built up.

Technology consultant Dan Terhorst-North likes to pose a thought experiment: if you could run a project again with the same team, the same organizational constraints, and the same context so that the only difference was the knowledge, experience, and learnings that the team had accumulated the first time, how long do you believe the work would take the second time? Answers usually range between half the time to one fifth of the time taken during the first run. That's the value of learning picked up by the team. To quote Dan: "Ignorance is the single greatest impediment to throughput."[6]

Back in 1936, Dr. T.P. Wright developed a theory of learning curves based on studies of aircraft cost. To put it simply, he found that the more you do something, the better you get at doing it. That experience and the knowledge it produces has a measurable value found in falling production costs. The knowledge delivers its full value to the organization only when it's shared across silos.[7]

ANTIPATTERN 8.2

Outputs over Outcomes

On an old automotive factory line there was always a direct correlation between "busyness" and productivity, the amount of output per unit of input. The more screws workers screwed and the more bolts they tightened, the higher the factory's productivity. That legacy is still very much alive.

Organizations are still trying to apply these principles to the world of knowledge workers. It doesn't work. Outputs like the number of lines of code produced, the number of story points delivered, the number of requirements fulfilled, or the number of features designed only shows how busy people are. They say nothing about organizational outcomes. Some companies go to the extreme of capturing time spent using *keyboards* and measuring the number of keystrokes made over a day to draw conclusions about developers' performance. It's like measuring the performance of soccer players by looking only at the number of miles covered during a game. A substitute who spent the entire match running around on the side of the pitch will have covered more miles over those ninety minutes than the goalkeeper. The goalkeeper, though, will have had a much bigger influence on the outcome of the game.

A focus on output rather than outcome remains common. At a conference, with positive intent and to be applauded for sharing the journey on the stage, a speaker described how the company had delivered more than 1,500 features the previous year. What wasn't articulated were the learnings from outcomes, such as the reaction of the customers, how many of those features were subscribed to, or what impact they had had on the organizational performance. Outputs are always much easier to define, monitor, and track than outcomes.

It is important to note that all the things that we ideate, design, build, and deliver, all the outputs we create, come from us, our teams, and the organization. However, learning whether we have delivered a valuable thing or not will not come from us; it comes from the customer. Thus, focusing more, or solely, on defining and tracking outputs instead of outcomes prevents potential learning. In addition, a focus on output requires little ongoing learning and reflection. Follow the prescribed plan, with learning backdated to the "end." Conversely, a focus on outcomes, with regular feedback loops builds learning into an everyday activity, as people reflect on how to best achieve the outcomes, for unique work in a rapidly changing environment.

ANTIPATTERN 8.3

The Bubble Effect

Amy Lynn Chua starts her book *Political Tribes: Group Instincts and the Fate of Nations* by noting that humans are tribal. "We need to belong to groups," she writes. "We crave bonds and attachments, which is why we love clubs, teams, fraternities, and family. Almost no one is a hermit. Even monks and friars belong to orders. But the tribal instinct is not just an instinct to belong. It is also an instinct to exclude."[8] This exclusion promotes the creation of social bubbles, whether consciously or unconsciously. Besides the positive benefits of these social structures, they all share some undesired antipatterns and bubble effects:

- **Silo mentality:** People and teams within the bubble develop a silo mentality. They want to protect their information, not share it with others in the same company.
- **Limited discoverability:** When learnings, knowledge, and information outside the bubble cannot be reached or discovery is limited. Are we living in a universe or multiverse?
- **Poor learning retention:** When people leave the company, their learnings are lost forever.
- **Duplication:** When sharing is limited, work is duplicated. The same ideas are developed and the same impediments tackled across multiple silos.

We can observe various forms of bubbles within organizations: role-based silos, agile, Scrum, Kanban teams, long-lived valuestream–aligned teams, and so on.

1: Waterfall Bubbles

On a conference call about the effectiveness of the new Jira set-ups, a lengthy discussion took place about how to configure notification mechanisms when tasks move from one state to the other. At one point, I asked why the notifications were needed. What would happen if the developer forgot to move a task on the board and the notification wasn't triggered?

The response was silence. No one could think of any other way that the person in the next stage in the process would know that they had work waiting for them. Knowledge workers have become so accustomed to working with tools and in their own silos that it didn't occur to them that they could actually speak to each other, pick up the phone, or bellow across the desks that they'd finished their task.

Traditional, waterfall, sequential delivery creates bubbles in each role-based silo. Analysts talk to analysts. Architects go to dinner together. Developers are down at the pub while the testers are testing. IT Ops are too busy fire-fighting. Information between waterfall bubbles travels by handoffs and document passing with loss of knowledge as described in Antipattern 8.1.

2: Agile Team Bubbles

The idea of agile teams comes with many positive behavioral patterns. They're small, cross-functional, multidisciplinary, long-lived entities with a clear focus, accountability, and the autonomy to self-organize. Their members build inward-looking behaviors, not connecting and sharing learnings with the rest of the organization. They collaborate daily in person to plan and discuss progress, impediments, and opportunities. When agile teams work well, their members build strong social connections and loyalty. The team succeeds or learns together.

As those connections strengthen, there is a risk that they form bubbles disconnected from the rest of the organization. Even with a positive organization for complex work, in the absence of deliberate intent, learning can be confined within invisible barriers instead of flowing freely throughout the organization.

3: Value Stream Bubbles

Long-lived teams built around long-lived value streams should provide an optimal, stable flow of communication and learning and enable teams to produce better designs. Even these teams-of-teams can become bubbles.

The challenge is balancing how and when to direct communications only through the value streams or share them with the rest of the organization. In an effort to optimize the value stream information and flow of learning, organizations sometimes go as far as inadvertently cutting communication lines beyond the value streams. This fails to optimize for overall organizational performance.

ANTIPATTERN 8.4

Applying a Deterministic Approach to an Emergent Domain

Even Albert Einstein sometimes gets things wrong. "God does not play dice," he once said, and that might literally be true. The world, though, is ruled by Heisenberg's uncertainty principle. Nothing is ever certain. We can only talk about risks and probabilities. The only thing we can say with anything approaching certainty is that we can expect to see the same mistakes occur again and again when applying deterministic, Taylorist approaches to an emergent domain of work, treating the unknowable as knowable.

Behind a deterministic mindset is a fear of uncertainty: the fear of not being able to tell when things are going to be done or a fear that people won't do the right thing if there is not a detailed plan. This traditionally leads to a lengthy, up-front planning process and big, up-front architecture and design, attempting to predict the future, in detail, at the point of knowing the least. This is a mismatch of the approach to work (deterministic) and domain of the work (emergent). With a charitable intent, it may be the case that there is a lack of awareness that product development is emergent or an internal fear of learning a new way to approach work that uses emergence as a lever to increase value over time. As per Chapter 5, it's still possible to have fixed dates and a roadmap, it's just done differently, exploiting emergence, learning, optimizing for flow, and the ability to pivot based on the learning in order to maximize *outcomes*.

A deterministic mindset typically comes with a command-and-control style leadership. Leaders who exhibit these behavioral patterns want deterministic plans with a set of milestones that will bear little relationship to the path that actually needs to be traveled. It may be a comfort blanket for some; however, it is a source of discomfort for many, by trying to lock in the future with unknown-unknowns. The focus is not on learning and pivoting to get to the best place. Instead, it's following orders, as per two technology revolutions ago.

As we've seen, when that happens targets are faked, not reached, and green lights signal that everything's fine until days before the launch deadline when suddenly everything turns red. That Watermelon Effect, when a project is green on the outside but red on the inside, occurs when the output is fixed in a context that is unknowable, as it's not been done before and the environment is changing at a faster pace than yesterday. It's also due to the burying of bad news that comes from a lack of psychological safety, the withholding of learning until firmly in the jaws of defeat.

This leads to no or limited space for learning for individuals and for the whole of the organization promoting ignorance with a Think Big, Start Big, Learn Slow approach, delaying time to react to when there is no time to react.

Taylor gives a sobering picture of this approach, which is the basis for traditional waterfall ways of working, in *Scientific Management*: "In our scheme, we do not ask the initiative of our men. We do not want any initiative. All we want of them is to obey the orders we give them, do what we say, and do it quick."[9] In other words, don't learn.

ANTIPATTERN 8.5

Weaponized Metrics

Writing about the difficulty of applying monetary policy on the basis of targets, Charles Goodhart noted that "any observed statistical regularity will tend to collapse once pressure is placed upon it for control purposes."[10] Marilyn Strathern, finding a similar difficulty in expectations of academic exam results, offered a simpler version. "When a measure becomes a target," she writes, "it ceases to be a good measure."[11] Using measures as targets pops up all the time at traditional organizations.

At an agile event, organizers could be seen wearing blue shirts with the following question on their backs: "How agile are you?" The charitable intent was to measure the agility of teams, and ultimately the agility of the company. The organization wanted to know the percentage of the software spend that went on work performed in an agile way. Senior leadership had asked for this number in order to have a measure of progress.

The response was four Agility Levels: mobilizing, transitioning, established, and optimizing.

The first two levels covered "doing agile." The second two were for teams who were "being agile." Each level had a set of criteria measured against organization, culture, process, and technical excellence. "Mobilizing," for example, required process improvement, regular retrospectives, an empowered Product Owner, cross-functional teams, coding and branching standards, etc. "Established" agility required small, long-lived, multidisciplinary teams aligned to a single product or platform, adaptive planning, a short release cycle time, automated build, a high level of automation of repetitive tasks, emergent architecture, and so on.

Teams periodically assessed themselves and reported on the progress of their journey. The hope was that by providing these definitions and criteria as guidance, teams would be able to better apply these practices and rise to the next level.

It didn't happen. As we've seen throughout this book, every context is unique. There is no single journey and no one size of agility that fits all. Impediments and focus priorities all differ according to the circumstances. Also, there is no "done." You are never done improving. You don't reach the top level and then stop.

Soon, the organization's business units were working toward set targets such as 30% "established" by the end of the year. This created the wrong behavior. Teams started gaming the metrics. As covered in Antipattern 1.1, it led to cargo cult behaviors. Individuals used it to define personal objectives. Even though the intention was positive, to provide guidance, the metrics had no correlation with the outcome-based benefits of **Better Value Sooner Safer Happier**, the job that agility is being hired to do.

In 2001, the UK's *Health Service Journal* described the use of the "hello nurse" in hospital accident and emergency departments. The job of a "hello nurse" is to meet a patient within five minutes of arrival—which they do, satisfying the relevant target. They then leave patients waiting for treatment for hours, which wasn't what the target intended.[12]

Meeting "how agile are you" target metrics does not necessarily correlate to improved outcomes. Usually it produces new labels with the same old behaviors. Daily standups or mandated bi-weekly sprint cycles (such as five analysis sprints, five Dev sprints, five testing sprints, or ten sprints in a Water-Scrum-Fall Gantt chart, predictively planned) does not necessarily result in better outcomes. A cross-functional team might still have role-based, tribal silos. An automated pipeline with a lack of technical excellence does not mean that the team is delivering the right thing; it might be functioning as a feature factory, pushing out low-quality code faster.

The focus is on meeting targets, not on inspecting and adapting in order to maximize outcomes. There is less focus on building a culture of learning when it's a case of following a checklist. By asking teams to use their own brains to decide how to improve outcomes, within guardrails, more emphasis is placed on building a culture of learning.

Also, as these examples highlight, trying to achieve targets sometimes promotes unethical behavioral patterns. This prevents learning on how to best achieve desired outcomes, with a focus on *doing Agile* instead of exhibiting agility.

From Antipatterns to Patterns

Connect and Share

These antipatterns are typical in traditional organizations. Information is lost in multiple handoffs; there is a focus on predetermined output rather than learning and pivoting to maximize outcomes; there are information bubbles without information sharing; and weaponized metrics focus the mind on achieving a target, however that's done, or on activities rather than outcomes.

These are the result of not optimizing for flow, a fear of uncertainty, a fear of losing mastery, a view that information is power so one should hold on to it, pathological or bureaucratic cultural norms, a silo mentality, focusing on "busyness" rather than outcomes, and no explicit actions being taken to increase transparency, share learning, or build a behavioral norm of feedback loops with early and often learning that is acted upon.

Each of these antipatterns has the same effect: they limit the creation and retention of learning and inhibit the sharing of information between individuals and across the company. They prevent the company from becoming a learning organization, failing to maximize **Better Value Sooner Safer Happier** outcomes.

Fortunately, there are a number of patterns that can encourage information flow and enable team members to share learnings.

PATTERN 8.1

Optimize for Learning

Once upon a time, individual knowledge stayed relevant for a lifetime—and even longer. A blacksmith would learn how to make horseshoes or swords as a youth and would continue making horseshoes or swords in the same way for the rest of his or her working life.

Before he or she died, the blacksmith would pass on his or her knowledge to a young apprentice. That apprentice would pass it on to the next generation, and so on. In the days of craft production, technology changed slowly and the work was repeatable and knowable, so the same knowledge remained valuable for a long time.

Today's knowledge becomes obsolete on a much quicker timescale. The half-life of the value of a new skill can be measured in years. Workers today need to unlearn and relearn much more quickly. In his bestselling book, *Unlearn*, Barry O'Reilly defines the cycle of unlearn and relearn in three steps: unlearn, relearn, and break through.[13] It starts with unlearning the behaviors and mindsets that prevent you and your business from moving forward followed by relearning new skills, and the last step in the cycle is to break through old mental models and habits by embracing new perspectives and ideas. There is a genuine mastery rather than rote learning. Indeed at a meta-level, the capability for an organization to do this quickly and effectively is essential in order to survive and thrive in the Age of Digital.

To optimize for learning, organizations must learn when knowledge is tacit versus explicit, and its implications on which practices to apply. They must identify and break silos, enable self-organizing teams, and establish channels for dialogue.

1: Tacit vs. Explicit Knowledge

Michael Polanyi described tacit knowledge as "information that is difficult to transfer," as opposed to the more formal, explicit knowledge for repetitive knowable tasks that can be written, transmitted, and easily understood by the recipient.[14] The steps to build a Lego model, for example, can be easily understood. Assuming that none of the parts are missing, someone who follows the instructions has a very high likelihood of producing an outcome that looks exactly like the model on the box's cover.

PATTERN 8.1

On the other hand, creating the detailed instructions needed to build the software that designed the model is much harder. By the time those instructions have been passed to the designers, then the developers, then the testers, the result will be very different to the original concepts.

As we saw in Antipattern 8.1, there is significant information loss at each handoff. Not all knowledge can be easily transmitted by writing it down and handing it over, which is why no swimming teacher has ever taught a student by giving them a swimming manual. They put their students in the pool and made them practice moving their arms and legs until they managed to stay afloat unaided and make their way to the end of the pool.

Some knowledge can only be shared by socialization, through the kind of shared learning experiences found in brainstorming sessions, pairing, face-to-face interactions, and a bias to action. Learning by doing, like a blacksmith training an apprentice.

In Chapter 0, we saw how work takes place in the five domains that Dave Snowden calls the Cynefin Framework. That framework can also be applied to knowledge as described in Figure 8.2. It provides a useful guide to how to optimize for learning depending on the domain. There is explicit knowledge on the right, which are the "ordered domains." There is tacit knowledge on the left, which are the "unordered domains."

In the **Clear** domain, workers follow the rules and apply best practices. This is the domain of explicit knowledge, where learnings can be shared through simple instructions, scripts, and guidelines—such as building a Lego model.

The **Complicated** domain requires experts who analyze and respond. This is not child's play. Work in this domain has been done many times before. There are known-unknowns. This is a domain of explicit knowledge where learnings can be documented and handed over even when they require plenty of detail.

The **Complex** domain is where people probe and respond. Work in this domain is unique, or the context is unique. It is emergent and there are unknown-unknowns. Workers need to apply a probabilistic approach and test hypotheses in order to learn. This is a domain of tacit knowledge. As we saw in Antipattern 8.1, tacit knowledge cannot travel by handoffs without significant loss of information, of learnings. In this emergent domain, skill-based silos present a strong antipattern. Instead, optimized learning takes place with a bias to action, by doing and co-creating in order to avoid a single person dependency.

The **Chaotic** domain has a blurry line between cause and effect. The rule here is to act first and hope something good happens. Any learnings generate tacit knowledge.

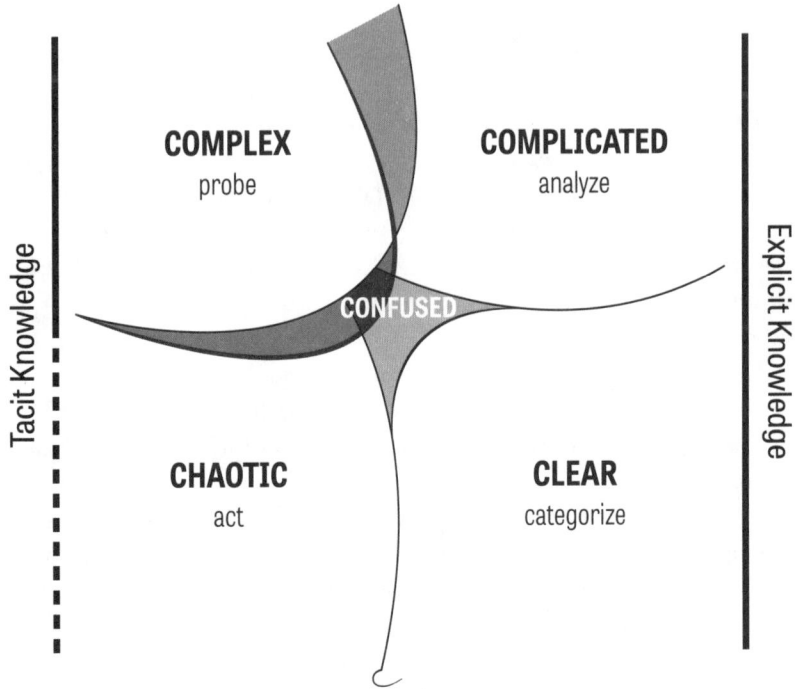

Figure 8.2: The Cynefin Knowledge Map

Confusion is when you are not sure what domain you are in. In this case, attempt to create a smaller domain of work.

The application of Cynefin in the context of information and knowledge provides useful guidance and insights on how the creation of learning happens and ways to optimize for it.

2: Identify and Break Silos

Installing end-to-end transparency will help make silos and bottlenecks visible, enabling identification of improvements to flow.

However the knowledge is created and regardless of whether it's tacit or explicit, it needs to be able to flow. Information and learning silos prevent the free, uninterrupted movement of knowledge. They block the creation of learning across a value stream. Value stream mapping can help identify the queues, handoffs, and information and learning silos that produce those blockages.

Representatives from each state of the workflow, from concept to production, should take part in the value stream mapping. Attendees can ignore their own cycles, whether they're sprints, flow-based, agile, or waterfall, and focus only on the flow of the work and the steps needed to go from left to right to complete production. The exercise could take two or more hours and will often require two or three long tables or a giant wall and a large amount of sticky notes. It is always a great learning exercise, as participants inevitably realize how little they know about the end-to-end flow of work, who does what, and how long it all takes.

The session installs transparency of silos, queues, impediments, and a number of improvement items to act on. It typically highlights bottlenecks, long wait times, and too much WIP. A typical outcome is the need to shift activities left, to build them in, collaborating early and often. Increasing transparency and collaboration leads to an improved flow of information, knowledge, and learning. Repeating this learning cycle regularly, such as once a quarter, results in continuous improvement of flow, information, learning, and ultimately better **BVSSH** outcomes.

3: Enable Self-Organizing Teams

Foster self-organizing teams, and teams-of-teams, with all the skills needed to ensure a fast flow of safe value, feedback, and learning end to end. This enables a shared understanding with minimal information loss and creates the ability to pivot quickly in order to maximize outcomes.

But having all the skill needed, aka cross-functional teams, alone does not prevent the team members from working in traditional skill-based silos— not unless the work also takes place through collaboration, pairing, and co-creation. Teams need to have the autonomy to organize themselves if the knowledge that they've acquired is to pass freely to where it's most needed.

Besides autonomy for teams to self-organize, there are other important enablers needed. Glenda Eoyang, founder of The Human Systems Dynamics Institute, has developed a theory and practice of human systems dynamics. Her model for self-organizing systems has three dimensions: containers, difference, and exchange.[15] Applying this concept in the organizational context, some examples are:

Containers: Long-lived, nested value streams with clear-cut strategic intent and shared strategic objectives, goals, business outcomes, shared beliefs, and mental models. Optimized for the fast flow of safe value and aligned to the customer. There should be high cohesion (do one thing well) and low coupling (minimize dependencies over time). Containers are interdependent services.

Difference: Diversity of skills, knowledge, experience, gender, and cultural background. This should be evident in multidisciplinary teams.

Exchange: Communication, feedback loops, and flow of information and learning.

Self-organizing patterns emerge in containers that hold diversity and allow free exchange of learning. People look to break specializations and develop new skills. They move from single, deep specializations to broad, cross-skill knowledge supported by multiple, deep specialist skills, from I-shaped to T-shaped to π-shaped and finally comb-shaped skills, as illustrated in Figure 8.3.

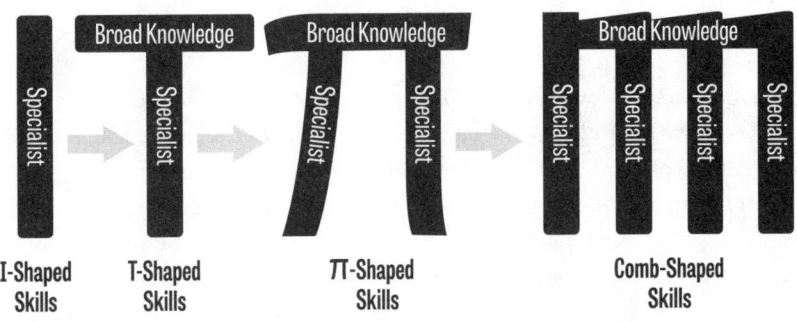

Figure 8.3: Skills Have Shapes

Physicist Jeremy England has argued that in nature, under certain conditions, matter will spontaneously self-organize.[16] This applies to teams and organizations as well, formally or informally. Teams should have the autonomy

PATTERN 8.1

to self-manage, self-design, and self-govern within their boundaries. Leaders can provide real empowerment to teams and individuals so that they decide how they want to work and what team-level processes they want to follow. Empowered teams and individuals are involved in goals and outcome roadmap settings. They set shared objectives and can decide how to get there.

Incentives should be aimed at teams rather than individuals and be based on shared, measurable, team-level outcomes. The old Taylorist approach of offering more pay to individuals who perform well can have negative outcomes in team-based work.

In 1968, the Ohio State Buckeyes football team introduced a tradition of rewarding the best individual players after each game. The coaches would give the best player a sticker depicting a buckeye leaf that they would place on their helmets. Everyone could see their acclaim and would work to win their own award. That year, the team won the national championship. Other teams soon copied the tradition.[17]

By 2001, with the same incentives still in place, the Buckeyes were a midleague, mediocre team with no apparent way back. Jim Tressel, the team's new coach, introduced a new way of rewarding effort and incentivizing players. Instead of rewarding individuals for scoring a touchdown, he started rewarding everyone when the team won or when they scored more than twenty-four points in a game. Rewarding teams over individuals paid off. The team went on to win the national championship and has been one of the most successful teams ever since.[18]

4: Dialogue

William Isaacs, co-founder of MIT's Organizational Learning Center and the director of the Institute's Dialogue Project, has described dialogue as the embrace of different points of view, literally the art of thinking together.[19]

Agile ways of working are based on dialogue. The Team Outcome Lead is responsible for encouraging dialogue, surfacing ideas from all team members, and making sure that everybody's voice is heard. They facilitate and coach to make sure that all voices and ideas are treated with respect, regardless of the source. They also prevent any power differences or antipatterns, like the HiPPO effect, taking over. Dialogue supports the optimization of learning. This is about diversity of opinion and thought and being actively and respectfully listened to by others, with everyone given a chance to speak. This can form part of a team charter and help to optimize for learning.

PATTERN 8.2
Nested Learning with Built-In Feedback Loops

A focus on output, rather than outcomes, guides behavior away from continuous learning, reflection, and adaptation and instead toward following a predetermined plan at the point of knowing the least, with learning coming in late, and with minimal time to respond to it.

In a learning organization, continuous learning happens at the individual level, the team level, and the organizational level at the same time. The absence of any of these layers prevents the creation of a learning organization and keeps knowledge siloed inside learning bubbles. Focusing on outcomes with nested learning loops promotes organizational learning and continuous improvement. This pattern is divided into the individual, team, and organizational levels.

1: Individual

Dan Pink, author of *Drive: The Surprising Truth About What Motivates Us*, describes personal mastery as one of the key factors that motivates individuals in addition to purpose and autonomy. Individuals, he says, have an intrinsic motivation to upskill, to gain new knowledge, and to self-develop.[20]

When information is able to flow through an organization, individuals can feel that they're constantly improving and always on a road to the next level. They want to pass through *Shu Ha Ri's* three distinct stages of a learning journey: the foundations when learners follow the rules, the mid-stage when they break the rules, and the advanced stage when they create new rules. They're always learning.

As we saw in Pattern 8.1, when there is autonomy, empowerment, intent, and purpose, individuals will look to develop skills and build mastery.

One of the obvious choices is training. Have you ever attended a classroom training session at which the trainer stood in front of the room and flipped through a long PowerPoint deck? How did you feel? Was it effective? How much learning did you take away? Did you have a good nap?

How information is delivered is important as it will determine how long the learnings will last. Sharon Bowman in her bestselling book *Training From the BACK of the Room!* introduces the technique of the four Cs: connections, concepts, concrete practice, conclusions.[21] The whole training and its sub-modules are designed as nested four Cs. In *connections*, learners connect to the topic through exploring prior experiences and knowledge. *Concepts* and *concrete practice* are largely self-learn, with a wide range of interactive, hands-on techniques. In *conclusions*, learners do self-reflection on the learning experience and teach back to the class.

A learners' own context is also vital. Learning happens when learners do the exercises and apply the practice in their own context. For example, if the concept is business outcomes, the trainer could give each group a flipchart and ask them to articulate a business outcome for their product. This provides tangible outcomes, takeaways, and enables continuation of using the concepts and practices.

There are other ways to develop skills and gain new knowledge, like participating in internal or external meet-ups, conferences, or through collaboration, breaking specialization. We will see more on these in the later parts of this pattern.

2: Team level

While individual learning is relatively straightforward, provided the right conditions as described in the previous section, learning at a team level is more complex and takes place in a number of different ways: nested learning loops, continuous improvement, and by working together.

Nested Learning Loops

Team events like daily coordinations, standups, weekly reviews, demos, retrospectives, and monthly show-and-tells are all team learning sessions. Besides learning about outcomes, these sessions are the mechanism to learn about team processes, policies, ways of working, their effectiveness, and what to improve. A specific case of retrospective is the debrief. It is used by fighter pilots and surgeons regularly after each mission or operation. The aim of the debrief is to share, communicate, and *learn* from what happened, why it happened, and how to improve. The most important ingredient of an effective retrospective or debrief is psychological safety, a safe environment where team members feel they can raise issues and concerns without fear that it will be held against them. Thus there is a rule of "no rank" in debriefs and similarly, optimally, "no reporting lines" in retrospectives.

In learning organizations, learning happens in loops that are nested on quarterly, yearly, and multi-year basis, and include measurable leading and lagging indicators. They allow regular learning on whether desired outcomes are being achieved or not. The learning loops include feature, story, and task breakdown feedback all on daily, weekly, and bi-weekly loops. This enables daily learning and feedback on strategic intent.

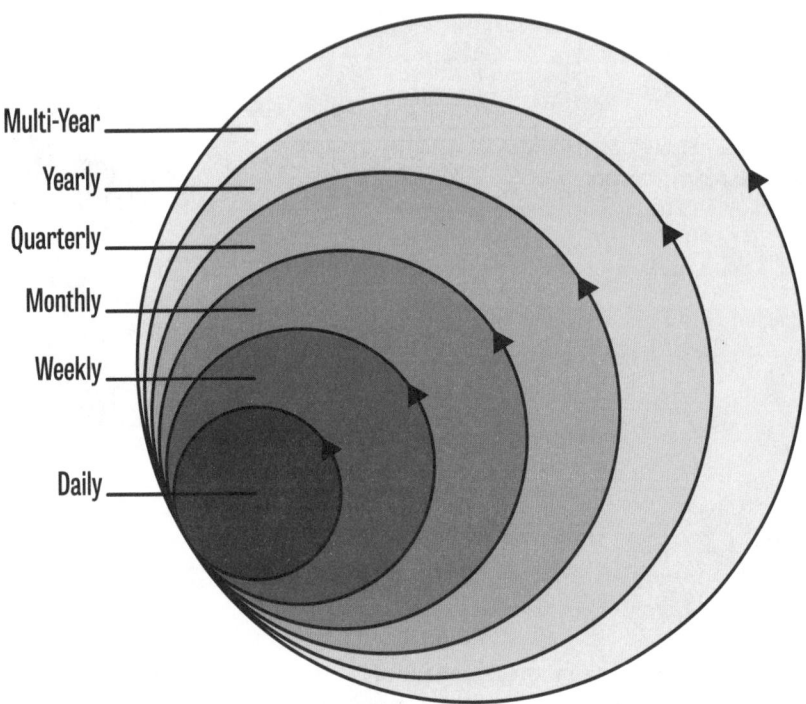

Multi-Year
Yearly
Quarterly
Monthly
Weekly
Daily

Figure 8.4: Nested Learning Loops

Continuous Improvement

Once we establish these routines of seeking and getting feedback, the next building block is to use these learnings to improve. One powerful practice described previously in this book is the Toyota Improvement Kata as articulated by Mike Rother.[22] It is a routine for moving from a current state to a new desired state iteratively, which uncovers obstacles that need to be worked on. In Figure 8.5, an evolution of Jimmy Janlen's "Improvement Theme,"[23] the left two quadrants show current (upper) and future (lower) states supported by data and articulation of leading and lagging indicators. In the upper right, is the next target state. The bottom right is a Kanban board with the steps required to reach the next target state.

PATTERN **8.2**

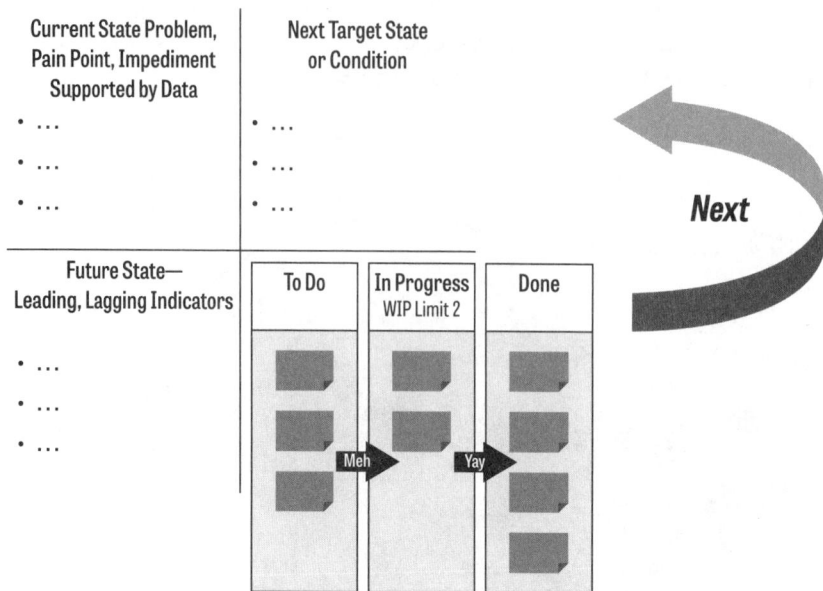

Figure 8.5: Toyota Improvement Kata Canvas

Adapted from Janlen, "Improvement Theme."

Work Together

One simple way to ensure the team is always receiving information is to enable everyone to see what's happening in their value stream. Kanban boards can produce that outcome, but so can working together.

Development is often lonely work, performed by individuals in front of a screen and wearing headphones. Agile pioneer Alistair Cockburn has described product development quite rightly as a "cooperative game,"[24] and it can be performed in groups. During pair programming, for example, two programmers sit together. The programmer in the hot seat writes the code while the programmer in the cold seat watches. After a time, they switch roles. Some people have compared pair programming to the roles of driver and navigator in rally driving. The driver focuses on the *what* and the *how* while the navigator looks at the *what* and the *why*.

Not all organizations see pair programming as a clear benefit. Two individuals working on the same task does not mean the loss of 50% productivity. According to studies by Alistair Cockburn and Laurie Williams, pair program-

PATTERN 8.2

ming increases development time by about 15%,[25] a great example of going slower to go faster, with the benefits of reducing production incidents, improving design quality, lowering staffing risk, enhancing technical skills, improving team communications, and being more enjoyable. It makes work Better, Safer, and Happier—and it ensures that any learning that takes place during that work is shared, which also leads to Sooner and better Value. It leads to collective code ownership and breaks specialization through a shared learning experience.

An organization can go even further. Mob programming is an extension of pair programming in which the whole team works together on the same code at the same time at the same computer. Although the practice is rooted in extreme programming, like pair programming it's not restricted to coding. It can also be used for other types of work like analysis, defining user stories, etc.

Creating a Dojo, a place for immersive learning, as US retailer Target has done, can be very valuable for learning together on your own product. It doesn't have to be any more than a meeting room large enough and equipped enough to enable collaboration. The objective is to learn new skills, whether technical or related to product excellence, through sharing and collaboration with the help of experts and coaches.

3: Organizational Level

Ensuring that learning takes place at the organizational level is the most complex and the most challenging to organize. There are many ways to share learning from individuals and teams across the organization as a whole. These include internal meet-ups, conferences, unconferences, webinars, brown-bag sessions, and show-and-tells. It is good to recognize and reward this behavior.

Unconferences are participant-driven sessions. Participants drive the agenda, bring their own ideas, and vote on the ideas that they discuss and develop. A popular style of unconference is Lean Coffee, where attendees write down their ideas on sticky notes, dot vote, and discuss the ideas with the most dots. The discussion is time-limited and participants can vote to continue discussing the same item for another period of time or move on to the next item with the most dots.

Open Space is another popular form of unconference. Like Lean Coffees, attendees bring their own ideas and topics to discuss. There is an empty timetable on the wall or flipchart with the timings (see Figure 8.6) and there are dedicated stations or break-out areas for discussions.

PATTERN **8.2**

	Room 1	Corner	Room 2
10:00 – 10:30	Internal Open Source	Leadership Coaching	Agility in HR
Break			
10:45 – 11:15	Agility in Accounting for OpEx, CapEx	What to Measure?	Internal Agility Awards

Figure 8.6: Open Space Timetable

Attendees announce their topics and place them in free slots on the agenda. Often there are more topics than free slots, so the facilitator helps to group them together. Each topic in each round is then discussed in the dedicated break-out areas in small groups for a set time.

Four principles drive Open Space: whoever comes are the right people, whatever happens is the only thing that could have happened, when it starts is the right time to start, and when it's over, it's over. The rule is to go where you want and where you feel you can contribute and learn.

PATTERN 8.3

Communicate, Communicate, Communicate

In Antipattern 8.3 we saw how various forms of learning bubbles emerge and promote undesired effects like silo mentality, limited discoverability, low learning retention, and duplication of work. Ways to pop the disconnected bubbles in the organization include awards, Communities of Practices (CoPs), and ASREDS loop.

1: Awards

Communication is essential for a learning organization, and that communication will take a variety of forms. Storytelling, case studies, and experience reports are all great for organizational learning. But unless we surface these stories and their insights, great things will remain in their bubbles and will struggle to bring benefits to other teams and to the organization as a whole.

Also, as we saw with the Diffusion of Innovation curve in Pattern 3.2, invite over inflict. It is necessary to generate social proof before the early majority will be willing to adopt something new. Once it's seen to be safe and is being recognized, then you'll get fast followers who—with continued communication, safety, and recognition—will help you reach the tipping point. People recognize that the change is working in context and this success is being recognized.

As a member of the ways-of-working team at an organization, I conducted interviews with teams that we published in the company newsletter and intranet. Scheduling interviews with busy people wasn't easy. The interviews went through multiple editing rounds and then had to be approved for publishing. Selection was limited. When we reached out for stories, offering special places for updates coming from senior leaders, we had few responses.

So we introduced the **Better Value Sooner Safer Happier** Awards. Submissions were open to any teams across the organization regardless of size or domain, whether IT-related product development or not. Over two weeks, we had over eighty submissions, considerably more stories than we had collected previously over a much longer time span.

Teams needed to provide factual evidence, data, and quotes from customers and colleagues to show how they had improved on agile, **BVSSH** dimensions:

- **Better:** Quality, such as a reduction in production incidents, faster mean time to recovery, and increased resilience.
- **Value:** Measured by quarterly business outcomes, with leading and lagging indicators, such as market share, customer retention, referrals, revenue, carbon emissions, and diversity.
- **Sooner:** A reduction in end-to-end lead time, an increase in throughput of items of value, and an improvement in flow efficiency.
- **Safer:** Continuous compliance so that the team was agile, not fragile. Examples of improved Safety, with leading indicators such as proactive work done and lagging improvement such as a reduction in control or compliance-related issues.

- **Happier:** Shown through an increase in NPS, retention, and referrals, as well as improved outcomes for citizens and for the climate.

We received data and quotes, delivering not just more stories but also richer insights. A panel of experienced practitioners across the business units reviewed the submissions. After the first contests, representatives of winning teams joined the panel for interviews, which led to the selection of winners, runners-up, and special commendations in multiple categories.

The Ways of Working conference and awards ceremony were not the end but the beginning of sharing these journeys and experience reports. We published them throughout the year in newsletters. Teams were asked to present in internal meet-ups and at show-and-tells attended by people across the organization. As a consequence, teams and individuals reached out, connected to their colleagues from winning teams, and asked for advice and hands-on help. The contest established connections, opened information channels, and accelerated learning across the organization. It also provided social proof and enabled a very visible team-level recognition.

Case Study: How Adidas Boosted Its Ways of Working Outcomes

It was early 2019, seventy years after the founding of adidas, when people started to explore more innovative ways to help teams make progress in improving ways of working for product development. Fernando Cornago, VP Platform Engineering, explains:

For us, it was not about "doing Agile." We acknowledged that only through both principles and practices would we perform at the speed needed in the most challenging industry of the time. With the "Retail Apocalypse," retail and digital eCommerce were the most challenging battlefields, as stated in the 2019 Accelerate State of DevOps survey.[26]

We all clearly agreed that we wanted to protect the team-level autonomy that had been cultivated with so much effort over the last five years. At the same time, we realized that the system needed more activation, more progress.

Adidas, as a company, has a strong DNA of sports and competition. You can feel it when entering a room in the HQ located in Herzogenaurach (Germany) or sitting in on any sprint retrospectives in the Tech Hub located in Zaragoza (Spain).

PATTERN 8.3

So we decided to play to the company's strengths, to its culture, in order to inject an extra dose of purpose, progress, and fun. We created the first "adidas DevOps Cup." It had the double goal of accelerating the improvement in outcomes *and* valuing the technical mastery of teams delivering business value through software.

We created a competition with the goal of teams improving their performance, measured by a set of metrics aligned to CALMS (culture, automation, lean, measurement, and sharing). Teams also had to demonstrate the business value obtained by these improvements.

The competition was a great success. Two hundred and twenty people volunteered to take part in twenty-two teams. They competed over a nine-month period, being coached by senior leaders from different departments, boosting knowledge sharing, and cross-pollinating learning, principles, and practices.

Teams improved by orders of magnitude on factors such as how often value was put in the hands of customers (Sooner) and time to recovery in the event of a system issue (Better). They reported huge revenue increases in areas (Value) due to releasing early and often (Sooner), and considerable savings via automation (Value and Sooner). Most importantly, business and technology teams got even closer due to the competition (Happier).

The final winners, the team behind the adidas mobile application, are still going around a virtual world tour to the different global adidas teams, telling their story and creating awareness about how important technical mastery is in order to create successful and sustainable digital products that add business value.

For adidas, given its culture, the competition was the perfect mechanism to accelerate and incentivize change while maintaining team ownership, accountability and motivation, which would not have been the case with a top-down mandate. The model is now continued with other internal competitions such as Game of Technical Debt (GOTD) or 008-Licence to Automate.

2: Communities of Practice (CoPs)

A very effective mechanism for shared learning is Communities of Practice, or CoPs. These are internal to a company, voluntary, open to all, and Darwinian.

If people meet, there is value. If they don't, there isn't. CoPs are not artificially kept alive. They may be aligned to a Center of Excellence, Guild, or Practice. The key is that they are open to all. This helps identify the natural champions, the innovators, the passionate people, the rebel alliance.

At one organization, after six years building CoPs, we had thirty-seven CoPs with 15,000 people in them, all voluntary. The Agile CoP had 2,500 people. Not all of the CoPs or members were active all of the time, which is by design. Whoever turns up are the right people. Whatever happens is the right thing. One full-time person supported the CoP of CoPs; everyone else volunteered to chair or contribute. The CoPs were also supported with internal social media.

In our experience, a successful CoP is made up of two co-chairs and a small group of core contributors (fewer than ten people).Chairs and core contributors ensure that there is a refined backlog of show-and-tells, both internal and external. There is an open invitation to *everyone and anyone*; those who turn up aren't always who you expect, helping make the company smaller and increase shared learning. And it's okay for people to be in listen-only mode. Use social media to help facilitate sharing and finding experts.

A good cadence for a CoP is meeting at least once every two weeks, a regular heartbeat. This is very important. The meeting could be a Lunch-and-Learn or it could be a meetup at the end of day that goes into the evening with an optional social activity such as drinks and pizza. For global organizations, start out in one location, getting the CoP working primarily in person if possible and with the ability to join virtually. As it grows, have regional chapters to build community.

In person meetings are preferable, in addition to dial-ins. Build networks and relationships. Have a roadmap of quarterly outcomes so there is an agreed North Star for each quarter aligned to longer-term organizational North Stars, ideally. Also, bearing in mind that it's voluntary, anything done is a bonus.

Each CoP should have a senior leader sponsor, for support, to act on ideas and to pass on top table challenges, concerns, or questions. Finally, have an overall Executive Committee sponsor who can help join the dots and move mountains if mountains need to be moved.

3: ASREDS Loop

When learnings become trapped in bubbles, knowledge is hidden. Teams face similar issues, run similar experiments, develop the same antipatterns, and fail to use each other's learnings. Our response to those antipatterns is the ASREDS learning loop (Figure 8.7).

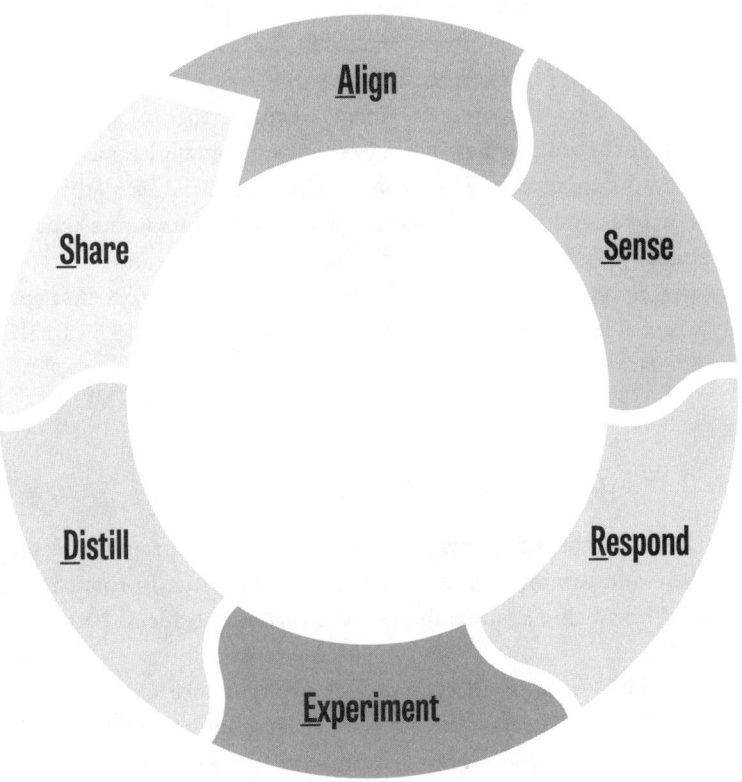

Figure 8.7: The ASREDS Learning Loop

The loop begins by clearly calling out *Align*, to ensure that there is clear alignment to the higher level intent, goal, North Star, mission, or outcome hypothesis. This is the first step of the learning loop—it installs vertical transparency (as we saw it in Pattern 5.3), and it connects the otherwise disconnected bubbles of strategy and delivery teams. Determine your aligned hypothesis that you want to learn about here.

Once aligned, it's time to *Sense* the context, the customer, terrain, history, behavioral patterns, antipatterns, underlying mental models, values, and one's own learning so far. It is fundamental to learn and understand the starting point, the unique context. As G.K. Chesterton is attributed as saying, "Don't ever take a fence down *until you know why it was put up*." Start where you are. Subscribe to learning from others, and sense the outside world to learn new potential patterns of success.

Next *Respond* by designing one or more experiments in order to test the hypothesis. These could be new or they could be the amplification or dampening of previous experiments. Then, run the *Experiment* and *Distill* the results to generate insights and metrics. Discuss it with participants in the experiment; run a retrospective or debrief to identify learnings.

Finally, *Share* by publishing the learning and updating doctrines and patterns. This enables others to pick it up when at the Sense step. This final Share step in the loop is essential, and I find it is rarely done.

PATTERN 8.4

Be Comfortable with Uncertainty

We saw in Antipattern 8.4 how the fear of uncertainty promotes deterministic culture and command-and-control style leadership. In this pattern we will look at how being comfortable with uncertainty leads to better **BVSSH** outcomes.

We live in a world of uncertainty. It's volatile, uncertain, complex, and ambiguous (VUCA). The pace of change is never going to be slower than it is today. Additionally, organizations are complex adaptive systems, they are emergent, and unique product development is emergent. Navigating this world, and optimizing for **BVSSH** outcomes, demands an experimental mindset. We have to embrace trial and error, define and run experiments, *continuously learn*, and use the results to define new experiments.

Carol Dweck has divided mindset into two forms: fixed and growth. Each describes different mental models of the development of abilities, talent, and intelligence.[27]

People with a fixed mindset, she argues, avoid challenges, give up easily, and feel threatened by the success of others. They tend to plateau early and achieve less than their full potential. "Fixed-mindset leaders, like fixed-mindset people in general, live in a world where some people are superior and some are inferior,"

PATTERN 8.4

says Dweck. "They must repeatedly affirm that they are superior, and the company is simply a platform for this."[28]

People with a growth mindset embrace challenges, persist in the face of setbacks, and find success stories inspiring. Dweck found that employees in growth-mindset organizations are 47% more likely than those in fixed-mindset organizations to see their colleagues as trustworthy. They're 34% more likely to feel a strong sense of ownership and commitment to the company, 65% more likely to say that the company supports risk-taking, and 49% more likely to say that the company fosters innovation.[29] These indicators of employee engagement are correlated with higher financial returns and a culture that serves as a recruiting tool.

Leaders with a growth-mindset encourage experimentation. They see innovation as part of everyday work and they share that innovation. General Stanley McChrystal has contrasted leaders who are like chess masters and feel a need to control every aspect of the organization, with leaders who are like gardeners. Gardeners don't try to command plants to grow with a detailed Work Breakdown Structure in a Gantt chart and milestones. With care, they tend to the garden, planting seeds, watering them, and when done well, producing a varied and flourishing garden.[30] In a leader-nurturing culture, people can build psychological safety, the single most important ingredient of a high-performing team. When a "gardener" leader is willing to risk a daisy growing where he thought a rose should grow, team members will feel safe enough to share their vulnerabilities.

PATTERN 8.5

Measure for Learning

As Douglas W. Hubbard points out in his bestselling book *How to Measure Anything*, "If a measurement matters at all, it is because it must have some conceivable effect on decisions and behavior. If we can't identify a decision that could be affected by a proposed measurement and how it could change those decisions, then the measurement simply has no value."[31] To avoid weaponized metrics, as we saw in Antipattern 8.5, we need to form the building blocks for metrics of learning.

Like an onion, the measure for learning is complex, comes in layers, starting with data in the innermost layer and builds up through metrics, analytics, and visualization. These are highly visible but do not create learning unless

PATTERN 8.5

there exists a supportive underlying mental model, a mindset for learning, which is the outermost layer. (See Figure 8.8.)

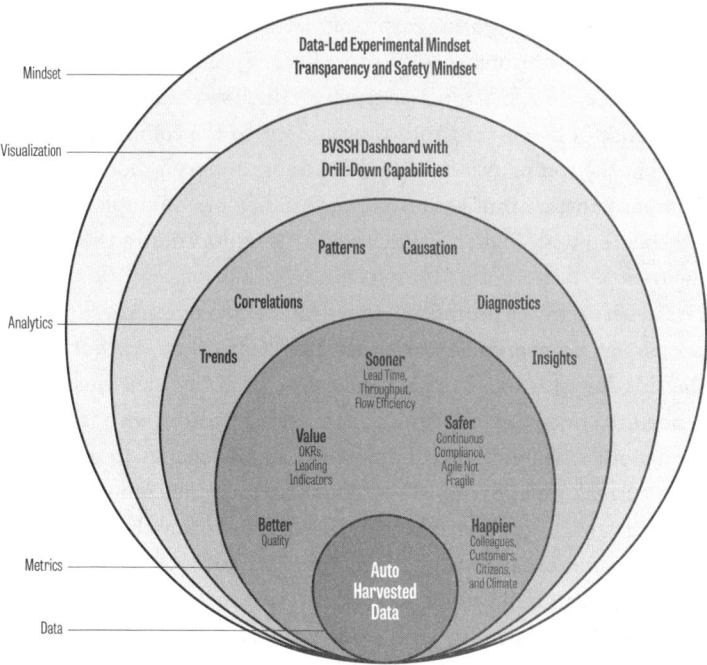

Figure 8.8: Measure for Learning Onion

1: Mindset for Learning

Encouraging a data-led, experimental mindset is fundamental in a volatile, uncertain, complex, and ambiguous world. The importance of being data-led is best articulated in the quote from Marissa Mayer: "It's not a Key Result unless it has a number."[32] These numbers are in the form of leading and lagging indicators as described in Pattern 5.2. It is equally important that leadership establishes an environment of psychological safety. In this context it means that there is no fear of revealing and sharing data. Data is not used as a stick but for learning and continuous improvement. Transparency and safety are required to establish any measure for learning.

You can't deliver sooner if you don't know how slowly you were delivering before and how quickly you're doing it now. Installing transparency and

PATTERN **8.5**

making work visible is the first building block in the fight against what Dominica DeGrandis calls "time thieves."[33] With transparency comes the ability to measure flow, to look at trends, and to see the impact on the changes we make on our ways of working.

2: Metrics on Outcomes for Learning

Pivot from output to outcome metrics. Measuring outputs like the number of specifications, enhancements, and features encourages the wrong behavior to create more and more, which leads to the busy trap. It does not bring any insights or learnings. If a company delivered more than 1,500 features last year, is that meaningful? An interesting insight would be to know how many features the customers have subscribed to. How many are unused? How many appear to be correlated to an increase in customer NPS scores or market share or reduction in carbon emissions?

Outcome metrics, on the other hand, are articulated with corresponding leading and lagging indicators. They are designed to help sense and generate insights and learnings.

Better Value Sooner Safer Happier measures include:

Better: Better is quality. Depending on your context, quality measures could include system outages, time to recovery, straight-through-processing exceptions, error rates, reconciliation breaks, rework, and so on.

Value: Value is unique to your business and is measured via OKRs, specifically the KRs, which are leading and lagging value measures. This could include revenue, market share, profit margin, site visits, new customer attraction, customer retention, trading volume, diversity, and more.

Sooner: Sooner is time to market. It's *lead time* from starting work on an item of value to getting it into the hands of a customer. It's *throughput*, which is the number of items of value over a given time period (which goes up as lead time comes down), and it's *flow efficiency*, which is a measure of the percentage of time that work is waiting. This is one of the most important things to focus on. *Look where the work* *isn't.* Alleviating impediments to flow enables lead time to reduce and throughput to rise. It increases "value-tivity"—the highest value in the shortest time.

Lead time distribution, as per Figure 8.9, is a useful visualization. It shows the number of days from when the work started on an item of value until it is in the hands of a customer (x-axis) versus the number of times that that same lead time occurred (y-axis). The curve typically shows a Weibull distribution, which is like a normal distribution skewed to the left. There is usually a long tail of long lead times. In this histogram view, it's recommended to measure the 85th percentile. This means that with empirical evidence, any similarly sized item of value (ideally all are roughly the same size, small), there is an 85% probability that it will be done within that amount of time. Plot this chart regularly to see how its shape is changing. When the 85th percentile point moves to the leftover time, then you are delivering value Sooner to customers. (See Figure 8.9.)

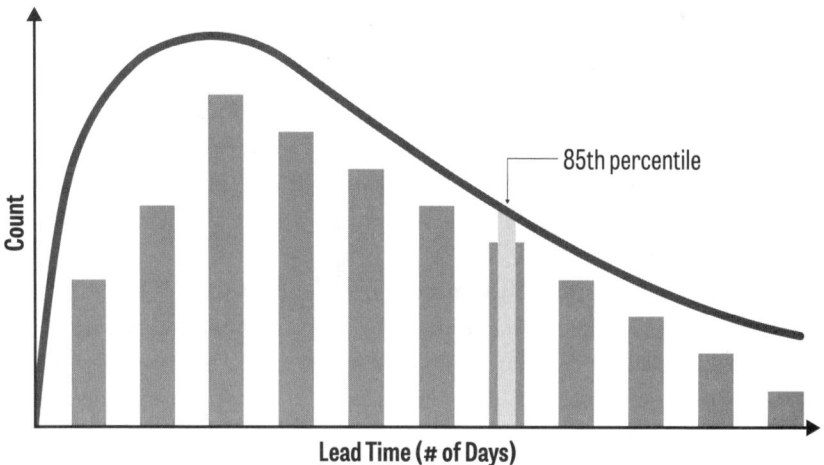

Figure 8.9: Lead Time Distribution

Safer: Safer is Governance, Risk, and Compliance (GRC). It's cyber, fraud, anti-money laundering, data privacy, not leaking your customer data, and avoiding news headlines. It's agile not fragile. In the context of software, measures include the percentage decrease in compliance breaches, such as mandatory risk stories not implemented, software binaries released without a link to the formal control environment, and safety incidents. It is also worth tracking the approximate percentage of time that Safety SMEs spend on reactive work (fire fighting) versus proactive work (building safety in up front). Safety is also cultural, keeping the conversation on risk alive, not taking past success as an indicator of future success, and having psychological safety within safety.

Happier: Happier covers colleagues, customers, citizens, and climate. More engaged colleagues, more satisfied customers, and corporate social responsibility (CSR) to benefit both society and the planet we live on. Measures can include customer Net Promoter Score (NPS), employee NPS, CSR outcome, and climate measures such as being carbon negative and reuse as per the renewable economy.

3: Analytics for Learning

Establishing measurability of flow and starting to measure lead time, throughput, and flow efficiency takes time. Often there is data available in existing work management tools that can be extracted to run diagnostics on, drawing early high-level insights on end-to-end flow. These diagnostics are essential, alongside anecdotes from teams and leadership, to establish a hypothesis of your current state.

Draw trends and find correlations (e.g., if release cadences are higher, are there fewer the incidents in production?) These insights help decide what levers to pull next to have a positive impact on ways of working.

Also note that correlation is not causation; just because two sets of data correlate does not mean that one causes the other. Checking conclusions with real-life narratives is important, as Jeff Bezos's famous quote articulates: "The thing I have noticed is when the anecdotes and the data disagree, the anecdotes are usually right. There's something wrong with the way you are measuring it."[34]

4: Visualization

Data needs to be turned into information and then into knowledge by being visualized and made available through a tool of choice. It could be just a physical board and a pen and paper (e.g., to count the number of tickets each day and calculate the number of days it takes for an average ticket to move across the board). If more data points are needed, more source systems and scale, and we want trends, correlations, automated calculation, and visualization, then we will need to create a dashboard.

A dashboard should be self-serve and accessible across the organization by teams and leadership. The best way to achieve this is to purchase or create a data engine that automatically harvests data from all the data sources across the pipeline. You can use that data layer to establish and visualize **Better Value Sooner Safer Happier** vector metrics, trends over time, and aggregate at different levels, such as application, team, product, value stream, and organization. You'll have the figures you need to provide transparency, a view of progress, and learning and feedback loops. Establish regular show-and-tells; provide training and workshop services for teams and leadership to learn how to self-consume data, how to slice and dice; and draw insights. Treat the dashboard as a product: establish hypotheses, run experiments, and collect feedback on how useful the provided metrics and services are. Create posters and infographics as information radiators on a regular basis (e.g., monthly).

Provide coaching services for teams and leadership on measures for learning. Why is it important to measure, what to measure, how does it help to enable continuous improvements and ultimately better **BVSSH** outcomes?

Another excellent tool for learning is surveys, harvesting the voice of colleagues and customers. As part of a Ways of Working team, I took part in conducting a semi-annual ways of working survey. We used the approach inspired by the work Gabrielle Benefield did at Yahoo! in 2005 when she looked at the effectiveness of Scrum and agile practices on 150 Yahoo! teams.[35] Our survey, too, asked participants to rate productivity, learning, development, growth, collaboration, customer satisfaction, quality, and time wasted.

We also asked whether participants would recommend this way of working to a colleague and whether they had any additional comments. The survey was anonymous and voluntary to establish safety and encourage honesty. On average, we received around a thousand responses, a quarter of which included additional comments. The survey questions were designed for self-assessment—it was comparison based. We asked colleagues to rate their team's ways of working using the questions on the scale of much worse, worse, neither better nor worse, better, or much better compared to how it was six months ago. Questions read like "collaboration within the team," "overall quality of what the team is delivering," or "ability to learn, develop, and grow."

Because we had asked the same questions each time, we could make comparisons, draw trends, and find correlations. Teams who felt they were at the beginning of their agility journey scored consistently lower on the benefits and Net Promoter Score (NPS). Teams who were, to use the earlier analogy, skiing proficiently rated benefits and NPS significantly higher. Perhaps not a surprise. We also saw the Kübler-Ross curve, described in Chapter 2, in action every time. We would see an initial rise, then a dip as people found it harder than they thought, and eventually a rise above the starting point. After three years, the externally run colleague engagement scores for product development teams were the highest they ever had been since records began. People were Happier with a more humane and rewarding way of working.

The most informative data was the free text. People sometimes left page-long comments that contributed to how we shaped our strategy, priorities, and our next outcome hypotheses. We generated word clouds to mine the free text data. The feedback became deeper and more sophisticated every time we ran the survey. It was a clear indicator that the organization was learning. And we used it for learning.

The free text in the first surveys showed that the majority of teams were at the very beginning of the journey. Their comments focused on team-level practices and questions around roles and agility itself. The issues raised in subsequent surveys trended toward organization-wide questions, budgeting, and how business, development, and operations work together. They became about whole enterprise agility and leadership behaviors. The organization was learning.

Summary

Pivot to a Learning Ecosystem

A silo mentality leads to disconnected learning bubbles, poor retention of learning, limited discoverability of knowledge, and duplicated work. A deterministic mindset and command-and-control culture leads to no or limited space for learning for individuals nor for the whole organization.

When teams and individuals have autonomy and empowerment, the right leadership support to self-organize, collaborate, develop new skills, and break specialization, you will experience better flow of information, knowledge, and

PATTERN **8.5**

learning. Nested learning with built-in feedback loops leads to continuous improvements and learnings at the individual, team, and organizational levels. Practices like ASREDS, awards, and CoPs help to pop the disconnected learning bubbles, and the combination of these patterns eventually promotes the creation of a learning ecosystem.

Detroit isn't what it used to be. In 2018, the US Census Bureau estimated the city's population at just under 673,000 a third of its peak size.[36] A survey in January 2020 ranked Detroit's job market last out of 182 US cities.[37] The days in which workers can stand on a production line without sharing their knowledge, their experience, or their learnings are over. Organizations today need to be relearning organizations.

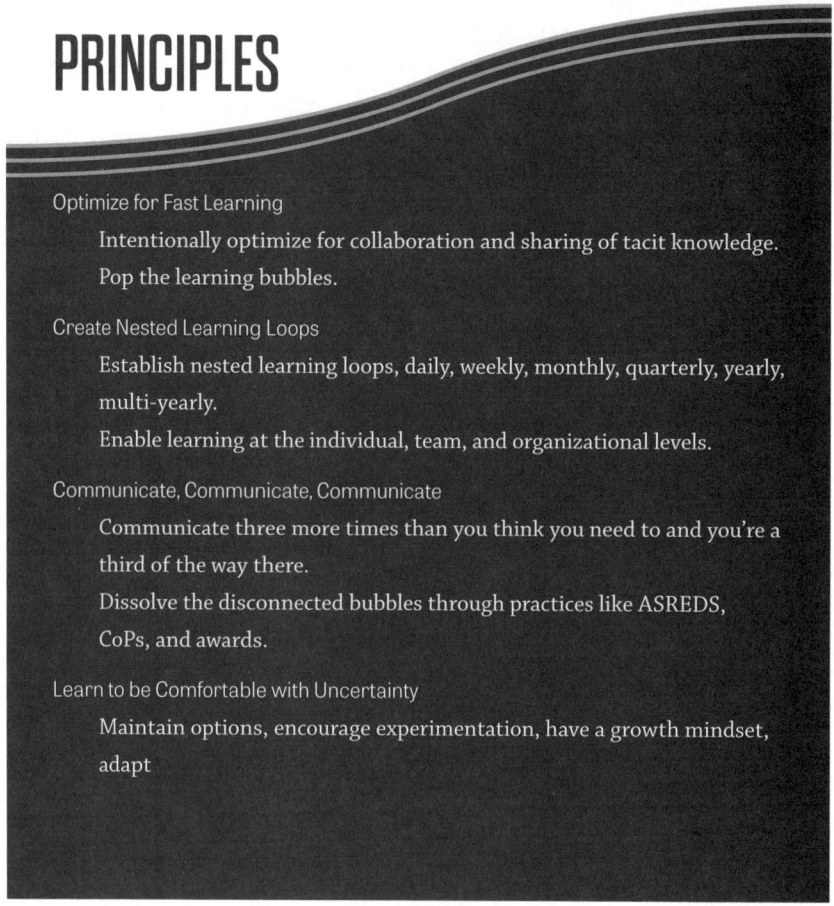

PRINCIPLES

Optimize for Fast Learning

Intentionally optimize for collaboration and sharing of tacit knowledge. Pop the learning bubbles.

Create Nested Learning Loops

Establish nested learning loops, daily, weekly, monthly, quarterly, yearly, multi-yearly.

Enable learning at the individual, team, and organizational levels.

Communicate, Communicate, Communicate

Communicate three more times than you think you need to and you're a third of the way there.

Dissolve the disconnected bubbles through practices like ASREDS, CoPs, and awards.

Learn to be Comfortable with Uncertainty

Maintain options, encourage experimentation, have a growth mindset, adapt

Measure for Learning

Have data-driven feedback loops.

Create the dials on the dashboard.

Support data-led experimental mindset and unlock measurability of Better Value Sooner Safer Happier.

9

THE BEST TIME TO PLANT A TREE IS TWENTY YEARS AGO; THE SECOND BEST TIME IS NOW

"**W**e were a classic conglomerate," wrote Jeffery R. Immelt, General Electric's then-CEO, in the *Harvard Business Review* in September 2017. "Now people are calling us a 125-year-old start-up—we're a digital industrial company that's defining the future of the internet of things. Although we're still on the journey, we've made great strides in revamping our strategy, portfolio, global footprint, workforce, and culture."[1]

Ten months later in June 2018, GE was removed from the Dow Jones index, the last remaining original constituent from 1896. From 2017 to 2018 GE's share price fell 75%, with dividends reduced an astounding 95% to $0.01 per share. A significant contributing factor was GE Power, which makes turbines for power plants. GE had been caught off guard by the shift from coal and gas toward renewable energy. Under Jeff Immelt, GE doubled down on fossil fuels, spending $9.5 billion in 2015 to acquire Alstom's power business. The deal turned out to be a disaster, with a $22 billion write off charge in 2018.[2] Continuing the buy-high, sell-low approach, GE completed its takeover of the oil and gas giant Baker Hughes in July 2017. Less than one year later, by June 2018, GE announced that it would divest its 62.5% stake[3] with an estimated write-off of $9.6 billion.[4] As of September 2019, Baker Hughes is an independent company again.

In 2019, GE's largest business area by revenue was aviation. With the coronavirus pandemic, like a lot of firms, its top revenue generating business was hit hard as the world stopped traveling. And in April 2020, due to the pandemic, the price of US oil turned negative for the first time in history over fears that storage capacity could run out.

We are living through a once in a forty- to sixty-year event, the Tipping Point from the Age of Oil and Mass Production to the Age of Digital,[5] with a global pandemic accelerating the demise of organizations who are victims of their past success, doing too little too late to move with the latest technological revolution and associated ways of working.

In the Age of Digital, every company is an Information Technology company if there is a desire to compete. Even for industrial firms, IT should not be viewed as a cost center, with capability outsourced. With self-driving vehicles, digital twins, fly-by-wire airplanes (an Airbus A380 has 25,000 sensors), jet engines collecting information at 5,000 data points per second, machine learning, the internet of things, beds that can sit you up via an app on your phone . . . in order to survive and thrive, organizations need to have competence in the new means of production and new ways of working.

As we saw in Chapter 7, evolution occurs with "Punctuated Gradualism"—that is, ongoing evolution and occasional revolution. The organizations that are the best at *kaizen* (continuous improvement) and *kaikaku* (disruptive innovation), with psychological safety, servant leadership, experimentation, a fast feedback loop, and a focus on outcomes rather than output, are the ones that will survive and thrive. The sea contains few living coelacanths.

Throughout this book, together with Zsolt Berend, Myles Ogilvie, and Simon Rohrer, we have looked at lessons learned the hard way: antipatterns and patterns in adopting better ways of working in order to deliver **Better Value Sooner Safer Happier** in the hope that they can help you avoid potholes and enjoy the journey to both a more humane and a more valuable way of working. These learnings are based on accumulated decades of practitioner experience, learned by doing and learned the hard way. That is, teams working together, experimenting, failing cheap and fast to succeed sooner, learning through the "scenius,"[6] pivoting and going again, trying to maintain courage and resilience to improve on outcomes. And sticking with it. The deepest learnings, in my experience, don't come in the first year or two, they come after that. Humans have a limited velocity to unlearn and relearn; behavior change takes time. Even prior to that it takes time for people to choose to want to unlearn. As per the Dunning-Kruger effect, we know that we still have a lot to learn and always will. This book will never be finished; it is never done. Not surprisingly, in the course of writing it, new insights have been learned. My intent is that this book will be emergent; that it will be updated over time; and that you can share your own observed antipatterns and patterns, and learn from others, via the companion website BVSSH.com.

Where to Begin?

Before beginning (or beginning again), it is important to recognize that it is extremely unlikely that any large organization is starting from 100% waterfall, traditional ways of working. Every firm, whether it's via a rebel alliance *despite* the organization or via activity *because* of the organization or people who have worked elsewhere will have some experience in agile and lean ways of working. That experience might be positive or negative or both depending on who you speak to, which will present a headwind, tailwind, or crosswind. There might be "agile islands" that are not connected. Hence, it's not really "Where to begin?" It's "How to continue from our current starting point and organizational memory to get better at fast learning in order to optimize for outcomes across the organization?" But that's too long a section title.

The important point is to exhibit *organizational empathy*. Riding roughshod over previous organizational scar tissue is unlikely to lead to good outcomes. Build situational awareness, be savvy to the history, to the people, to emotions, to fears. Seek to understand the terrain and start where you are. As we looked at in depth in Pattern 3.1, your context is unique. There is no one size fits all.

What follows is a getting started (or getting restarted) list. It is itself a pattern, an approach that has been found to be successful more often than not, and *your mileage may vary*. The suggested steps are:

1. Start with Why
2. Focus on Outcomes: BVSSH
3. Leaders Go First
4. Create a Ways of Working Center of Enablement
5. Start Small and Create an S-Curve Change
6. Invite over Inflict
7. Involve Everyone from Top to Bottom
8. Bias to Action
9. Become a Relearning Organization: You're Never Done

Ultimately, you are looking for a series of cultural ninja moves unique to your organization, amplifying the ones that move the dials on the dashboard in the right direction. Eventually, this should become a new habit, where everyone is learning and acting on the learning in order to optimize outcomes.

1: Start with Why

As we saw in Pattern 1.2, start with why if the why is not already clearly understood. The question to be answered is not "Why Agile?" or "Why Lean?" It is "Why change?" Agile and lean are the means to an end, they are not the end. With change, there is a hurdle of learning anxiety to be reduced and then overcome. There will be decades of ingrained habits. What if the status quo is maintained? What's the "so what?" Why do people need to go through the discomfort of change and a lack of mastery? What appeals to the selfish gene? People will have a range of emotions from "Thank goodness; at last," to "What if I can't change?" or "Here we go again" and even "Hell will freeze over first."

There should be a compelling *why* unique to your organization, which is the call to action. "We want to be more agile" is an insufficient call to action, as is "more for less." Why be more agile? Why more for less?

I have found doing a "five whys" exercise is useful, a technique originally developed at Toyota. A team breaks into pairs with the starting question of "Why change?" and take turns asking why five times with each answer forming the basis of the next question. This enables deeper than the usual surface level thinking. Usually I find that someone comes up with the existential point. "If we don't change, we won't exist as an organization."

The why should not be solely about short-term shareholder returns, financials, or cost cutting, as it often is. People don't want to work themselves or their colleagues out of a job. The why should cover society, climate, customer, company, team, and individual.

Happier in **BVSSH** includes colleagues, customers, citizens, and climate. This is a key part of why. It is a more humane way of working, with higher levels of engagement. Customer satisfaction is higher with better quality and sooner delivery. And there should be societal and climatic benefits. Part of better ways of working has to be helping those less fortunate and urgently turning the tide on the ever increasing burning of fossil fuels, leading to irreversible climate change.

There is an important concept here, which is obliquity, a term coined by economist John Kay.[7] In a complex domain, if you focus on a goal directly, such as financials, you are likely to have a detrimental outcome. For example, Boeing's troubles as we looked at in Chapter 6. If you come at your goals from an oblique angle, such as a primary focus on quality, value, time to market, safety, and the happiness of colleagues, customers, citizens, and the climate, you are more likely to achieve your financial goals.

2: Focus on Outcomes: Better Value Sooner Safer Happier

Knowing *why* change is needed, the next step is to articulate Values and Principles (as per the VOICE acronym from Pattern 3.1) and agree on desired outcomes (as per Pattern 1.1). Values and Principles guide every decision from everyone, every day. They provide behavioral guidelines and indicate what to optimize for if there are tradeoffs. They also allow people in more junior roles to constructively challenge people in more senior roles. As per Pattern 3.1, there are many sources of inspiration for suitable principles for ways of working, including the intentionally long list of principles in this book. Don't strive for perfection; start somewhere and have an intent that the principles most suited to your organization will iterate over time.

Having an initial list of principles that will guide behavior, the next thing to focus on is desired outcomes. Doing Agile is not the goal, as Nokia Mobile found (see Antipattern 1.1). The teams were "doing Agile" (i.e., following an Agile process); however, due to a lack of psychological safety, long lead times for the Symbian operating system were not bubbled up. It's not Agile for Agile's sake or Lean for Lean's sake. Instead, the goal is to improve on **Better Value Sooner Safer Happier** outcomes. Agile, Lean, DevOps, Systems Thinking, Design Thinking, Theory of Constraints, and so on are all metaphorical tools in the toolbox, bodies of knowledge, wisdom, principles, and practices to be applied in context to achieve desired outcomes.

In recent years, "Agile" has itself developed into a deliverable. This can be described as the Agile Industrial Complex, Agile-in-a-Box, cookie-cutter Agile, or Agile Snake Oil. People must be living under a rock to not hear about competitors undergoing an "Agile Transformation" and believe that they should do the same if they want to stay relevant and competitive. There is also the threat from non-traditional competitors, the "born agile" unicorns. As well as attracting market share, they are attracting talented people away from more bureaucratic traditional organizations. With a charitable intent, people with a traditional deterministic mindset, new to modern ways of working, seek to apply it in the only way they know how. That is, as a project, an initiative to be rolled out, top down, with a detailed plan, a start date and an end date, milestones and a twelve-month countdown before declaring reinvention. And there are plenty of people willing to sell that type of Agile installation. As Erasmus wrote circa 1500, "In the land of the blind, the one-eyed man is king."

Equally, a cloud transformation does not by itself lead to an improvement in **BVSSH** outcomes. It is often an answer looking for a question. An organization can spend considerable sums of money on elastic infrastructure and find that they have a Formula 1 racing engine sitting inside their 1950s tractor of an organization, with the F1 engine throttled back to 5% of its capability and most innovation disabled. Cloud is an enabler of agility. It is not the headline act, it is a tool in the toolbox to be used if infrastructure is the biggest impediment.

Leaving ways of working unchanged and adopting cloud will have little bearing on **BVSSH** outcomes, other than maybe computing more and storing more of something that you are already doing. There will still be a long lead time to perhaps not the most valuable activity, with a low level of organizational agility and a new economic model to adjust to, which itself requires agility. It may be that finance or PMO processes in your organization are a bigger blocker to valuable outcomes than elastic infrastructure. Focus on the outcomes first, then identify the biggest impediments. When it's no longer the weakest link in the chain, stop strengthening it. Identify what might be the next biggest impediment. Alleviate it. Repeat. Forever.

As we saw in Antipattern 6.1, some people in senior positions take a passive role, not role modeling desired behaviors, not seeking to unlearn and relearn, thinking that change is an org chart update, the adoption of Scrum, and the installation of JIRA and Jenkins. With a charitable intent, this may be due to a lack of understanding that the behavioral norms in an organization are the biggest lever to better outcomes. It's all about people.

The goal is to improve on outcomes, to deliver **Better Value Sooner Safer Happier** as we saw in Pattern 1.1. There is no end date. It is a case of building new muscle memory, the ability to continuously improve, to be a relearning organization, to be the best at being better, with balance.

Together, **Better Value Sooner Safer Happier** outcomes reinforce and balance each other. It's hard to game these outcomes. Forcing one shows a decline in others. For example, forcing Sooner by working people harder leads to a reduction in Better, Safer, and Happier and eventually a reduction in Value. By improving the system of work, empowering and supporting people, it is possible to get into a virtuous circle. It's easier to get stuff done, which results in Sooner. This leads to Happier as people see the fruits of their labor more often and there is clear cause and effect. Happier and Sooner lead to positive trends in Better and Safer, with more engaged people, complexity that fits in your head, and smaller safe-to-fail experiments. In turn, with faster feedback, less rework, less fire-fighting, and less time spent on "run" activities, this leads to an increase in Value, which leads to Happier customers, and so on.

These **BVSSH** outcomes should be measured and visualized. They are the dials on the dashboard. All of them, apart from any unique business unit Value measures, can be aggregated up to the organizational level and disaggregated to the value stream or team level. Importantly, focus on the trend over time and relative ranking on improvement rather than on absolutes, as everyone has a different starting point. The goal is improving over time.

3: Leaders Go First

As per Pattern 6.1, leaders should lead. The leadership team is team number one. Ideally this is the executive committee, the C-suite. Improving ways of working will likely need to involve all parts of an organization over time. Impediments could be anywhere, including legal, finance, HR, internal audit, real estate, or procurement. There should be nothing not in scope. There will be a bubble of better ways of working anchored at the top by the most senior person supporting it.

There is a need to engage the leadership team. With a starting hypothesis on the why, the principles, and the outcomes, there is a need to reach a shared understanding, refine the starting hypothesis, agree on priority, and invite participation. There will be champions and critics. History will add a tailwind or a headwind. There will be wildly different levels of understanding, knowledge, experience, and beliefs. From exploring the why, if change is not needed, don't change. If it is agreed that change is needed then there is a need to commit as a team.

Delivering **Better Value Sooner Safer Happier** should be articulated as one of a handful of top priorities for the organization, with support provided without being prescriptive as to how and without targets. Or it becomes one of a limited number of enduring values across the organization. This creates incentivization for action. People can only prioritize so many things; improving ways of working needs to be articulated as a priority. Knowing that it will lead to recognition and reward, that it will inform bonus, pay, and promotion, that it incentivizes behavior—it helps doors to open, creating a tailwind. It accelerates improving outcomes.

Change is a social activity. As we saw in Chapter 6, people in senior roles have a disproportionate impact on behavioral norms. Trust and role modeling are essential. Central to modern ways of working is creating high alignment and high autonomy. Ensure that the nested North Star outcome hypotheses are in place and are understood (see Chapter 5) and then provide autonomy within minimal viable guardrails (see Chapter 6). Enable teams to run fast, safe-to-learn experiments to optimally achieve the outcomes, acting as a servant leader, supporting teams, creating psychological safety, and mobilizing the organization's resources to alleviate impediments. Create a generative culture, move authority to the information, and create leaders at all levels. Getting there will take time, depending on the starting point. Like learning to ski, it is beneficial to have coaching. That is, leadership coaching specifically for ways of working. This is a chance to learn in a psychologically safe environment, to hold the mirror up, to reflect and improve.

4: Create a Ways of Working Center of Enablement

In order to be successful, there is a need for people who are dedicated full time in a servant leader capacity to orchestrate the improvement of the system of work across an organization, as we looked at in Pattern 1.2. This is typically a small, agile team with multidisciplinary skills, complemented with a team of coaches and teams focused on key enablers as needed. For a large organization, the success pattern is to have federated Ways of Working Centers of Enablement (WoW CoEs), with one for each business unit or value stream and a central one providing the team-of-teams coordination.

The federated WoW CoEs deal with impediments to **BVSSH** that bubble up, with a goal of solving them at the lowest possible level. They are not a department of continuous improvement where improvement actions are lobbed over a fence. The "servant part" of "servant leader" is to support teams to be able to deliver **Better Value Sooner Safer Happier**. There should be an impediment backlog, with the WoW CoE orchestrating the right people in the organization to help alleviate the top-priority impediments where this is beyond the sphere of influence of a team. For example, it may be a case of ensuring that on-demand training and coaching is available.

The "leader" part of "servant leader" is leadership in ways of working, being coaches, ski instructors, guiding people on the journey, sharing learning internally and externally, communicating, creating community, rewarding and recognizing desired behaviors and outcomes. To be able to lead on this topic, ideally the WoW CoE lead or co-lead will have prior experience guiding an organization on a similar journey. As a multi-disciplinary team, it is also beneficial to include people who are already well networked in the organization and know how to get stuff done informally. People in the WoW CoE should be framework agnostic—that is, have experience in multiple approaches so that there is no framework fundamentalism. The optimal approach for a context can be experimented with and then evolved within minimal viable compliance guardrails (as per Chapter 5).

5: Start Small and Create an S-Curve Change

As we saw in Chapter 2, achieve big through small instead of big through big. This type of work is emergent, and a group of people trying to do something (an organization) is also emergent. There is a need to minimize time to learning by running fast, safe-to-learn experiments. Amplify the ones that work well and quickly dampen the ones that don't. Through this, you will be able to apply an agile mindset to agility.

Remember that people have a limited velocity to unlearn and relearn. You cannot force the pace of change. If you do, you will only get new labels on existing behavior, and you will simply create a "cargo cult" behavior. Trying to force the pace of change will create a prolonged period of chaos, a longer and deeper dip in the Kübler-Ross curve, a lower probability of optimizing outcomes, and organizational scar tissue that makes a hard job harder. You can give change a tailwind or a headwind. As per the Diffusion of Innovation curve, as we looked at in Pattern 1.1, humans adopt change with an S-curve. It is best to leverage this to your advantage.

Think Big, Start Small, and Learn Fast. The Rule of One means running one experiment with one team or customer in a production environment. When it's working, then it's time for the second team, second customer, or second transaction. Once it's working well with ten teams, then gradually increase the rate of adoption, with maybe five teams at a time, then ten teams at a time, and so on. This is the rise in the gradient of the line at the beginning of the S-curve. It's hardest at the beginning. As a complex adaptive system, see how the organization responds.

As per Antipattern 3.1, there is no one size fits all. Context matters. Every environment is unique. Starting small makes it safe to learn, keeps change within risk appetite, and generates social proof unique to your context. It reduces fear and lowers the bar to change. Over time, the gradient of adoption can be increased as an initial path has been beaten through the organizational jungle and as social proof is created. Eventually the Pareto principle kicks in at 80% and the rate of adoption starts to slow, getting into the Laggards and more tricky edge cases.

The journey will be frustrating, messy, and bumpy. Personal resilience will be needed. It will be hardest at the beginning, and then as social proof is created, as breakthroughs happen, it will start to get easier. Eventually it will get its own momentum.

6: Invite over Inflict: Start with the Natural Champions

As per Pattern 3.2: *invite over inflict*. Allow people to satisfy their psychological need for agency and control, the need to feel in control of one's own destiny. Allow the Innovators, the natural champions, to identify themselves. There should be a colleague engagement model, a way to allow everyone to volunteer to contribute and shape their own destiny. Invite participation and get behind the champions. In addition to more obvious ways to invite participation, a great approach is to run a voluntary Ways of Working Community of Practice. It's a regular, open-to-all, internal meet-up with spotlights, demos, and external speakers for shared learning. The Law of Mobility applies. Turn up if you want to, leave when you want to. Whatever happens is the right thing and whoever turns up are the right people. The people who always turn up, every single time, are your natural champions.

Give the champions the coaching and the support they need in order to deliver better outcomes. As the benefits are seen, recognized, and communicated via every mechanism available, the Early Adopters will want to join in. These are the fast followers. They can see that it's safe to put a toe in the water; someone else has gone first and has been recognized for it. The water is warm, come in! Gradually invite them in too, within the pace of unlearning and relearning and within risk appetite. The words "convince" or "resistance" should not enter the vocabulary. If they do, then change is being done wrong. It will take time, so be patient, because it will bring better results.

To *inflict* forced change brings fear and extrinsic motivation, with the psychological need for agency and control not being satisfied. *Inviting* participants attracts the pioneers, those who are passionate, who are willing to take the bumpy journey, to do the hard yards and to face into the highest level of impediments. Inevitably, for any change there will be Laggards. In my experience they either jump in when it's clear that they are now the odd ones out, not wanting to stand out, or will choose to work elsewhere. Both are voluntary decisions and either is a good outcome.

7: Involve Everyone from Top to Bottom

Having identified the natural champions, as we've just seen, don't just inflict top-down change. Equally, bottom-up grassroots change soon hits a grass ceiling. There is a need for both top-down and bottom-up. Invite one or more vertical slices of the organization, starting small, as per Pattern 2.3. Those in the most difficult position are the pressurized middle, who have to deliver, come what may, and are now being asked to change ways of working as well as continuing to deliver. It's a difficult role and is often missed during a change that is sponsored from the top table and implemented at grass roots.

The Toyota Improvement Kata and Coaching Kata are a great approach to implement scientific thinking, running experiments in order to achieve an outcome. The Coaching Kata in particular provides a great role for leaders at all levels, including the pressurized middle, to coach teams on their thinking process and on how impediments or improvements are being approached, without being directive.

8: Bias to Action: Communicate, Communicate, Communicate

A traditional waterfall approach in the context of product development has a deterministic mindset, as we saw in Antipattern 6.3. There is an incorrect view that unique knowledge work is knowable and predictable, like making thousands of identical widgets in a factory. It results in big, up-front design at the point of knowing the least, a detailed plan, tasks allocated to people, deadlines set and output predicted. Optionality is removed. Learning comes in late, when there is little time to respond. There is no excuse for a Think Big, Start Big, Learn Slow approach. Even the first known writing about it in the 1970s, in the context of product development, described it as "risky and invites failure."[8] Why would you do that?

In the Age of Digital, with a new means of production and an increased pace of change, more than ever work is *emergent*. Product development is emergent. Improvement of repetitive tasks is emergent. Organizations are complex adaptive systems, which are emergent. A butterfly flaps its wings and there is a tornado a thousand miles away. Improving **Better Value Sooner Safer Happier** outcomes is emergent. This is the Complex domain in Cynefin, as we looked at in Chapter 0. There are *unknown-unknowns*; the link between cause and effect is not known. The only way to know if an intervention will have the hypothesized effect is to run safe-to-learn experiments with fast feedback.

There is a need for a *bias to action*, starting small and within risk appetite. Experiments are then amplified or dampened. As causality is not known in advance, it's the only way to determine what the next action could be in order to get closer to the desired outcomes. To quote Kurt Lewin, a pioneer of social and organizational psychology, "You cannot understand a system until you try to change it."[9] A lengthy diagnosis followed by a detailed plan, without learning by doing, is not an optimal approach. It is applying an old way of thinking to a new way of working, as we saw in Antipattern 1.2. Instead, Think Big, Start Small, Learn Fast.

Communicate three more times than you think you need to and you are a third of the way there. Communicate, communicate, communicate. Change is a social activity. Use every communication channel at your disposal and add some more. Use the communication channels to reinforce the why, the values and principles, the outcomes, to recognize desired behaviors and to do story-telling. Have senior leaders recognize the great work of teams in improving outcomes and have teams share their stories. As per the ASREDS Learning Loop described in Chapter 8, as lessons are learned they should be shared and broadcast to anyone who has chosen to subscribe. I have found that in addition to a Community of Practice, running internal ways of working conferences is a great way to share learning and raise the bar.

9. Become a Relearning Organization: You're Never Done

Stick at it. It requires commitment and resilience. It takes years for sustainable, lasting culture change, for genuine *agility*. For a large organization with a tailwind, it's three to five years, longer with a headwind. There are no shortcuts. Forcing the pace of change doesn't really force the pace of change. It's not applying agility to agility. It leaves people behind. There is a bigger and deeper dip in the change curve, and it's high risk. Instead, with an S-curve, there is progress toward an organizational capability where everyone continuously inspects, learns, and adapts, aligned to outcomes, with leadership and coaching at all levels. Become a relearning organization. Be the best at being better.

Better Value Sooner Safer Happier

There is no one way of working, and no one way to improve ways of working. There are antipatterns and patterns that have been observed more often than not to hinder or to help the delivery of **Better Value Sooner Safer Happier**. Use them as inspiration and experiment to find what works in your context.

Whatever patterns you choose to adopt, whichever road you choose to take, the destination, which will always be just over the horizon as you are never done improving, should be a place with each of the balanced **Better Value Sooner Safer Happier** outcomes.

Your organization should enjoy Better quality, whether that's measured in lower customer complaints, fewer production incidents, quicker recovery time, or any other measure that works in your context.

Your organization should benefit from greater Value. This is the reason your organization is in business, the benefits it delivers. You might see it reflected in higher revenues, profits, league table position, or in declining carbon emissions, falling crime figures, or falling hospital admissions.

Your organization should get where it wants to go Sooner. Flow should improve so that, like impatient coffee drinkers in a café, work spends less time waiting in queues. There should be quicker learning and a faster delivery of the highest value.

Your organization should be Safer. This covers Governance, Risk, and Compliance (GRC), such as information security, cyber, data privacy, and fraud. You don't want customer credit card details leaked onto the internet. Depending on context, this might also include physical safety. This is agile, not fragile, having both speed and control. The better your brakes, the faster you can go.

And your organization should be Happier, where that happiness covers customers, colleagues, citizens, and climate. A goal of **BVSSH** is to make the world of work more humane, more engaging, and more rewarding—and to do that in a socially responsible manner, to improve society, and to care for the one planet we live on.

The journey IS the destination.
Enjoy the journey!

We want to hear your stories, your antipatterns and patterns.
We are all on a shared learning journey.
For more information, go to BVSSH.com

RESOURCES

PRINCIPLES

CHAPTER 1
Focus on Outcomes
> Better Value Sooner Safer Happier.

Whole Organization Value
> Agile in IT only is a local optimization.
> Everything is in scope.

CHAPTER 2
Achieve Big Through Small
> Think Big, Start Small, Learn Fast.
> Apply agility to agility.

S-Curve Approach to Change
> People have a limited velocity to unlearn.
> People adopt change in an S-curve.

Descale Before You Scale
> Scaling agility *is* descaling the work and the system of work.

Scale Agility Vertically Then Sideways
> Join up, top down, and bottom up.

CHAPTER 3
One Size Does Not Fit All
> Organizations are complex adaptive systems.
> You have a unique VOICE.
> If the path ahead is clear, you're on someone else's path.

Invite over Inflict
> Invite participation with intrinsic motivation and empowerment.
> The words "resist" or "convince" should not enter the vocabulary.

CHAPTER 4
Leaders Go First
> Leaders lead.
> Role model desired behaviours.
> Exhibit courage and vulnerability.
> Tell stories; reward desired behaviors in others.

Foster Psychological Safety
> Invite participation.
> Foster an open culture of learning through intelligent failure.
> Listen and act.
> Foster a blame-free culture.

PRINCIPLES

Leverage Emergence
> Leverage emergence to maximize outcomes.
> Adopt an emergent mindset.
> Move authority to the information, with transparency.
> Coach and support; supporting lines over reporting lines.

CHAPTER 5
Optimize for Sustainable Fast Flow of Safe Value
> Long lived multi-disciplinary teams, on long lived products, on long lived value streams, aligned to the customer.

Tribal Identity by Value Stream
> Humans are tribal; primary identity should be to the value stream and the customer over job role specialism.

Outcome Hypotheses over Solution Milestones
> Outcome hypotheses and experimentation to leverage emergence to your advantage.
> Nested outcomes for strategic alignment.

Stop Starting, Start Finishing
> Limit WIP at every level.
> The fewer cars on the road, the faster they go.

Pull Work, Don't Push it
> Pulling work shines a light on the natural capacity of the system and impediments to flow.
> Impediments are not in the path, impediments ARE the path.

CHAPTER 6
Safety within Safety
> Foster psychological safety.
> Seek the presence of positives, not only the absence of negatives.

Safety Teams Aligned to Value Streams
> Long-lived Safety teams on long-lived value streams.
> Optimize for the sustainably fast flow of safe value.
> Shared ownership of Safety.
> Keep the discussion on risk alive.

Minimal Viable Compliance (MVC)
> Right size risk mitigation taking context and risk appetite into account.

People, Process, Tooling, In That Order
> Behavior, collaboration, conversation is the biggest lever.

PRINCIPLES

CHAPTER 7
Continuous Attention to Technical Excellence
> Technical excellence, operational excellence, good design,
>> and good designers are key to sustainable business agility.
> If you're living with legacy, allocate more time to pay off the debt.

Architect For Flow
> Sustainably fast flow of value is the primary goal of software delivery.

Punctuated Gradualism (Multiple Speeds in Parallel)
> Evolution and periodic revolution in order to realize most value.
> From daily continuous attention to periodic revolutionary architectural change.

Autonomation: People and Machines In Harmony
> DevOps doesn't mean automating smart people out of a job.
> Use automation and tooling judiciously to make good people even better.
> Culture is the biggest lever; sometimes tools won't improve outcomes.

CHAPTER 8
Optimize for Fast Learning
> Intentionally optimize for collaboration and sharing of tacit knowledge.
> Pop the learning bubbles.

Create Nested Learning Loops
> Establish nested learning loops, daily, weekly, monthly, quarterly, yearly,
>> multi-yearly.
> Enable learning at the individual, team, and organizational levels.

Communicate, Communicate, Communicate
> Communicate three more times than you think you need to and you're a
>> third
>> of the way there.
> Dissolve the disconnected bubbles through practices like ASREDS,
>> CoPs and awards.

Learn to be Comfortable with Uncertainty
> Maintain options, encourage experimentation, have a growth mindset,
>> adapt.

Measure For Learning
> Have data-driven feedback loops.
> Create the dials on the dashboard.
> Support data led experimental mindset and unlock measurability of
>> Better Value Sooner Safer Happier.

GLOSSARY

Agentic State: A concept from Stanley Milgram's Agency Theory. An *agentic state* is a state of mind in which a person will allow other people to direct their behaviors and pass responsibility for the consequences of the behaviors to the person giving the orders.

Agile: (1) A state of being, exhibiting agility, being nimble, able to learn fast and pivot fast in order to optimize for desired outcomes. (2) A body of knowledge for ways of working suited to *unique* change, where the work and or the environment are *emergent* and there are *unknown-unknowns*. Origins in Japan in the 1970s and 1980s, for product development in manufacturing (e.g., Xerox and Honda). Learnings from manufacturing transferred to software development in the early 1990s. Originally called "lightweight processes" ("heavyweight" referring to sequential, big-batch waterfall processes). Articulated as a set of Values and Principles in the Agile Manifesto in 2001. Now being applied more broadly for whole business agility. There are many practices that are best applied in context in order to optimize for outcomes rather than as one size fits all.

Antipattern: An antipattern is a response to a situation that, more often than not, is ineffective and risks being counterproductive; acting as a headwind rather than a tailwind. Antipatterns are behaviors and approaches that can make a hard job harder, setting an organization back many years, creating organizational scar tissue and an organizational memory, and strengthening antibodies to repel any future desired change. As there is no "best practice" in an emergent domain of work, very occasionally an antipattern for the majority of organizations might be a pattern for one organization. For example, a scenario where cashflow is about to run out and it's a high-risk, do-or-die strategy for an organization.

Architecture Outcome Lead: One of the triumvirate of roles, along with the Value Outcome Lead and Team Outcome Lead. These three roles exist as equal partners at each nested value stream level. This role has primary accountability for the technical "how", the technical excellence, ensuring that the technology is enabling the delivery of Better Value Sooner Safer Happier. There is a capability-based reporting line up the nested value streams, ultimately to the CTO for a business. For example, this role should ensure that the technical architecture enables agility and resilience, meets broader architectural principles, and will engage in business risk based conversations around technical debt, safety, and business value.

BVSSH: Better Value Sooner Safer Happier. *Better* is quality. *Value* is unique and why you are doing what you are doing. *Sooner* is lead time, throughput, and flow efficiency. *Safer* is continuous compliance, "Governance, Risk and Compliance (GRC)", agile not fragile, trust. *Happier* covers colleagues, customers, citizens, and climate. They are outcomes to be continuously improved (you're never done improving). Agile, lean, and other bodies of knowledge are learnings to help improve these outcomes.

Cynefin: A conceptual framework used to aid decision making with five domains: Clear, Complicated, Complex, Chaos, and Confusion.

Deterministic: Behavior is entirely determined by initial state and input and can be predicted. The outcome and output is predetermined. Repeating the behavior will result in the same outcome and output each time, such as a machine mass producing widgets. A belief that a complex system is no more than the sum of its parts and that the parts are interchangeable. There is an inevitability of causation. Everything that happens is the only possible thing that could happen. The domain is "knowable", now and in the future, there is nothing new to learn.

DevOps: DevOps is a portmanteau that combines development and operations. DevOps focuses on flow. That is, on breaking down the historical barriers between siloed teams responsible for developing a product and teams responsible for deploying and operating the product. DevOps can have a narrow IT Dev plus IT Ops meaning or a broader enterprise DevOps meaning. The broader enterprise meaning of DevOps is delivering Better Value Sooner Safer Happier, organization-wide. It is the application of better ways of working, end to end, to deliver business and customer value, leveraging many bodies of knowledge, including agile and lean.

Domain: A domain of work is the context within which you are operating. For example the domain of work could be emergent (see Complex and Chaos in Cynefin) or deterministic (see Complicated and Clear in Cynefin). Work can move around domains. For example, the agile creation of a new model of car (an emergent domain) and then identical mass production of that model of car (a deterministic domain of work).

Emergent: Behavior, outcomes and output cannot be predetermined. The domain is "unknowable". The only way to learn is by doing and seeking a feedback loop. Acting in the space changes the space. Individual and collective behavior mutates and self-organizes in response to change. Repeating an action will result in different outcomes. A perfect understanding of the individual parts does not automatically convey a perfect understanding of the whole system's behavior. The whole is more complex than its parts.

Flow: The flow of value, end-to-end, from *concept* to *cash*, from *need identified* to *need met*. Optimizing for flow is optimizing for the shortest time, to a sliver of hypothesised value, with the least effort, in order to learn fast and pivot and to maximize desired outcomes. See also Flow Efficiency, Lead Time, Throughput, and Outcomes.

Flow Efficiency: The percentage of value-add time within the elapsed end-to-end Lead Time. For example, a Flow Efficiency of 10% means that work is waiting 90% of the time (i.e., doing too much work in parallel, having role-based handoffs, bureaucratic one-size-fits-all processes and big-batch, stage-gate processes, all lead to work waiting).

GRC: The acronym refers to supervisory Governance, Risk, and Compliance functions of an organization. See Safety Teams.

Lead time: The end-to-end time to value, from concept to cash, from *need identified* to *need met*.

Lean: "Lean production" is a term coined by John Krafcick, the first American engineer hired at the Toyota-General Motors joint venture, NUMMI, referring to the Toyota Production System. "Lean production is lean, because it uses less of everything compared with mass production, half the human effort in the factory, half the manufacturing space, half the investment in tools, half the engineering hours, in half the time."[1] As lean production has evolved in the context of mass production, it is suited to repetitive, knowable activities. Lean includes concepts such as a focus on flow, specifying value from the perspective of the customer, identifying the value stream and all steps in it, a pull-based system of work (enabling smaller inventories to be held), continuous improvement (which includes eliminating waste), respect for people, servant leadership, building quality in rather than inspecting it in later (stopping the line), and "autonomation" (machine and person in harmony). Lean and agile have a common root in post–World War II Japan, influenced by the work of W. Edwards Deming; Lean being suited to mass production, agile being suited to unique product development (such as designing a new model of car before mass producing it).

OKR: Objectives and Key Results. See Outcome.

Outcome: In the context of unique change, an outcome is articulated as a *hypothesis* of a desired future state, which is to be tested to try to achieve or to prove wrong. It is a hypothesis as the domain of work is emergent and the future cannot be predicted. The outcome hypothesis is informed by data-led insights or by a belief. An outcome is articulated as a desired *business outcome*, not as an activity, a predetermined solution, or an IT-only task. Outcomes are all "our business" in scope, not "the business" and IT as separate entities. Outcomes have leading and lagging value measures (the "KR" in OKR). Leading value measures provide an early feedback loop on the hypothesis (e.g., downloads of an app, clicks on a website, customer enquiries), lagging measures indicate a change in behavior and value (e.g., more mortgages sold, increased customer satisfaction, diversity, carbon emissions, revenue, profitability, and so on). Outcomes exist at multiple cadences and are nested, providing strategy alignment. For example, quarterly, annual, and multi-year. The quarterly outcomes are comprised of monthly experiments, weekly iterations, and daily stories (requirements), providing a fast feedback loop on strategic intent. The cadences provide dates (with an outcome rather than output focus) and regular cadences to inspect and adapt. There is continuous planning, with a rolling twelve month roadmap of quarterly outcomes.

Pattern: A pattern is a response to a situation that, more often than not, is effective and improves desired outcomes, acting as a tailwind. Patterns come with their own ups and downs, back and forths, swings and roundabouts, as change is social and it's all about people. Patterns can lead to change being more "sticky". As with antipatterns, there is no such thing as "best practice" in this domain of work. Your mileage may vary. In some contexts, based on culture and history, a pattern might be an antipattern at a given point in time. Timing and pace is important. People have a limited velocity to unlearn and relearn. In most cases, start with the patterns, experiment, and pivot based on fast learning. Think Big, Start Small, Learn Fast.

Product: A product is long lived, is produced by and aligned to a long lived value stream, is of value to one or more customers, and is worked on by one or more long lived multidisciplinary teams. A product has a corresponding service level. Experimenting on desired *outcome hypotheses* leads to work being done on long-lived products. Products are long lived, with evolutionary revolution. That is, they evolve over time, such as continuously upgrading a plane mid-flight, similar to evolutionary biology. Products might not include IT at all, might partially include IT, or might be entirely an IT product. Examples of products include internal audit report, mortgage, credit card, helicopter engine, car, movie, generation of renewable energy, shipping goods from A to B, cloud computing, operating system, protecting law and order and so on. Some products are clearly aligned to customers and one value stream. Other products may be used within an organization, aligned to a shared service value stream, or used by the many customer aligned value streams (e.g., general ledger and sub ledgers (Finance), recruitment (HR), physical environment (Real Estate), desktop compute (Infrastructure) and so on).

Project: A project is temporal, with a start date and an end date. A project involves people who don't usually work together, who come together temporarily into a project team and then disband. Projects are typically sequential in nature, with stages such as Initiate, Plan, Execute, Monitor and Control, and Close, often with work passing between role-based silos with role-based incentivization. Typically a project plan is put together early on (at the point of knowing the least), which lays out a predetermined output and set of actions, along with a corresponding prediction of time, cost, quality, and scope. Usually, there is a focus on the plan rather than on the desired outcome, with change being tightly controlled and inhibited. Typically there is a long lead time from starting to realizing value, resulting in late learning and making causality of action, leading to value being hard to measure. Typically, projects are deterministic, treating the future as knowable. Projects originate from two technological revolutions ago, in the context of manual labor in factories in the early 1900s. Projects do not optimize for outcomes in an emergent domain of work. See Outcomes, Product, Value Stream.

Risk Appetite: Risk appetite is the level of risk that an organization is prepared to accept in pursuit of its objectives before action is deemed necessary to reduce the risk. It represents a balance between the potential benefits of innovation and the threats that change inevitably brings. The ISO 31000 risk management standard refers to risk appetite as the "Amount and type of risk that an organization is prepared to pursue, retain, or take."

Safety Team: A Safety Team is a long-lived multi-disciplinary team providing governance, risk, and compliance (GRC) subject matter expert (SME) support with a long-lived alignment to one or more value streams. For example the Safety Team will include SMEs for Information Security, Data Privacy, Fraud, Compliance, and so on. The Safety Team shares the goals and objectives of the value stream(s) and is accountable to the value stream and GRC leadership for judgements about appropriate risk mitigation with a Minimal Viable Compliance approach in order to right size the compliance requirements to the context (rather than a one-size-fits-all, lowest-common-denominator approach). The members of the Safety Team are accountable for determining which regulatory requirements and organizational controls are mandatory for the unique context of the work within their value stream. As the teams are long-lived, there are long lived working relationships and the Safety SMEs get to understand the unarticulated needs of the customer, allowing for safety innovation (e.g., biometrics) leading to better outcomes. There is early and often interaction with the value stream aligned teams and a continuous compliance approach, keeping the conversation on risk alive.

Throughput: Throughput is a count of the number of items of value produced over a given period of time. In the context of unique change, this could be a count of Stories (i.e., a sliver of value). As Lead Time comes down, it is possible for Throughput to increase.

Team Outcome Lead: One of the triumvirate of roles, along with the Value Outcome Lead and Architecture Outcome Lead. These three roles exist as equal partners at each nested value stream level. This role has primary accountability for the "how", in particular the people and processes. This role supports the long-lived multi-disciplinary team as a servant leader, helps to improve the system of work aligned to desired outcomes (such as Better Value Sooner Safer Happier), coaches the team in continuous improvement, supports the removal of impediments, mitigates people and process risks, and facilitates regular shared learning and retrospective activities. The focus is on continuously and sustainably experimenting to optimally achieve the desired nested outcomes or to pivot quickly. This role is also known as "Delivery Lead", "Team Lead", or "Scrum Master" if a team has adopted Scrum. At the team-of-teams value stream level, this role is the "Value Stream Outcome Lead" or "VS Delivery Lead". At higher level value streams, this role is the "Business Unit Head of Change" or the "Business Unit CIO" (particularly for organizations where change is predominately IT change, with multi-disciplinary teams).

Technical Debt: Technical debt is the implied increased cost and time of adding new features caused by choosing to make design or implementation shortcuts during software development (i.e., "I'll fix that later"). Technical debt is sometimes consciously taken on for short periods as a business risk versus value decision (e.g., first mover advantage in order to capture market share). This form of debt is invisible and often poorly understood. It creates drag, inertia, and fragility for subsequent changes and often results in a significantly higher long-term cost (effectively paying compound interest on the debt) rather than the lower cost of paying down debt early and often. In large traditional enterprises it is much easier for project-oriented teams with short-term incentives to accept (invisible) technical debt during their work in order to meet fixed milestones for (visible) functional delivery then ending the project with the debt left unpaid. When multiplied across years and thousands of projects, the technical debt load of an enterprise can be significant and presents a high risk. In some cases, a high level of technical debt (e.g., unsupported technologies and a hard-to-maintain change system) results in a high cost, high risk, complete system rewrite, often repeating the cycle. It leads to increased cost of "change" and "run," squeezing out discretionary innovation spending and leading to slower realization of less value. This contrasts with a Value Stream organizational construct, with long-lived continuously evolving Products with a focus on Flow, where the incentives of long-lived teams align more closely to the long-term goals of the enterprise, technical debt repayment is a continuous business risk conversation and goes hand in hand with optimizing for outcomes.

Value Curve: A pictorial representation of value over time.

Value Outcome Lead: One of the triumvirate of roles, along with Team Outcome Lead and Architecture Outcome Lead. These three roles exit as equal partners at each nested value stream level. This role has primary accountability for the "what," for Value, prioritizing the backlog of outcomes and experiments. This role, crucially, has accountability for what is not done in order to limit work in progress and reduce lead time. This role engages in risk-based conversations with the two peer roles to balance new features with process improvement and technical improvements, enabling ongoing pace, efficiency, and agility. Also known as "Product Owner." This role is often the leader for the business value stream. At higher level value streams, this role is the "Business Head" or "CEO".

Value Stream: A value stream is long-lived, with long-lived multi-disciplinary teams who produce one or more long-lived Products that are of value to customers. The value stream covers all the steps end to end, from *concept* to *cash*, from *need identified* to *need me*t, and are usually represented horizontally as the flow of value from left to right. The term originates from Lean. Value streams are nested. For example, Bank → Investment Bank → Markets → Equity Trading. Value streams should have high cohesion (do one job well, avoid duplication, aim for simplicity) and low coupling (ability to exhibit agility within minimal viable guardrails). The long-lived teams work on Outcomes that are aligned to the Value Stream. The majority of Value Streams are aligned to customers; some are internal Shared Service Value Streams, such as HR, Finance, Real Estate, and Legal. Value streams are not customer journeys (which may span Value Streams) nor are they aligned to customer personas (e.g., retired couple, young student).

Value Stream Network: The network formed by the connections between Value Streams. To enable agility, there should be minimal coupling between Value Streams with dependencies eliminated or minimized over time where possible.

Valuetivity: Amount of value realized over a time period with minimal output and effort. Productivity is the number of units of output per unit of input. In an emergent domain, we don't want to maximize output. We want to maximize for most value in the quickest time with the least output.

VOICE: Values and principles, Outcomes and purpose, Intent-based leadership, Coaching and support, Experimentation. An approach to outcome-oriented continuous transformation.

Ways of Working: Approaches to work using many bodies of knowledge. For example, agile, lean, waterfall, design thinking, systems thinking, theory of constraints, Self Managing Organizations (SMOs), Teal organizations, and so on. The way of working should be suited to the unique context of an organization and aligned to desired outcomes such as Better Value Sooner Safer Happier.

BIBLIOGRAPHY

"787 Deferred Production Cost, Unamortized Tooling & Other Non-Recurring Cost balances," Boeing.com. Accessed May 1, 2020. https://www.boeing.com/investors/accounting-consid erations.page/.

Ahonen, Tomi T. "Nokia Final Q4 Smartphones As Expected: 6.6M Total means Market Share now 3% (from 29% exactly 2 years ago)," Communities-Dominate.blogs.com (January 24, 2013). https://communities-dominate.blogs.com/brands/2013/01/nokia-final-q4-smartphones -as-expected-66m-total-means-market-share-now-3-from-29-exactly-2-years-ag.html.

American Psychological Association. "Multitasking: Switching costs," APA.org (March 20, 2006). https://www.apa.org/research/action/multitask.

Andreessen, Marc. "Why Software Is Eating the World," *Wall Street Journal*, August 20, 2011. https://www.wsj.com/articles/SB10001424053111903480904576512250915629460.

Anti-Corruption Digest. "Total WannaCry losses pegged at $4 billion," *Anti-Corruption Digest* (October 2, 2017). https://anticorruptiondigest.com/2017/10/02/total-wannacry-losses -pegged-at-4-billion/#axzz6NR0jbWtl.

Anthony, Scott D., S. Patrick Viguerie, Evan I. Schwartz, and John Van Landeghem. *2018 Corporate Longevity Forecast: Creative Destruction is Accelerating, Executive Briefing.* Boston, MA: Inno-sight, 2018. https://www.innosight.com/wp-content/uploads/2017/11/Innosight-Corporate -Longevity-2018.pdf.

Badenhausen, Kurt. "The World's Most Valuable Brands 2019: Apple On Top At $206 Billion," Forbes.com (May 22, 2019). https://www.forbes.com/sites/kurtbadenhausen/2019/05/22 /the-worlds-most-valuable-brands-2019-apple-on-top-at-206-billion/#231fb04b37c2.

Bajkowski, Julian. "ANZ's boss hits pause button on massive agile expansion," iTnews.com (May 2, 2019). https://www.itnews.com.au/news/anzs-boss-hits-pause-button-on-massive-agile-expansion-524529.

Bass, Bernard. *Leadership and Performance Beyond Expectations*. NY: Free Press, 1985.

Bass, Bernard, and Ronald E. Riggio. *Transformational Leadership*. London: Taylor & Francis, 2005.

Bavel, Jay van, and Dominic Packer. "The Problem with Rewarding Individual Performers," *Harvard Business Review* (December 27, 2016). https://hbr.org/2016/12/the-problem-with-rewarding-individual-performers.

Beck, Kent, et al. *Manifesto for Agile Software Development*, AgileManifesto.org. Accessed May 1, 2020. https://agilemanifesto.org/.

Benefield, Gabrielle. "Rolling Out Agile in a Large Enterprise," Proceedings of the 41st Annual Hawaii International Conference on System Sciences (HICSS 2008). https://ieeexplore.ieee.org/xpl/conhome/4438695/proceeding.

Berger, Eric. "New document reveals significant fall from grace for Boeing's space program," *arcTechnica* (April 10, 2020). https://arstechnica.com/science/2020/04/a-nasa-analysis-of-boeings-lunar-cargo-delivery-plan-is-very-unflattering/.

"Boeing Sets New Airplane Delivery Records, Expands Order Backlog," Boeing.com (January 8, 2019). https://boeing.mediaroom.com/2019-01-08-Boeing-Sets-New-Airplane-Delivery-Records-Expands-Order-Backlog

"Boeing Statement on Employee Messages Provided to U.S. Congress and FAA," Boeing.com (January 9, 2020). https://boeing.mediaroom.com/news-releases-statements?item=130600

Bolton, Michael, and James Bach. "Testing and Checking Refined," Satisfice.com (blog) Accessed May 1, 2020. https://www.satisfice.com/blog/archives/856.

Bort, Julie and Business Insider. "Amazon Founder Jeff Bezos Explains Why He Sends Single Character '?' Emails," *Inc.* (Apr 23, 2018). https://www.inc.com/business-insider/amazon-founder-ceo-jeff-bezos-customer-emails-forward-managers-fix-issues.html.

Bowman, Sharon L. *Training from the Back of the Room!: 65 Ways to Step Aside and Let Them Learn*. San Francisco, CA: Pfeiffer, 2008.

"Brian Eno of 'Scenius,'" Facebook post, posted by Art With Teeth (August 31, 2016). https://www.facebook.com/watch/?v=1045575582215934.

Burgess, Matt. "What is the Petya ransomware spreading across Europe? WIRED explains," *Wired* (July 3, 2017). https://www.wired.co.uk/article/petya-malware-ransomware-attack-outbreak-june-2017.

Burns, James M. *Leadership*. NY: HarperCollins, 1978.

Byrnes, Jonathan. "Middle Management Excellence," *Working Knowledge* (December 5, 2005). https://hbswk.hbs.edu/archive/middle-management-excellence.

Callahan, Patricia. "So why does Harry Stonecipher think he can turn around Boeing?" *Chicago Tribune* (February 29, 2004). https://www.chicagotribune.com/chi-0402290256feb29-story.html

"Capital One data breach: Arrest after details of 106m people stolen," BBC (July 30, 2019). https://www.bbc.co.uk/news/world-us-canada-49159859.

Carrington, Damian. "'Our leaders are like children,' school strike founder tells climate summit," *The Guradian* (December 4, 2018). https://www.theguardian.com/environment/2018/dec/04/leaders-like-children-school-strike-founder-greta-thunberg-tells-un-climate-summit.

Catmull, Ed. "Inside the Pixar Braintrust," *Fast Company* (March 12, 2014). https://www.fastcompany.com/3027135/inside-the-pixar-braintrust.

Centre for Retail Research. "The Crises in Retailing: Closures and Job Losses," RetailResearch.org. Accessed May 1, 2020. https://www.retailresearch.org/retail-crisis.html.

"Chart your Agile Pathway," AgileFluency.org. Accessed February 24, 2020. https://www.agilefluency.org.

Chen, Jui-Chen, and Colin Silverthorne. "The impact of locus of control on job stress, job performance and job satisfaction in Taiwan," *Leadership & Organization Development Journal* 29, no. 7 (2008): 575–582.

Chernoff, Allan. "Study: Deepwater Horizon workers were afraid to report safety issues," *CNN* (July 22, 2010). https://edition.cnn.com/2010/US/07/22/gulf.oil.rig.safety/index.html.

Chua, Amy. *Political Tribes: Group Instincts and the Fate of Nations*. NY: Penguin, 2019.

Clark, Wallace. *The Gantt Chart: A Working Tool of Management*. NY: Ronald Press Company, 1923.

Cockburn, Alistair, and Laurie William. "The costs and benefits of pair programming," in *Proceedings of the First International Conference on Extreme Programming and Flexible Processes in Software Engineering (XP2000)*, Cagilari, Sardinia (2001).

"Columbia verdict reveals bizarre Challenger parallels," *The Sydney Morning Herald* (July 14, 2003). https://www.smh.com.au/world/columbia-verdict-reveals-bizarre-challenger-parallels-20030714-gdh3eq.html.

"command," Online Etymology Dictionary. Accessed May 1, 2020. https://www.etymonline.com/word/command.

"commander," Online Etymology Dictionary. Accessed May 1, 2020. https://www.etymonline.com/word/commander.

Conway, Melvin E. "How do Committees Invent?" Datamation (April 1968). http://www.melconway.com/Home/pdf/committees.pdf.

Coutu, Diane. "The Anxiety of Learning," *Harvard Business Review* (March 2002). https://hbr.org/2002/03/the-anxiety-of-learning.

Coyne, Allie. "ANZ to make the whole bank agile," iTnews.com (May 2, 2017). https://www.itnews.com.au/news/anz-to-make-the-whole-bank-agile-460213.

Cremen, Louis. "Introducing the InfoSec colour wheel—blending developers with red and blue security teams," *HackerNoon* (November 29, 2019). https://hackernoon.com/introducing-the-infosec-colour-wheel-blending-developers-with-red-and-blue-security-teams-6437c1a07700.

DeGrandis, Dominica. "5 Time Thieves and How to Beat Them," *The Enterprisers Project* (January 2018). https://enterprisersproject.com/article/2018/1/5-time-thieves-and-how-beat-them.

DeGrandis, Dominica. *Making Work Visible: Exposing Time Theft to Optimize Work & Flow*. Portland, OR: IT Revolution, 2017.

Dekker, Sidney W.A. "The Bureaucratization of Safety" *Safety Science* 70 (2014): 348–357. https://www.safetydifferently.com/wp-content/uploads/2014/08/BureaucratizationSafety.pdf.

Dekker, Sidney. "Safety Differently Lecture," YouTube video, 26:48, posted by sidneydekker, December 1, 2015. https://youtu.be/oMtLS0FNDZs.

Democratic Staff of the House Committee on Transportation and Infrastructure. *The Boeing 737 MAX Aircraft: Costs, Consequences, and Lessons from its Design, Development, and Certification—Preliminary Investigative Findings*. Washington, DC: The House Committee of Transportation & Infrastructure, March 2020. https://transportation.house.gov/imo/media/doc/TI%20Preliminary%20Investigative%20Findings%20Boeing%20737%20MAX%20March%202020.pdf.

Dewar, Carolyn, and Scott Keller. "The irrational side of change management," *McKinsey Quarterly* (April 1, 2009). https://www.mckinsey.com/business-functions/organization/our-insights/the-irrational-side-of-change-management.

"Digital, Data and Technology Profession Capability Framework," Gov.uk (March 23, 2017) https://www.gov.uk/government/collections/digital-data-and-technology-profession-capability-framework.

Dixon, Matthew, and Brent Adamson, *The Challenger Sale: How To Take Control of the Customer Conversation*. NY: Portfolio Penguin, 2013.

Doctorow, Cory. "The true story of Notpetya: a Russian cyberweapon that escaped and did $10B in worldwide damage," *BoingBoing* (August 22, 2018). https://boingboing.net/2018/08/22/andy-greenberg.html.

Dweck, Carol S. *Mindset: The New Psychology of Success Paperback*. NY: Ballantine, 2007.

Eavis, Peter. "The Lessons for Finance in the GE Capital Retreat," *The New York Times*, April 10, 2015. https://www.nytimes.com/2015/04/11/business/dealbook/the-lessons-for-finance-in-the-ge-capital-retreat.html.

Edmondson, Amy. *The Fearless Organization: Creating Psychological Safety in the Workplace for Learning, Innovation, and Growth*. Hoboken, NJ: John Wiley & Sons, 2018.

Edmondson, Amy, and Zhike Lei, "Psychological Safety: The History, Renaissance, and Future of an Interpersonal Conduct," *Annual Review of Organizational Psychology and Organizational Behavior* 1 (2014):23–43. https://www.annualreviews.org/doi/pdf/10.1146/annurev-orgpsych-031413-091305.

Egan, Matt. "GE Slashes 119-year old dividend to a penny," *CNN* (October 30, 2018). https://edition.cnn.com/2018/10/30/investing/ge-dividend-cut-earnings-culp/index.html.

Egan, Matt. "GE to raise $4 billion by selling chunk of Baker Hughes," *CNN* (November 13, 2018). https://edition.cnn.com/2018/11/13/business/ge-baker-hughes-oil/index.html.

Eoyang, Glenda. "Conditions for Self-Organizing in Human Systems," HSDinstitute.org. Accessed May 2020. https://www.hsdinstitute.org/resources/conditions-for-self-organizing-in-human-systems.html.

Farfan, Barbara. "What is Apple's Mission Statement," TheBalancesmb.com (November 20, 2019). https://www.thebalancesmb.com/apple-mission-statement-4068547.

Feathers, Michael. "Unit Tests Are Tests of Modularity," *Itemis* (blog) (August 21, 2019). http://blogs.itemis.com/en/unit-tests-are-tests-of-modularity.

Feathers, Michael. *Working Effectively with Legacy Code*. Upper Saddle River, NJ: Prentice Hall, 2004.

Field, Matthew. "WannaCry cyber attack cost the NHS £92m as 19,000 appointments cancelled," *Telegraph* (October 11, 2018). https://www.telegraph.co.uk/technology/2018/10/11/wannacry-cyber-attack-cost-nhs-92m-19000-appointments-cancelled/.

Financial Conduct Authority, *FCA Handbook*, Release 47, February 2020, 5.1.8 https://www.handbook.fca.org.uk/handbook/SYSC/5.pdf clause 5.1.8

Floryan, Marcin. "There is No Spotify Model," *InfoQ*, presented at Spark the Change 2016. Accessed May 1, 2020. https://www.infoq.com/presentations/spotify-culture-stc/.

Forsgren, Dr. Nicole, Dr. Dustin Smith, Jez Humble, Jessie Frazelle. *Accelerate State of DevOps 2019*. DORA and Google Cloud, 2019. https://services.google.com/fh/files/misc/state-of-devops-2019.pdf.

Forsgren, Dr. Nicole, Jez Humble, Gene Kim, Alanna Brown, and Nigel Kersten. *State of DevOps Report 2017*. Puppet + DORA, 2017. https://puppet.com/resources/report/2017-state-devops-report/.

Fowler, Martin. "AgileImposition," MartinFowler.com (October 2, 2006) https://martinfowler.com/bliki/AgileImposition.html.

Fowler, Martin. "FlaccidScrum," MartinFowler.com (blog) (January 29, 2009). https://martinfowler.com/bliki/FlaccidScrum.html.

Fowler, Martin. "The State of Agile Software in 2018," presented at Agile Australia, August 25, 2018. https://martinfowler.com/articles/agile-aus-2018.html.

Fowler, Martin. "StranglerFigApplication," MartinFowler.com (blog) (June 29, 2004). https://martinfowler.com/bliki/StranglerFigApplication.html.

Fukuyama, Francis. *Trust: Human Nature and the Reconstitution of Social Order*. NY: Free Press, 1995.

Gates, Dominic, Steve Miletich, and Lewis Kamb. "Boeing rejected 737 MAX safety upgrades before fatal crashes, whistleblower says," *Seattle Times* (October 2, 2019).

https://www.seattletimes.com/business/boeing-aerospace/boeing-whistleblowers-complaint-says-737-max-safety-upgrades-were-rejected-over-cost/.

"GDPR Fines/Penalties," GDPR-Info.eu. Accessed May 20, 2020. https://gdpr-info.eu/issues/fines-penalties/.

Gelles, David. "'I Honestly Don't Trust Many People at Boeing': A Broken Culture Exposed," *New York Times* (January 10, 2020). https://www.nytimes.com/2020/01/10/business/boeing-737-employees-messages.html

Gelles, David, and Natalie Kitroeff. "Boeing Board to Call for Safety Changes After 737 Max Crashes," *New York Times* (September 15, 2019). https://www.nytimes.com/2019/09/15/business/boeing-safety-737-max.html.

Gerndt, Ulrich. *Frederic Laloux "Reinventing organizations": Excerpt and Summaries.* Change Factory, (2014). http://www.reinventingorganizations.com/uploads/2/1/9/8/21988088/140305_laloux_reinventing_organizations.pdf.

Glassman, James K. "World of Investing: The Dividend Makes a Return," *New York Times* (March 6, 2004). https://www.nytimes.com/2004/03/06/your-money/IHT-world-of-investing-the-dividend-makes-a-return.html

Goodhart, Charles. "Problems of Monetary Management: The U.K. Experience," in Courakis, Anthony S. (ed.). *Inflation, Depression, and Economic Policy in the West.* Barnes and Noble Books, 1981: 111–146.

Greenberg, Andy. "The Untold Story of NotPetya, the Most Devastating Cyberattack in History," *Wired* (August 22, 2018). https://www.wired.com/story/notpetya-cyberattack-ukraine-russia-code-crashed-the-world/.

Greenleaf, Robert K. *Servant Leadership: A Journey Into the Nature of Legitimate Power and Greatness,* 25th Anniversary Edition. NY: Paulist Press, 2002.

Gov.uk. *Digital, Data and Technology Profession Capability Framework* (March 23, 2017). http://www.gov.uk/government/collections/digital-data-and-technology-profession-capability-framework.

"Guide: Understand team effectiveness," *re:Work.* Accessed May 1, 2020. https://rework.withgoogle.com/print/guides/5721312655835136/.

Handwerk, Brian. "China's Three Gorges Dam, by the Numbers," NationalGeographic.com, June 9, 2006. https://www.nationalgeographic.com/science/2006/06/china-three-gorges-dam-how-big/.

Harter, Jim. "Employee Engagement on the Rise in the U.S.," *Gallup* (August 26, 2018). https://news.gallup.com/poll/241649/employee-engagement-rise.aspx.

Hawkins, Andrew J. "Tesla relied on too many robots to build the Model 3, Elon Musk says," *The Verge* (April 13, 2018). https://www.theverge.com/2018/4/13/17234296/tesla-model-3-robots-production-hell-elon-musk.

Hearing: "The Boeing 737 MAX: Examining the Federal Aviation Administration's Oversight of the Aircraft's Certification. 116th Congress (2019) (statement of Edward F. Pierson, retired Boeing employee). https://transportation.house.gov/imo/media/doc/Pierson%20Testimony.pdf

Herway, Jake. "How to Create a Culture of Psychological Safety," *Gallup* (December 7, 2017). https://www.gallup.com/workplace/236198/create-culture-psychological-safety.aspx.

Hipple, Kathy, Tom Sanzillo, and Tim Bucley. "GE's $7.4 Billion Loss, Write-off on Baker Hughes: Another Bad Bet on Fossil Fuels," *Institute for Energy Economics and Finacial Analysis* (October 2019). http://ieefa.org/wp-content/uploads/2019/10/GE-Writeoff-on-Baker-Hughes-Sale-Another-Bad-Bet-on-Fossil-Fuels_October-2019.pdf.

Hollnagel, Erik, Robert Wears, and Jeffrey Braithwaite. *From Safety I to Safety II: A White Paper.* Self-published: August 1, 2015. https://www.researchgate.net/publication/282441875_From_Safety-I_to_Safety-II_A_White_Paper.

Holmes, Carson, and Julian Holmes, "I want to run an agile project," YouTube video, 10:00, posted by holmesUPMFMC, June 13, 2011. https://youtu.be/4u5N00ApR_k.

Howland, Daphne. "Digitally native brands set to open 850 stores in 5 years," *Retail Dive* (October 10, 2018). https://www.retaildive.com/news/e-commerce-pure-plays-set-to-open -850-stores-in-five-years/539320/.

Hubbard, Douglas W. *How to Measure Anything: Finding the Value of "Intangibles" in Business.* Hoboken, NJ: Wiley & Sons, 2014.

Hubbard, Douglas. "The IT Measurement Inversion: Are your IT Investment Decisions Based on the Right Information?" CIO.com (June 13, 2007). https://www.cio.com/article/2438748 /the-it-measurement-inversion.html?page=2.

Immelt, Jeffery R. "How I Remade GE," *Harvard Business Review* (September-October 2017). https://hbr.org/2017/09/inside-ges-transformation.

Improving the Delivery of Government IT Projects, prepared by the House of Commons Public Accounts Committee (London, 2000). https://publications.parliament.uk/pa/cm199900 /cmselect/cmpubacc/65/6502.htm.

"Introduction to Disciplined Agile (DA)," Disciplined Agile website (Accessed February 6, 2020). https://disciplinedagiledelivery.com/agility-at-scale/disciplined-agile-2/.

Isaacs, William. *Dialogue and the Art of Thinking Together: A Pioneering Approach to Communicating in Business and in Life.* NY: Crown Business, 2008.

Janlen, Jimmy. "Improvement Theme—Simple and practice Toyota Kata," Jimmy Jalen's blog, May 14, 2013. https://blog.crisp.se/2013/05/14/jimmyjanlen/improvement-theme-simple -and-practical-toyota-kata.

Jones, Carrie Melissa. "Here is Duolingo's Playbook for Creating Community-Generated Content for over 50 Million Learners," CMXhub.com. Accessed February 12, 2020. https://cmxhub .com/duolingo-ugc-challenges/.

Jones, Daniel T. and James P. Womack. *Lean Thinking: Banish Waste and Create Wealth in Your Corporation.* NY: Simon and Schuster, 1996.

Kanter, Rosabeth Moss. "Ten Reasons People Resist Change," *Harvard Business Review* (September 25, 2012). https://hbr.org/2012/09/ten-reasons-people-resist-chang.

Kay, John. "Obliquity," JohnKay.com (blog) (January 17, 2004). https://www.johnkay.com/2004 /01/17/obliquity/.

Kersten, Mik. *Project To Product: How to Survive and Thrive in the Age of Digital Disruption with the Flow Framework.* Portland, OR: IT Revolution, 2018.

Khaleel, Sonia. "Detroit Ranked Last in Report on Best Cities for Jobs," *Metro Times* (January 3, 2020). https://www.metrotimes.com/news-hits/archives/2020/01/03/detroit-ranked-last -in-report-on-best-cities-for-jobs.

Kim, Gene. *The Unicorn Project: A Novel about Developers, Digital Disruption, and Thriving in the Age of Data.* Portland, OR: IT Revolution, 2019.

Kissler, Courtney. "Starbucks Technology Transformation - Courtney Kissler," YouTube video, 28:25, posted by IT Revolution, July 27, 2018. https://www.youtube.com/watch?v=uImY-8iWYWu8.

Kitroeff, Natalie. "Boeing 737 Max Safety System Was Vetoed, Engineer Says," *New York Times* (October 2, 2019). https://www.nytimes.com/2019/10/02/business/boeing-737-max -crashes.html.

Kitroeff, Natalie, and David Gelles. "Claims of Shoddy Production Draw Scrutiny to a Second Boeing Jet," *New York Times* (April 20, 2019). https://www.nytimes.com/2019/04/20/business /boeing-dreamliner-production-problems.html.

Kniberg, Henrik. "Spotify Engineering Culture (Part 2)," Spotify R&D (September 20, 2014). https://engineering.atspotify.com/2014/09/20/spotify-engineering-culture-part-2/.

Kniberg, Henrik, and Anders Ivarsson. *Scaling Agile @ Spotify with Tribes, Squads, Chapters and Guilds* (October 2012) https://blog.crisp.se/wp-content/uploads/2012/11/SpotifyScaling .pdf.

Kruger, Justin, and David Dunning, "Unskilled and Unaware of It: How Difficulties in Recognizing One's Own Incompetence Lead to Inflated Self-Assessments," *Journal of Personality and Social Psychology* 77, no. 6 (Dec 1999): 1121–1134.

Kübler-Ross, Elisabeth, and David Kessler, *On Grief and Grieving: Finding the Meaning of Grief Through the Five Stages of Loss.* NY: Scribner, 2014.

Kübler-Ross, Elisabeth. *On Death and Dying.* London, UK: Routledge, 1969.

Laloux, Frédéric. *Reinventing Organizations: A Guide to Creating Organizations Inspired by the Next Stage of Human Consciousness.* Nelson Parker, 2014

Langfit, Frank. "The End of the Line for GM-Toyota Joint Venture," *All Things Considered* (March 26, 2010). https://www.npr.org/templates/story/story.php?storyId=125229157.

Larman, Craig. *Large-Scale Scrum: More with Less.* Upper-Saddle River, NJ: Addison-Wesley Signature Series, 2016.

Larman, Craig, and Bas Vodde. *Practices for Scaling Lean & Agile Development.* Upper-Saddle River, NJ: Addison-Wesley Professional, 2010.

Larman, Craig, and Bas Vodde. *Scaling Lean & Agile Development Thinking and Organizational Tools for Large-Scale Scrum.* Upper-Saddle River, NJ: Addison-Wesley Professional, 2008.

"lead," Online Etymology Dictionary. Accessed May 1, 2020. https://www.etymonline.com/word /lead.

"leader," Online Etymology Dictionary. Accessed May 1, 2020. https://www.etymonline.com /word/leader.

"Leadership Principles," Amazon website. Accessed February 5, 2020. https://www.amazon.jobs /en/principles.

Leitz, Shannon. "Shifting Security to the Left," DevSecOps.org (June 5, 2016). https://www .devsecops.org/blog?author=54dc6220e4b085335dd9d630.

Leopold, Klaus. *Rethinking Agile: Why Agile Teams Have Nothing to do With Business Agility.* Vienna, Austria: LEANability GmbH, 2018.

MacCormack, Alan D., John Rusnak, and Carliss Y Baldwin. "Exploring the Duality between Product and Organizational Architectures: A Test of the Mirroring Hypothesis," *Working Knowledge* (March 27, 2008). https://hbswk.hbs.edu/item/exploring-the-duality-between-product -and-organizational-architectures-a-test-of-the-mirroring-hypothesis.

Magee, David. *How Toyota Became #1: Leadership Lessons from the World's Greatest Car Company.* NY: Penguin, 2007.

"Manifesto," DevSecOps.org. Accessed February 17, 2020. https://www.devsecops.org/.

Marquet, L. David, Stephen R. Covey. *Turn the Ship Around!: A True Story of Turning Leaders into Followers.* NY: Portfolio, 2013.

Mathieson, Steve. "Take Aim . . ." HSJ.co.uk, June 14, 2001. https://www.hsj.co.uk/news/take -aim-/24372.article.

Maurer, Robert. *One Small Step Can Change Your Life: The Kaizen Way.* NY: Workman, 2014.

McChrystal, Gen. Stanley, Tantum Collins, David Silverman, and Chris Fussell. *Team of Teams: New Rules of Engagement for a Complex World.* NY: Portfolio, 2015.

McFadden, Cynthia, Anna Schecter, Kevin Monahan, and Rich Schapiro. "Former Boeing manager says he warned company of problems prior to 737 crashes," NBC News (December 9, 2019). https://www.nbcnews.com/news/us-news/former-boeing-manager-says-he-warned -company-problems-prior-737-n1098536.

McLean, Iain, and Martin Johnes. *Aberfan: Government and Disaster.* Cardiff, UK: Welsh Academic Press, 2018.

Mezick, Daniel. "The Agile Industrial Complex," *New Technology Solutions* (December 12, 2016). https://newtechusa.net/aic/.

Microsoft, *Diversity and Inclusion Report 2019*. Microsoft, 2019. https://query.prod.cms.rt .microsoft.com/cms/api/am/binary/RE4aqv1

Milgram, Stanley. "Behavioral Study of Obedience," *Journal of Abnormal and Social Psychology* 67, no. 4 (1963): 371–378.

Mindock, Clark. "Apple is the first trillion dollar company: What was the first billion dollar valuation?," *Independent* (August 2, 2018). https://www.independent.co.uk/news/business/apple -valuation-shares-trillion-billion-latest-money-tech-google-alphabet-amazon-a8472026 .html.

Moore, Geoffrey A. *Crossing the Chasm: Marketing and Selling High-Tech Products to Mainstream Customers*. NY: Harper Business Essentials, 199.1

National Audit Office. *The Cancellation of the Benefits Payment Card Project*, The Stationary Office: London, 2000. https://www.jfsa.org.uk/uploads/5/4/3/1/54312921/the_full_report_on_the _cancelled_dhss_card.pdf.

National Commission on the BP Deepwater Horizon Oil Spill and Offshore Drilling. *Deep Water: The Gulf Oil Disaster and the Future of Offshore Drilling, Report to the President*. Washington, DC: National Commission on the BP Deepwater Horizon Oil Spill and Offshore Drilling, January 2011. https://www.govinfo.gov/content/pkg/GPO-OILCOMMISSION/pdf/GPO-OIL COMMISSION.pdf.

Newman, Jared. "This app will file an unemployment claim on your behalf," *Fast Company* (April 14, 2020). https://www.fastcompany.com/90490163/this-app-will-file-an-unemployment -claim-on-your-behalf

North, Dan. "Microservices: Software that Fits in Your Head," *InfoQ* (August 9, 2015). https:// www.infoq.com/presentations/microservices-replaceability-consistency/.

North, Dan, and Katherine Kirk. "Scaling Without a Religious Methodology," SpeakerDeck.com . Accessed February 3, 2020. https://speakerdeck.com/tastapod/swarming.

North, Dan. "Kicking the Complexity Habit," presented at GOTO Chicago 2014. http://gotocon .com/dl/goto-chicago-2014/slides/DanNorth_KickingTheComplexityHabit.pdf

"Online Nexus Guide," Scrum.org (Accessed February 6, 2020) https://www.scrum.org/resources /online-nexus-guide.

O'Reilly, Barry. *Unlearn: Let Go of Past Success to Achieve Extraordinary Results*. NY: McGraw-Hill Education, 2018.

Ostrower, Jon. "Inside Boeing: Sadness, frustration, anger, uncertainty & focus after 737 Max crashes," *The Aire Current* (May 16, 2019).https://theaircurrent.com/company-culture/inside -boeing-sadness-frustration-anger-uncertainty-focus-after-737-max-crashes/.

Parkinson, C. Northcote. "Parkinson's Law," *The Economist* (November 15, 1955).

Perez, Carlota. *Technological Revolutions and Financial Capital: The Dynamics of Bubbles and Golden Ages*. Cheltenham, UK: Edward Elgar Pub, 2003.

Perry, Gina. *Behind the Shock Machine: The Untold Story of the Notorious Milgram Psychology Experiments*. NY: The New Press, 2013.

Phillips, Matt. "G.E. Dropped From the Dow After More Than a Century," *New York Times* (June 19, 2008). https://www.nytimes.com/2018/06/19/business/dealbook/general-electric-dow -jones.html.

"PI Planning," ScaledAgileFramework.com (Accessed February 6, 2020). https://www.scaledagile framework.com/pi-planning/.

Pink, Daniel. *Drive: The Surprising Truth About What Motivates Us*. NY: Riverhead Books, 2011.

Polanyi, Michael. *The Tacit Dimension*. University of Chicago Press, 1966

Poppendieck, Mary, and Tom Poppendieck. *Implementing Lean Software Development: From Concept to Cash*. Upper Saddle River, NJ: Addison-Wesley, 2006.

"Principles behind the Agile Manifesto," AgileManifesto.org. Accessed May 1, 2020. https://agile manifesto.org/principles.html.

PWC. *Global Top 100 Companies by market capitalization*. London, UK: PriceWaterhouseCoopers, 2016. https://www.pwc.com/gr/en/publications/assets/global-top-100-companies-by-market -capitalisation.pdf.

"Questions and Answers About Large Dams," InternationalRivers.org. Accessed May 1, 2020. https://www.internationalrivers.org/questions-and-answers-about-large-dams.

"Quick Facts: Detroit city, Michigan; United States," Census.gov. Accessed May 1, 2020. https:// www.census.gov/quickfacts/fact/table/detroitcitymichigan,US/PST045218

Radtac. *Nokia transforms their software division using Agile at unprecedented scale*. Radtac. Accessed May 1, 2020. https://www.radtac.com/wp-content/uploads/2016/05/Nokia-and-Radtac-case -study.pdf.

Rafferty, John D. "9 of the Biggest Oil Spills in History," *Britannica*. Accessed June 1, 2020. https:// www.britannica.com/list/9-of-the-biggest-oil-spills-in-history.

Reinertsen Donald G., and Preston G. Smith. *Developing Products in Half the Time: New Rules, New Tools*. Hoboken, NJ: Wiley & Sons, 1997.

"Renton rolls out 47th 737 built at new 47-er-month rate," Boeing.com (July 31, 2017). https:// www.boeing.com/company/about-bca/washington/737-rate-increase-07-28-17.page.

Report of the Tribunal appointed to inquire into the Disaster at Aberfan on October 21st, 1966. London: Her Majesty's Stationary Office, 1967. http://www.mineaccidents.com.au/uploads/aberfan -report-original.pdf.

Rigby, Darrell K., Jeff Sutherland, and Andy Noble. "Agile at Scale," *Harvard Business Review* (May– June 2018).

"Risk," Prince2.wiki. Accessed February 17, 2020. https://prince2.wiki/theme/risk/.

Ritchie, Rae. "Maersk: Springing Back from a Catastrophic Cyber-Attack," *I-Global Intelligence for the CIO* (August 2019). https://www.i-cio.com/management/insight/item /maersk-springing-back-from-a-catastrophic-cyber-attack.

Robison, Peter. "Former Boeing Engineers Say Relentless Cost-Cutting Sacrificed Safety," *Bloomberg* (May 8, 2019). https://www.bloomberg.com/news/features/2019-05-09/former -boeing-engineers-say-relentless-cost-cutting-sacrificed-safety.

Rogers, E.M. *Diffusion of innovations* (5th ed.). NY: Free Press, 2003.

Rother, Mike. "The Coaching Kata: Managing Through Coaching," University of Michigan website. Accessed February 5, 2020. http://www-personal.umich.edu/~mrother/The_Coaching_Kata .html.

Rother, Mike. *Toyota Kata: Managing People for Improvement, Adaptiveness and Superior Results*. NY: McGraw-Hill Education, 2004.

Royce, Dr. Winston W. "Managing the Development of Large Software Systems," *IEEE* (August 1970), 1–9.

Sahota, Michael. "How to Make Your Culture Work (Schneider)," Agilitrix.com (Marcy 23, 2011). http://agilitrix.com/2011/03/how-to-make-your-culture-work/.

Schein, Edgar H. "Kurt Lewin's Change Theory in the Field and in the Classroom: Notes Toward a Model of Managed Learning," *Reflections* 1, no. 1 (February 1996): 27–47. http://citeseerx .ist.psu.edu/viewdoc/download?doi=10.1.1.475.3285&rep=rep1&type=pdf.

Schwaber, Ken. *SCRUM Development Process*, from OOPSLA '95 Workshop Proceedings, October 16, 1995. http://www.jeffsutherland.org/oopsla/schwapub.pdf.

Senge, Peter M. *The Fifth Discipline: The Art & Practice of the Learning Organization*. NY: Random House, 1990.

Sensenbrenner, Joseph. "Quality Comes to City Hall," *Harvard Business Review* (March-April 1991). https://hbr.org/1991/03/quality-comes-to-city-hall.

Shih, Willy. "Inside Toyota's Giant Kentucky Factory: Japanese Production Techniques, Made in America," *Forbes* (April 17, 2018). https://www.forbes.com/sites/willyshih/2018/04/17/inside-toyotas-giant-kentucky-factory-japanese-production-techniques-made-in-america/#1f51e9d233e4.

Shook, John. "How to Change a Culture: Lessons From NUMMI," *MIT Sloan Management Review* 51, no. 2 (Winter 2010): 63–68. https://www.lean.org/Search/Documents/35.pdf.

Siilasmaa, Risto. *Transforming NOKIA: The Power of Paranoid Optimism to Lead Through Colossal Change*. NY: McGraw-Hill Education, 2018.

Simon, Herbert A. "Rational Choice and the Structure of the Environment," *Psychological Review* 63, no. 2 (1956): 129–138.

Sinek, Simon. "Start with why—how great leaders inspire action | Simon Sinek | TEDxPugetSound," YouTube video, 18:01, published by TEDx Talks, September 29, 2009. https://youtu.be/u4ZoJKF_VuA.

Sinek, Simon. *Start with Why: How Great Leaders Inspire Everyone to Take Action*. NY: Portfolio, 2009.

Skelton, Matthew, and Manuel Pais. "Monoliths Vs Microservices Is Missing The Point—Start With Team Cognitive Load," IT Revolution (blog) (September 17, 2019). https://itrevolution.com/team-cognitive-load-team-topologies/.

Skelton, Matthew, and Manuel Pais. *Team Topologies: Organizing Business and Technology Teams for Fast Flow*. Portland, OR: IT Revolution, 2019.

Smart, Jonathan. "The PMO is Dead, Long Live the PMO—Barclays," YouTube video, 33:33, posted by IT Revolution, July 3, 2018. https://www.youtube.com/watch?v=R-fol1vkPlM.

Snowden, Dave. "Scaling in complex systems," Cognitive-Edge.com (October 1, 2017). https://cognitive-edge.com/blog/scaling-in-complex-systems/.

Snowden, David J., and Mary E. Boone. "A Leader's Framework for Decision Making," *Harvard Business Review* (November 2007). https://hbr.org/2007/11/a-leaders-framework-for-decision-making.

Society for Personality and Social Psychology. "How we form habits, change existing ones," *ScienceDaily*. (August 8, 2014). www.sciencedaily.com/releases/2014/08/140808111931.htm.

Sorscher, Stan. "What will it be, Boeing? Great airplanes that generate cash flow or great cash flow, period?

"Statement from Boeing," submitted to Emily Siegel at NBC News. Accessed May 1, 2020. https://www.documentcloud.org/documents/6571701-BOEING-STATEMENT.html.

Strathern, Marilyn. "Improving Ratings: Audit in the British University System," *European Review* 5, no. 3 (July 1997) : 305–321. https://www.cambridge.org/core/journals/european-review/article/improving-ratings-audit-in-the-british-university-system/FC2EE640C0C44E3DB87C29FB666E9AAB.

Sundén, Joakim. "How things don't quite work at Spotify . . . and how we're trying to solve it," presented at Agile Boston. (October 23, 2016). http://www.agileboston.org/wp-content/uploads/2016/05/Spotify-talk-Agile-Boston.pdf.

Sutherland, Jeff. "Nokia Test 'aka the ScrumButt Test,'" JeffSutherland.com. (March 25, 2009). http://jeffsutherland.com/scrum/nokiatest.pdf.

Sutherland, Jeff. "Nokia Test: Where did it come from?" Scruminc.com. (February 28, 2010). https://www.scruminc.com/nokia-test-where-did-it-come-from/.

Takeuchi, Hirotaka, and Ikujiro Nonaka. "The New New Product Development Game," *Harvard Business Review* (January 1986).

Taylor, Frederick Winslow. *Principles of Scientific Management*. New York, Harper & Brothers, 1911.

Teller, Astro. "A Peek Inside the Moonshot Factory Operating Model," X Company blog (July 23, 2016). https://blog.x.company/a-peek-inside-the-moonshot-factory-operating-manual-f5c-33c9ab4d7.

Teller, Astro. "The Head of 'X' Explains How to Make Audacity the Path of Least Resistance," *Wired* (April 15, 2016). https://www.wired.com/2016/04/the-head-of-x-explains-how-to-make-audacity-the-path-of-least-resistance/#.rmrppjtip.

"Ten things we know to be true," Google.com. Accessed May 1, 2020. https://www.google.com/about/philosophy.html.

Terhorst-North, Daniel. "Introducing Deliberate Discovery," DanNorth.net (August 30, 2010). https://dannorth.net/2010/08/30/introducing-deliberate-discovery/.

Terhorst-North, Dan. "Microservices: software that fits in your head," Speakerdeck.com, posted by Daniel Terhorst-North (March 6, 2015). https://speakerdeck.com/tastapod/microservices-software-that-fits-in-your-head.

"The Agile FluencyTM Model," AgileFluency.org. Accessed May 20, 2020. https://www.agilefluency.org/model.php.

"The Architecture Owner Role: How Architects Fit in on Agile Teams," AgileModeling.com. Accessed May 1, 2020. http://www.agilemodeling.com/essays/architectureOwner.htm.

"The Fearless Organization Scan," FearlessOrganization.com. Accessed May 1, 2020. https://fearlessorganization.com/.

"The Kanban Method," Kanban University website (Accessed May 1, 2020). https://edu.kanban.university/kanban-method

"The Pursuit of Success & Averting Drift into Failure - Sidney Dekker," YouTube video, 28:09, posted by IT Revolution, November 19, 2017. https://www.youtube.com/watch?v=pmZ6w-tOmTZU

"The Scrum at Scale Guide," ScrumatScale.com (November 26, 2019). https://www.scrumatscale.com/scrum-at-scale-guide-read-online/#End_Note.

"The Scrum Guide," ScrumGuides.org. (Accessed February 6, 2020). https://scrumguides.org/scrum-guide.html#endnote.

The Standish Group, *Chaos Report 2015*. The Standish Group, 2015. https://standishgroup.com/sample_research_files/CHAOSReport2015-Final.pdf

Thomas, Lauren. "25,000 Stores Are Predicted to Close in 2020, As the Coronavirus Pandemic Accelerates Industry Upheaval," CNBC (June 9, 2020). https://www.cnbc.com/2020/06/09/coresight-predicts-record-25000-retail-stores-will-close-in-2020.html.

Trevitchick, Joseph. "The Air Force's Troubled Boeing KC-46 Tankers Leak Fuel Excessively," TheDrive.com (March 30, 2020). https://www.thedrive.com/the-war-zone/32818/the-air-force-has-revealed-that-its-troubled-kc-46-tankers-leak-fuel-excessively.

Tuckman, Bruce W. "Developmental sequence in small groups," *Psychological Bulletin* 63, no. 6 (1965): 384–399.

Turner, Barry A. "The Organizational and Interorganizational Development of Disasters," *Administrative Science Quarterly* 21, no. 3 (1976): 378-397.

"US refuses to ground Boeing 737 Max crash aircraft," BBC News (March 13, 2019). https://www.bbc.co.uk/news/business-47548083.

Useem, Jerry. "The Long-Forgotten Flight That Sent Boeing Off Course," *The Atlantic* (November 20, 2019). https://www.theatlantic.com/ideas/archive/2019/11/how-boeing-lost-its-bearings/602188/.

Van Hasster, Kelsey. "Road-mapping Your Way to Agile Fluency," *ThoughtWorks* (April 18, 2016). https://www.thoughtworks.com/insights/blog/road-mapping-your-way-agile-fluency.

Varhol, Peter. "To Agility and Beyond: The History—and Legacy—of Agile Development," *TechBeacon* (August 26, 2015). https://techbeacon.com/app-dev-testing/agility-beyond-history-legacy-agile-development.

Wagner, I. "Automotive electronics cost as a percentage of total car cost worldwide from 1950 to 2030," Statista.com, October 23, 2019. https://www.statista.com/statistics/277931/automotive-electronics-cost-as-a-share-of-total-car-cost-worldwide/.

Weinberg, Gerald M. *The Secrets of Consulting: A Guide to Giving and Getting Advice Successfully*. NY: Dorset House Publishing, 1985.

Weinberg, Samantha. *A Fish Caught in Time: The Search for the Coelacanth*. NY: Perennial, 2000.

Westrum, Ron. "A typology of organizational culture," *BMJ Quality & Safety* 13, no. 2 (2004): 1122–1127. https://qualitysafety.bmj.com/content/13/suppl_2/ii22.

"What is Lean?" Lean Enterprise Institute website, Accessed May 1, 2020. https://www.lean.org/WhatsLean/.

Wikipedia. "Agile Construction," Wikipedia.org. Last modified September 13, 2019. https://en.wikipedia.org/wiki/Agile_construction.

Wikipedia. "Boeing 787 Dreamliner," Wikipedia.org. Last modified May 20, 2020. https://en.wikipedia.org/wiki/Boeing_787_Dreamliner.

Wikipedia. "Cargo cult," Wikipedia.org. Last modified May 15, 2020. https://en.wikipedia.org/wiki/Cargo_cult.

Wikipedia. "Deepwater Horizon," Wikipedia.org. Last modified May 26, 2020. https://en.wikipedia.org/wiki/Deepwater_Horizon.

Wikipedia, "Greta Thunberg," Wikipedia.org. Last modified May 16, 2020. https://en.wikipedia.org/wiki/Greta_Thunberg.

Wikipedia. "HealthCare.gov." Wikipedia.org. Last modified July 27, 2020. https://en.wikipedia.org/wiki/HealthCare.gov.

Wikipedia. "List of manufacturers by motor vehicle production," Wikipedia.org. Last modified April 18, 2020. https://en.wikipedia.org/wiki/List_of_manufacturers_by_motor_vehicle_production.

Wikipedia. "List of public corporations by market capitalization." Last modified April 2020. https://en.wikipedia.org/wiki/List_of_public_corporations_by_market_capitalization.

Wikipedia, "Loss aversion," Wikipedia.org. Last modified May 9, 2020. https://en.wikipedia.org/wiki/Loss_aversion.

Wikipedia. "Pixar," Wikipedia.org. Last modified May 19, 2020. https://en.wikipedia.org/wiki/Pixar.

Wikipedia. "Roman roads," Wikipedia.org. Last modified May 31, 2020. https://en.wikipedia.org/wiki/Roman_roads#Milestones_and_markers.

Williams, Neil. "Experiments in roadmapping at GOV.UK," *Mind the Product* (blog) (July 28, 2014. https://www.mindtheproduct.com/experiments-roadmapping-gov-uk/.

Willis, John. "DevOps Culture (Part 1)," IT Revolution (blog) (May 1, 2012. https://itrevolution.com/devops-culture-part-1/.

Wolchover, Natalie. "A New Physics Theory of Life," *Quanta Magazine* (January 28, 2014). https://www.scientificamerican.com/article/a-new-physics-theory-of-life/.

Womack, James P., Daniel T. Jones, and Daniel Roos. *The Machine That Changed the World: The Story of Lean Production*. NY: Harper Perennial, , 1991.

World Economic Forum. "Securing a Common Future in Cyberspace," YouTube video, 3:50, posted by World Economic Forum, January 24, 2018. https://youtu.be/Tqe3K3D7TnI.

Wright, T.P. "Factors Affecting the Cost of Airplanes," *JAS Aeronautical Sciences* 3 no. 4 (1936): 122–128. https://www.uvm.edu/pdodds/research/papers/others/1936/wright1936a.pdf.

"Your 'Deadline' Won't Kill You: Or Will It," Merriam-Webster.com. Accessed May 31, 2020. https://www.merriam-webster.com/words-at-play/your-deadline-wont-kill-you.

NOTES

A Sense of Urgency

1. Phillips, "G.E. Dropped From the Dow."
2. Perez, *Technological Revolutions and Financial Capital*.
3. Glassman, "World of Investing."
4. PWC, *Global Top 100 Companies*.
5. Eavis, "The Lessons for Finance in the GE Capital Retreat."
6. Anthony et al., *2018 Corporate Longevity Forecast*.
7. Wikipedia, "List of Public Corporations by Market Capitalization."
8. Wagner, "Automotive electronics cost."
9. Shih, "Inside Toyota's Giant Kentucky Factory."
10. Takeuchi and Nonaka, "The New New Product Development Game."
11. Perez, *Technological Revolutions and Financial Capital*.
12. Terhorst-North, "Microservices."

Chapter 0

1. Handwerk, "China's Three Gorges Dam."
2. Handwerk, "China's Three Gorges Dam."
3. National Audit Office, *The Cancellation of the Benefits Payment Card Project*.
4. *Improving the Delivery of Government IT Projects*.
5. Wikipedia, "Healthcare.gov."
6. "Questions and Answers About Large Dams," InternationalRivers.org.
7. Taylor, *Principles of Scientific Management*, 39.

8. Taylor, *Principles of Scientific Management*, 59.

9. Clark, *The Gantt Chart*.

10. Andreessen, "Why Software Is Eating the World."

11. Mindock, "Apple is the first trillion dollar company."

12. Thomas, "25,000 Stores Are Predicted to Close."

13. Centre for Retail Research, "The Crises in Retailing."

14. Howland, "Digitally native brands."

15. Takeuchi and Nonaka, "The New New Product Development Game."

16. Schwaber, Ken, *SCRUM Development Process*.

17. O'Reilly, *Unlearn*.

18. Beck et al., *Manifesto for Agile Software Development*.

19. Mezick, "The Agile Industrial Complex."

20. Senge, *The Fifth Discipline*.

21. Womack, Jones, and Roos, *The Machine That Changed the World*.

22. "What is Lean?" Lean Enterprise Institute.

23. Jones and Womack, *Lean Thinking*.

24. Kim, *The Unicorn Project*.

25. Varhol, "To Agility and Beyond."

26. Royce, "Managing the Development of Large Software Systems."

27. Wikipedia, "Agile Construction."

28. Forsgren et al., *State of DevOps Report 2019*.

Chapter 1

1. Wikipedia, "Cargo cult."

2. Radtac, *Nokia transforms their software*.

3. Sutherland, "Nokia Test."

4. Sutherland, "Nokia Test."

5. Ahonen, "Nokia Final Q4 Smartphones."

6. Siilasmaa, *Transforming NOKIA*, 71–72.

7. Siilasmaa, *Transforming NOKIA*, 72.

8. Fowler, "AgileImposition."

9. Kanter, "Ten Reasons People Resist Change."

10. Maurer, *One Small Step Can Change Your Life*, 43.

11. Maurer, *One Small Step Can Change Your Life*, 43.

12. Wikipedia, "Loss aversion."

13. Milgram, "Behavioral Study of Obedience."

14. Perry, *Behind the Shock Machine*.

15. Pink, *Drive*.

16. Senge, *The Fifth Discipline*, 58.

17. Rogers, *Diffusion of Innovations*.

18. Pink, *Drive*.

19. Sinek, *Start with Why*.

20. Sinek, *Start with Why*, 209.

21. Farfan, "What is Apple's Mission Statement."

22. Badenhausen, "The World's Most Valuable Brands 2019."

23. Sinek, "Start with why—how great leaders inspire action."

24. Coutu, "The Anxiety of Learning."

25. Dewar and Keller, "The irrational side of change management."

Chapter 2

1. Kübler-Ross, *On Death and Dying*.
2. Kübler-Ross, *On Death and Dying*.
3. Society for Personality and Social Psychology, "How we form habits."
4. Wendy Wood as quoted in Society for Personality and Social Psychology, "How we form habits."
5. Coyne, "ANZ to make the whole bank agile."
6. Bajkowski, "ANZ's boss hits pause button on massive agile expansion."
7. Parkinson, "Parkinson's Law."
8. Parkinson, "Parkinson's Law."
9. Parkinson, "Parkinson's Law."
10. Parkinson, "Parkinson's Law."
11. Byrnes, "Middle Management Excellence."
12. Snowden, "Scaling in complex systems."
13. Rigby, Sutherland, and Noble, "Agile at Scale."
14. Rigby, Sutherland, and Noble, "Agile at Scale."
15. Laloux, *Reinventing Organizations*, 17.
16. Rother, *Toyota Kata*.

Chapter 3

1. "Principles behind the Agile Manifesto," AgileManifesto.org.
2. Westrum, "A typology of organizational cultures."
3. North and Kirk, "Scaling Without a Religious Methodology."
4. Fowler, "AgileImposition."
5. Fowler, "AgileImposition."
6. Fowler, "The State of Agile Software in 2018."
7. Fowler, "The State of Agile Software in 2018."
8. Fowler, "The State of Agile Software in 2018."
9. Chen and Silverthorne, "The impact of locus of control on job stress."
10. "Leadership Principles," Amazon website.
11. North, "Kicking the Complexity Habit."
12. Forsgren et al., *State of Devops Report 2017*.
13. "Guide: Understand team effectiveness," *re:Work*.
14. Kruger, "Unskilled and Unaware of It."
15. North and Kirk, "Scaling Without a Religious Methodology.
16. Rother, "The Coaching Kata."
17. Schein, "Kurt Lewin's Change Theory."
18. "The Scrum Guide," ScrumGuides.org.
19. "The Kanban Method," Kanban University website.
20. "Introduction to Disciplined Agile (DA)," Disciplined Agile website.
21. "The Scrum Guide," ScrumGuides.org.
22. Senge, *The Fifth Discipline*.
23. "PI Planning," ScaledAgileFramework.com.
24. "The Scrum At Scale Guide," ScrumatScale.com.
25. "Online Nexus Guide," Scrum.org.
26. Larman, *Large-Scale Scrum*.
27. Larman and Vodde, *Scaling Lean & Agile Development*.
28. Kniberg and Ivarsson, *Scaling Agile @ Spotify*.
29. Sundén, "How things don't quite work at Spotify."
30. Floryan, "There is no Spotify Model," presented at Spark the Change 2016.

31. Ulrich, "Reinventing organizations."
32. Kniberg, "Spotify Engineering Culture."

Chapter 4

1. *Report of the Tribunal appointed to inquire into the Disaster at Aberfan*, 11.
2. Turner, "The Organizational and Interorganizational Development of Disasters."
3. "lead," Online Etymology Dictionary; "leader," Online Etymology Dictionary.
4. "leadership," Online Etymology Dictionary.
5. "command," Online Etymology Dictionary.
6. "commander," Online Etymology Dictionary.
7. Carrington, "'Our leaders are like children.'"
8. Wikipedia, "Greta Thunberg."
9. Forsgren et al., *State of Devops Report 2017*.
10. McLean and Johnes, *Aberfan*.
11. Kitroeff and Gelles, "Claims of Shoddy Production."
12. Kitroeff and Gelles, "Claims of Shoddy Production."
13. Robison, "Former Boeing Engineers Say Relentless Cost-Cutting Sacrificed Safety."
14. *Hearing: "The Boeing 737 MAX."*
15. "Renton rolls out 47th 737."
16. McFadden et al., "Former Boeing manager says he warned company."
17. *Hearing: "The Boeing 737 MAX."*
18. "Boeing Statement on Employee Messages Provided to U.S. Congress and FAA."
19. Peter, "Former Boeing Engineers Say Relentless Cost-Cutting Sacrificed Safety."
20. Peter, "Former Boeing Engineers Say Relentless Cost-Cutting Sacrificed Safety."
21. Peter, "Former Boeing Engineers Say Relentless Cost-Cutting Sacrificed Safety."
22. Peter, "Former Boeing Engineers Say Relentless Cost-Cutting Sacrificed Safety."
23. Gates, Miletich, and Kamb, "Boeing rejected 737 MAX safety upgrades."
24. Gates, Miletich, and Kamb, "Boeing rejected 737 MAX safety upgrades."
25. Gates, Miletich, and Kamb, "Boeing rejected 737 MAX safety upgrades."
26. Gelles, "'I Honestly Don't Trust Many People at Boeing.'"
27. "Boeing Statement on Employee Messages Provided to U.S. Congress and FAA."
28. Democratic Staff of the House Committee on Transportation and Infrastructure, *The Boeing 737 MAX Aircraft*.
29. "US refuses to ground Boeing 737 Max crash aircraft," BBC News.
30. Wikipedia, "Boeing 787 Dreamliner."
31. Kitroeff and Gelles, "Claims of Shoddy Production."
32. Trevitchick, "The Air Force's Troubled Boeing KC-46."
33. Berger, "New document reveals significant fall from grace."
34. Democratic Staff of the House Committee on Transportation and Infrastructure, *The Boeing 737 MAX Aircraft*, 5.
35. Democratic Staff of the House Committee on Transportation and Infrastructure, *The Boeing 737 MAX Aircraft*, 6.
36. Gelles, "'I Honestly Don't Trust Many People at Boeing.'"
37. Useem, "The Long-Forgotten Flight That Sent Boeing Off Course."
38. Useem, "The Long-Forgotten Flight That Sent Boeing Off Course."
39. Kay, "Obliquity."
40. Useem, "The Long-Forgotten Flight That Sent Boeing Off Course."
41. Useem, "The Long-Forgotten Flight That Sent Boeing Off Course."
42. Useem, "The Long-Forgotten Flight That Sent Boeing Off Course."

43. Useem, "The Long-Forgotten Flight That Sent Boeing Off Course."

44. Gelles and Kitroeff, "Boeing Board to Call for Safety Changes."

45. Callahan, "So why does Harry Stonecipher think he can turn around Boeing?"

46. Callahan, "So why does Harry Stonecipher think he can turn around Boeing?"

47. Useem, "The Long-Forgotten Flight That Sent Boeing Off Course."

48. Democratic Staff of the House Committee on Transportation and Infrastructure, *The Boeing 737 MAX Aircraft.*

49. Sorscher, "What will it be, Boeing?"

50. "787 Deferred Production Cost, Unamortized Tooling & Other Non-Recurring Cost balances."

51. Ostrower, "Inside Boeing."

52. McFadden et al., "Former Boeing manager says he warned company."

53. Kitroeff, "Boeing 737 Max Safety System Was Vetoed, Engineer Says."

54. Milgram, "Behavioral Study of Obedience."

55. Edmondson, *The Fearless Organization.*

56. Dekker, "The Bureaucratization of Safety."

57. "Guide: Understand team effectiveness," *re:Work.*

58. Gerndt, Frederic Laloux *"Reinventing organizations."*

59. Rother, *Toyota Kata.*

60. Burns, *Leadership.*

61. Bass, *Leadership and Performance Beyond Expectations.*

62. Forsgren et al., *State of DevOps Report 2017.*

63. Bass and Riggio, Transformational Leadership.

64. Magee, *How Toyota Became #1.*

65. Frank, "The End of the Line for GM-Toyota Joint Venture.

66. Frank, "The End of the Line for GM-Toyota Joint Venture.

67. Wikipedia, "List of manufacturers by motor vehicle production."

68. "Guide: Understand team effectiveness," *re:Work.*

69. Teller, "A Peek Inside the Moonshot Factory Operating Model."

70. Teller, "The Head of 'X' Explains How to Make Audacity the Path of Least Resistance."

71. Teller, "The Head of 'X' Explains How to Make Audacity the Path of Least Resistance."

72. Wikipedia, "Pixar."

73. Catmull, "Inside the Pixar Braintrust."

74. Catmull, "Inside the Pixar Braintrust."

75. Catmull, "Inside the Pixar Braintrust."

76. Edmondson, *The Fearless Organization.*

77. Hollnagel, Wears, and Braithwaite, *From Safety I to Safety II.*

78. Marquet and Covey, *Turn the Ship Around!*, 18.

79. Marquet and Covey, *Turn the Ship Around!*, 79.

80. Marquet and Covey, *Turn the Ship Around!*, 49.

81. Marquet and Covey, *Turn the Ship Around!*, 203.

82. Greenleaf, *Servant Leadership*, 22.

83. Greenleaf, *Servant Leadership*, 10.

84. "Columbia verdict reveals bizarre Challenger parallels," *The Sydney Morning Herald.*

Chapter 5

1. Courtney, "Starbucks Technology Transformation."

2. Reinertsen and Smith, *Developing Products in Half the Time.*

3. Wikipedia, "Roman roads."

4. "Your 'Deadline' Won't Kill You: Or Will It," Merriam-Webster.com.

5. The Standish Group, *Chaos Report 2015*.

6. Harter, "Employee Engagement on the Rise."

7. American Psychological Association, "Multitasking: Switching costs."

8. Tuckman, "Developmental sequence in small groups."

9. "The Architecture Owner Role," AgileModeling.com.

10. Rother, *Toyota Kata*.

11. Hubbard, "The IT Measurement Inversion."

12. "Ten things we know to be true," Google.com.

13. Williams, "Experiments in roadmapping at GOV.UK."

14. Smart, "The PMO is Dead, Long Live the PMO."

Chapter 6

1. World Economic Forum, "Securing a Common Future in Cyberspace."

2. Greenberg, "The Untold Story of NotPetya."

3. Burgess, "What is the Petya ransomware."

4. World Economic Forum, "Securing a Common Future in Cyberspace."

5. "GDPR Fines/Penalties," GDPR-Info.eu.

6. "Capital One data breach," BBC.

7. Field, "WannaCry cyber attack;" Anti-Corruption Digest. "Total WannaCry losses."

8. Greenberg, "The Untold Story of NotPetya."

9. "The Pursuit of Success & Averting Drift into Failure - Sidney Dekker."

10. "The Pursuit of Success & Averting Drift into Failure - Sidney Dekker."

11. Anonymous, Personal communication with the authors.

12. Rafferty, "9 of the Biggest Oil Spills in History."

13. National Commission on the BP Deepwater Horizon Oil Spill and Offshore Drilling, *Deep Water*, vii.

14. National Commission on the BP Deepwater Horizon Oil Spill and Offshore Drilling, *Deep Water*, ix.

15. National Commission on the BP Deepwater Horizon Oil Spill and Offshore Drilling, *Deep Water*, ix.

16. National Commission on the BP Deepwater Horizon Oil Spill and Offshore Drilling, *Deep Water*, ix.

17. National Commission on the BP Deepwater Horizon Oil Spill and Offshore Drilling, *Deep Water*, 224.

18. Chernoff, "Study: Deepwater Horizon workers were afraid to report safety issues."

19. National Commission on the BP Deepwater Horizon Oil Spill and Offshore Drilling, *Deep Water*, 126.

20. Edmondson, *The Fearless Organization*.

21. Anonymous personal communication with the authors.

22. Holmes and, Holmes, "I want to run an agile project."

23. Financial Conduct Authority, *FCA Handbook*.

24. Dixon and Adamson, *The Challenger Sale*.

25. Anonymous, personal communication with the authors.

26. Anonymous, personal communication with the authors.

27. Anonymous, personal communication with the authors.

28. Dekker, "Safety Differently Lecture."

29. "Risk," Prince2.wiki.

30. Adam Banks, as quoted in Ritchie, "Maersk."

31. Edmondson and Lei, "Psychological Safety."

32. Herway, "How to Create a Culture of Psychological Safety."
33. Edmondson, *The Fearless Organization.*
34. "The Pursuit of Success & Averting Drift into Failure—Sidney Dekker."
35. Takeuchi and Nonaka, "The New New Product Development Game."
36. Leitz, "Shifting Security to the Left."
37. Cremen, "Introducing the InfoSec colour wheel?."
38. "Manifesto," DevSecOps.org.
39. Doctorow, "The True Story of Notpetya."

Chapter 7

1. Weinberg, *A Fish Caught in Time.*
2. Weinberg, *A Fish Caught in Time.*
3. Weinberg, *A Fish Caught in Time.*
4. Beck et al., *Manifesto for Agile Software Development.*
5. Fowler, "FlaccidScrum."
6. Conway, "How do Committees Invent?"
7. MacCormack, Rusnak, and Baldwin, "Exploring the Duality between Product and Organizational Architectures."
8. Forsgren et al., *State of DevOps Report 2017*; Forsgren, Humble, and Kim, *Accelerate.*
9. Skelton and Pais, *Team Topologies*, 24.
10. Willis, "DevOps Culture—Part 1."
11. Hawkins, "Tesla relied on too many robots to build the Model 3."
12. Feathers, "Unit Tests Are Tests of Modularity."
13. Bolton and Bach, "Testing and Checking Refined."
14. Simon, "Rational Choice and the Structure of the Environment."
15. DeGrandis, *Making Work Visible.*
16. Kersten, *Project to Product*, 78.
17. Anonymous, personal communication with the authors.
18. Kim, *The Un,icorn Project*, 110 (my emphasis).
19. van Hasster, "Road-mapping Your Way to Agile Fluency"; "The Agile FluencyTM Model," Agile-Fluency.org.
20. "The Agile FluencyTM Model," AgileFluency.org.
21. "The Agile FluencyTM Model," AgileFluency.org.
22. Forsgren, Humble, and Kim, *Accelerate.*
23. Fowler, "StranglerFigApplication."
24. Skelton and Pais, *Team Topologies*, 15–29.
25. Skelton and Pais, "Monoliths Vs Microservices."
26. North, "Microservices."
27. Weinberg, *The Secrets of Consulting.*
28. Shook, "How to Change a Culture."
29. Gov.uk, *Digital, Data and Technology Profession Capability Framework.*

Chapter 8

1. Fukuyama, *Trust.*
2. Microsoft, *Diversity and Inclusion Report 2019.*
3. Polanyi, *The Tacit Dimension.*
4. Poppendieck and Poppendieck, *Implementing Lean Software Development.*
5. Tuckman, "Developmental sequence in small groups."

6. Terhorst-North, "Introducing Deliberate Discovery."

7. Wright, "Factors Affecting the Cost of Airplanes."

8. Chua, *Political Tribes*, Introduction.

9. Taylor, *Principles of Scientific Management*, 11.

10. Goodhart, "Problems of Monetary Management."

11. Strathern, "Improving Ratings."

12. Mathieson, "Take Aim . . ."

13. O'Reilly, *Unlearn*.

14. Polanyi, *The Tacit Dimension*, 4.

15. Eoyang, "Conditions for Self-Organizing in Human Systems."

16. Wolchover, "A New Physics Theory of Life."

17. van Bavel and Packer, "The Problem with Rewarding Individual Performers."

18. van Bavel and Packer, "The Problem with Rewarding Individual Performers."

19. Isaacs, *Dialogue and the Art of Thinking Together*.

20. Pink, *Drive*, 35–41.

21. Bowman, *Training from the Back of the Room!*

22. Rother, *Toyota Kata*.

23. Janlen, "Improvement Theme."

24. Cockburn and William, "The costs and benefits of pair programming."

25. Cockburn and William, "The costs and benefits of pair programming."

26. Forsgren et al., *Accelerate State of DevOps 2019*.

27. Dweck, *Mindset*.

28. Dweck, *Mindset*.

29. Dweck, *Mindset*, 112.

30. McChrystal et al., *Team of Teams*.

31. Hubbard, *How to Measure Anything*, 47.

32. Mayer, "It's not a Key Result unless it has a number."

33. DeGrandis, "5 Time Thieves and How to Beat Them."

34. Jeff Bezos as quoted in Bort, *Business Insider*.

35. Benefield, "Rolling Out Agile in a Large Enterprise."

36. "Quick Facts: Detroit city, Michigan; United States," Census.gov.

37. Khaleel, "Detroit Ranked Last in Report on Best Cities for Jobs."

CHAPTER 9

1. Immelt, "How I Remade GE."

2. Egan, "GE Slashes 119-year old dividend to a penny."

3. Egan, "GE to raise $4 billion by selling chunk of Baker Hughes."

4. Hipple, Sanzillo, and Bucley, "GE's $7.4 Billion Loss, Write-off on Baker Hughes."

5. Perez, *Technological Revolutions and Financial Capital*.

6. "Brian Eno of 'Scenius,'" Facebook post.

7. Kay, "Obliquity."

8. Royce, "Managing the Development of Large Software Systems."

9. Schein, "Kurt Lewin's Change Theory in the Field and in the Classroom."

INDEX

#BVSSH

ACKNOWLEDGMENTS

We would like to thank the many courageous people we have worked with, talked to, and learned from over the years, from many organizations. People who are willing to exhibit courage and vulnerability, to experiment, to be like a sponge open to re-learning, willing to change direction, to be pragmatic, to challenge the status quo, to be a force for good, to create more humane and engaging ways of working, all while enjoying the journey along the way. People who do something about change for the better within their sphere of influence, fostering psychological safety, inspiring others to follow, irrespective of seniority. We are grateful for having met so many passionate people, sharing learnings through sometimes failing and sometimes succeeding, with a personal resilience to keep on going. We are grateful to be surrounded by so many amazing people who we are learning from all the time, during this once in a working lifetime pivot in ways of working to a new normal. This book is a reflection of the learnings and insights from the many people we've got to know so far on our continuous journeys.

In particular, we are deeply grateful to the following people who put considerable time and effort into reviewing drafts of the manuscript or individual chapters (alphabetical by first name): Barry O'Reilly, Courtney Kissler, Fernando Cornago, Gene Kim, Jenny Wood, John Cutler, Leah Jochim, Maria Muir, Mik Kersten, and Richard James. We would also like to thank the following people who read the manuscript and provided feedback, a quote or a case study: Adam Banks, Ahmed Sidkey, Amanda Colpoys, Brijesh Ammanath, Chris Orson, Christian Metzler, Daniel Cahill, Dave Snowden, Dave Whyte, David Marquet, David Silverman, Dawie Olivier, Dean Leffingwell, Ellie Taylor, Evan Leybourn, Ian Buchanan, Prof. Julian Birkinshaw, Mark Lines, Manuel Pais, Matthew Skelton, Michael Harte, Nick Higginbottom, Patrick Eltridge, Pete Jarvis, Ralf Waltram, Russ Warman, Sally Clarke, Scott Ambler, Scott Prugh, Steven Sanders, and Werner Loots.

A special thanks goes to the team at IT Revolution, especially Anna Noak and Leah Brown for patience and faith in helping guide us through the book writing process. Thanks to Devon Smith at IT Revolution and also to Tamsin Ogilvie for the book design. And a special shout out to Gene and Margueritte Kim for attracting and organizing a "scenius" (a term coined by musician Brian Eno) of like minded people in a humble manner and centered around shared learning. Thank you.

We would like to thank the passionate people who we worked with together at Barclays. These people exhibited personal courage in challenging the status quo in order to get to better outcomes, including, and not limited to (apologies to the many people we have missed), Adam Furgal, Alex Brown, Allan Southward, Amol Pradhan, Andy Clapham, Andy Smith, Andy Spence, Angie Main, Barry Chandler, Brijesh Ammanath, Graham Zabel, Hardeep Bath, Derek White, Donal Quinn, Ian Buchanan, Ian Dugmore, James Foster, Jess Long, Jessica Edwards, John Stinson, Kate Mulligan, Kamila Sledz, Li Chung, Manoj Kulkarni, Mark Williams, Martin Craven-Wickes, Martin Mersey, Michael Harte, Mike Webb, Milan Juza, Morag McCall, Nej D'jelal, Nick Funnell, Owen Gardner, Paulo Dias, Paul Cavanagh, Richard Chester, Sally Clarke, Samantha Randall, Shweta Chawla, Simon Birch, Simon Pattinson, Simon Paynter, Simone Steele, Sonali Barat, Stephen West, Susan Scott, Tracy Norris, and Tony Caink.

Jon: I would like to thank my wife and soulmate, Kate, for her love and support, enabling the book to be delivered sooner, safer, and happier. Without Kate the book would be (even) late(r). I would also like to thank our grown-up children, Annabelle and Oscar, for their support, encouragement, and understanding when I'm head down and balk at going for a walk. I'd like to thank Gene Kim for enabling a corridor conversation about tips for writing which turned into my own lessons learned on writing and for this book to become a reality. The seed of an idea for writing was planted over breakfast with Barry O'Reilly in Canary Wharf, London. I'd like to thank Barry for being an inspiration and for his support. I'd like to thank Michael Harte and Ian Buchanan for providing the opportunity, for enabling me to step out of my comfort zone with shared learning and psychological safety. And finally, I'd like to thank my co-authors, Myles, Simon, and Zsolt, for having fun together on the journey and for the teamwork. I really appreciate the brainstorming, the learning, and going on a shared journey together.

Myles: My sincere thanks to Jon for his inspiration over the past few years, for helping me to grow, and for inviting my contribution to this book. It is one more example of what can happen when positive feedback loops are established, when there is the right focus on Happier outcomes. My equally warm thanks go to Simon and Zsolt for their wisdom and friendship over the years, also to so many of our colleagues mentioned above. I'd also like to thank Tamsin Ogilvie for the investment of her professional expertise to collaborate with IT Revolution, iterating the book design into the product that you have in your hands today.

Simon: I'd like to thank Jon for the mass of opportunities to work in and contribute to an area that I've been passionate about for two decades with an incredibly inspiring group of people, not least Zsolt and Myles. I'd also like to thank the team at Saxo Bank—Ashok Kalyanswamy, Ashish Kurana, and Jimmy Casey among many others—for the opportunity to learn lessons and to help an inspiring company get even better. And thanks always to Bronwyn for endless patience and support.

Zsolt: I would like to thank Jon for taking me on the journey, asking me to contribute to the book, for being a mentor and an inspiration for many years, and for all the learnings. I would also like to thank Simon and Myles for working together, for all the feedback, chats, and fun. Finally, I would like to thank my wife, Zsuzsa, and my children, Zsofi and Dani, for their unconditional support.

ABOUT THE AUTHORS

Jonathan Smart has been leading an agile approach to change as a business technologist for nearly thirty years, starting out as a developer on the trading floor in investment banking. Today, Smart leads Deloitte's Business Agility practice, helping organizations deliver better value sooner, safer, and happier through the application of agile, lean, and DevOps principles and practices organization wide.

Previously Smart led Ways of Working globally for Barclays Bank where after 4 years, teams were delivering, on average, three times as much in a third of the time, with twenty times fewer production incidents and the highest ever employee engagement scores. He and his team won the Best Internal Agile Team award at the Agile Awards in 2016.

Smart is also the founder of the Enterprise Agility Leaders Network, a member of the Programming Committee for the DevOps Enterprise Summit, a member of the Business Agility Institute Advisory Council, a guest speaker at London Business School, and speaks at numerous conferences a year.

Myles Ogilvie has led, supported, and coached change initiatives within large and small enterprises for over twenty-five years. An advocate of no-nonsense problem-solving, he seeks to build transparency, improve collaboration, and enable outcomes that produce Better Value Sooner Safer Happier During 2016, when leading ways of working for a major UK investment bank during a period of intense regulatory and controls scrutiny, Myles applied lean and agile principles to risk management in the product development process. He is now a passionate advocate of patterns that can help foster a safer, leaner, and more innovative controls culture.

Zsolt Berend is a business agility practitioner, coach, and trainer. He helps global organizations on their journey to achieving Better Value Sooner Safer Happier. He began his early career as a research fellow in astronomy, and then spent twenty years across industry sectors in various roles applying agile and lean practices, mainly in telecom, healthcare, financial services, and consulting. He was the global chair of the Agile Community of Practice at Barclays with more than 2,500 members, and with the Ways of Working Center of Enablement team, won "Best Internal Agile Team" at the Agile Awards 2016. He writes on Medium and is a speaker at conferences and meetups. His passion is data, measurements, insights, and the creation of learning organizations.

Simon Rohrer has been a hands on practitioner across both software engineering and enterprise architecture for over twenty-six years, and has had a passion for agile software development since picking up the eXtreme Programming white book in 1999. He's passionate about an eclectic and pragmatic approach to modern ways of working, incorporating lean, agile, systems thinking, DevOps and other principles and practices at the right pace and in a human context in enterprises, typically with a legacy of existing technology and a drive to do things better.